WILEY **CPA** Examination Review

Fast Track

Study Guide

Third Edition

O. Ray Whittington, CPA, PhD

WILEY

JOHN WILEY & SONS, INC.

ISBN: 0-471-45390-0

Printed in the United States of America.

10 9 8 7 6 5 4 3 2 1

TABLE OF CONTENTS

AUDITING AND ATTESTATION

FINANCIAL ACCOUNTING AND REPORTING

REGULATION

BUSINESS ENVIRONMENT AND CONCEPTS

INTRODUCTION

We have had the good fortune of assisting an almost countless number of wonderful folks as they have prepared for the CPA Exam. After working with so many people, we are firmly convinced that every candidate can pass the CPA Exam. If a person uses good quality materials and prepares properly, that person should have every reason to anticipate success. Everyone knows that the failure rate is high but there are good reasons not to let those percentages be discouraging. Many people take the exam without proper preparation. They have not allocated enough time or they have not been able to put in an adequate effort because of job or family commitments or they have not had good materials available to provide them with the organized structure and clear explanations that they need. For others, the sheer amount of material to be mastered is simply overwhelming. They have never faced so much information and they just do not know where to start. Do not take the CPA Exam until you are able to put in an adequate amount of effort so that you can be in a position to be successful. Furthermore, when you do prepare, use the best review guides that you can find. Do not settle for mediocre materials.

When we work with candidates, we stress that a fundamental level of knowledge must be mastered for each topic. Almost an unlimited amount of material can actually appear on the CPA Exam. Fortunately, you are not trying to make a perfect score; you are only trying to answer enough questions correctly in order to pass. A key step in achieving that success is to realize that for each topic (from contracts to leases to government accounting to qualified audit opinions) a core of basic knowledge exists that needs to be understood. The purpose of this book is to present that same core coverage to you. In addition, this book has been thoroughly revised for the content of the new computerized CPA exam. It provides essential outlines of topics that you need to be successful.

In working with candidates for the CPA Exam, we stress three steps: **Learn**, **Practice**, **Retain**. First, each person must learn the essential information about every topic. That basic material is presented in the outlines that follow. Second, candidates must practice using that knowledge to make certain that they know it well enough to be able to answer exam questions. The best way to practice is to simply work questions and carefully review the answers. For each topic, we have included a number of questions that we wrote to assist you in practicing what you have learned. After covering the essential information presented in an outline, work the practice questions to ensure that you understand the material well enough to arrive at appropriate answers. Use the knowledge you have obtained to add points to your score. For additional practice, we would suggest the purchase of Wiley CPA Examination Review for Windows, a computer program, or Wiley CPA Examination Review 2004 edition, each of which has thousands of questions and answers, including the new simulation type questions.

The final step to success is to retain the knowledge that has been obtained until time for the test. Over the course of three or four months, your understanding of a topic will begin to fade. Therefore, periodically review the outlines in this book to keep all of the essential material in your memory. When taking the CPA Exam, you need to have this knowledge fresh in your mind; thus, schedule in some time every week or two to go back through the outlines just to remind yourself of the key points, terms, calculations, and the like.

Learn the essential core level of information about each potential topic.

Practice the use of that knowledge by working as many questions and problems as you can.

Retain your understanding by reviewing these outlines as often as possible.

You can be successful on the very next CPA Exam and I hope that the outlines and problems in this book will help you achieve that passing grade that you are seeking to obtain.

DO THE WORK AND PASS THE NEXT CPA EXAM! YOU CAN DO IT!

Ray Whittington, CPA, CMA, CIA
Chicago, Illinois

TABLE OF CONTENTS
AUDITING AND ATTESTATION

Topic	Page

AUDITING AND ATTESTATION

TOPIC	For additional information see Wiley CPA Examination Review
Overview of Attest Function	Module 1
Audit Opinions	Module 4
Use of Report of Another Auditor	Module 4
Comparative Financial Statements	Module 4
Compilations and Reviews	Module 3
Audit Risk	Module 1
Internal Control	Module 2
Evidence Gathering	Module 3
Accounts Receivable and Revenues	Module 3
Statistical Sampling	Module 5
Inventory and Accounts Payable	Module 3
Auditing with Technology	Module 6
Flowcharting	Module 6
Cash Receipts and Cash Balances	Module 3
Special Reports and Other Reports	Module 4
Long-Term Liabilities and Contingencies	Module 3
Payroll	Module 3
Land, Buildings, and Equipment	Module 3
Investments	Module 3

OVERVIEW OF AN ATTEST FUNCTION

The Attest Function

(1) In an attest engagement a CPA is engaged to issue or does issue an examination, a review, or agreed-upon procedures report on subject matter, or an assertion about subject matter, that is the responsibility of another party.

(2) To perform an attest engagement there must be suitable criteria to judge the fairness of the information being reported on.

(3) The attestation standards establish three forms of CPA attestation engagements—examinations, reviews, and the performance of agreed-upon procedures.

   (A) An **examination** referred to as an audit when it involves financial statements, normally results in a positive opinion, the highest form of assurance about whether the information follows the criteria.

   (B) A **review** is substantially less in scope than an audit and provides negative assurance ("nothing came to our attention") rather than positive assurance.

   (C) For the third form of attestation engagement, a CPA and a specified party that wishes to use the information may mutually decide on specific **agreed-upon procedures** that the CPA will perform. Agreed-upon procedures engagements result in a report that describes the procedures performed and related findings

(4) **Statements on Standards for Attestation Engagements** provide guidance on how to perform attestation engagements.

(5) **Statements on Standards for Accounting and Review Services** provide guidance for work done for a nonpublic company that is less than an audit.

(6) An **independent audit** is made up of two separate steps.

   (A) First step is the examination of a set of financial statements that have been produced by the management of the reporting entity.

      (1) Purpose of examination is to gather sufficient, competent evidence on which to form an opinion as to the fair presentation of the statements in accordance with generally accepted accounting principles.

      (2) For each group of accounts and for the statements taken as a whole, management makes five **assertions**.

         (a) **Valuation** - all accounts are shown at proper amounts based on generally accepted accounting principles.

         (b) **Existence or occurrence** - all reported assets and liabilities actually exist; all other balances did occur. The account is not overstated.

         (c) **Presentation and disclosure** - all accounts are properly classified and all relevant information is disclosed.

         (d) **Completeness** - all transactions and accounts have been included within the financial statements. The account is not understated.

         (e) **Obligations and rights** - all assets and liabilities are those of the reporting entity.

      (3) Auditor attempts to corroborate these assertions in order to provide reasonable assurance that no material misstatements exist in any of the assertions.

(a) The term "**material**" means anything of a size or type that would influence the judgment of a reasonable person relying on the information. A preliminary judgment of the size component of materiality is set at the beginning of an audit but is continuously reassessed as new information is gathered.

(b) A **misstatement** is an **error** (an unintentional mistake), **fraud** (an intentional manipulation of the assets or the records).

(B) Second step is the report of the findings to outside parties, primarily to stockholders and other parties outside of the reporting entity. The report is intended to add credibility to the financial information being distributed.

(7) All of the auditor's work must follow **generally accepted auditing standards** (GAAS) which are currently established by means of **Statements of Auditing Standards** that are produced by the Auditing Standards Board. If the audit is of a public company, the audit must be performed in accordance with auditing standards adopted or issued by the **Public Company Accounting Oversight Board (PCAOB).**

(8) There are ten basic generally accepted auditing standards that provide the basis for an auditing engagement.

(A) **General Standards**

(1) The audit is to be performed by a person or persons having adequate technical training and proficiency as an auditor. The auditor should have sufficient education and experience in (1) auditing, (2) accounting, and (3) the industry in which the client operates in order to make the decisions necessary to evaluate whether any material misstatements exist in any of the management's five assertions.

(2) In all matters relating to the assignment, **independence** in mental attitude is to be maintained by the auditor.

(a) Independence in mental attitude cannot be regulated. However, to encourage independence in fact and to maintain the appearance of independence, the auditor can have no **direct financial interest** in the client. "Direct" includes the auditor and members of immediate family. "Financial interest" is ownership of equity shares, other client financial instruments, or any other potential financial benefit.

(b) In addition, there can be no material **indirect financial interest** such as ownership through a mutual fund.

(c) To ensure independence, auditor cannot render an opinion on statements of one year until all fees from the prior year audit have been paid.

(d) To emphasize independence from management, auditor is usually appointed by audit committee of the board of directors.

(3) **Due professional care** is to be exercised in the performance of the audit and preparation of the report.

(a) Auditor must do at least what any average auditor would do and never less.

(B) **Standards of Fieldwork**

(1) The work is to be adequately planned and assistants, if any, are to be properly supervised.

(a)   Audit program is developed before substantive testing to ensure that adequate planning has occurred.

(b)   All evidence is recorded on working papers that are reviewed by qualified personnel to ensure supervision. Even a partner other than the partner in charge of the engagement should review the working papers.

(2)   A sufficient understanding of **internal control** is to be obtained to help determine the nature, extent, and timing of the substantive testing to be performed.

     (a)   Assessment is made of control risk. If that risk is high, the auditor will have to gather more evidence than anticipated or a better quality of evidence.

(3)   Sufficient, competent **evidential matter** is to be obtained through inspection, observation, inquiries, confirmations, and the like to afford a reasonable basis for an opinion regarding the financial statements under audit.

     (a)   Evidence gathering is sometimes called **substantive testing**. Any testing that confirms the ending balance of an account is known as a test of a balance. Evidence gathered to support an account by looking at the various transactions that have affected it during the period is called a test of details.

     (b)   The actual amount and quality of evidence to be gathered depends on the judgment of the auditor.

(C)   Standards of Reporting

(1)   The report shall state whether the financial statements are presented in accordance with **generally accepted accounting principles**. (This assurance is stated explicitly.)

     (a)   The determination of what specific generally accepted accounting principle (GAAP) applies to a situation can be difficult because various sources can give conflicting guidelines. A **GAAP Hierarchy** has been established with five levels of authority. The higher levels have highest priority. In the top level (for businesses) are FASB Statements and Interpretations, APB Opinions, and AICPA Accounting Research Bulletins.

(2)   The report shall identify those circumstances in which such principles have not been consistently observed in the current period in relation to the preceding period. (Assurance of **consistency** is implied.)

(3)   Informative disclosures in the financial statements are to be regarded as reasonably adequate unless otherwise stated in report. (Assurance of adequate disclosure is implied.)

(4)   The report shall either contain an **expression of opinion** regarding the financial statements, taken as a whole, or an assertion to the effect that an opinion cannot be expressed. When an overall opinion cannot be rendered, the reasons should be stated. A clear-cut indication of the character of the auditor's work should be included along with the degree of responsibility that the auditor is taking.

PROBLEMS AND SOLUTIONS
OVERVIEW OF AUDIT FUNCTION

ONE – Because of the attest function, financial statements are the responsibility of the independent auditor. (True or False?)

Answer – Financial statements are the responsibility of the management of the reporting entity. The independent auditor examines and reports on these financial statements. (Number One is False.)

TWO – In an audit, the independent auditor attempts to corroborate five assertions made by the company's management in connection with each account or group of accounts found in a set of financial statements. These assertions are: valuation, timing, relevance, presentation, and completeness. (True or False?)

Answer – The five assertions to be corroborated by the independent auditor are: (1) valuation, (2) existence or occurrence, (3) presentation and disclosure, (4) completeness, and (5) obligations and rights. (Number Two is False.)

THREE – An independent auditor seeks to provide reasonable assurance that no material misstatements exist in any of the five assertions made by management. (True or False?)

Answer – The role of the independent auditor is to gain sufficient, competent evidence so as to provide reasonable (not perfect) assurance that material misstatements do not exist in any of the assertions made by management. (Number Three is True.)

FOUR – The term "materiality" refers to any factor of a size or type that would impact an outside decision-maker's decision about a set of financial statements. (True or False?)

Answer – A material item is anything that – because of either its size or its type – would influence the judgment of a reasonable person relying on the information being presented. (Number Four is True.)

FIVE – A misstatement is either due to error or fraud. (True or False?)

Answer – A misstatement is an error (an unintentional mistake), or fraud (an intentional manipulation of the assets or the records. (Number Five is True.)

SIX – The spouse of an auditor holds a small number of shares in a company. The auditor is not independent as to that particular company. (True or False?)

Answer – To maintain the appearance of independence, independence is assumed to be lacking if the auditor has either a direct financial interest or a material indirect financial interest in the reporting company. Ownership of the shares by the spouse is considered a direct financial interest and would be prohibited. (Number Six is True.)

SEVEN – According to generally accepted auditing standards, the standard audit report explicitly states that the financial statements are in accordance with generally accepted accounting principles applied on a consistent basis. (True or False?)

Answer – The standard audit report must specify that the statements are in accordance with generally accepted accounting principles. However, consistency is not mentioned unless a problem exists. Thus, consistency is implied in the standard audit report. (Number Seven is False.)

EIGHT – Auditing standards for audits of public companies are issued by the Auditing Standards Board. (True or False?)

Answer – The AICPA Auditing Standards Board issues auditing standards for audits of nonpublic companies. The Public Company Accounting Oversight Board issues auditing standards for audits of public companies. (Number Eight is False.)

AUDIT OPINIONS

(1)   An **unqualified opinion** (also called a standard auditor's report) is given when auditor's examination provides sufficient evidence that statements are presented fairly in accordance with generally accepted accounting principles (GAAP). It provides the users of financial statements with **reasonable assurance** that no material misstatements exist in any of the five assertions made by management.

(2)   A **standard unqualified opinion** should contain several specific elements

    (A)   The heading should state: Independent Auditor's Report.

    (B)   The report is normally dated as of the final day of the auditor's field work and can never be dated prior to the final day of field work. Under normal circumstances, this concludes the auditor's responsibility for any type of evidence gathering.

        (1)   If an account has to be changed or a footnote added after the conclusion of the audit, management can request that the auditor return and audit that particular change. If that is done, the report must be dual dated ("March 22, 2005 except for Note Y as of April 2, 2005") to indicate that the auditor's work and responsibility have been extended for that one item.

    (C)   The first paragraph is called the **introductory paragraph**.

        (1)   Indicates that an audit has been carried out (and not a preparation) of the financial statements

        (2)   Identifies the financial statements by name, by name of the company, and by the dates.

            (a)   Balance sheet is for a particular date; statements of income, retained earnings, and cash flows are for a period of time.

        (3)   Specifies that the statements are the responsibility of the company's management.

        (4)   States that the auditor's responsibility is to express an opinion on statements based on audit.

    (D)   The second paragraph is called the **scope paragraph**.

        (1)   Specifies that the audit was conducted according to the auditing standards generally accepted in the United States.

        (2)   Indicates that audit was planned and performed to obtain reasonable assurance that the statements were free from material misstatements. Perfect assurance is not given for many reasons: not every transaction is examined, human error might occur in audit, fraud and illegal acts might be hidden, etc.

        (3)   Explains that evidence supporting amounts and disclosures has been examined but only on a test basis.

            (a)   This statement shows that not every transaction was examined

            (b)   Stresses reliance on auditor's judgment

        (4)   Indicates that an assessment was made of accounting principles, significant estimations, and statement presentation.

        (5)   States the belief that audit provides a reasonable basis for the opinion.

    (E)   The third paragraph is called the **opinion paragraph**.

        (1)   Starts with the phrase "in our opinion" to show that this is not a guarantee but only an expert judgment

             (2)   Says that statements present fairly in all material respects the financial position, operations, and cash flows.

             (3)   States that financial statements conform to accounting principles generally accepted in the United States.

(3)   An **explanatory fourth paragraph** should be added in several specific instances. In these cases, the extra paragraph is placed after the opinion paragraph and does not affect the wording of the other three paragraphs.

     (A)   **Emphasis of a matter** - the paragraph is added to draw attention to a matter of particular importance such as significant related party transactions or a subsequent event.

     (B)   Lack of consistency - the paragraph is added to draw attention to a footnote that explains a change in accounting principle. Paragraph mentions change but does not provide any judgment of it.

             (1)   If auditor does not concur that change is appropriate, the opinion should be qualified rather than relying on this explanatory paragraph.

     (C)   **Going concern problem** - the paragraph is added if substantial doubt exists as to company's ability to stay in business for 12 months from the date of the balance sheet. In this case, auditor does have the option to disclaim an opinion instead of adding an extra paragraph.

     (D)   **Other information attached to audited financial statements** - auditor is required to read all information attached to financial statements to determine if it is consistent with the information presented in the financial statements. If inconsistency is discovered and the financial statements are judged to be fairly presented, an extra paragraph is added to describe the problem. A qualified opinion is not rendered because the problem lies outside of the financial statements.

(4)   If a problem arises and an unqualified opinion cannot be given, the appropriate wording depends on the type of problem. In each case, an additional paragraph is added to describe the problem but it always comes before the opinion paragraph and not after.

     (A)   There can be a **qualification because of a scope limitation**; the auditor fails to follow one or more of the generally accepted auditing standards. Frequently, the auditor is unable to obtain sufficient, competent evidence to provide reasonable assurance that a material misstatement does not exist in one of the assertions made by management

             (1)   Introductory paragraph does not change but scope paragraph indicates that GAAS was followed "except as discussed below" in the explanatory paragraph. As indicated above, explanatory paragraph describes problem and may direct the reader to a footnote where more information is provided.

             (2)   Opinion paragraph says that statements are fairly presented "except for adjustments, if any, that might have been found had we been able to . . ."

             (3)   If the lack of evidence is so material that auditor cannot add any credibility to financial statements, **disclaimer** (no opinion) should be given rather than a scope qualification.

                  (a)   For a disclaimer, the last sentence in introductory paragraph about auditor's responsibility is removed.

                  (b)   Scope paragraph is omitted completely.

        (c)   Opinion paragraph reiterates problem identified in explanatory paragraph and indicates that "the scope of our work was not sufficient to enable us to express and we do not express, an opinion on these statements.

        (d)   Even in a disclaimer, auditor must spell out any GAAP problems that were discovered

        (e)   If independence is lacking, auditor always issues a disclaimer but never gives the specific reason for the problem. In this case, the disclaimer is often just a single sentence: "I am not independent; I have no opinion."

(B)   Statements can contain a departure from GAAP. For example, disclosure might not be adequate or a balance might not be capitalized properly. If the problem is material but some credibility can be given to the statements as a whole, the auditor issues an **opinion qualification**.

     (1)   The introductory and scope paragraphs are both left with standard wording. As always, an explanatory paragraph is added before opinion paragraph

     (2)   In opinion paragraph, the wording is changed to warn of the problem: "In our opinion, except for the effects of . . ."

     (3)   In severe cases, a departure from GAAP can have such an impact that the entire statements cannot be viewed as fairly presented in any capacity. An **adverse opinion** is appropriate. Again, the first two paragraphs are standard and the explanatory paragraph is added. The opinion paragraph states that "because of the effects . . . the financial statement referred to above do not present fairly . . ."

(C)   Auditor can give different opinions for different statements (for example, an unqualified opinion on the balance sheet but a disclaimer on the other statements) but cannot give an opinion on specific accounts presented within a set of financial statements.

PROBLEMS AND SOLUTIONS
AUDIT OPINIONS

ONE – In a standard audit report, the responsibility of the management is stated in the first paragraph and the responsibility of the independent auditor is stated in the second paragraph. (True or False?)

Answer – The responsibility of the management for information in the financial statements is spelled out in the first paragraph. In addition, the auditor's responsibility to express an opinion based on the audit is also stated in this first paragraph. The second paragraph is used to detail the scope of the auditor's work. (Number One is False.)

TWO – In the second (scope) paragraph of a standard audit report, the auditor states that all appropriate evidence was examined. (True or False?)

> *Answer – The auditor cannot possibly examine all evidence, too much would be available. Therefore, in the second (scope) paragraph of the report, the auditor states that evidence was examined on a test basis. (Number Two is False.)*

THREE – An auditor has examined a set of financial statements and is willing to provide reasonable assurance that the statements are free of material misstatements. However, the auditor wants to draw attention to a particular event that could be of special interest to readers of the statements. The auditor adds a separate fourth paragraph at the end of the report for this purpose. In addition, the opinion paragraph should begin with "in our opinion, except for the information spelled out in the following paragraph." (True or False?)

> *Answer – In this case, the auditor wants to emphasize a particular matter in the audit report. To do this, the auditor adds a paragraph at the end of the report, after the opinion paragraph. However, because the auditor is simply drawing the readers' attention to this matter, no change should be made in the wording of the other three paragraphs. The "except for" wording seems to indicate a qualification of the opinion and should not be included. (Number Three is False.)*

FOUR – In each of the following cases, an auditor may add an extra paragraph at the end of an audit report but should not change the wording of the other paragraphs: a change in an accounting principle with which the auditor concurs, the emphasis of a matter, and where there is substantial doubt that the company can remain in business for 12 months from the balance sheet date. (True or False?)

> *Answer – In each of these three situations, the auditor should not qualify the report but should provide additional information at the end of the report. No change should be made in the wording of the other paragraphs. Information on these three situations should be added to provide adequate information for the readers of the financial statements. (Number Four is True.)*

FIVE – An auditor is not able to gather sufficient, competent evidence to corroborate an account balance. Because of this problem, the auditor is not willing to provide reasonable assurance that the statements are free of material misstatements. The auditor should give either a qualified opinion or an adverse opinion. (True or False?)

> *Answer – Where the auditor is unable to gather sufficient, competent evidence on which to render an opinion, the auditor has not followed generally accepted auditing standards. Because of the failure to follow generally accepted auditing standards, the auditor must provide either a qualified opinion or a disclaimer of opinion. (Number Five is False.)*

SIX – An auditor discovers that the reporting company has not followed generally accepted accounting principles in the reporting of its lease obligations. The problem is considered to be material by the auditor. The auditor must provide either a qualified opinion or a disclaimer of opinion. (True or False?)

Answer – When financial statements are not free of material misstatements, the auditor provides either a qualified opinion or an adverse opinion. (Number Six is False.)

SEVEN - An auditor is unable to gather sufficient, competent evidence to corroborate an account balance. Because of this problem, the auditor is not able to provide reasonable assurance that the statements are free of material misstatements. The auditor is planning to provide a qualified audit opinion. In that report, the scope paragraph and the opinion paragraph must both be changed. In addition, an explanatory paragraph is added before the opinion paragraph to provide information and may direct the reader to a note to the statements for more information. (True or False?)

Answer – When a qualified opinion is given because the auditor has not followed generally accepted auditing standards, the wording of both the scope paragraph and the opinion paragraph are affected. In addition, an extra paragraph is added before the opinion paragraph to provide the reader with more information. (Number Seven is True.)

EIGHT – An auditor has discovered a material misstatement in the application of an accounting principle in a company's financial statements. Because of this problem, the auditor is going to provide a qualified audit opinion. In that report, the scope paragraph and the opinion paragraph must both be changed. Furthermore, an explanatory paragraph is added before the opinion paragraph to provide information and may direct the reader to a footnote for more information. (True or False?)

Answer – When an audit report is qualified because of a departure from generally accepted accounting principles, a paragraph is added before the opinion paragraph to explain the problem. In addition, the wording of the opinion paragraph is altered. However, no change is made in the scope paragraph because the problem was not a result of the auditor's examination. (Number Eight is False.)

NINE – An audit report is dated as of March 29, Year Two. That date indicates the last day of the audit fieldwork. (True or False?)

Answer – An audit report is dated as of the last day of the auditor's fieldwork in order to indicate the point in time that standard audit procedures were completed. (Number Nine is True.)

TEN – An audit report is dated as of "March 29, Year Two, except for Note Y as of April 17, Year Two." This report has been dual dated. The auditor apparently finished standard audit procedures on March 29 but returned to apply audit procedures to the information provided in Note Y. This later work was completed on April 17. (True or False?)

Answer – The report here has a dual dated opinion. The earlier date reflects the completion of the audit. However, the client (or perhaps the auditor) decided that Note Y should be added (or modified) to provide more complete information. Since this change occurred after the auditor's fieldwork, the auditor must have returned to gain satisfactory information so that reasonable assurance could also be given in connection with this new material. (Number Ten is True.)

USE OF REPORT OF ANOTHER AUDITOR

(1)   Most large companies are actually made up of many separate corporations. On occasion, one auditing firm will examine the statements of a portion of these companies while a different firm (an **other auditor**) audits the rest. Having two auditors may occur because a part of the company is in a separate geographical area.

    (A)   Management designates a **principal auditor** to sign the audit report and be the auditor clearly visible to the public. The principal auditor is usually the firm that audits the parent company.

        (1)   Before accepting the role as principal auditor, firm must have knowledge of entire business and audit a large enough portion of the company to take responsibility as principal auditor.

    (B)   If other auditor did only a small portion of the work, there often will be no division reported; opinion of principal auditor is standard with no mention made of the other auditor.

    (C)   Principal auditor can also decide to indicate the presence of the other auditor (called "dividing the responsibility").

        (1)   If responsibility is divided, the introductory paragraph provides several pieces of information.

            (a)   Mentions existence of other auditor but rarely identifies other auditor by name. Can only mention name with permission of the other auditor.

            (b)   States the size of the division by giving the total assets and revenue of the part of the company that was examined by the other auditor.

            (c)   States that the opinion being rendered is based on principal's audit and the report of the other auditor.

        (2)   If responsibility is to be divided, the last sentence of the scope paragraph mentions that the principal's audit "and the report of the other auditor" provided basis for opinion.

        (3)   If responsibility is to be divided, opinion paragraph states that opinion is "based on our audit and the report of the other auditor."

        (4)   A qualification given by the other auditor does not necessarily lead to a qualification of the entire financial statements. Opinion depends on overall materiality of problem.

    (D)   Principal auditor has responsibilities in connection with other auditor.

        (1)   Must always verify the professional reputation of the other auditor.

        (2)   Must always verify the independence of the other auditor.

        (3)   May possibly need to ascertain that other auditor understands applicable GAAP, SEC regulations, tax laws, etc. This step is most likely if other auditor is a very small firm or is located in a foreign country.

        (4)   May also want to review evidence gathered about intercompany balances.

        (5)   If responsibility is not divided, principal auditor should gain assurance of the quality of the work performed by the other auditor. In that case, principal may choose to do some or all of the following.

            (a)   Review other auditor's audit program.

            (b)   Review the evidence that was gathered and the handling of any problems that were discovered.

(c)   Do some audit testing to confirm work of other auditor.

PROBLEMS AND SOLUTIONS **USE OF REPORT OF ANOTHER AUDITOR**

ONE – The firm of ABC audits the Jones Company. The Jones Company has a wholly owned subsidiary that was audited by the firm of XYZ. Jones Company plans to release consolidated financial statements and ABC has agreed to serve as the principal auditor. In preparing its report, ABC has decided not to divide the responsibility for the audit with the firm of XYZ. For that reason, the work of XYZ will be noted in the audit report although the name of this other firm will probably not be mentioned. (True or False?)

Answer – When another auditor is involved in an audit and the principal auditor decides not to divide the responsibility, all mention of the other auditor is omitted. Unless some other problem exists, the standard audit report is rendered. (Number One is False.)

TWO – When another auditor has done a portion of an engagement and the principal auditor has decided not to divide the responsibility, the principal auditor must examine the other auditor's audit program and a portion of the evidence gathered. (True or False?)

Answer – When no division of responsibility is being made, the principal auditor has to verify the professional reputation and independence of the other auditor. In addition, the principal auditor should consider determining whether the other auditor has adequate knowledge of applicable accounting principles and laws. The principal also needs to consider examining the other auditor's audit program and the evidence that was gathered. However, the principal is not required to do so. (Number Two is False.)

THREE – The firm of ABC audits the Jones Company. The Jones Company has a wholly owned subsidiary that was audited by the firm of XYZ. Jones Company plans to release consolidated financial statements and ABC has agreed to serve as the principal auditor. In preparing its report, ABC has decided to divide the responsibility for the audit with XYZ. The report produced by ABC will have three paragraphs but each of these paragraphs will differ from the standard audit report. (True or False?)

Answer – In order to divide the responsibility for an audit, the principal auditor must make changes in each of the three paragraphs of the audit report. In the first paragraph, the existence of the other auditor is noted by giving the size of the assets and revenue examined by this other group. Furthermore, in all three paragraphs, the principal auditor indicates its reliance on the report of the other auditor in arriving at its opinion. (Number Three is True.)

FOUR - When another auditor has performed a portion of an engagement and the principal auditor has decided to divide the responsibility, the principal auditor must verify the other auditor's professional reputation and independence. (True or False?)

Answer – Whether the principal auditor divides the responsibility for the engagement or not, the principal is relying on the work of this other party. Consequently, the principal auditor must verify the professional reputation of the other firm as well as its independence from the reporting company. (Number Four is True.)

COMPARATIVE FINANCIAL STATEMENTS

(1)   A company may change auditors. Subsequently, in connection with **comparative statements**, the new auditor reports on current year statements but previous opinion is still applicable for the earlier set of financial statements.

    (A)   Previous opinion can simply be included along with the current audit report. However, previous auditor must agree to inclusion of report. Before giving permission, previous auditor must make certain that original opinion is still appropriate.

        (1)   Previous auditor should review earlier financial statements to make certain that nothing has been changed since original examination.

        (2)   Must also read the current statements and compare to earlier statements to determine that no obvious discrepancies are present.

        (3)   Must obtain a representation letter from current auditors stating that nothing has been found to indicate that the previous statements require adjustment.

        (4)   Must also obtain an updated representation letter from management similar to the one that is required at the end of an audit.

    (B)   The previous report can be omitted but then current auditor must refer to the earlier report. In that case, the introductory paragraph is changed to include several pieces of information.

        (1)   The statements being presented that were audited by the previous auditor must be identified but the name of that firm cannot be given.

        (2)   Date of the previous report must be included.

        (3)   Type of opinion given in previous report should be noted along with an explanation if the report varied from a standard unqualified opinion.

(2)   For nonpublic companies, different levels of assurance may be appropriate for the statements of different years. For example, an audit may be performed in one year but only a review or compilation in another.

    (A)   The report for the current year should be generated as is appropriate.

    (B)   A separate paragraph at the end of the current report should be included to indicate the following about the previous statements.

        (1)   Identification of the previous statements.

        (2)   Indication of the type of engagement that was performed.

        (3)   Date and contents of the previous report.

(3)   Auditor may decide to change an opinion given on an earlier set of financial statements that is being included for comparative purposes.

    (A)   For example, statements may have been restated to conform with generally accepted accounting principles.

    (B)   Within current report, an explanatory paragraph is added prior to the opinion paragraph.

        (1)   Should include date and opinion of previous report.

        (2)   Should indicate updated opinion on earlier statements and reasons for change.

| PROBLEMS AND SOLUTIONS |
| COMPARATIVE FINANCIAL STATEMENTS |

ONE – The audit firm of ABC prepares an audit report for the Year One financial statements of Smith Company. The audit firm of XYZ provides an audit report on the Year Two financial statements of that same company. Smith now wants to present the financial statements for these years together in comparative form. If both years are to be included, both audit reports must also be presented. (True or False?)

> *Answer – Under certain conditions, Smith Company may present both audit reports along with its comparative financial statements. However, the report of the previous auditor (ABC) need not be included if the current auditor (XYZ) provides specific information about the previous report within its own audit report. (Number One is False.)*

TWO - The audit firm of ABC provides an audit report for the Year One financial statements of Wilson Company. The audit firm of XYZ provides an audit report on the Year Two financial statements of that same company. Wilson now wants to present the financial statements for these years together in comparative form. Wilson has asked ABC for permission to include its original report. ABC can grant permission as long as it has performed certain procedures including reading the current financial statements. (True or False?)

> *Answer – In order to give permission to reissue a previous audit report, the previous auditor must take several actions: (1) review the original financial statements to make certain that nothing has been changed, (2) read the current statements and compare to earlier statements to ensure that no obvious discrepancies exist, (3) obtain a representation letter from the current auditors indicating that no adjustments are needed to the original financial statements, and (4) obtain an updated representation letter from the management of the reporting company. (Number Two is True.)*

THREE - The firm of ABC provides an audit report for the Year One financial statements of Aaron Company. The firm of XYZ provides an audit report on the Year Two financial statements of that same company. Aaron now wants to present the financial statements for these years together in comparative form. ABC performs the required activities and grants permission to include the original audit report. That report should have the same date as was used when it was originally issued. (True or False?)

> *Answer – When a statement is reissued, the previous auditor must perform certain tasks. However, these procedures do not necessitate the dual dating of the audit report. Thus, the original date continues to be appropriate. (Number Three is True.)*

FOUR - The firm of ABC provides an audit report for the Year One financial statements of Harkins Company. The firm of XYZ provides an audit report on the Year Two financial statements of that same company. Harkins now wants to present the financial statements for these years together in comparative form. The report issued by ABC is not going to be included. Thus, the current audit firm (XYZ) must provide specific information about the previous report in the opening paragraph of its current report. (True or False?)

> *Answer – When comparative statements are presented and the audit report of the previous auditor is not included, the current auditor must refer to that report. In the first paragraph of the current report, the auditor should identify the statements examined by the previous auditor, the date of that report, the type of opinion that was rendered, and an explanation if that report was not a standard unqualified opinion. (Number Four is True.)*

FIVE - The firm of ABC provides a review report for the Year One financial statements of Cheen Company (a nonpublic company). The firm of XYZ provides an audit report on the Year Two financial statements of that same company. Cheen now wants to present the financial statements for these years together in comparative form. The review report issued by ABC is not going to be included. Thus, the current firm (XYZ) must refer to this previous report in the opening paragraph of its audit report. (True or False?)

> *Answer – Because the previous report is not being included, the audit report of the current auditors must refer to it. However, since different levels of assurance are being given (reasonable assurance for the audit and limited assurance for the review), readers might be confused. Therefore, to draw attention to the difference, relevant information about the previous report should be disclosed in a separate paragraph at the end of the current audit report. This paragraph should spell out (1) the identification of the previous statements,(2) an indication of the type of engagement, and (3) the date and contents of the previous report. (Number Five is False.)*

COMPILATIONS AND REVIEWS

(1)   Anytime that a CPA is associated with financial statements, a report must be issued to avoid any possible misunderstanding.

  (A)   This report should indicate level of assurance, if any, that is being given.

  (B)   A CPA is **associated with statements** when he or she prepares or assists in preparing statements or putting information into the form of financial statements.

(2)   If CPA is associated with the statements of a publicly-held company but has not performed an audit, CPA must state so clearly ("I have not performed an examination and, therefore, have no opinion.")

  (A)   No negative assurance should be given. For example, CPA cannot say "I did not perform an audit but I saw nothing wrong."

  (B)   Each page should be stamped "Unaudited."

  (C)   If CPA is aware of a problem with the application of GAAP, that information must be included in report.

(3)   For the **interim financial statements** of a publicly-held company, CPAs perform **reviews**.

  (A)   CPA carries out specified procedures and, if no problems are discovered, states that he or she is not aware of any material modifications that are needed to be in conformity with GAAP.

    (1)   This wording is known as **negative assurance** or **limited assurance**.

    (2)   Assurance being given is less than that of an audit (reasonable assurance) because no evaluation is made of internal control and insufficient evidence is gathered to form an opinion as to whether material misstatements exist in any of the five assertions made by management about the accounts and the financial statements.

(4)   If a company is privately-held and an audit is not performed, CPA carries out either a **review** or a **compilation**. These services can be done on either interim or annual statements. The CPA's work must adhere to the **Statements on Standards for Accounting and Review Services**.

  (A)   A review is essentially the same as a limited review performed on the interim financial statements of a public company.

  (B)   There are specific procedures that CPA should do in a review.

    (1)   Obtain a general knowledge of the company, its systems, its control structure, and the industry in which it operates.

    (2)   Perform **analytical procedures**. Client balances, percentages, and ratios are compared to auditor's expectations for those same figures. Significant differences indicate areas where risk of misstatement is greatest.

      (a)   Auditor expectations are usually stated within a range and the client figures would be expected to fall within that range.

      (b)   Auditor expectations can be based on past years' figures, budgets, financial statements of competitors, industry averages, related nonfinancial information (the local economy has declined so that bad debt expense would be expected to increase), and related financial information (sales have gone up so cost of goods sold should have also gone up).

(3) Make inquiries of the client management looking for potential problems. Areas of inquiry would include the following.
    (a) Method of preparing the statements
    (b) Any changes in internal control
    (c) Any changes in the application of GAAP.
    (d) Outcome of problems found in previous engagements.
    (e) Changes in the company, its systems, or its personnel.
(4) Read the financial statements and verify the math on those statements.
(5) Read **minutes of board of directors and stockholders' meetings** looking for discussion of unusual events or problems.
(6) Get **representation letter** from the management.

(5) A **review report** normally has three paragraphs.
  (A) First paragraph states that a review was performed and identifies the statements.
    (1) Also indicates that the work was in accordance with the Statements on Standards for Accounting and Review Services issued by the American institute of Certified Public Accountants (AICPA).
    (2) Specifies that financial statements are the representations of the management.
  (B) Second paragraph explains the steps and purpose of a review.
    (1) Indicates that a review is mainly inquiries of company personnel and analytical procedures applied to financial data.
    (2) Explains that a review is substantially less than an examination made in an audit.
    (3) Specifies that no opinion is being expressed.
  (C) Third paragraph provides **negative (limited) assurance**: "Because of my review, I am not aware of any material modifications that should be made . . . to be in conformity with GAAP."
  (D) Each page of the financial statements must be stamped "see accountant's review report."
  (E) If need for modification to be in conformity with GAAP is found, CPA discusses the problem with management and, if not resolved, with the audit committee. If still not resolved, CPA adds a fourth paragraph to explain. This extra paragraph is placed at the end of the report. The third paragraph (described above) makes mention of the problem and the inclusion of the additional paragraph.
  (F) Situations (such as an emphasis of a matter) that lead in an audit to the inclusion of an **explanatory paragraph** are not mentioned in a review because the financial statements do not need modification.

(6) For a nonpublic company, the CPA can also perform a **compilation** which provides no assurance in connection with the statements.
  (A) A compilation is sometimes referred to as write up work and means that the CPA took client information and put it into the form of financial statements.
    (1) Footnote disclosure is often omitted in such statements but, in that case, an extra paragraph should be added to report to indicate that the statements are only intended for people aware of the missing disclosures.
    (2) In performing a compilation, CPA should have a general knowledge of the company: its transactions, records, personnel, applicable GAAP, and the industry in which it operates.

        (3)   CPA must read the final statements and verify the math in order to catch any obvious errors. However, no evidence gathering is performed.

        (4)   A compilation is one service that can be performed by a CPA who is not independent of the reporting company although the lack of independence must be disclosed in the report.

(B)   A compilation report normally has two paragraphs.

        (1)   The first paragraph identifies the financial statements that were compiled and indicates that the work was done in accordance with the Statements on Standards for Accounting and Review Services issued by the AICPA.

        (2)   The second paragraph describes the purpose of a compilation as presenting the representations of management in the form of financial statements. An indication is made that no audit or review was made and that no opinion or assurance is being given.

        (3)   If the CPA is aware of any departure from GAAP, a sentence is added to the second paragraph of the report to note that departure. Then, a third paragraph is added to describe the problem.

        (4)   Each page of the financial statements must be stamped "see accountant's compilation report."

PROBLEMS AND SOLUTIONS
COMPILATIONS AND REVIEW

ONE – A compilation and a review can only be performed for nonpublic companies. (True or False?)

    Answer – Either a compilation or a review can be performed on the financial statements of a nonpublicly-owned company. Normally, compilations and reviews are not appropriate for companies that are publicly owned. However, the interim financial statements of a publicly-owned company can be subjected to a limited review. (Number One is False.)

TWO – In a review, the auditor can provide limited assurance. However, in a compilation, the auditor is not allowed to provide any assurance. (True or False?)

    Answer – Limited (sometimes called negative) assurance is appropriate in a review. When providing limited assurance, the CPA states that he or she is not aware of any material modifications that are needed for the financial statements to be in conformity with generally accepted accounting principles. For a compilation, the CPA provides no assurance of any type. A compilation is usually no more than the taking of client data and putting it into the form of financial statements. (Number Two is True.)

THREE – In a review, the CPA does not assess control risk and does not gather corroborating information about particular accounts. The primary work done by the CPA is limited to performing analytical procedures and making inquiries of the client management. (True or False?)

Answer – For a review, the CPA does not perform essential audit tasks such as assessing control risk and performing traditional audit tests of transactions and account balances. A review is an overview of the financial information in search of potential problems. The two main steps are analytical procedures and inquiries made of the client's management. In performing analytical procedures, the auditor arrives at estimations for significant client figures, ratios and the like. These auditor expectations are then compared to the client data looking for unusual variations that would indicate possible reporting problems. (Number Three is True.)

FOUR – In a review, a large part of the work is carried out by making inquiries of the company's management. The CPA should ask about relevant issues such as the method of preparing the statements, changes in internal control and the application of generally accepted accounting principles, the composition of large account balances, and the outcome of problems found in previous examinations. (True or False?)

Answer – For a review, numerous inquiries should be made of the company management. These questions address the financial reporting process in general. The CPA will be interested in changes that have occurred in the company and the statements as well as the settlement of any reporting problems previously noted. However, in a review, the CPA does not get involved with the composition of account balances. That is appropriate as an audit test of a specific account. (Number Four is False.)

FIVE – A standard review report contains three paragraphs. The first paragraph indicates that a review is composed mainly of inquiries of company personnel and analytical procedures and is substantially less than an audit. (True or False?)

Answer – The first paragraph of a review report indicates that a review was performed and identifies the financial statements. It also states that the Statements on Standards of the American Institute of Certified Public Accountants were followed and that the financial statements are the representations of the company management. The second paragraph explains that a review is primarily inquiries and analytical procedures and is substantially less than an audit examination. (Number Five is False.)

SIX – In a compilation, the CPA need not be independent. (True or False?)

Answer – A CPA normally has to be independent of all clients. One exception, though, is a compilation. Since no assurance is provided, independence is not required. However, disclosure must be made in the CPA's report of any lack of independence. (Number Six is True.)

SEVEN – In performing a compilation, the CPA provides limited assurance for all information that was actually tested. No assurance is provided for the remainder of the financial information. (True or False?)

Answer – In a compilation, the CPA provides no assurance. The CPA must read the finished statements and verify the math in order to catch obvious errors. However, no testing is done and no assurance is given. (Number Seven is False.)

EIGHT – A CPA performs a compilation for a client. The compilation report should contain three paragraphs and describe any testing that was actually performed. (True or False?)

Answer – A compilation report has only two paragraphs. The first paragraph identifies the financial statements and specifies that the CPA followed the Statements on Standards for Accounting and Review Services. The second explains that a compilation is the presentation of representations made by management in the form of financial statements and that no assurance of any type is being provided. (Number Eight is False.)

AUDIT RISK

(1) An independent auditor provides reasonable assurance that the five **assertions** made by management (and described earlier) are free from material misstatements. Misstatements result from errors, fraud, and direct illegal acts.

   (A) **Errors** are unintentional mistakes that affect the financial statements such as accidentally capitalizing a repair expense.

   (B) **Fraud** is an intentional action that leads to distortion of financial statements. Auditor may encounter two types of fraud.

   (1) **Fraudulent financial reporting** is the manipulation of the financial records to make the reporting entity appear either better or worse than it really is.

   (2) **Misappropriation of assets** (also known as **defalcation**) is the theft of assets, an action that causes the financial statements to be misstated.

   (C) Three conditions must be present for fraud to occur.

   (1) Incentive/pressure.

   (2) Opportunity.

   (3) Attitude/rationalization.

   (D) A **direct-effect illegal act** is one that has an immediate impact on the financial statements. Income tax evasion is an example because the reported balances for income tax payable and income tax expense are wrong.

   (E) Auditor provides only reasonable assurance because (1) not every transaction is examined, (2) human error can occur in the testing, and (3) both fraud and illegal acts are usually hidden.

(2) **Audit risk** is the possibility that a material misstatement will occur and be reported within an entity's financial statements. For each group of accounts, the auditor is not satisfied until audit risk is reduced to an acceptable level. Acceptable audit risk is the amount of risk that the auditor is willing to assume and still provide reasonable assurance of no material misstatements. Audit risk has three components, each of which may be judged quantitatively (for example, a 20% risk of misstatement might be said to exist) or nonquantitatively (one account may be assessed as having maximum risk of misstatement whereas another has minimum risk).

   (A) The auditor estimates the severity of the first two components of audit risk based on an assessment of the client and the particular group of accounts. Auditor must evaluate the likelihood of a problem.

   (1) **Inherent risk** is the possibility that a material misstatement will occur within the company's accounting system

   (2) **Control risk** is the possibility that a material misstatement that has occurred will not be detected by the company's control system.

   (B) The final component of audit risk is based on the quality and quantity of evidence gathered by the auditor.

   (1) **Detection risk** is the possibility that a material misstatement will not be caught by the auditor's testing (often referred to as substantive testing). Auditor continues testing an account group (thereby decreasing detection risk) until the three components taken together indicate that overall audit risk has been reduced to the level judged to be acceptable by the auditor.

(a) If inherent risk and/or control risk are assessed as high, auditor may have to reduce detection risk further than expected in order for overall audit risk to be acceptable.

(b) Detection risk decreases whenever auditor gathers more evidence or obtains evidence of a better quality. Evidence is considered to be of a better quality if it is gathered (1) closer to year end, (2) by more experienced auditors, or (3) using more sophisticated techniques (such as statistical sampling rather than judgment sampling).

(3) Early in the audit, the auditor should have a staff discussion (brainstorming session) regarding the risk of material misstatement due to fraud. The discussion should focus on how fraud might be perpetrated and emphasize the need for professional skepticism.

(4) Obtain the information needed to identify risks of material misstatement due to fraud through

(A) Inquiries of management and others within the organization.

(B) Considering the results of planning analytical procedures.

(C) Considering the existence of **fraud risk factors**.

    (1) SAS 99 contains lists of fraud risk factors organized around the conditions of

        (a) Incentive/pressure, (e.g., management or directors' financial situation threatened by significant financial interests in company).

        (b) Opportunity (e.g., internal control deficiencies).

        (c) Attitude/rationalization (e.g., known history of violations of securities or other laws).

(5) Identify fraud risks

(A) There is a presumption that misstatement of revenue will be a fraud risk.

(6) Responding to fraud risks

(A) Overall responses—assignment of personnel, careful consideration of accounting policies, and make audit procedures less predictable.

(B) Specific responses—alterations in the nature, extent, or timing of auditing procedures.

(C) Responses to further address the risk of management override of controls.

    (1) Examination of journal entries and other adjustments.

    (2) Retrospective review of prior accounting estimates for evidence of bias.

    (3) Evaluation of the business rationale for significant unusual transactions.

(7) The auditor should document: the audit team discussion, procedures performed to identify fraud risks, specific fraud risks identified and the auditor's response, the reason why revenue was not identified as a fraud risk (if it was not), results of procedures to further assess the risk of management override of controls, and the nature of communications about fraud made to management, the audit committee, and others.

(8) At any time during an audit, auditor may discover evidence that indicates that a misstatement could possibly exist in the financial records.

(A) Auditor must assess whether the possible misstatement could be material. If not, the auditor need only inform members of management at least one level above those involved about the potential problem.

(B) If possible misstatement could be material, auditor gathers more evidence to determine if misstatement actually exists.

(C)   If misstatement does exist, auditor assesses if it is material. If not, auditor tells management and has no other responsibility.

    (1)   If misstatement is material, auditor talks with management because the statements are the responsibility of management.

    (2)   Even if material problem is resolved, the audit committee of the board of directors must be informed because the issue had a significant impact on the financial reporting of the company.

    (3)   If material misstatement is not corrected, auditor gives an opinion qualification or an adverse opinion.

(9)   Auditor's responsibility for detecting illegal acts.

(A)   **Direct illegal acts** - auditor must provide reasonable assurance that no illegal acts have occurred that have a direct and material effect on financial statements. Auditor's responsibility is the same here as it is for errors and fraud.

(B)   Other illegal acts such as insider trading and safety hazards only have indirect effects on the financial statements. No account is currently wrong but a contingency exists; if the act is discovered, company could be punished.

    (1)   Auditor has no responsibility to look for or find illegal acts that have an indirect impact on financial statements. These actions are outside scope of the audit; in addition, they may well be hidden.

    (2)   However, auditors must maintain skeptical attitude and, thus, may discover such illegal acts or situations pointing to illegal acts. Questionable events would include unauthorized transactions, improper or slow reporting, and large cash or unspecified payments

(C)   Even for an indirect illegal act, if suspicious situation is encountered, auditor must investigate. If illegal act is discovered, auditor considers potential effect on the fair presentation of financial statements

    (1)   Must determine, by talking with management or through investigation, whether a contingency has been incurred that should be disclosed.

    (2)   If contingency has been incurred, auditor gathers evidence as to amount and proper presentation.

(D)   If a material indirect illegal act is found and company will not disclose, auditor renders an opinion qualification. If an act is discovered but its legality cannot be established, the auditor can provide a scope qualification

PROBLEMS AND SOLUTIONS
AUDIT RISK

ONE – Audit risk is the possibility that a material misstatement will occur and be reported within an entity's financial statements. For each group of accounts, the auditor must carry out substantive testing until audit risk is reduced to zero. (True or False?)

> *Answer – The auditor provides reasonable assurance of no material misstatements and not perfect assurance. Therefore, the auditor must continue to gather corroborating evidence until reasonable assurance can be given. Conveyance of reasonable assurance is possible when audit risk has been reduced to an acceptable level. (Number One is False.)*

TWO – Audit risk has three components: nonsampling risk, control risk, and sampling risk. (True or False?)

Answer – Audit risk does have three components but they are inherent risk, control risk, and detection risk. (Number Two is False.)

THREE – Inherent risk is the possibility that a material misstatement will occur within the reporting company's accounting system. The auditor examines the client's accounting system and assesses the amount of inherent risk that is present. (True or False?)

Answer – Inherent risk reflects a characteristic found in a particular company. Therefore, an auditor cannot alter inherent risk but can only estimate how much risk is present based on assessing the people and systems in place within the company. (Number Three is True.)

FOUR – Control risk is the possibility that a material misstatement that has occurred in a company's accounting system will not be detected by the internal control. The auditor examines the client's control components and may test certain control activities in order to assess the amount of control risk that is present. (True or False?)

Answer – Control risk reflects a characteristic of a particular company. Therefore, an auditor cannot change control risk but can only estimate the amount of risk based on the testing that is performed. (Number Four is True.)

FIVE – Detection risk is assessed by the auditor by examining the client company and the method by which it prepares its financial statements. (True or False?)

Answer – Detection risk is the possibility that a material misstatement exists that will not be discovered by the independent auditor's own testing. It is not a characteristic of the company but is a function of the amount and quality of work performed by the auditor. (Number Five is False.)

SIX – The auditor assesses both the inherent risk and control risk for a particular account or assertion to be high. The auditor must set the acceptable level of detection risk for that account or assertion at a relatively low level. (True or False?)

Answer – The assessments of inherent and control risk will vary inversely with the level of detection risk that is considered to be acceptable. If inherent risk and control risk are estimated as being high for a particular account or assertion, detection risk will have to be reduced to a relatively low level in order to be acceptable. (Number Six is True.)

SEVEN – The auditor assesses both the inherent risk and control risk for a particular account or assertion to be high. The auditor must set the acceptable level of detection risk for that account or assertion at a low level. In order to reduce detection risk to this acceptable level, the auditor must perform additional substantive testing. (True or False?)

Answer – Detection risk can be reduced to an acceptable level by additional substantive testing or by obtaining evidence of a higher quality. Evidence is considered to be of a higher quality if it is gathered closer to the end of the year, is obtained by more experienced auditors, or is generated by more sophisticated techniques such as positive confirmations rather than negative confirmations. Additional substantive testing will reduce detection risk but obtaining a higher quality of corroborating evidence also decreases this risk. (Number Seven is False.)

EIGHT – In assessing fraud risk, the auditor must be aware of management incentives to commit fraud. For example, a lack of internal control might provide the incentive. (True or False?)

Answer – Management incentives to commit fraud include such factors as threats to financial stability or profitability, excessive pressure on management to meet requirements or third-party expectations, or management or director's financial situation threatened. A lack of internal controls provides an opportunity to commit fraud. (Number Eight is False.)

NINE – The presence of an undisclosed direct-effect illegal act creates a misstatement. Because an auditor provides reasonable assurance that financial statements are free of material misstatements, the auditor's responsibility extends to direct illegal acts. In addition, the auditor provides negative assurance about the absence of indirect illegal acts. (True or False?)

Answer – The auditor has no responsibility to search for or discover illegal acts that have an indirect impact on financial statements. Therefore, the auditor provides no assurance about the absence of such indirect illegal acts. However, the auditor must remain suspicious and follow up if events indicate the possible presence of an indirect illegal act. (Number Nine is False.)

TEN – Income tax evasion is an example of a direct-effect illegal act and water pollution is an example of an illegal act that has only an indirect effect on financial statements. (True or False?)

Answer – With a direct-effect illegal act, figures currently reported within the financial statements are stated incorrectly. Thus, income tax evasion is a direct illegal act because the Income Tax Expense account and the Income Tax Payable account are both misstated. Illegal acts are said to have an indirect effect on financial statements if they create a contingency for the company. If the act is discovered, the company may be fined or penalized in some way. Thus, water pollution creates an indirect impact; the financial statements will only be affected if the crime is discovered. (Number Ten is True.)

ELEVEN – The procedures required to further address the risk of management override of controls include tests for unrecorded revenue and examination of the business rationale for significant unusual transactions. (True or False?)

Answer – The procedures required to further address the risk of management override of controls include examination of journal entries and other adjustments, retrospective review of prior year accounting estimates for biases, and evaluation of the business rationale for significant unusual transactions. (Number Eleven is False.)

TWELVE – The risk of fraudulent misstatement of revenue generally must be presumed to be a fraud risk on every audit. (True or False?)

Answer – SAS 99 indicates that revenue recognition should be considered a fraud risk unless the auditor can justify otherwise. (Number Twelve is True.)

INTERNAL CONTROL

(1) **Internal control** is a process set up by board of directors and management to provide reasonable assurance that company goals will be achieved as to (1) the reliability of financial reporting, (2) effectiveness and efficiency of operations, and (3) compliance with laws and regulations.

    (A) **Control risk** is the chance that a material misstatement will not be prevented or detected by the company's internal control.

    (B) An inverse relationship exists between assessed level of control risk and the acceptable level of detection risk that has to be achieved through auditor's substantive testing. Thus, assessment of control risk affects nature, extent, and timing of substantive testing.

(2) Auditor must always come to an understanding of five components of client's internal control. Knowledge of components must be documented. Documentation can be by questionnaire, flowchart, memorandum, or a combination of these.

    (A) **Control environment** - company's commitment to integrity, ethical values, and competence; management's philosophy and style (the amount of risk that the company is willing to take, for example, or conservative nature of reporting); delegation of authority and responsibility; and human resource policies.

    (B) **Risk assessment** - company's ability to anticipate potential misstatements and work to prevent them before they occur. Control system should recognize that risk increases because of new people, new operating systems, rapid growth, change in company or environment, new technology, new products, geographical separation and the like.

    (C) **Control activities** - policies and procedures installed by company to reduce risk of misstatements to an acceptable level. Can be separated into several classifications.

        (1) **Performance reviews** (such as comparing reported figures to budgets, standards, forecasts, past year figures, etc.) to highlight differences and indicate to officials the possible need for investigation and corrective action.

        (2) **General controls** to help ensure the accuracy of all data processing activities.

        (3) **Application controls** applied to individual transactions to ensure that all transactions are valid, authorized, and properly processed.

        (4) **Physical controls** to safeguard assets.

        (5) **Segregation of duties** within the organization so that different individuals/departments (1) authorize transactions, (2) record transactions, and (3) maintain custody of assets.

    (D) **Information and communication** - ability of the accounting system to generate reliable information. System must be able to identify and record all transactions in a timely manner and convey information to those parties who can make use of it.

    (E) **Monitoring** - regular assessment of internal control over time so that it does not become outdated or lose its dependability.

(3) While assessing control risk, auditor must watch for factors, such as the following, that indicate a particular **risk of fraud**.

    (A) Failure of management to monitor significant controls.

        (B)   Failure to screen new employees who will be in positions to steal.

        (C)   Inadequate recording of assets that could be easily stolen.

        (D)   Lack of proper segregation of duties.

        (E)   Lack of system for authorizing and approving transactions.

        (F)   Poor physical safeguards.

        (G)   Failure to record transactions in a timely fashion.

        (H)   Lack of mandatory vacations.

        (I)   Failure to correct problems found in internal control system.

(4)   After coming to an understanding of control components, auditor makes a **preliminary assessment of control risk** based on the quality of these components, evaluations made in previous audits, discovery of fraud risk factors, competence and objectivity of internal audit department, review of client control documentation, observation of employee performance, and by tracing a sample of transactions through various systems to note proper application of control procedures.

        (A)   Based on this preliminary assessment, significant problems may be apparent and the auditor will assess control risk at a maximum level. Auditor then relies solely on substantive testing to reduce detection risk so that overall audit risk is reduced to acceptable level. Auditor has no reason to perform tests of controls.

        (B)   Based on preliminary assessment, control risk for some assertions may appear to possibly be below maximum. If control risk is eventually assessed as being below the maximum level, auditor will be required to do less substantive testing or can rely on tests of a lower quality.

        (C)   To finalize a preliminary assessment that control risk is below the maximum, the auditor performs **tests of specific control activities**.

               (1)   Must determine **design of internal control** within individual accounting systems. Once again this understanding can be documented by a questionnaire, flowchart, and/or memorandum.

               (2)   **Control activities** are identified within these systems that should help to reduce control risk. Auditor anticipates types of misstatements that could occur and then searches for control activities that would prevent these problems.

               (3)   The identified control activities are tested to verify that they are actually operating effectively and efficiently as intended. Auditor can take several actions.

                     (a)   Talk with personnel about procedures that they follow.

                     (b)   Observe employees as they perform critical tasks.

                     (c)   Trace the processing of transactions through the system to see if control activities were properly performed. In most cases, control activities are designed to leave some physical proof such as a check mark.

                     (d)   Reperform the activities to ensure that all problems were caught.

        (D)   Even if control risk appears low after preliminary assessment of the five components, further testing of specific controls may take more effort than the potential savings in substantive testing. In those cases, it is more efficient for auditor to assume maximum control risk and move directly to substantive testing.

        (E)   If control risk is assessed at the maximum, auditor must document understanding of the control components and specify the conclusion. If control risk is assessed below the maximum, auditor must also provide basis for this conclusion and understanding of the control activities relied on in the individual systems.

- (F) In a system where information is transmitted, processed, or maintained electronically, auditor may be unable to carry out enough substantive testing to reduce detection risk to an acceptable level. Auditor should perform additional tests of controls to gather evidence that might provide adequate assurance.

(5) **Inherent limitations** exist for all systems of internal control. Some amount of risk will always exist; internal control cannot provide perfect assurance.

- (A) Collusion by employees can get around most control activities.
- (B) Management can override control activities.
- (C) Human errors can prevent control activities from working properly.
- (D) At some point, the cost of additional control is not worth the additional benefits that accrue.
- (E) Internal control as well as the company itself can change quickly over time. Even though control may be excellent at one point in time, that is no assurance that it will continue to be sufficient.

(6) **Internal audit department** is responsible for monitoring internal control within a company. It appraises the design and helps assure compliance with all controls (as compared to independent auditor who just assesses financial controls). Fair presentation of financial statements is only an indirect interest of the internal audit department.

- (A) Independent auditor determines the actual function of the internal audit department by looking at job descriptions, status in the company, audit plans, etc.
- (B) If internal audit department is competent and objective (independent), assessed level of control risk might be reduced so that less substantive testing is needed.
  - (1) **Competence of internal audit department** is judged by looking at education, certification, and experience of the individuals. Auditor should also review some of the work of the internal audit department as it relates to financial reporting
  - (2) **Objectivity of internal audit department** is judged by determining whether reporting is done directly to audit committee and/or board of directors. It is also important to make sure that no limitations are placed on work of internal audit department.
- (C) If risk of material misstatements is very low for certain assertions (value of prepaid expenses, for example), the work of the internal audit department alone may provide sufficient evidence for the independent auditor.

(7) If auditor discovers a **reportable condition** (a significant deficiency) in a company's internal control, auditor must inform the audit committee.

- (A) Communication can be written or oral.
- (B) If problem has been previously reported and acknowledged by board but not fixed, auditor has no responsibility to communicate again.
- (C) If problem constitutes a **material weakness in internal control** (high level of risk), communication should be made immediately. Otherwise communication can wait until end of the audit.

PROBLEMS AND SOLUTIONS
INTERNAL CONTROL

ONE – An auditor is assessing a company's control risk and determines that less risk exists than was anticipated originally. Consequently, the auditor will probably reduce the amount of substantive testing to be performed. (True or False?)

Answer – When the assessment of control risk is reduced, the level of detection risk that is considered acceptable can be increased. Because the acceptable level of detection risk is higher, the auditor will be required to do less substantive testing (or can gather evidence of a lower quality than was originally expected). (Number One is True.)

TWO – Regardless of the anticipated level of control risk, the auditor must gain an understanding of the components of a reporting company's internal control. There are five such components. (True or False?)

Answer – In following generally accepted auditing standards, an auditor must come to an understanding of five components of internal control. These components are (1) the control environment, (2) risk assessment, (3) control activities, (4) information and communication, and (5) monitoring. (Number Two is True.)

THREE – The auditor seeks to determine whether a company has the ability to anticipate and prevent potential misstatements. This component of internal control is known as the control environment. (True or False?)

Answer – Assessing whether an accounting system and its related controls can anticipate potential misstatements and take actions to prevent them is a component of internal control known as risk assessment. The term "control environment" refers to factors such as the company's commitment to integrity and management's philosophy toward financial reporting. (Number Three is False.)

FOUR – A company's accounting system is able to identify all transactions and report them in a proper and timely fashion to the people within the organization who need the information. The auditor is assessing the company's control activities, one of the five components of internal control. (True or False?)

Answer – The auditor does assess whether the reporting company can gather all essential information in a timely manner and report it to the appropriate individuals. However, this component of internal control is known as "information and communication." Control activities relate to policies and procedures used by the company to reduce misstatements within its accounting system. (Number Four is False.)

FIVE – During the assessment of control risk, an auditor must watch for fraud risk factors that may be present. For example, the failure of the company to require mandatory vacations would be one such fraud risk factor. (True or False?)

Answer – Factors that might indicate the presence of fraud within the internal control of the reporting company would include: failure of management to monitor significant controls, lack of proper segregation of duties, poor physical safeguards, failure to correct problems in internal control, and lack of mandatory vacations. An employee's failure to take a vacation may indicate that the individual is hiding either theft or a manipulation of the accounting records and is afraid to take time off because of the chance of discovery. (Number Five is True.)

SIX – After making a preliminary assessment of the five components of internal control, the auditor believes that control risk is high because of weaknesses that are discovered. The auditor should test those controls further before beginning substantive testing in order to reduce detection risk to the level that is considered acceptable. (True or False?)

Answer – If control risk is high because of identified weaknesses, there is no reason to do additional testing of those controls. The auditor should move directly to substantive testing. Control risk will be assessed at the maximum level. As a result, the auditor has to set the acceptable level of detection risk relatively low. Increased substantive testing will be performed or evidence of a better quality must be obtained. (Number Six is False.)

SEVEN – After making a preliminary assessment of the five components of internal control, the auditor believes that control risk might be low for one or more assertions. The auditor may then choose to test those controls but may also decide not to test those controls. (True or False?)

Answer – Where control risk appears to be below the maximum level, the auditor must decide whether to test those controls or not. If a reduction in control risk is expected to cause a decrease in overall audit time and effort, the controls should be tested further. However, if the effort needed to reduce control risk will not lead to a drop in overall audit time and effort, control risk should be set at the maximum level. The auditor then immediately begins substantive testing procedures. (Number Seven is True.)

EIGHT – A preliminary assessment has been made of the five components of internal control. If the auditor decides to perform tests of controls, the design of specific systems and the control activities within those systems should be determined. A flowchart must be created in order to reflect the auditor's understanding of those systems and controls. (True or False?)

Answer – In performing tests of controls, the design of the internal control within individual systems must be determined and documented. For that purpose, a flowchart, a memorandum, or a questionnaire can be used. (Number Eight is False.)

NINE – If an auditor has decided to perform tests of controls, the auditor must determine the design of internal control within the various accounting systems, identify control activities that could reduce control risk, and verify that those activities are operating effectively and efficiently. The auditor performs substantive testing procedures to determine whether specified control activities are operating as intended. (True or False?)

> *Answer – Testing of controls does consist of three steps: determining the design of the systems and the internal control within those systems, identifying control activities that would reduce risk, and testing to see if those activities are actually functioning as intended. To verify that the designated activities are operating effectively and efficiently, the auditor can make inquiries, observe employees performing the controls, look for physical proof that the activities have been performed, or reperform some of the activities to ensure that all problems are being detected. These actions are considered tests of controls and not substantive tests. (Number Nine is False.)*

TEN – Collusion among employees is an inherent limitation of internal control. (True or False?)

> *Answer – Internal control can only provide reasonable assurance that material misstatements are prevented or detected. It cannot provide perfect assurance because certain inherent limitations are impossible to overcome completely. These inherent limitations include (1) overriding the system of control by members of the management, (2) human errors, (3) changes in the company that occur over time, and (4) collusion among company employees. (Number Ten is True.)*

ELEVEN – If an independent auditor discovers a significant deficiency (a reportable condition) in a company's internal control, the auditor must inform the management and the audit committee immediately. (True or False?)

> *Answer – In assessing control risk, an auditor may discover a significant deficiency in internal control which is known as a "reportable condition." This information must be communicated to management and to the audit committee. This communication can be orally or in writing and can be made immediately or delayed until the end of the audit. (Number Eleven is False.)*

EVIDENCE GATHERING

(1)   The **audit program** is a list of substantive testing procedures to be performed. It is required in an audit; it shows that the work has been adequately planned.

    (A)   Preliminary draft is often written at the beginning of the audit.

    (B)   Audit program is finalized after assessment is made of inherent risk and control risk. At that point, auditor knows the level of detection risk that has to be achieved which affects the nature, extent, and timing of the substantive tests to be carried out.

(2)   In the year that an auditing firm takes a new engagement, information should be sought from the **predecessor auditor**. Predecessor auditor is one who did previous audit but who has been terminated or resigned or has been told that termination may occur.

    (A)   Current auditor must always get the client's permission before talking with past auditor (or anyone else). If client refuses to give permission, auditor normally resigns because of fear that management cannot be trusted. However, resignation is not required; auditor should assess reason for refusal.

    (B)   **Successor auditor** is required to communicate with predecessor before accepting engagement but should not seek this discussion until after engagement has been offered. If predecessor's response is limited (if, for example, because of litigation), the limitation should be indicated. Required communications include the following:

        (1)   Information as to the integrity of management.

        (2)   Disagreements with management on either accounting or auditing issues.

        (3)   Communications with audit committee regarding fraud, illegal acts, and internal control related matters.

        (4)   The predecessor's understanding of the reason for changing auditors.

    (C)   After accepting an engagement, the successor is urged (but not required) to communicate with predecessor again so as to review prior **working papers**.

        (1)   This review can help the auditor identify accounting methods that were used in the past so that consistent application can be substantiated.

        (2)   Successor also needs to substantiate the opening balances of the balance sheet accounts. Successor does not rely on the predecessor's working papers but rather the review of those working papers is one method of gathering the needed evidence.

(3)   Auditor is required to establish an **understanding with the client about each engagement** (an audit as well as other attestation services).

    (A)   This understanding must include four areas:

        (1)   Objective of the work (for an audit, it is the expression of an opinion on the financial statements).

        (2)   Management's responsibilities - the financial statements, effective internal control, compliance with laws and regulations, making all records available, and a representation letter to the auditor.

        (3)   Auditor's responsibilities - following generally accepted auditing standards and letting the audit committee know of any reportable conditions.

        (4)   Limitations of the engagement - reasonable assurance is given and not absolute assurance, a disclaimer will be rendered if no opinion can be

given, and that internal control is only evaluated in order to determine the nature, extent, and timing of audit testing.

    (B)   Other matters can also be included in the understanding: the use of a specialist, the use of internal auditors, discussions with predecessor auditors, etc.

    (C)   Understanding with client must be documented. An **engagement letter** is recommended for this purpose but not required. A signed memo describing an oral discussion will be adequate as will a formal contract.

(4)   **Representation letter** is obtained by auditor, usually on the last day of fieldwork. Can be dated later than the audit report but no earlier.

    (A)   It is a letter from representatives of the management (signed by both the CEO and CFO and anyone else with sufficient knowledge of financial statements).

    (B)   If representation letter is not received, auditor must give qualified opinion because of the scope limitation. Auditor also has the right to give a disclaimer or withdraw from the engagement.

    (C)   The letter requires management to acknowledge responsibility for financial statements. Management must also state its belief that the financial statements are presented fairly according to generally accepted accounting principles. Management indicates that it is also responsible for correcting any material misstatements and that any uncorrected misstatements are not material. In addition, letter confirms and documents the representations made to the auditors during the audit. It also helps to reduce misunderstandings between the parties.

    (D)   Can include a number of representations such as the following:

        (1)   Management acknowledges responsibility for financial statements and states belief that they are presented fairly.

        (2)   States that all records, data, and minutes have been made available.

        (3)   States that all material transactions have been properly recorded.

        (4)   States that no fraud has occurred involving management with a significant role in internal control and that no fraud has occurred that has a material effect on the financial statements.

        (5)   States that the following have been properly disclosed and reported: related party transactions, guarantees, significant estimates, unasserted claims, contingencies and the like.

    (E)   Can include information on materiality, in either qualitative or quantitative terms.

(5)   **Audit committee** is composed of independent members of the board of directors (members who are not part of management).

    (A)   Committee oversees the internal audit function and serves as liaison with independent auditors.

    (B)   Independent auditor should ensure that committee knows of anything that has a significant effect on financial statements including: accounting policy decisions by management, method of deriving estimates, and proposed adjustments discovered by auditor.

    (C)   Auditor must also tell audit committee about any misstatements not corrected by management even though the misstatements were not considered to be material, either individually or in the aggregate.

    (D)   For an SEC client, an auditor must talk with the audit committee about the quality (as well as the acceptability) of the company's accounting principles and estimations.

(6) **Analytical procedures** are used in reviews and they are also required in an audit engagement.

    (A)   Analytical procedures must be performed in the planning stage of an audit to help auditor assess inherent risk. They also must be carried out in the final review stage of the audit to make certain that no suspicious changes occurred during the audit that were overlooked. Analytical procedures can be used as substantive tests but this use is optional.

    (B)   Auditor anticipates client figures, ratios, and relationships such as sales, current ratio, age of inventory, gross profit percentage, etc. These estimations are made within a range. If client figures lie outside of this range, the risk of misstatement increases.

    (C)   Expected figures come from budgets, figures of previous years, industry averages, reports by competitors, changes in environment or in the company and the like.

    (D)   The credibility of auditor expectation is improved if information was derived from (1) several sources, (2) outside of company, (3) an independent party inside of company, or (4) audited data.

(7) In every engagement, auditor must maintain an attitude of **professional skepticism**. During substantive testing, auditor should watch for factors that might indicate a particular risk of fraud. **Fraud risk factors** in this stage of the audit include the following.

    (A)   Transactions that were not recorded in a complete and timely manner or were recorded incorrectly.

    (B)   Discovery of unsupported or unauthorized balances or transactions.

    (C)   Significant adjustments made by the client near the end of the year.

    (D)   Missing documents or only photocopies available when the originals should exist.

    (E)   Unexplained items appearing on reconciliations.

    (F)   Inconsistent or vague responses from management to auditor inquiry.

    (G)   Unusual discrepancies found in financial records.

    (H)   Auditor denied access to certain records.

    (I)   Missing assets.

    (J)   Unusual delays in getting requested information from management.

(8) If auditor has reason to suspect fraud, certain actions may be needed.

    (A)   Surprise inspection of assets.

    (B)   Requiring a count of assets closer to year's end.

    (C)   Oral confirmations of balances as well as written ones.

    (D)   Detailed review of large transactions and adjustments.

    (E)   Analytical procedures on a more detailed basis (sales by location, for example).

    (F)   Interviews with employees in high risk areas.

(9) Auditor can make use of an outside **specialist** in gathering evidence.

    (A)   In some areas, an auditor will not have the expertise necessary for making required judgments. In those cases, auditor may hire and rely on a specialist. For example, this may be done in inventory valuation (diamonds), estimations (percentage of completion), litigation analysis, etc.

    (B)   Before relying on specialist, auditor must verify the reliability of that party's work.

        (1)   Auditor checks specialist's professional reputation by examining licenses, certifications, references, client list, etc.

> (2) Auditor checks independence. Specialist does not have to be independent but that would weigh on credibility of evidence
>
> (C) Auditor is responsible for making certain that specialist understands what is needed and how the information will be used.
>
> (D) If there is a difference between client figures and the results of a specialist, auditor should seek a resolution or get opinion of a second specialist or consider qualifying opinion.
>
> > (1) Using the name of specialist in audit opinion is allowed but only if the work of the specialist lead to an opinion that was other than the standard unqualified opinion.

(10) Material **related party transactions** must be disclosed in the footnotes. Auditor must make sure that all have been found and disclosed.

> (A) Related parties include affiliates of the company, substantial owners, management and their immediate family, and anyone who exerts significant influence over the company
>
> (B) Auditor first gets a list of all related parties by asking client, looking at SEC reports and annual reports, getting a list of management and stockholders, and looking at information found in previous audits.
>
> (C) Auditor attempts to find all related party transactions by asking client, giving staff a list of related parties, reading minutes, scanning accounts for unusual amounts or familiar names, and watching for transactions with unusual terms especially if they occur near the end of the year.
>
> (D) If related party transactions have occurred, the nature of the relationship and the terms of the transactions must be disclosed
>
> > (1) Client can also state that transactions were at same terms as transactions with an outside party but only if that assertion can be substantiated.

(11) Auditor has special problem in corroborating **estimations** because there is usually a lack of objective evidence.

> (A) Estimates are found throughout statements: collectibility of receivables, outcome of lawsuits, life of equipment, etc.
>
> (B) Auditor evaluates (a) management's system of identifying need for estimates and (b) the method used in making specific estimations.
>
> (C) Auditor must also evaluate reasonableness of each significant estimate by (a) looking at past results (for example, how long equipment is normally used), (b) having an independent estimation made possibly by using an outside specialist, and (c) reviewing subsequent events to determine if they confirm estimations.

(12) Auditor must evaluate whether substantial doubt exists that company can remain in business for one year from balance sheet date. Auditor looks for indications of possible evidence that warn of **going concern problems**.

> (A) Indicators of possible problems include recurring losses, negative cash flows from operations, a negative working capital position, restructuring of debt, default on loans, lawsuits, unpaid dividends, loss of key customers, etc.
>
> (B) If problems are discovered, auditor seeks management's plans as to how problem will be resolved so that the company can continue to operate.
>
> (C) If auditor is not satisfied with management's plans, an **explanatory paragraph** is added after the opinion paragraph to warn readers that substantial doubt exists as to whether company can remain as a going concern. As an alternative, a disclaimer is allowed.

(13)   The evidence that is gathered in an audit is recorded in **working papers** (audit documentation). **Audit documentation** serves mainly to provide support for the auditor's report and aid the auditor in the conduct and supervision of the audit. It should be sufficient to show that the standards of fieldwork have been observed.

  (A)   Audit documentation should be sufficient to enable reviewers to (1) determine the nature, timing, and extent of the work performed and the results, (2) indicate who performed and reviewed the work, and (3) show that the accounting records agree or reconcile with the financial statements. Significant findings and issues and actions taken to address them should also be documented.

  (B)   **Current file** includes (a) the audit program to indicate planning, (b) all evidence gathered to substantiate opinion, (c) indication of proper supervision, and (d) an explanation of all problems encountered and their resolution.

    (1)   Quality of evidence affects need for quantity. Best quality evidence is any direct personal evidence acquired by auditor (inspection, observation, computation) especially if it is based on information derived from outside of client. Poorest evidence is anything produced by client and given directly to auditor (bill of lading, receiving reports, etc.).

  (C)   **Permanent file** includes client data that will stay the same for a number of years: account numbers, bond contracts, the company charter, organizational chart, etc.

(14)   In an audit, the **subsequent period** is the time between the end of the client's fiscal year and the last day of the auditor's fieldwork.

  (A)   Auditor's investigation during this period should provide evidence about the possibility of misstatements in year-end balances. Such testing would include reviewing (a) cash payments as a search for unrecorded liabilities, (b) cash receipts to verify collectibility of receivables, (c) sales to prove reported value of inventory, (d) sales returns to substantiate reported Sales figure, etc.

  (B)   Some subsequent events have no impact on year-end balances but are so significant that they should be disclosed in the footnotes. Examples would include the issuance of capital stock, a large casualty loss, or the incurrence of a large debt.

(15)   After issuance of an opinion, auditor may discover new information about the financial statements or the audit examination.

  (A)   After audit is finished, auditor has no further responsibility to do any further investigation. However, information may come to the auditor's attention that indicates a potential problem. In that situation, the auditor's concern is whether the original opinion can still be justified.

  (B)   Auditor should determine if original opinion continues to be appropriate. If necessary, client should be contacted and asked for help in the investigation.

PROBLEMS AND SOLUTIONS
EVIDENCE GATHERING

ONE – An audit program is a requirement of an audit. It is normally not finalized until after the auditor's assessments of inherent and control risks have been made. (True or False?)

Answer – An auditor is required to create an audit program to demonstrate that the work was planned properly. Frequently, a tentative program will be developed in the early stages of the audit. However, until the auditor has assessed both inherent risk and control risk, the acceptable level of detection risk is unknown. Since this determination will impact the amount of substantive testing to be done, the audit program cannot be finalized until those assessments have been made. (Number One is True.)

TWO – A new auditor will seek permission from a client to talk with the audit firm that did the engagement in previous years. To avoid burdening the predecessor, the new auditor should wait until the client has offered the engagement. In the initial conversation with the predecessor, the new auditor is most interested in asking about accounts that are likely to contain material misstatements. (True or False?)

Answer – When talking with the predecessor auditor prior to accepting an engagement, the new auditor is most interested in information about the integrity of the company's management. This information helps the new auditor determine whether to take the engagement. For this reason, the new auditor should ask about disagreements that arose with the management and communications made with the audit committee because of matters such as fraud or illegal acts. The new auditor should also seek information about the reason for the change being made in auditors. (Number Two is False.)

THREE – An auditor must write up an engagement letter and have it signed by the management of the client company. (True or False?)

Answer – The auditor has to establish an understanding with the client company about the objective and limitations of the work as well as the responsibilities of both parties. This understanding must be documented. An engagement letter can be used for this purpose but is not required. (Number Three is False.)

FOUR – An auditor fails to obtain a representation letter from the client company at the end of an audit engagement. The auditor cannot give a standard unqualified audit opinion. (True or False?)

Answer – According to generally accepted auditing standards, a representation letter is required in order to have sufficient, competent evidence on which to base an opinion. Failure to receive a representation letter will prevent the auditor from giving a standard unqualified audit opinion. (Number Four is True.)

FIVE – A representation letter has to be signed by the president of the reporting company as well as the head of the board of directors. (True or False?)

Answer – A representation letter should be signed by the chief executive officer of the reporting company as well as the chief financial officer and any other person with sufficient knowledge of the financial statements. (Number Five is False.)

SIX – A representation letter should have the same date as the audit report. (True or False?)

Answer – A representation letter should be received (and dated) as of the last day of the audit fieldwork. That is the same date that is applied to the audit report. In the representation letter, the management acknowledges its responsibility for the financial statements and states its belief that they are presented fairly in accordance with generally accepted accounting principles. The letter also serves to document specific representations made during the audit by the management. (Number Six is True.)

SEVEN – The auditor only needs to inform the audit committee of issues that will lead to an opinion that is other than a standard audit report. (True or False?)

Answer – The auditor must make certain that the audit committee is aware of anything that will have a significant effect on the financial statements. Disclosure to that group should include accounting policy decisions, methods of deriving important estimations, and proposed adjustments (even if agreed to by management). (Number Seven is False.)

EIGHT – Analytical procedures must be performed by the auditor in both the planning stage and review stage of the audit. (True or False?)

Answer – Analytical procedures are carried out in the planning stage of the audit to highlight areas of particularly high risk. The procedures are done in connection with the assessment of inherent risk. Analytical procedures are also required during the final review stage of the audit to help make certain that no suspicious changes have been missed. Analytical procedures can also be used for substantive testing purposes although that is an optional method of gathering evidence. (Number Eight is True.)

NINE – In performing analytical procedures, auditor expectations of account balances, ratios, and the like are compared to client records. The auditor is looking for any large or unusual differences. The amounts anticipated by the auditor are normally based on the budgets and forecasts prepared by the client company for the period. (True or False?)

Answer – The amounts, ratios, and the like anticipated by the auditor are derived from numerous sources such as historical figures, budgets and forecasts, industry averages, figures reported by competing companies, and other financial and nonfinancial information. (Number Nine is False.)

TEN – The firm of XYZ is auditing a mining company that has based its depletion expense for the year on an estimation that 10,000 tons of ore are located in a particular mine. The audit firm hires an outside specialist who indicates no material difference with this estimation. The audit firm must render a qualified opinion because of reliance on this outside expert. (True or False?)

Answer – An auditing firm will occasionally need to corroborate information through the use of an outside expert. As long as certain procedures are followed, such testing is acceptable and normal. Because the specialist found no evidence of a material misstatement in the company's estimation, the audit firm can provide a standard unqualified audit report. (Number Ten is False.)

ELEVEN – An auditor notes that a company did not pay its normal dividend during the past year because of cash flow problems. The auditor is not certain that the company can remain in business for the next five years because of such problems. The auditor should qualify the audit opinion because of this concern. (True or False?)

Answer – The auditor must be aware of any indications that substantial doubt might exist that the reporting company will not remain a going concern for at least 12 months from the balance sheet date. Such factors as unpaid dividends, default on debt, and major litigation can all point to this type of concern. If the company cannot show how it will stay in operation for at least 12 months, the auditor should add a paragraph at the end of the audit report to draw attention to this uncertainty. As an alternative, the auditor can give a disclaimer of opinion. (Number Eleven is False.)

TWELVE – A company's balance sheet is dated December 31, Year One. The date of the audit report is March 4, Year Two. On February 8, Year Two, a major fire creates a material loss for the company. Even though the fire occurred after the balance sheet date, the loss should be disclosed in the Year One financial statements. (True or False?)

Answer – Any significant event that occurs between the end of the fiscal period and the date of the audit report must still be disclosed even if the entire impact relates to the subsequent time period. This information is considered useful to the users of the financial statements. (Number Twelve is True.)

ACCOUNTS RECEIVABLE AND REVENUES

(1)   In auditing accounts receivable and related revenue balances, several potential problems exist that could create material misstatements. Some of these would be errors whereas others would indicate fraud.

    (A)   Reported receivables and sales could be false. Amounts were recorded to manipulate reported amount of income. **False sales** are especially likely if (a) income to be reported is down for the period, (b) employee compensation or bonuses are based on profits, or (c) company plans to issue capital stock or borrow money in the near future.

    (B)   Incoming cash is stolen and theft is hidden by writing off the receivable as a bad debt.

    (C)   **Lapping** is being carried out. Cash from one receivable is stolen and covered with cash received from a second customer during the following day or two

    (D)   The **year-end cut-off** of transactions is incorrect. Transactions occurring before the end of year could be recorded in the subsequent period (thus, reporting for the initial year is not complete). Transactions after the end of year could be recorded prematurely in the initial year (reported transactions in initial year did not actually exist at the time of the financial statements).

    (E)   Customer is billed incorrectly (because of math errors, wrong quantity, wrong price, wrong items) or customer is just not billed at all for goods that were actually shipped (inventory is gone but no collection is ever made)

    (F)   Transaction is with a related party so that disclosure is needed

(2)   Company should have a system in place to record sale, make proper shipment, and control and collect receivable balance.

    (A)   A customer order is received. May be by mail or over telephone or given directly to company employees.

    (B)   On a pre-printed, pre-numbered **sales order** form, the **sales department** lists all relevant information: quantity, description, terms, buyer, address, method of payment, etc.

    (C)   **Credit department** reviews **credit file** (which can hold credit report, references, financial statements, payment history of client, etc.). Approval or disapproval of credit is then indicated on the sales order form.

    (D)   If approved, sales order goes to finished goods **warehouse** where goods are gathered and sent to **shipping department**. Separate departments are maintained so that goods being removed must be documented. Since asset is being transferred, shipping department should verify description and quantity against sales order form. Condition of goods should also be checked. Shipping then signs and returns a copy of sales order which is kept by warehouse as a receipt to prove that transfer was made.

    (E)   Shipping department sends goods to customer and prepares a shipping document, often known as a **bill of lading**. One copy goes with merchandise and a second copy is sent directly to customer.

    (F)   Copy of bill of lading is sent to **inventory accounting department** which should maintain a perpetual listing of all inventory. An entry is made to remove item from records. Entries are accumulated and forwarded to **general accounting department** for posting of the overall reduction of Inventory account.

(G)   Copies of all documents go to **billings department**. Comparison is made of quantity and description. If all information agrees, a **sales invoice** is prepared and sent to client. It is also recorded in **sales journal**. Summary of sales journal is forwarded to general accounting for recording.

(H)   Copy of sales invoice is sent to **accounts receivable department**. Amount is recorded in **accounts receivable master file** by customer name.

(I)   Periodically, an **aged accounts receivable trial balance** is prepared which lists each account by age. Old accounts are turned over to a **collection department**.

(J)   If balance still proves to be uncollectible, both collection and accounts receivable departments file documentation to indicate actions taken. Independent party reviews information before final write-off of balance is approved.

(3)   A number of substantive testing procedures should be performed to verify the five assertions made by client about accounts receivable and related balances.

    (A)   Perform **analytical procedures** to identify areas where client figures differ from auditor expectations. Look at: overall balance of each account, age of receivables, gross profit percentage, sales returns as a percentage of sales, write off of accounts as compared to previous years, etc.

        (1)   Analytical procedures are required in planning stage of audit to help assess inherent risk. They are also required in final review stage of audit as a last check. Use as a substantive test of an account balance is optional.

    (B)   Trace one or more transactions through the entire system to see if recording is appropriate at each step. Start with customer order and check all steps until account and collection are recorded. Auditor is especially interested that all shipments are properly billed.

        (1)   Whenever auditor starts with transactions at their inception, the **completeness assertion** is being tested.

    (C)   Vouch one or more entries in the T-account back through system to see if there is adequate support. Whenever auditor starts with a reported balance and seeks corroboration, the **existence assertion** is being tested.

    (D)   Check math and accuracy of client work where applicable. Re-add accounts receivable master file and compare it to the general ledger account. Verify that aged accounts receivable trial balance is added correctly and individual amounts agree with master file. Re-add sales journal.

    (E)   For 3-4 days before and 3-4 days after year end, verify client cut-off procedures to make sure transactions were recorded in correct period. Use the bill of lading and sales invoice to determine when receivable and sale should be recorded. Cash receipts listing provides date for removal of receivable.

    (F)   Auditor reviews any evidence generated in **subsequent period** (the time from the balance sheet date until the end of fieldwork). For example, cash collections prove the balance and collectibility of a receivable, sales returns should be matched with sales, and bad debts written off may have been uncollectible at year's end.

    (G)   Look for **related party transactions** that have to be disclosed. For example, the **representation letter** asks about their existence.

    (H)   **Confirm balances directly with customers** to prove **existence assertion**. Usually done early in audit unless inherent and/or control risks are high. In that case, confirmation is carried out closer to year's end.

(1) All confirmations are signed by client but controlled, mailed, and responses received by auditor

(2) **Negative confirmations** ask customer for a response only if reported balance is wrong. It is less costly but provides a poorer quality of evidence since nothing tangible is received unless a problem exists. Normally used for small balances, balances that are not old, and where risk appears low.

(3) **Positive confirmations** ask for response from customer whether balance is correct or incorrect. Because an actual response should be received in all cases, this is viewed as a better technique. Normally used for old balances, large balances, or where risk is high.

    (a) If no response to positive request is received, a second confirmation can be sent or a direct call made. If auditor still does not get a response, alternative testing must be expanded. All documents should be compared and cash receipts should be reviewed for subsequent payment.

    (b) In either type of confirmation, reported discrepancies should be investigated to determine whether a problem exists.

(4) Accounts which have been written off or which have a zero balance can be confirmed just to make certain that reported facts are accurate.

(5) If a confirmation is returned by e-mail or by fax, the auditor may need to call the customer or request that the confirmation be mailed to the auditor in order to get adequate support.

(I) Method of estimating bad debt expense should be examined. Auditor wants to make sure that no evidence exists to indicate that client's estimation is not justified. Auditor must be aware of changes that may affect client's previous experience.

(J) Auditor must ensure balance sheet presentation and disclosure is appropriate. For example, pledged accounts must be noted.

PROBLEMS AND SOLUTIONS
ACCOUNTS RECEIVABLE AND REVENUES

ONE – The shipping department of a company should be a department separate from the warehouse. (True or False?)

Answer – The warehouse has custody of assets (inventory) and is, thus, in a position to steal. To add control and to prevent theft, a separate shipping department should be in operation. Thus, the assets must pass through a different department (shipping) before they can be taken from the company. This organizational separation reduces the potential for theft. (Number One is True.)

TWO – A company's billings department produces a sales invoice. Immediately after preparation, the document should be sent to the accounts receivable department for recording purposes. (True or False?)

Answer – To avoid possible misstatements within a system, all documents are normally reviewed and authorized before any other step occurs. After that, a record should be made of the document and a copy should be kept in case of loss. (Number Two is False.)

THREE – Company X has a receivable from a customer that is never collected. The collection department attempts to force payment but no amount is received. The account is now to be written off as uncollectible. Before this account is removed from the records, the cashier must give final approval. (True or False?)

> *Answer – Accounts being written off are a concern because the balance may have been collected and then stolen. As a second problem, perhaps the sale should not have been made to this particular credit risk. Therefore, before any account is declared uncollectible, it should be reviewed and authorized by an independent party. The cashier is not considered independent because that person may have stolen the incoming money. Therefore, some other party unrelated to the transaction needs to review the documentation and approve the write off. (Number Three is False.)*

FOUR – A company has an account receivable from a customer with a balance of $11,000 as of the end of the year. The auditor finds documentation such as a sales order and a shipping document to support that balance. The auditor is testing the existence assertion. (True or False?)

> *Answer – Typically, when an auditor selects a balance found in the financial records and seeks to corroborate or support it by looking for documentation, the auditor is attempting to make sure the balance did exist and was not falsified. (Number Four is True.)*

FIVE – An auditor randomly selects a sales order that is from a customer who wants five large pieces of furniture. The auditor finds a shipping document that matches this sales order. The auditor also locates a copy of the sales invoice for this transaction. Then, the auditor discovers that the appropriate amount is included in the accounts receivable subsidiary ledger. The auditor is testing the completeness assertion. (True or False?)

> *Answer – Whenever an auditor starts with the origination of a transaction and traces it through the system into the financial statements, the auditor is seeking to verify the completeness assertion. The auditor is making certain that information is not changed or lost while the documents make their way through the system. All relevant information is supposed to get into the financial statements. (Number Five is True.)*

SIX – A company makes several sales and records them just before the end of Year One. The auditor examines the appropriate documentation to be sure that the transactions should have been recorded in Year One and not Year Two. The auditor is testing the completeness assertion. (True or False?)

> *Answer – These accounts have been recorded in the current year. The auditor is interested in ascertaining whether they actually existed prior to the end of the year. Thus, the auditor is testing the existence assertion. Whenever the auditor is*

concerned that an account may be overstated by the inclusion of extra transactions, the existence assertion will be tested. If the auditor is worried that accounts are understated by the omission of transactions, the completeness assertion is tested. (Number Six is False.)

SEVEN – Confirmations are signed by the client but mailed by the auditor with all responses directed back to the auditor. (True or False?)

Answer – To avoid the chance for the client to manipulate the information, confirmations remain in the custody of the auditor. However, because of confidentiality, they must be signed by a representative of the client. (Number Seven is True.)

EIGHT – If control risk is assessed as high, the auditor is more likely to rely on negative rather than positive confirmations of account receivable balances. (True or False?)

Answer – When control risk is viewed as high, the acceptable level of detection risk will have to be relatively low to compensate. In order to reduce detection risk, the auditor has to carry out more substantive testing or gather evidence of a higher quality. Positive confirmations provide a better quality of audit evidence since a response is requested in all cases. Thus, positive confirmations are more likely when control risk is assessed at a high level. (Number Eight is False.)

NINE – An auditor sends a first and a second positive confirmation to a client of the reporting entity but receives no response. The auditor will likely look at cash receipts in the period subsequent to the end of the year in hopes of corroborating the balance. (True or False?)

Answer – The confirmation process has failed to support the balance. This lack of response may indicate that the receivable is false. One alternative auditing procedure is to examine subsequent cash receipts to determine if the receivable is collected and, if so, if the receipt corresponds with the reported balance. A subsequent collection will provide evidence of the existence of the receivable. (Number Nine is True.)

STATISTICAL SAMPLING

(1)   Sampling is used in virtually every aspect of auditing. The term refers to making a decision about a whole (a population) by testing only a part of that group (called a sample).

    (A)   Sampling creates a problem; because auditor does not look at every piece of evidence, a chance exists that a material misstatement could be missed. Thus, some risk always remains that the audit opinion will be wrong.

    (B)   There are two reasons why auditor only provides reasonable assurance and not perfect assurance.

        (1)   **Sampling risk** is the chance that auditor's conclusion will be wrong because only a portion of the population was examined. A sample may not be representative of the population.

        (2)   **Nonsampling risk** is the chance that auditor's conclusion will be wrong for reasons that would happen even if every item had been tested. Includes human errors such as the failure to recognize a misstatement and the misinterpretation of results.

    (C)   **Judgment sampling** estimates the amount of sampling risk that the auditor faces purely by human guess.

    (D)   **Statistical sampling** determines sampling risk mathematically

        (1)   Auditor sets an acceptable level of sampling risk before beginning a test and statistical sampling computes the number of items to be tested to reduce risk to that desired level.

        (2)   Auditor can also perform a test and then use statistical sampling to determine the amount of sampling risk that is present. For example, the auditor might use statistical sampling in making the following evaluation: "Based on the results of this test, there is a 10 percent chance that the client figure is not fairly presented."

(2)   In general, there are two types of statistical sampling.

    (A)   **Attributes sampling** estimates a percentage and is often used in the **tests of controls** because the auditor is interested in the **error rate** that has occurred in connection with a particular control activity. Auditor is attempting to determine if activity is functioning as intended.

    (B)   **Variables sampling** estimates a total and is often used in substantive tests where the auditor is attempting to corroborate a reported account balance.

(3)   Auditor carries out several steps in following an attributes sampling plan.

    (A)   Anticipates the **deviation rate** for the control activity (or other application) being tested. Expected rate is based on difficulty of activity, experience of person performing the control, results found in previous audits, etc. The more deviations that are anticipated the larger the sample must be.

    (B)   Sets a **tolerable deviation rate**. This is the maximum error rate that the auditor could tolerate and still believe the control activity was operating effectively and efficiently. As the rate that the auditor can tolerate gets smaller, sample size must get larger.

(C)   Sets allowable level of risk that the sample will be misleading. For this particular testing, auditor is especially worried that the sample will look better than the actual population. In that case, auditor may think that the control activity is functioning properly and will set control risk too low and do less substantive testing than is needed. To reduce the level of risk that the sample will be misleading, the size of the sample must be increased.

(D)   Based on these three figures, a calculation or a chart is used to determine proper sample size. Except with very small populations, the number of items in the population has little or no effect on the sample size.

(E)   The appropriate number of items is selected from the population. Items must be picked randomly, each item should have an equal chance of selection.

(F)   Sample items are examined and the number of deviations (usually errors) is determined. That number is restated as a percentage based on sample size.

(G)   Another chart is used to convert the actual deviation rate of the sample to the potential **upper deviation rate of the population**. Difference between the actual rate and upper deviation rate is called the **allowance for sampling risk**.

(H)   Upper deviation rate is compared to maximum tolerable rate. If upper deviation rate is lower, auditor assumes control activity is functioning as intended and will probably set control risk at a low level. If upper deviation rate is more, auditor assumes activity is not functioning as intended; control risk is high

(I)   Auditor also examines both the cause and size of the errors that were found. Even if rate is low, the type of deviation may indicate a serious problem.

(4)   Auditor carries out several steps in a variables sampling plan. There are several variations but following is an example of classical mean-per-unit sampling.

(A)   Sets the level of a **tolerable misstatement**. This is the size of the largest misstatement in the account being examined that (when combined with misstatements in all other accounts) would still not cause the financial statements to be materially misstated. If auditor reduces the size of a misstatement that can be tolerated, a bigger sample will be required.

(B)   Sets allowable risk levels that sample will be misleading. To reduce these risk levels, a larger sample size must be selected.

(1)   A misleading sample can cause **incorrect acceptance**. There is a risk that a sample will substantiate client figure when the population is actually materially misstated. This problem leads to an unqualified opinion being given on statements that are not fairly presented.

(2)   A misleading sample can cause **incorrect rejection**. There is a risk that a sample will not substantiate the client figure even though the population is not materially misstated. This problem leads to additional (unnecessary) testing being performed.

(C)   Estimates the amount of misstatement in the population. This figure is usually affected by the efficiency of the accounting system and staff. The bigger the expected misstatement the larger the required sample size.

(D)   Again, population size has only a little impact on sample size.

(E)   Auditor takes a preliminary sample to estimate the variability of the items in the population. If the items are all about the same amount, variability is low. Variability is measured by estimating the **standard deviation**. The higher the variability, the more items that have to be selected to get a representative sample.

(F)   The various factors are entered into mathematical formulas to determine the appropriate sample size.

(G)   Auditor randomly selects items for the sample and measures the average value of these items. The average of the sample is then extended to the entire population to give a total. Difference between this total and client figure is the **projected misstatement**. If projected misstatement is less than tolerable misstatement, the test has provided evidence that reported balance is fairly presented. If projected misstatement is more, the test has not provided evidence that balance is fairly presented.

(5)   In variables sampling, the variability of the items in the population can often be so great that sample size has to be large, causing the auditor to do extensive testing.

(A)   One alternative is to stratify the population. Items are divided into two or three separate populations based on size. Because they are grouped by size, the variability of each population will be relatively small and the required sample will be reduced.

(B)   Two other alternatives are **ratio and difference estimations**. These methods do not estimate the average item in the population but rather the average of differences between book values and audited values or the ratio of book values to audited values.

(6)   **Probability proportional to size sampling** (PPS sampling) is another way of estimating a total while keeping sample size small. The sampling unit is each dollar in the population and not each document. This approach is also called monetary unit sampling and dollar unit sampling.

(A)   Instead of selecting every Nth item (every 50th invoice, for example), auditor picks every Nth dollar (every $5,000th, for example, in a list of invoices). Although the Nth dollar is selected, the entire document is tested.

(1)   Bigger items have more dollars so they are more likely to get picked. Stratification and the degree of variability are not important.

(2)   Sample size is determined mathematically based on tolerable misstatement, expected misstatement in population, allowable risk of incorrect acceptance, and expected number of errors.

(3)   Total dollar figure of population is divided by sample size to get sampling interval (such as every $5,000th dollar).

(B)   If sample has no errors, population total is accepted. If misstatements are found, the size of a projected misstatement must be determined.

(1)   For items that are larger than the interval (in this example, an invoice that is over $5,000), the amount of the misstatement is just used in arriving at the projected misstatement.

(2)   For items that are smaller than interval, the percentage of the misstatement (called the tainting percentage) is determined and multiplied by the interval. If a $500 item has a 2% error, 2% is multiplied by sampling interval to get figure to include in projected misstatement.

PROBLEMS AND SOLUTIONS
STATISTICAL SAMPLING

ONE – When control risk is assessed as being high, an auditor is more likely to use statistical sampling. (True or False?)

Answer – If control risk is high, the level of detection risk that must be achieved to be acceptable will have to be low. To lower the achieved level of detection risk, the auditor must do more substantive testing or gather evidence of a higher quality. Substantive testing provides higher quality evidence if it is performed closer to the end of the year, uses more experienced audit personnel, or incorporates more sophisticated audit techniques. Statistical sampling is viewed as a more sophisticated audit technique than judgment sampling so its use is more likely when control risk is viewed as being high. (Number One is True.)

TWO – The benefit of using statistical sampling is that it reduces the amount of risk that the auditor faces in performing a test. (True or False?)

Answer – Two audit benefits are associated with statistical sampling. First, it can be used to determine mathematically the size of the sample that should be selected to achieve the desired amount of reliability. Second, after the testing has been conducted, statistical sampling can be applied to evaluate mathematically the results that have been found. It does not reduce risk; it helps the auditor determine the amount of risk that is present. (Number Two is False.)

THREE – In auditing, most statistical sampling can be divided into two different general types. (True or False?)

Answer – When applying statistical sampling, the auditor is usually attempting to estimate either a rate or a balance. If a rate is being estimated, the auditor is sometimes said to be sampling for attributes. When estimating a balance, the auditor is said to be sampling for variables. (Number Three is True.)

FOUR – When using statistical sampling to estimate a rate (sampling for attributes), the auditor is frequently assessing control risk. When using statistical sampling to estimate a balance (sampling for variables), the auditor is frequently attempting to gather evidence about a particular account. (True or False?)

Answer – In assessing control risk, an auditor often wants to estimate the error rate that is associated with a particular control activity. In order to reduce detection risk, an auditor may want to estimate a balance that is being reported by the client. Hence, estimation of a rate (sampling for attributes) is associated with the assessment of control risk whereas estimation of a balance (sampling for variables) is more often used in the substantive testing done to reduce detection risk. (Number Four is True.)

FIVE – Whether an auditor is estimating a rate or a balance, assume that the sample size is determined to be 100 out of a population size of 10,000. If the population size had been 20,000 instead of 10,000, the sample size would have been 200. (True or False?)

Answer – Except in very small populations, the size of the population has little impact on sample size. Doubling the population size might increase the sample size from 100 to 103 but would not have come close to doubling the required sample size. (Number Five is False.)

SIX – Whether an auditor is estimating an error rate or an account balance, assume that the auditor determines that more errors (or attributes) exist in the population than was originally expected. This discovery will necessitate a smaller sample size. (True or False?)

Answer – In either method of sampling, the presence of more errors (or attributes) will cause the auditor to select a larger number of items in order to get a representative sample. (Number Six is False.)

SEVEN – An auditor carries out a test of a population and comes to the wrong conclusion. The auditor may have come to the wrong conclusion for either of two different reasons. (True or False?)

Answer – In testing, an auditor may arrive at the wrong conclusion for either of two reasons. First, the auditor faces sampling risk – the chance that the sample did not look like the population as a whole. There is always some possibility that any sample will not have the same characteristics as the population and, hence, the auditor will be lead into making the wrong conclusion. That risk is always present whenever an auditor chooses to sample rather than look at every item. Second, the auditor has some amount of nonsampling risk – the chance that a human error will lead the auditor into making the wrong conclusion. Perhaps the auditor incorrectly looked at a document or the auditor's judgment was simply incorrect. (Number Seven is True.)

EIGHT – Whether an auditor is estimating an error rate or an account balance, the auditor must set an acceptable level of sampling risk. For some reason, the auditor decides to reduce the acceptable level of sampling risk for a particular test. The auditor will have to select a larger sample. (True or False?)

Answer – In order to reduce sampling risk, the auditor will always have to sample a larger proportion of the population. (Number Eight is True.)

NINE – An auditor is attempting to estimate a balance. The auditor must estimate the amount of variability of the items in the population. For example, if one item is $12 and the next item is $989, there appears to be a high degree of variability among the items. If variability is high, the auditor will have to select a larger sample. (True or False?)

Answer – When variability is high, the auditor must sample more items in order to get a representative sample. (Number Nine is True.)

TEN – When an auditor is attempting to estimate a balance, if the variability of the items in the population is high, the sample size will be quite large. In order to reduce this problem, the auditor may choose to stratify the population so that the sample size will be lower. (True or False?)

Answer – Stratifying a population means that the larger items are pulled out and tested separately. The items that remain in the population will have a much smaller variability and, therefore, will necessitate a smaller sample size. The same effect can be achieved by using alternative methods of statistical sampling such as difference estimation, ratio estimation, and probability proportionate to size sampling. (Number Ten is True.)

ELEVEN - Whether an auditor is estimating an error rate or an account balance, the auditor must set the highest amount of problem that can be tolerated. In other words, a tolerate error rate must be set or a tolerable amount of difference from the client balance must be established. As the rate or the amount that an auditor can tolerate rises, the sample size must go up. (True or False?)

Answer – If the auditor can tolerate a higher error rate, or if the auditor can tolerate a bigger misstatement in the client balance, the auditor will need to sample fewer items. (Number Eleven is False.)

TWELVE – The auditor performs a test to estimate an error rate. The sample indicates that the error rate is 2 percent but statistical sampling indicates that the population rate could be as high as 3 percent (the upper deviation rate). The auditor had previously established a tolerable error rate of 2.4 percent. Because the sample error rate (2 percent) is below the tolerable rate (2.4 percent), the auditor will assume that this particular control activity is operating effectively. (True or False?)

Answer – Because the upper deviation rate (3 percent) is above the tolerable rate (2.4 percent), the auditor concludes that the control activity is not being performed effectively. The assessment of control risk will probably be set at a higher level. (Number Twelve is False.)

THIRTEEN – The auditor performs a test to estimate an error rate. The sample indicates that the error rate is 2 percent but statistical sampling indicates that the population rate could be as high as 3 percent (the upper deviation rate). The 1 percent difference between the sample rate (2 percent) and the upper rate estimated for the population as a whole (the 3 percent upper deviation rate) is known as the allowance for sampling risk. (True or False?)

Answer – Because only a sample is being selected, a difference will exist between the rate determined for the sample and the upper deviation rate that is estimated for the population. That difference (1 percent in this case) is known as the allowance for sampling risk. (Number Thirteen is True.)

INVENTORY AND ACCOUNTS PAYABLE

(1)   Auditor should anticipate certain potential problems in auditing **inventory, accounts payable**, and related accounts.

    (A)   Inventory may include **damaged or obsolete items** so that recorded value must be reduced to net realizable value. This possibility relates to valuation assertion.

    (B)   Inventory might be miscounted either accidentally or intentionally. Overcounting inflates currently reported earnings; undercounting reduces reported income. If overcounted, problem is with existence assertion. If undercounted, problem is with completeness assertion.

    (C)   End of year cut off could be recorded incorrectly in connection with receipt and shipment of inventory. Again, possible overstatement relates to existence assertion whereas understatement affects completeness assertion.

    (D)   End of year liabilities may have been omitted because invoice has not been received or because company wants to improve its reported debt position. Problem relates to completeness assertion.

    (E)   Inventory being held by client is on **consignment** or inventory owned by client is out on consignment.

(2)   Company should have a system in place to record purchase of inventory (or fixed assets) and the related liability as well as subsequent payment.

    (A)   For example, assume that a department or individual within company needs an item. A **requisition** (sometimes referred to as a material requisition) is completed. A person with appropriate authority reviews and authorizes requisition.

        (1)   Whenever any document is created, it should be reviewed, authorized, recorded, and a copy kept.

    (B)   Copy of approved requisition goes to **warehouse** (or store room).

    (C)   If item is available, order is filled. If not, **purchase requisition** is created and sent to **purchasing department**.

    (D)   Purchasing department verifies request by checking against budget. Should also check that all documents have been properly authorized. A **purchase order** should be created after going through a set of prescribed steps such as getting bids (for expensive items) or checking with a number of vendors (for cheaper items).

        (1)   Should only buy from vendors listed on a **preapproved vendor list**.

    (E)   Copy of purchase order goes to **receiving room** to alert that a shipment is to be expected. On this copy, quantity is blanked out to ensure that goods will be counted.

    (F)   Goods are received by receiving room and compared to copy of purchase order to verify make, model, description of item, and condition. If there is a discrepancy or if goods are damaged, they are not accepted. If accepted, a **receiving report** is prepared giving all information about goods.

        (1)   Copy is sent to **inventory accounting department** to update **perpetual inventory records**.

        (2)   Receiving room is separate from warehouse in order to ensure adequate documentation of goods that are received.

    (G)   Goods are transferred to warehouse. Warehouse employees verify quantity, description, and condition and then return a signed copy of the receiving report so that the receiving room has a receipt to verify transfer of goods.

(H) **Purchase invoice** is eventually received from vendor. The price charged, terms of payment, and math need to be verified.

(I) Copies of all documents (requisition, purchase requisition, purchase order, receiving report, and purchase invoice) are forwarded to **accounts payable department** (also referred to as **vouchers payable department**). Agreement and authorization of all documents is verified.

(J) A **voucher** is prepared by accounts payable to indicate approval to make payment. It is reviewed and authorized. Liability and purchase are recorded in **voucher register**. Summary of voucher register is forwarded periodically to general accounting to record in general ledger.

(K) Voucher and back-up documentation (sometimes referred to as a voucher package) are sent to **cash disbursements department** and filed by due date.

(L) On due date, voucher is reviewed for reasonableness and compared one final time to documentation. **Check** is written.

(M) Second party compares check and voucher and signs check. Amount is recorded in **cash disbursements journal** as a reduction in cash and liability. Again, a summary will be made and forwarded to general accounting for recording. Voucher is defaced in some manner to avoid repayment. Check is mailed to vendor.

(3) A number of substantive testing procedures should be performed to verify the five assertions made by client about inventory, accounts payable, and any related balances.

(A) **Analytical procedures** are performed, both at beginning and end of audit. Auditor expectations are compared to client figures such as the age of inventory, gross profit percentage, balance of year-end inventory and liabilities, cost per unit, percentage of inventory that is recorded below cost, etc.

(B) Trace one or more transactions through the entire system to see if recording is appropriate at each step. Start with requisition and check all steps until liability is recorded and paid. Whenever auditor starts with initiation of a transaction and follows it through system, the **completeness assertion** is being tested.

(C) Vouch one or more entries in the T-account back through system to see if there is adequate support. Whenever auditor starts with a reported balance and seeks support, the **existence assertion** is being tested.

(D) Check math as well as client work where applicable. Re-add voucher register and cash disbursements journal and compare totals to the general ledger account. Application of LIFO/FIFO should be checked. For manufacturing company, inventory cost figures should be verified.

(E) For the 3-4 days before and 3-4 days after the end of the year, verify client **cut-off procedures** to ensure that transactions were recorded in correct period. Use receiving report and purchase invoice to determine when inventory and payable should be recorded. Need to know FOB point and location of inventory on last day of year. Cash disbursements journal provides date for removal of payable.

(F) Auditor reviews any evidence generated in **subsequent period** (the time from the balance sheet date until the end of fieldwork). For example, auditor investigates the following.

(1) Inventory that does not sell in subsequent period should be examined for obsolescence or damage.

(2)   Cash payments in subsequent period are reviewed to see if they indicate an unrecorded year-end liability.

(3)   Invoices received should be reviewed to see if an unrecorded liability existed at year's end.

(4)   Accounts payable can be confirmed but that is not usually done since invoice is received from vendor.

(G)   **Representation letter** should ask about presence of obsolete inventory.

(H)   Auditor looks for evidence that inventory might be out on **consignment** or that goods are being held on consignment.

(1)   Contract file should be examined for evidence of consignment transactions.

(2)   Preparation of a **bill of lading** without a subsequent sales invoice may indicate consignment-out transactions. Receipt of goods without a subsequent purchase invoice may indicate consignment-in transactions.

(3)   Collections and payments made at irregular intervals may indicate that cash is transferred whenever a sale is made.

(4)   Confirmations may expose inventory out on consignment that has been recorded by company as a receivable.

(5)   Auditor should confirm consignment-out balances and may want to make a test count.

(I)   Auditor should observe client's taking of a **physical inventory**. If company uses a periodic system, count will be at year's end. If it has a perpetual system, count can be any time during year unless risk levels are high. Auditor performs a number of tasks.

(1)   Makes sure that counters know what they are doing.

(2)   Looks for damaged or obsolete items.

(3)   Makes and records a number of test counts.

(4)   If tag system is used, records last tag number so no additional inventory can be added at a later time.

(J)   Client adds cost to ending list of inventory items and arrives at a final total of the inventory cost. Auditor must verify this listing.

(1)   Makes sure that quantity listed for the items that were test counted agrees with recorded amounts.

(2)   Verify that last tag number is the same.

(3)   Checks a sample of cost figures.

(4)   Checks a sample of extensions and footings.

PROBLEMS AND SOLUTIONS
INVENTORY AND ACCOUNTS PAYABLE

ONE – When examining the Accounts Payable account, the auditor is most concerned with corroborating the existence assertion. (True or False?)

Answer – For most liabilities, the auditor wants to ensure that the balance is not understated. Omitting liabilities improves the company's debt to equity ratio and can often increase net income. In addition, initial documentation for many liabilities (such as an invoice) may come from outside of the company and not be

---

generated internally. *Whenever an auditor fears that a balance may be understated, special emphasis will be placed on the completeness assertion. (Number One is False.)*

TWO – The auditor finds a receiving report for 25 refrigerators. However, the related purchase invoice is for 28 refrigerators. The problem is never caught and payment is made based on the invoice. The accounts payable account will be understated. (True or False?)

Answer – The payable was recorded for 28 refrigerators and then paid so that the balance in the liability is now reported as zero. Since no further liability exists, that balance is correct. However, the company appears to be due a refund for the extra three refrigerators so that accounts receivable is understated by that amount. (Number Two is False.)

THREE – Company A ships inventory costing $300,000 to Company Z on consignment. The total sales price of this merchandise is $390,000. Company A incorrectly reports a $390,000 balance as an account receivable. The auditor may discover this problem by confirmation. (True or False?)

Answer – The confirmation process is intended primarily to ascertain that a reported balance does exist. Here, the auditor will need to seek evidence that the $390,000 amount does exist as a receivable. Obviously, when the confirmation arrives, Company Z will respond that there is no debt between the companies until the merchandise is sold. (Number Three is True.)

FOUR – When merchandise is received by a company's receiving department, the goods should be counted and inspected before being accepted. In addition, receiving department personnel should verify that the proper merchandise was delivered. For that purpose, the Receiving department should have a copy of the approved purchase order. (True or False?)

Answer – Normally, whenever any asset is conveyed, the receiving party should make a count, inspect the asset, and verify its description. For inventory, that is especially important since a large amount of merchandise may be received on a regular basis. Thus, the receiving department should have a copy of a purchase order to ascertain that the appropriate merchandise is being accepted. Furthermore, the quantity should be deleted on this copy of the purchase order to encourage a careful count of the goods. (Number Four is True.)

FIVE – A voucher is an approval to pay a liability and is recorded in the voucher register. (True or False?)

Answer – After ensuring that a debt is legitimate, a voucher is prepared as approval for the company to make payment. It is then reviewed and authorized. If appropriate, the voucher is entered in the voucher register which serves to record the debits and credits created by the debt. (Number Five is True.)

SIX – A voucher is prepared in the cash disbursements department. (True or False?)

Answer – As an approval to pay a liability, the voucher is prepared in the accounts payable (or vouchers payable) department. It is then forwarded to cash disbursements for payment. (Number Six is False.)

SEVEN – Accounts payable balances are usually confirmed. (True or False?)

Answer – Confirmations are primarily used to gather information about the existence assertion. With liabilities, the auditor is most concerned that the balance is understated (the reported balance is too low or the debt has been omitted entirely). Therefore, the completeness assertion is of primary interest. Because confirmations are not viewed as a good test of the completeness assertion, they are rarely utilized in connection with accounts payable. However, they can be used if the existence of a particular balance is in question. (Number Seven is False.)

EIGHT – In testing accounts payable, the auditor is more likely to look at cash payments just after the end of the year than at payments made before the end of the year. (True or False?)

Answer – Payments made after the end of the year might well signal liabilities that had been improperly omitted on the balance sheet date. However, if a payment is made before the end of the year, the liability will probably have been recorded as a step in the system that led to the payment. (Number Eight is True.)

NINE – An auditor has assessed control risk at the maximum level in connection with inventory. As a result, the auditor is more likely to ask for a physical count of inventory to be held as early in the audit as possible. (True or False?)

Answer – When control risk is high, the acceptable level of detection risk will be relatively low. To reduce detection risk to this desired level, the auditor must carry out a substantial amount of substantive testing or perform tests that generate a better quality of evidence. Evidence resulting from tests performed closer to the balance sheet date is viewed as having a better quality. When control risk is high, the auditor is likely to insist that the physical inventory count be carried out nearer to the end of the year in order to reduce detection risk to the acceptable level. (Number Nine is False.)

TEN – An auditor fails to observe the taking of the client's physical inventory but is satisfied by other testing that the reported balance is fairly presented. The auditor must render either a qualified opinion or a disclaimer of opinion. (True or False?)

Answer – If a legitimate reason exists for the failure to observe the physical inventory and if alternative procedures can be applied to gain satisfactory evidence, the auditor may still give a standard unqualified audit report. (Number Ten is False.)

AUDITING WITH TECHNOLOGY[1]

(1)   The auditor's responsibility with regard to internal control over information technology (IT) systems remains the same as with a manual system. However, the auditor's consideration may be affected by the fact that IT systems

    (A)   Result in transaction trails that exist for a short period of time or only in machine readable form.

    (B)   May allow data to be altered without any visible evidence.

    (C)   Include computer controls that may not be tested by observation.

(2)   IT specialists may be needed to assist the auditor with the audit of complex systems.

(3)   **Computerized audit tools (CAATs)** and other automated audit tools

    (A)   Program analysis

        (1)   **Code review**—actual analysis of the logic of the program's processing routines.

        (2)   **Flowcharting software**—automatically flowcharts the logic of programs.

        (3)   **Program tracing and mapping**—trace or map the logic of programs.

        (4)   **Snapshot**—"takes a picture" of the status of program execution and results at a specified point.

    (B)   Program testing techniques.

        (1)   **Test data**—a set of dummy transactions used to test computer controls.

        (2)   **Integrated test facility**—processes dummy (test) transactions with live processing.

        (3)   **Controlled program**—auditor testing of a copy of the company's program at the auditor's facility.

    (C)   Techniques for continuous testing.

        (1)   **Embedded audit modules and audit hooks**—embedded audit functions.

        (2)   **Systems control audit review files (SCARF)**—embedded audit modules that capture unusual transactions.

        (3)   **Transaction tagging**—used to follow a transaction through processing.

    (D)   The auditor may use a **generalized computer audit software package**.

        (1)   It is designed with considerable flexibility so that it can be adapted to the client's computer.

        (2)   It provides auditor with independent access into computer so that the data can be gathered without having to rely on client personnel and programs.

        (3)   Programs can serve as a **controlled program** so that a **parallel simulation** of data can be carried out and compared to the output of client's programs.

        (4)   Can test data stored within computer. Can do mechanical testing such as selecting old accounts, internal comparisons, verification of year-end cut-off, and the like.

    (E)   Spreadsheets can be developed to do many audit tasks. Data can then be entered into the spreadsheet to verify calculations such as depreciation and interest. Analytical procedures as well as statistical sampling tests can be performed using such spreadsheets.

---

[1] *You should also review the Information Technology chapter in the Business Environment and Concepts section of this Guide.*

(F)   Working papers can be placed on diskettes for easy storage. Items such as flowcharts, questionnaires, representation letters, and engagement letters can be kept on file and printed out when needed.

(G)   Testing typically done to control computer such as the use of test data, code comparison programs, and integrated test facilities an also be applied by external auditor.

PROBLEMS AND SOLUTIONS
AUDITING WITH TECHNOLOGY

ONE – A major problem with auditing sophisticated IT systems is that transaction trails do not exist. (True or False?)

Answer – In IT systems transaction trails may exist on-line for only a short period of time. In addition, the trails are often only machine readable. This requires the auditor to adopt different approaches to auditing transactions. However, the trails exist in all systems. (Number One is False.)

TWO – In testing computer program controls auditors often rely on computerized audit tools. A program testing technique that is commonly used is the test data approach. (True or False?)

Answer – An audit difficulty with respect to auditing IT systems is the fact that many controls exist in the software and often can only be tested using computerized audit tools. A commonly used technique is the test data approach. (Number Two is True.)

THREE – A continuous testing technique that is often used by internal auditors and may also be used by external auditors is embedded audit modules and audit hooks. (True or False?)

Answer – Techniques for continuous testing of computer systems include embedded audit modules and audit hooks, systems control audit review files, and transaction tagging. (Number Three is True.)

FOUR – Generalized computer audit software is most often used to perform substantive tests directly on the company's computerized records. (True or False?)

Answer – Generalized computer audit software can test data stored within the IT system. It can do mechanical testing such as selecting old accounts, internal comparisons, verification of year-end cut-off, and preparation of confirmations. Generalized computer audit software is most often used for substantive testing of client records. (Number Four is True.)

FLOWCHARTING

(1)   In assessing control risk, the auditor evaluates five **internal control components**. Auditor must also decide whether to perform tests of controls such as investigating the design of individual accounting systems and the control activities in use. Three approaches can be used in achieving an understanding of controls and systems.

   (A)   **Internal control questionnaire** is a list of questions about internal control with "yes" answers indicating good control and "no" being a problem.

      (1)   Auditor anticipates problems that might happen and the control activities that should be in use, both general controls and controls specifically for the system being studied. Each question is designed to ascertain whether a particular control exists and is functioning appropriately.

      (2)   Thus, a "no" answer would indicate that a control is not functioning properly and, if a misstatement occurs, it may not be caught.

      (3)   The advantages of using a questionnaire are that this is a very thorough technique and problems are noted immediately. The disadvantage is that company personnel often know the appropriate response and may not be completely truthful.

   (B)   Using a **memorandum** means that auditor physically writes out a description of a system and its control activities.

      (1)   The advantages are that anyone can produce a memo and it requires auditor to gain a good knowledge of a system. The disadvantages are that it takes a long time, problems are not always apparent, and changes are difficult to record.

   (C)   **Flowcharting** is the symbolic presentation of a system in a sequential order. It is designed to show what each department does as well as the creation and disposition of all documents.

      (1)   The advantages are that it provides an excellent depiction of the system and problems may be easier to spot. The disadvantage is that creating and reading a flowchart both take a particular skill.

      (2)   Numerous flowchart symbols are used. Below are some of the most common.

Document	Computer Operation	Manual Operation	Disk Storage	Input/ Output

Off-line Storage (File)	On-line Storage	Manual Data Entry	Annotation	On Page Connector

Off Page Connector	Decision	Auxiliary Operation	Display on Computer Screen	Magnetic Tape

PROBLEMS AND SOLUTIONS
FLOWCHARTING

ONE – A flowchart is a symbolic representation of an auditor's understanding of the design of a system or of particular control activities. Because of the increased sophistication of accounting systems, a flowchart must be used whenever an auditor anticipates that control risk will be assessed at below the maximum level. (True or False?)

Answer – A flowchart is one method by which auditors can depict their understanding of the design of a company's various systems or particular control activities within those systems. However, a memorandum can be written for this same purpose or a questionnaire may also be used as an alternative. A flowchart has some advantages in that it provides a visual display of all documents, departments, and activities. Unfortunately, control weaknesses and strengths may not be obvious to a person without experience in working with flowcharts. (Number One is False.)

TWO – In flowcharting, the auditor is especially interested in the activities of each department and the source and disposal of documents within a system. (True or False?)

Answer – Flowcharts should follow all documents within a system or process from their creation to disposal. In addition, the activities of each department should be clearly marked. (Number Two is True.)

THREE – The flowcharting symbol for a computer operation or process is the diamond. (True or False?)

Answer – The diamond symbol is used to indicate that a decision must be made. A computer operation or process is represented by a rectangle. (Number Three is False.)

FOUR – A document symbol is shown on a flowchart and is followed by a triangle. The document has been sent to a different system within the company or to a recipient outside of the company. (True or False?)

Answer – A triangle represents a file; thus, the document has been filed. A connector (as might be used to show that a document has been sent to another part of a company or to a party outside of the company) is shown by the use of a five-sided symbol. (Number Four is False.)

FIVE – On a flowchart, a square symbol indicates an auxiliary operation. (True or False?)

Answer – An auxiliary operation is any procedure or process that is helpful but not essential to an activity. On a flowchart, it is symbolized by a square. (Number Five is True.)

CASH RECEIPTS AND CASH BALANCES

(1)   For auditor, **cash receipts** and resulting cash balances provide several concerns. Most problems deal with the theft of company's cash and ability of company's internal control to prevent such theft.

(2)   Company should have a system to record the inflow of cash into company.

    (A)   As with any transaction, there should be an immediate recording. However, because of the possibility of theft, this step is especially important in connection with cash receipts. The use of a cash register is quite common for this purpose. Cash register tape can be used to make sure money is deposited correctly.

    (B)   If checks are accepted, they should be required to be in the name of the company and immediately endorsed "For Deposit Only."

    (C)   Periodically, all cash is delivered to **cashier** and a signed receipt is used to document conveyance of asset.

    (D)   Cashier prepares a daily cash summary of all incoming cash with a copy going to general accounting for journal entry purposes.

    (E)   Money should be deposited in the bank on a daily basis for security purposes and to provide an additional record of the cash amounts.

    (F)   Cashier prepares **bank deposit slip** listing individual items. This document is reviewed and approved by second party who makes deposit.

    (G)   **Validated bank deposit slip** is mailed by bank directly back to independent party in company who compares total and individual items with daily cash summary to make certain that appropriate cash was deposited each day.

    (H)   Independent party in company performs **reconciliation of bank account** on a regular basis. Second party reviews reconciliation, especially looking at deposits in transit, outstanding checks, and other items included to get balances to reconcile.

(3)   If money is mailed into company (for sales or on account), additional control steps should be taken to prevent theft.

    (A)   Ask for payment by check (not cash). Request that checks be made out in the name of the company.

    (B)   Have customer return a **remittance slip** with the payment which includes information about account. Customer should enter amount of the payment being made.

    (C)   One person opens mail, counts money, and takes custody. A second person records names and amounts, collects remittance slips, and prepares a cash remittance list (which can be used to make certain that money is deposited correctly and that proper reductions are made to accounts receivable).

    (D)   As in any cash system, checks are immediately endorsed "For Deposit Only" and money is conveyed to cashier for inclusion on daily cash summary.

    (E)   Remittance slips go to accounts receivable department to update master file of customer balances.

(4)   A number of substantive testing procedures should be performed by the auditor to verify the five assertions made by client about cash and cash receipts.

    (A)   Carry out **analytical procedures**. For example, compare expected cash inflows to actual cash inflows, compare cash inflows by month looking for any unusual amount, compare items on bank reconciliation to previous reconciliations.

(B) Trace a sample of all documents through system to test for completeness: remittance slips, cash remittance list, cash register tape, daily cash summary, bank deposit slip, and journal entries.

(C) Vouch entries in Cash account to find support to test for existence. Look for documentation that substantiates entries.

(D) Cash remittance list and daily cash summary should be re-added on a test basis.

(E) Request a bank cutoff statement for all items clearing account for the first 7 to 10 days after the end of the year for all checking accounts. As with any confirmation, it is signed by client but controlled by auditor.

(F) Year-end **bank reconciliation** should be reviewed. Math is checked. Items from bank cutoff statement are used to verify outstanding checks and deposits in transit.

(G) Test year-end cut-off by looking at receipts and disbursements for a few days before and a few days after the end of the year to make certain transactions are recorded in proper time period.

    (1) One of the big concerns at year-end is the chance of **kiting**. In kiting, money is transferred from one account to another with deposit recorded in first period and withdrawal recorded in second period.

    (2) Kiting is used to inflate cash in order to (1) allow for recording of false sales or (2) cover stolen funds.

    (3) Auditor reviews **bank cutoff statement** to uncover transfers at year-end which are then scheduled to ensure that they have been recorded correctly.

(H) Cash is only counted if a significant amount is held by client. Should count marketable securities and any other liquid assets at the same time so that funds cannot be moved around to cover a cash shortage.

(I) Request a **bank confirmation** from all banks with which the company has dealt. Confirmations should even be sent to banks where accounts have been closed to make certain that balances have not been hidden. It asks for information about checking accounts, savings accounts, loans and other debts, etc. Confirmation will ask for all balances and terms including interest rates and security arrangements.

(J) Look in subsequent time periods for any unusual cash receipts or cash disbursements. Also watch for any returned checks

---

PROBLEMS AND SOLUTIONS
CASH RECEIPTS AND CASH BALANCES

ONE – Kiting is a process by which employees can steal money from a company by using funds collected from one receivable to cover a theft of an earlier cash collection. (True or False?)

> *Answer – The term "lapping" refers to the misappropriation of funds collected from one customer to cover a balance stolen from an earlier receipt. Kiting is a practice whereby money is transferred from one bank account to another with the receipt being recorded in one period and the disbursement in the following period. In this way, cash balances can be inflated for a short period of time or a shortage can be camouflaged. (Number One is False.)*

TWO – A bank cutoff statement is used to corroborate balances shown on a bank reconciliation. (True or False?)

> *Answer – A bank reconciliation will include balances such as deposits in transit and outstanding checks that appear in the financial records but have not yet been recorded by the bank. To support such figures, the auditor requests a cutoff statement directly from the bank. This statement includes all account activity for a few days after the end of the year to enable the auditor to determine that reconciling items actually did exist. (Number Two is True.)*

THREE – A variety of information can be gathered by means of a bank confirmation: checking, savings, and debt balances, interest rates, security agreements and restrictions, and the like. The auditor mails the confirmation and the bank is requested to send the information directly to the auditor. (True or False?)

> *Answer – The client must sign any confirmation to authorize release of the information. However, the auditor retains custody of the confirmation and all information should be sent directly to the auditor to prevent any possible manipulation by the client. (Number Three is True.)*

FOUR – During the current year, the reporting company closes out a checking account with a particular bank. No other activity was carried out with that bank. At the end of the year, the auditor should still send a confirmation request to that bank. (True or False?)

> *Answer – Company officials may say that a bank account has been closed out but then use that particular account to steal money from the company or make illegal payments. Therefore, even if an account has been apparently closed during the year, the auditor will normally mail a bank confirmation simply for additional corroboration. (Number Four is True.)*

FIVE – A company receives cash payments in the mail. One employee should take immediate custody of the cash while another lists each payment. If this control procedure is not in place, the auditor will be especially concerned with corroborating the existence assertion. (True or False?)

> *Answer – With cash, the auditor realizes that the risk of theft is particularly high. Thus, at every point within the cash receipts system (and the cash disbursements system), a clear separation should be maintained between the party responsible for custody of the asset and the party in charge of the recordkeeping function. If this segregation of responsibilities is not maintained, the risk of theft increases. In this case, the money could be stolen when the mail is opened with no record being made of the cash receipt. Since the auditor is concerned about the balance being understated or omitted, the completeness assertion will need to be corroborated. (Number Five is False.)*

SIX – A company requires that its cashier prepare a bank reconciliation for each account on a monthly basis. Because of this responsibility, the auditor will probably set control risk at a particularly high level. (True or False?)

Answer – Every reconciliation should be prepared by a party who is independent of both the custody of the asset in question and the recordkeeping function. The cashier is an employee directly connected to the custody of cash and would, therefore, not be an independent party. (Number Six is True.)

SPECIAL REPORTS AND OTHER REPORTS

(1)   Several types of **special reports** exist where auditor can examine information not in the form of financial statements presented according to US generally accepted accounting principles.

    (A)   One common form of special report is prepared to report on statements produced using a comprehensive basis of accounting other than US generally accepted accounting principles. One example would be reporting on statements prepared on the cash basis.

        (1)   An additional paragraph is inserted before the opinion paragraph of the report to identify the method of accounting being applied and specify that it is not GAAP.

        (2)   The opinion paragraph then states whether there is fair presentation based on the specified method in use.

    (B)   Another type of special report is based on the examination of a single account or schedule – such as sales revenue at a certain location. The CPA can audit the information and give an opinion based on GAAP (or whatever basis of accounting has been used).

        (1)   If the basis of accounting is anything other than GAAP, a fourth paragraph is added after opinion paragraph to restrict the distribution of report to those parties who understand what basis was utilized.

(2)   The attestation function covers any examination and report made by a CPA and can go far beyond the traditional audit of financial statements.

    (A)   **Statements on Standards for Attestation Engagements** of the AICPA provide rules for any attestation other than an audit.

    (B)   One type of attestation is the application of agreed-upon procedures where the CPA is engaged to issue a report of findings based on specific procedures that were performed. In this way, the CPA can report on almost anything – such as the number of votes at the Academy Awards.

        (1)   CPA may evaluate either a particular subject matter or an assertion.

        (2)   CPA and the hiring party must agree on work to be carried out and this party must take responsibility for sufficiency of those procedures.

        (3)   The matter to be examined must be subject to consistent measurement and the criteria must be agreed on by all parties.

        (4)   The report must be restricted to specified parties who understand what was done.

        (5)   The report should indicate the subject matter (or assertion), the specified parties to receive the report, the party who was responsible for the subject matter, the procedures performed, and the findings.

(3)   CPA can be associated with **financial forecasts** and **projections** (sometimes known as **prospective financial statements**).

    (A)   Financial forecast is a general anticipation of a company's future statements. Distribution may be limited or may be given to the general public.

    (B)   Financial projection indicates effect that a hypothetical event would have on future financial statements. Distribution is restricted to party responsible for projection and to anyone with whom this party is negotiating directly.

    (C)   CPA may compile statements (no assurance), apply agreed upon procedures (indicate findings), or exam statements (give positive assurance that assumptions are reasonable). CPA never gives any assurance as to the achievability of the figures.

    (D)   In an examination, CPA also makes certain that all assumptions are disclosed and followed. In report, CPA warns that results will usually be different than projected.

(4)   **Pro forma financial statements** are created to indicate effect that a hypothetical event (a merger, for example) would have had on past statements. CPA may either review or exam. Examination and report are similar to that done for a financial projection.

(5)   **Registration statements** must be filed by a company with the SEC before new securities can be issued. Normally, these securities are transferred to underwriting companies (stock brokerage houses) which then sell them to the public. Legally, the underwriters must make a reasonable investigation to be certain that information they are using is not false or misleading.

    (A)   To help an underwriter meet these legal requirements, it will seek assurance from auditor who furnishes what is called a **comfort letter** (or a **letter for underwriters**). This letter provides assurance beyond that which was given on the financial statements included in the registration statement.

    (B)   Auditor provides positive assurance about independence and that audit followed SEC standards.

    (C)   Auditor provides limited (or negative) assurance for specified information (such as interim data) that is included within the registration statement.

(6)   An auditor may be engaged to provide an examination and **report on internal control**.

    (A)   In an audit, internal control is studied solely to determine amount of control risk. Any **reportable conditions** or material weaknesses noted in internal control must be indicated to the board of directors and appropriate members of management.

    (B)   In a separate engagement, examination of internal control is more comprehensive. First, management makes an assertion that internal control is effective. Auditor then makes examination and reports on internal control. As an alternative, auditor can report on management's assertion.

    (C)   Auditor's standard report on internal control has four paragraphs.

        (1)   First paragraph indicates nature of examination and outlines responsibilities.

        (2)   Second paragraph indicates that standards established by the AICPA were followed. Also specifies that auditor (1) obtained understanding, (2) tested, and (3) evaluated both design and effectiveness of internal control.

        (3)   Third paragraph spells out inherent limitations of internal control.

        (4)   Fourth paragraph indicates whether the company has maintained effective internal control over financial reporting based on criteria established in "Internal Control-Integrated Framework" issued by the organizations sponsoring the Treadway Commission.

(7)   If auditor is asked to issue a report on statements that have been condensed, report indicates that the audit was performed on the basic financial statements, gives the date and type of opinion, and indicates whether the condensed statements are fairly stated in all material respects in relation to the basic financial statements.

(8)   CPA can accept a **WebTrust** engagement to help give customers assurance about the security of transactions placed through a web site.

    (A)   CPA examines and reports on three principles

        (1)   Business Practices Disclosure – all business operating practices used in the web site are disclosed and followed appropriately.

        (2)   Transaction Integrity – company controls are effective in making certain that customer orders are complete and properly filled.

        (3)   Information Protection – all information provided by customers is protected.

    (B)   CPA grants company the user of the WebTrust seal. Consumer can then click on this seal to read the CPA's report.

    (C)   The CPA's report will include the following information.

        (1)   Indication that the web site does conform to the three principles listed above.

        (2)   Company is responsible for the assertions made about the web site.

        (3)   CPA has obtained reasonable assurance that management's assertion about the web site is not materially misstated.

        (4)   Projections of assurance into future periods are subject to risk.

(9)   Auditor can perform engagements for governments and agencies receiving government funding. Guidelines may require auditor to follow GAAS, GAS (**government audit standards**), and/or the Single Audit Act.

    (A)   In a financial audit carried out according to GAS, audit may cover an entire set of financial statements or just a segment or schedule.

        (1)   Reporting is extended. Three different areas must be covered in a combined report or in separate reports.

            (a)   An audit report is provided to indicate whether information is fairly presented according to GAAP.

            (b)   An indication is provided as to whether entity has complied with laws and regulations for all material transactions and events. Any material noncompliance must be reported. Positive assurance is given for tested items; negative assurance is given for items not tested.

            (c)   A listing is provided of any material weaknesses or reportable conditions found in internal control.

    (B)   Auditor can also carry out **performance audits**.

        (1)   In an **economy and efficiency audit**, auditor indicates whether entity protected and used financial resources efficiently and effectively.

        (2)   In a **program audit**, auditor indicates whether desired benefits or results are being achieved.

PROBLEMS AND SOLUTIONS
SPECIAL REPORTS AND OTHER REPORTS

ONE – A company prepares its financial statement on the cash basis of accounting. In the report of the independent auditor, an additional paragraph must be included before the opinion paragraph to draw attention to the method being applied. The auditor must then render a qualified audit opinion because generally accepted accounting principles were not followed. (True or False?)

Answer – When a comprehensive basis of accounting other than generally accepted accounting principles has been applied, a special report is given. The auditor does include an extra paragraph in this report to indicate the method in use. Then, in the final paragraph, the auditor renders an opinion on whether the financial statements are presented fairly according to that particular method. If so, the opinion is unqualified. (Number One is False.)

TWO – An audit firm has been asked to perform an audit on the Royalty Expense account of a particular publishing company because of a dispute. The auditor is to determine whether the balance is in conformity with generally accepted accounting principles. Because of the narrow scope of this engagement, the auditor must restrict the release of the report to the parties who are involved in the dispute. (True or False?)

Answer – There are times when an accountant or auditor must restrict the distribution of a report. However, if an audit is performed and the account is being evaluated according to generally accepted accounting principles, no reason exists for restriction even if the report only concerns a single account or schedule. Conversely, if a different criteria is used or if the accountant or auditor is carrying out agreed-upon procedures, the report should be restricted to parties with an adequate knowledge of the situation. (Number Two is False.)

THREE – In a comfort letter (a letter for an underwriter), the auditor will provide limited assurance. (True or False?)

Answer – In connection with the issuance of new securities to the public, a registration statement must be produced by the reporting company. The underwriter that will actually sell these securities to the public is required by law to carry out a reasonable investigation to ensure that the information in the registration statement is not false or misleading. As part of this responsibility, the underwriter requests a letter from the auditor (a comfort letter) that provides positive assurance as to independence and limited (or negative) assurance on any data in the registration statement that was reviewed by the auditor. (Number Three is True.)

FOUR – A financial forecast can be issued to the public. (True or False?)

Answer – A financial forecast is a general anticipation of future financial statements for a company. Distribution may be restricted but the forecast can also be given to the public. In contrast, a financial projection is a measure of the impact that a hypothetical event will have on future statements and must be restricted to parties having adequate knowledge. (Number Four is True.)

FIVE – An audit firm has been auditing the financial statements of ABX Company for a number of years. This year the company wants the firm to perform a separate examination of its internal control. The techniques used by the audit firm will be different for this engagement than those used in assessing control risk as part of the annual audit. (True or False?)

Answer – The work carried out in an examination of internal control is very similar to that done in the assessment of control risk. The auditor comes to an understanding of the five components of internal control and then documents the understanding of each system to determine the design of control activities so that they can be tested for effectiveness. However, the auditor's work will be much more extensive in this engagement. When hired to evaluate internal control, the auditor looks more carefully at each significant control activity. (Number Five is False.)

SIX – In a report on internal control, the auditor will describe reasons that errors or fraud may occur regardless of the internal control. (True or False?)

Answer – The third paragraph of a report on internal control indicates that inherent limitations (such as human error or management overriding of the system) may always allow misstatements to occur and not be detected. In addition, changes in conditions over time may cause the internal control to become inadequate. Thus, the reader is warned that errors or fraud may still occur despite the presence at the current time of internal control activities and procedures. (Number Six is True.)

SEVEN – An audit is conducted in accordance with government audit standards (GAS) because the reporting entity receives certain federal financial assistance. The report is more extensive than is prepared traditionally because it includes references to both internal control and the efficiency of the federal program in meeting its stated objectives. (True or False?)

Answer – When an audit is conducted in accordance with GAS, an audit report on the financial statements must be made. In addition, either in a separate or combined report, the auditor must report on both internal control and compliance with laws and regulations. (Number Seven is False.)

EIGHT – An audit is conducted in accordance with government audit standards (GAS). The auditor must include a report on internal control that is primarily designed to disclose any material weaknesses that are discovered. (True or False?)

Answer – Within an audit conducted according to GAS, an internal control report is included to report any reportable conditions that were discovered. A separate discussion is only required if any of the reportable conditions is so serious as to be considered material weaknesses. (Number Eight is False.)

NINE – An audit is conducted in accordance with government audit standards (GAS). As part of this examination, the auditor must test the reporting entity's compliance with laws that have both a direct and a material effect on the financial statements. (True or False?)

Answer – In following GAS, evidence must be gathered concerning compliance with laws. These tests concern laws and regulations that have a direct and material effect on the financial reporting of the entity. (Number Nine is True.)

TEN – An audit is conducted in accordance with the Single Audit Act. As part of this audit, the auditor is required to test internal control activities and procedures over federal programs in order to determine if they are effective. (True or False?)

Answer – When a company or other organization is governed by the regulations of the Single Audit Act, the auditor is required to test the controls that are in place in connection with the federal programs of the reporting entity. (Number Ten is True.)

LONG-TERM LIABILITIES AND CONTINGENCIES

(1)   In looking at **long-term liabilities** and **contingencies**, auditor should be aware of certain potential problems.

   (A)   Auditor is always concerned about the understatement of debt because that would improve the company's reported debt to equity position. Consequently, completeness is a particular worry.

   (B)   Because of lack of documentation, the mere discovery of contingencies can be difficult. Once discovered, evaluating the likelihood of occurrence and possible amounts poses special problems.

   (C)   For debts that have been issued, amortization of any discounts and premiums must be verified.

   (D)   **Loan covenants** must be properly disclosed. Auditor should also make certain that no covenants have been broken; failure to meet covenants can necessitate debts being reported as current liabilities.

(2)   Auditor would expect to find certain actions taken by company in connection with long-term liability balances.

   (A)   Normally, approval for incurring additional debt must be made by board of directors and/or stockholders.

   (B)   A formal contract (indenture) should be drawn up by lawyers and signed by company officials so that all terms are clearly understood.

   (C)   The issuance of bonds or other long-term debt may be made through the use of an independent trustee.

   (D)   Cash received should be recorded in cash summary or **cash receipts journal** and bank deposit slip to provide documentation.

   (E)   Unpaid interest should be accrued at end of year along with the recording of any discount or premium amortization.

(3)   A number of substantive testing procedures should be performed to verify the five **assertions** made by management about long-term liabilities.

   (A)   **Analytical procedures** are carried out. For example, cash receipts and interest expense are compared with previous years or with anticipated figures.

   (B)   Debt transactions are traced from initiation through the accounting system to the formal recording in order to substantiate completeness. Because debt must usually be approved by board of directors, minutes should be read to check for approval and for mention of debts that may have gone unrecorded.

   (C)   Entries in ledger are vouched back to source documents to substantiate existence and, possibly, valuation.

   (D)   Amortization of any discount or premium should be recomputed.

   (E)   Interest expense is reconciled to debt balance. If interest is higher than expected, unrecorded liabilities may be present.

   (F)   Verify that any unpaid interest at end of year is accrued.

   (G)   Examine events in subsequent period for evidence of the incurrence of any new debts, a transaction that might require disclosure. Also in subsequent period, look for any payments on debts. May indicate unrecorded liabilities or substantiate balances being reported.

   (H)   On representation letter, ask about any unrecorded debts.

(I)   Read loan indentures to determine nature of covenants so that a verification can be made that they have not been broken.

(J)   If risk is high, auditor can confirm balances with creditors. Transactions during the year can be confirmed with trustee.

(K)   **Bank confirmations** should be reviewed for existence and terms of long-term liabilities.

(4)   Additional testing should be performed in connection with contingencies.

(A)   Ask client for (1) a list of contingencies, (2) an evaluation of the possibility of loss for each, and (3) the amounts, if any, expected to be lost.

(B)   Check files for correspondence with lawyers or insurance companies that might relate to contingencies. Look at invoices from lawyers that might indicate existence of contingencies.

(C)   Read contracts to see if failure to meet requirements creates a contingency.

(D)   **Lawyers letter** should be sent by auditor to company's outside attorneys to substantiate information. Should list all contingencies as well as company's evaluation of each.

(1)   Lawyer responds directly to auditor indicating any disagreements. Lawyer should also mention any asserted claims that were not included.

(2)   Lawyers do not have to respond about contingencies where they lack adequate knowledge. However, the lawyer must indicate any limitation in the response.

(3)   If **unasserted claim** has been omitted and lawyer believes auditor should be told, lawyer suggests client make disclosure. If not disclosed, lawyer considers resigning.

PROBLEMS AND SOLUTIONS
LONG-TERM LIABILITIES AND CONTINGENCIES

ONE – In auditing long-term liabilities, the auditor should read all debt indentures to determine the existence of any loan covenants. The auditor is attempting to corroborate the valuation assertion. (True or False?)

Answer – If loan covenants are in existence, the financial statements will probably need to disclose their nature and presence. Thus, the auditor is obtaining support for the presentation and disclosure assertion. (Number One is False.)

TWO – In searching for unrecorded liabilities, the auditor will probably read the minutes of the meetings of the board of directors. (True or False?)

Answer – In most companies, incurring long-term debt requires approval by the board of directors. Thus, the auditor will read the minutes of those meetings looking (at least in part) for the mention of additional debt that might not have been reported properly. (Number Two is True.)

THREE – A company is reporting a total of $1 million in long-term debt that bears an annual 8 percent interest rate. The company also reports an Interest Expense account of $240,000. The auditor's primary concern is that net income may be misstated. (True or False?)

Answer – The $1 million in debt would indicate interest expense of $80,000 based on the 8 percent annual rate. Thus, the $240,000 amount reported for interest could well be in error by $160,000. However, the large Interest Expense balance could also indicate that debts of several million dollars have been left off of the financial records by the company. Because of the size of the potential problem, the omission of the debt would probably be a bigger concern for the auditor. (Number Three is False.)

FOUR – In auditing contingencies, the auditor is most concerned with the completeness and the valuation assertions. (True or False?)

Answer – Because records may not be readily available for contingent losses, balances may be omitted from the financial statements. Thus, the auditor must always attempt to corroborate the completeness assertion for contingencies. In addition, since the actual loss (if any) will not be determined until the future, the valuation assertion is another primary worry for the auditor. (Number Four is True.)

FIVE – A company lists all of its contingencies and then evaluates the likelihood of loss and the anticipated amount. The auditor forwards this information to the company's outside law firm. The firm refuses to corroborate the information. The auditor will normally have to render either a qualified or an adverse opinion. (True or False?)

Answer – Failure of the outside attorney to substantiate the information provided by the client in connection with contingencies will normally lead to either a qualified opinion or a disclaimer of opinion. Whenever a problem is based on a lack of evidence, one of these reports is appropriate. (Number Five is False.)

SIX – A company lists all of its contingencies and evaluates the likelihood of occurrence and the anticipated amount of loss. This information is forwarded to the company's law firm. If the firm disagrees with the amounts listed, the law firm must contact the client and ask that the information be modified. (True or False?)

Answer – Unless an unasserted claim has been omitted, the law firm should contact the independent auditor directly in order to express reservations about the information that was provided concerning contingencies. (Number Six is False.)

PAYROLL

(1)   When auditing payroll balances, auditor should be aware of several potential problems.

    (A)   Because money is being removed from company, theft is biggest concern. Overpayment can occur for several reasons.

        (1)   Payment may be for more hours than employee actually worked or for a higher rate than employee earned.

        (2)   Extra deductions may be taken from one employee in order to increase another employee's paycheck.

        (3)   Paychecks may be issued in the name of false employees or employees who have quit or been fired. These checks are stolen and cashed.

(2)   Company should have a well designed payroll system to ensure that records are correct and payments appropriate.

    (A)   **Personnel department** hires employees and sets up a personnel file to accumulate information for computing payroll.

        (1)   W-4 form lists marital status and number of dependents.

        (2)   Employee or union contract gives pay rate and terms of fringe benefits.

        (3)   Deduction authorizations are signed by employee as approval for deducting money for medical insurance, savings bonds, union fees, donations, etc.

        (4)   Personnel department prepares a payroll input record for each pay period giving list of employees, marital status, pay rate, deductions, etc. Copy is sent to payroll department so that wages can be computed.

    (B)   For employees paid an hourly rate, number of hours worked is maintained by **timekeeping department**. Clock cards or other system is used to determine exact time spent at work.

    (C)   Where applicable, employees keep record of their work on **time tickets** (or job order cards). This information can be used in determining labor costs charged to each job.

    (D)   Employee's supervisor reviews number of hours being reported and provides authorization. Since overtime hours are usually paid at a higher rate, a special authorization may be necessary.

    (E)   **Payroll department** computes each employee's gross wages, deductions and net pay based on hours worked and information from payroll input record.

        (1)   Salary information is recorded for each employee in payroll register. Totals are forwarded to general accounting for reporting purposes.

        (2)   Second employee verifies all figures and computations and provides authorization.

    (F)   **Payroll register** is sent to cash disbursements department in treasurer's office. It is reviewed and approved unless discrepancies are apparent.

    (G)   Paychecks are written on a separate payroll bank account which has no money in it except when payroll is issued. Use of second account reduces the chance and potential amount of theft.

        (1)   Second employee compares checks to register and signs.

    (H)   **Paymaster** distributes checks to employees but only after they provide proper identification.

       (I)   Unclaimed paychecks are recorded by paymaster and given to independent party for follow up.

(3)   A number of substantive testing procedures should be performed to verify the five assertions made by client about payroll.

      (A)   **Analytical procedures** should be carried out such as comparing expense to previous years, budgeted figures, and number of employees. May want to compare expense from month to month to note any unusual amounts.

      (B)   Select a sample of employees and trace payroll information from personnel file to payroll input form to clock cards to payroll register to general ledger account to canceled check.

      (C)   Vouch a sample of payroll checks to find supporting documentation.

      (D)   Verify mathematical computation of individual paychecks including all deductions.

      (E)   Verify extensions and footings in payroll register.

      (F)   Recompute year-end accrual of any unpaid salaries.

      (G)   Observe paymaster's distribution of checks to verify that each employee has proper identification. Investigate the handled of any unclaimed checks.

PROBLEMS AND SOLUTIONS
PAYROLL

ONE – The personnel department calculates the amount of gross wages earned by each employee in a company. (True or False?)

    Answer – The personnel department makes decisions about hiring and firing employees. It also maintains employee records and provides information such as pay rates and marital status. However, the actual computation of gross wages for each employee is handled by the payroll department. (Number One is False.)

TWO – In auditing the Salary Expense account, the auditor is especially concerned with supporting the existence assertion. (True or False?)

    Answer – Theft of company cash is often accomplished by issuing paychecks to false employees or to employees who have quit or retired. The checks are simply stolen and cashed by other individuals who are usually employees of the company. Thus, the auditor is especially interested in ascertaining that each employee who is to receive a paycheck actually does exist. (Number Two is True.)

THREE – A company has a paymaster who distributes paychecks after verifying the appropriate identification of each recipient. Any paychecks that are not distributed should be turned over to an independent party within the company for verification purposes. (True or False?)

    Answer – When a paycheck is not claimed, the problem may be that no employee exists with that identification. The check was requested or issued in hopes of misappropriating the funds. Thus, some party who is independent of both the

---

payroll and the personnel departments should investigate any unclaimed checks. (Number Three is True.)

FOUR – The payroll register is used to capture all information about each employee's paycheck so that an appropriate recording can be made. (True or False?)

Answer – The payroll register indicates the amounts earned by each employee as well as deductions and withholding and the actual payment made. These balances are used in the general accounting department to record the entire impact of the payroll payment. (Number Four is True.)

LAND, BUILDINGS, AND EQUIPMENT

(1)   In looking at **land, buildings, and equipment**, auditor is aware that several problems could prevent fair presentation.

    (A)   The cost of new items are not properly capitalized. The cost of additions and other changes in items already in use has not been recorded correctly.

    (B)   Depreciation is computed incorrectly or is based on estimations that are not reasonable.

    (C)   Assets are retired or disposed of in some manner without being removed from the accounting records.

(2)   Auditor performs a number of substantive tests in connection with land, buildings, and equipment.

    (A)   On a test basis, recompute depreciation amounts.

    (B)   Physically inspect a sample of assets and compare to records maintained by company.

    (C)   For assets retired, compare life and residual value to amounts that were anticipated.

    (D)   Review Repair Expense account and Maintenance Expense accounts to determine if any capitalized amounts have been expensed.

    (E)   For **constructed assets**, review all cost records for appropriate classification. Make certain that capitalized interest has been appropriately recorded.

    (F)   For new acquisitions, review vendor invoice and search for any other normal and necessary costs that should be capitalized.

    (G)   For all additions to land, buildings, and equipment, vouch entries back to source documentation to substantiate balances.

    (H)   During tours of facilities, look for **idle assets** that should be reclassified.

    (I)   For capitalized leased assets, review contract and computations.

    (J)   Review cash receipts for an amount that might indicate the sale of a fixed asset. Company may have recorded transaction as miscellaneous income without removing asset.

    (K)   Look over loan agreements to see if any assets have been pledged as security. If so, that information must be disclosed.

PROBLEMS AND SOLUTIONS
LAND, BUILDINGS, AND EQUIPMENT

ONE – A company is in the process of constructing a new building. In examining this account, the auditor is concerned with the presentation and disclosure assertion. (True or False?)

Answer – A long-lived asset is classified as an "other asset" until the time that it begins to generate revenues. At that point, the reported balance should be reclassified as "land, buildings, and equipment." Thus, the auditor needs to verify the appropriate placement of the account within the company's balance sheet. (Number One is True.)

TWO – An auditor discovers a cash receipt of $18,000 with the notation "amount received from sale of equipment." The auditor also finds an equal amount recorded within miscellaneous income. Net income is likely to be overstated while the total reported for assets is understated. (True or False?)

Answer – Unless the equipment was fully depreciated, the amount of cash received should not be recorded as an increase in net income but only the amount (if any) that is in excess of book value. Since the entire amount was recorded as miscellaneous income, the book value of the asset was apparently not removed from the books. Thus, income is probably overstated and, because the book value of the equipment was not removed, assets are also overstated. (Number Two is False.)

THREE – In performing analytical procedures, the amount reported by the company in its Repair Expense account is lower than the auditor's anticipated figure. The auditor should be concerned that the client may be attempting to inflate net income. (True or False?)

Answer – Whenever a Repair Expense or a Maintenance Expense account is lower than expected, the auditor must be aware that company officials may be incorrectly capitalizing expense expenditures in order to increase net income artificially. (Number Three is True.)

INVESTMENTS

(1)   Investments include securities and derivative instruments. In looking at investments, auditor is aware that several problems could prevent the fair presentation of reported balances.

     (A)   If control or significant influence exists, the investments must be recorded through consolidation or the equity method. Company may not be aware of this need or may not know how to apply these accounting methods.

     (B)   Interest or dividends can be received by the company and then be stolen.

     (C)   Most securities must be valued at fair value. The company may not appropriately apply GAAP with respect to valuing the securities.

     (D)   A change in market value creates an income effect for a trading security but only a stockholders' equity effect for a security available for sale. Company may manipulate these classifications in order to impact reported net income.

     (E)   Securities may be sold with the money misappropriated by an employee. At the end of the year, the stock is repurchased and replaced.

     (F)   For **bonds being held to maturity**, any discount or premium must be properly amortized.

     (G)   Accounting for and valuing derivative instruments is complex.

     (H)   GAAP may require developing assumptions about future conditions.

     (I)   Strict GAAP requirements apply to the use of derivatives for hedging. The company may not appropriately apply these rules.

(2)   The auditor may need specialized knowledge to plan and perform auditing procedures for certain assertions about derivatives and securities.

(3)   Auditor should perform a number of substantive tests in connection with investments.

     (A)   Should investigate whether control or significant influence is present. If so, auditor verifies that the proper method of reporting is being utilized and that amounts are being reported properly. Audited financial statements furnished by the investee should be used to verify appropriate financial reporting.

     (B)   For each new purchase, the auditor should review documentation to ensure that capitalized cost figure is correct.

     (C)   For each sale, auditor recomputes gain or loss that is reported.

     (D)   Auditor uses reported amounts of dividend and interest payments to verify amount being reported by company. Dates that individual amounts are recorded should be checked with distribution dates for any unusual delays.

     (E)   If certificates are being held by an independent trustee, auditor should confirm these securities.

     (F)   If certificates are being held within the company, auditor should consider making a surprise inspection to be sure that all documentation is present. Auditor should verify name of company, number of shares or face value, and serial numbers on all stocks and bonds to make sure they have not been switched or replaced.

     (G)   Review company's justification for classifying marketable securities as trading securities, securities available for sale, or bonds to be held until maturity. Look at past history to determine how long investments are usually held.

         (1)   Auditor may also want to determine company's intentions by examining recorded investment strategy as well as the **minutes of meetings of the board of directors** and any investment committees.

      (2)   Auditor should also consider company's ability to hold securities for an extended period by looking at current financial position, working capital needs, debt agreements and the like.

(H)   Inspect derivative contracts.

(I)   Request counterparties or holders to confirm terms of agreements and whether there are any side agreements or agreements to repurchase securities sold.

(J)   Inspect financial instruments and other agreements to identify embedded derivatives.

(K)   For derivatives accounted for as hedges, the auditor should gather evidence that management (1) complied with GAAP, (2) originally expected and documented that the hedging relationship would be highly effective, and (3) periodically assessed the hedge's ongoing effectiveness.

(L)   Review company's application of fair market value to securities and derivatives. Market value can be determined in one of several ways.

      (1)   Get a quoted market price.

      (2)   Talk with broker who makes a market in the investment.

      (3)   If no market price is available, a valuation pricing model may be used to estimate fair value. In such cases the auditor can use one or a combination of the following approaches.

            (a)   Review and test management's process.

            (b)   Independently develop and estimate.

            (c)   Review subsequent events.

(M)   Recompute the amortization of any premium or discount on bonds being held to maturity.

(N)   For investments being held until maturity, a write-down in book value is necessary if a permanent drop in market value has occurred.

      (1)   A permanent drop in market value should be suspected if one of several events occurs: fair market value is significantly below cost, the entire industry or geographic region is in decline, decline in market value has persisted for an extended period of time, financial condition of issuer has deteriorated, there has been a reduction in dividend distributions, etc.

PROBLEMS AND SOLUTIONS
INVESTMENTS

ONE - A company buys ownership shares of a large company during the current year. By year end, the value of this investment has risen rather substantially on a national stock exchange. Company officials indicate that they plan to report these shares as trading securities. Unless evidence to the contrary is indicated, the auditor must allow this classification. (True or False?)

Answer – As trading securities, the rise in value of the investment will increase net income rather than being reported within stockholders' equity. Thus, the company may have reason to report the investment in this manner regardless of its actual intentions. The auditor should look for evidence to support this placement. For example, the auditor may search for any investment strategies put forth by the company as well as indications by the board of directors of its objectives for the investments. If evidence exists that the company plans to hold the investments indefinitely, a reclassification will be necessary to "securities available for sale." (Number One is False.)

TWO – A company holds ownership shares of a stock that is not publicly traded. Thus, without a market value, the company will have to leave this investment on its books at historical cost. (True or False?)

Answer – If a market price is not readily available for an investment in securities, the auditor should attempt to determine an approximate market value by the use of a valuation pricing model or by discussions with investment brokers. (Number Two is False.)

THREE – A company acquires $500,000 in bonds for $470,000. The company plans to hold this investment until the maturity date of the bonds. Thereafter, the value of these bonds drops rather significantly. Because the investment is being held until maturity, it will be reported at amortized cost rather than at fair market value. (True or False?)

Answer – Normally, a change in the market value of bonds being held until maturity has no impact on amounts to be reported. Any associated discount or premium will be amortized using either the effective rate method or the straight-line method. However, if a drop in market value is permanent, the reported value of the investment must be reduced. For example, if a decline in market value is significant and has persisted for an extended period of time, a reduction may be necessary. (Number Three is False.)

FOUR – Derivatives are often hard to discover because they may be embedded in other financial agreements. (True or False?)

Answer – Derivatives can be embedded in a manner of different types of financial agreements (e.g., loan agreements). (Number Four is True.)

FIVE – If management has elected to account for a financial instrument as a hedge, the auditor must inspect documentation of management's basis for concluding that the hedge would be effective. (True or False?)

Answer – To account for a financial instrument as a hedge management must document this fact and the basis for concluding that the hedge will be highly effective. (Number Five is True.)

INDEX

TABLE OF CONTENTS
FINANCIAL ACCOUNTING AND REPORTING

Topic	Page

FINANCIAL ACCOUNTING AND REPORTING

TOPIC	For additional information see Wiley CPA Examination Review
Accounts Receivable and Bad Debt Expense	Module 10
Present Value Computations	Module 11
Land, Buildings, and Equipment	Module 9
Bonds and Notes; Payables and Investments	Module 11
Miscellaneous Financial Statements	Module 18
Stockholders' Equity	Module 13
Accounting for Leases	Module 11
Miscellaneous Accounting Concepts	Module 7
Marketable Securities	Module 14
Long-Term Construction Contracts	Module 8
Installment Sales Method	Module 7
Structure of an Income Statement	Module 7
Contingencies and Other Losses and Liabilities	Module 10
Deferred Income Taxes	Module 12
Equity Method of Accounting for Investments	Module 14
Consolidated Financial Information	Module 16
Statement of Cash Flows	Module 15
Intangible Assets	Module 9
Pension Accounting	Module 11
Inventory	Module 8
Accounting Changes	Module 7
Partnership Accounting	Module 18
Financial Instruments	Module 17
Earnings Per Share	Module 13
Foreign Currency Balances	Module 18
Disposal of a Segment	Module 7
Reporting Segments of an Enterprise	Module 18
Governmental Accounting – Fund Accounting and Financial Statements	Module 19
Governmental Accounting – Financial Reporting Process	Module 19
Not-for-Profit Accounting	Module 20

ACCOUNTS RECEIVABLE AND BAD DEBT EXPENSE

(1)   **Accounts Receivable** - amounts owed to the reporting entity, frequently owed to it by customers for sales made on credit.
    (A)   Shown as a current asset unless payment is to be delayed.
    (B)   Made up of four separate figures:
        (1)   Beginning balance for the period.
        (2)   Increased by credit sales for the period.
        (3)   Decreased by collections made.
        (4)   Decreased by balances written off because of returns or discounts or because they are uncollectible.

(2)   **Allowance for Doubtful Accounts** - an estimation of the amount of receivables being reported that will not be collected.
    (A)   Balance is shown as a contra (negative) account to accounts receivable to report these receivables at net realizable value.
        (1)   **Net realizable value** is the amount (of any asset) that is expected to be collected in cash.
    (B)   Final balance in the Allowance account is a credit and is the result of four figures:
        (1)   Beginning balance for the period (starts with credit).
        (2)   Decreased by the write off of an account receivable as bad.
        (3)   Increased by the subsequent collection of an account previously written off as bad. Cash is debited (increase) and allowance for doubtful accounts is credited (increase).
        (4)   Increased by the recognition of bad debt expense for the current period.
    (C)   **Bad debt expense** is frequently recorded just prior to producing financial statements. Expense for current period is estimated and recorded so that it will be recognized in the same period as the sale - an example of the matching principle.
        (1)   Estimation can be made by the **percentage of sales method** which calculates and then records bad debt expense based on an estimated percentage of sales. The percentage is derived from past experience. (Sales times specified percentage) = Bad Debt Expense
            (a)   This calculated figure is the expense recognized for period with an accompanying increase in the allowance for doubtful accounts.
            (b)   The sales figure for this computation can be "gross" or "net" (with discounts, allowances, etc. subtracted)
        (2)   An alternative method is the **percentage of receivables method** (and the **aging method** which is a variation). It calculates the ending credit balance for the Allowance account based on an estimated percentage of ending receivables. (Receivables times specified percentage) = Ending Allowance Balance
            (a)   Allowance will already have a balance - in this method that figure is increased to the credit balance computed above.
            (b)   Bad debt expense is the increase in the allowance.
        (3)   Company may use percentage of sales during the year for interim reporting and switch to receivables method at end.
            (a)   Expense is recognized during the year as a percentage of sales.

        (b)   Allowance is adjusted at end of year to appropriate balance based on percentage of receivables (or aging).

(D)   Actual **write-off of a bad account** can occur at any time and is a debit to allowance (decrease) and a credit to accounts receivable (decrease). Has no effect on bad debt expense, net income, or the net balance reported for the receivables.

(3)   Direct Write-Off Method - sometimes used by smaller businesses to report bad debts although it is not considered as generally accepted. No allowance account is established; bad debt expense is not recognized until account is written off.

    (A)   Accounts receivable is decreased and bad debt expense is increased.

    (B)   Receivable is reported at an amount above what will be collected. Expenses are not being matched in the same period as revenues.

(4)   Receivables can be used to generate immediate cash flows. Assignment means that cash collected from a receivable must be used to pay off a specific liability. Pledging means that if a debt is not paid as it comes due, the creditor can force the liquidation of the pledged asset (such as accounts receivable). Discounting refers to the sale of a note receivable whereas **factoring** and **securitization** reflect the sale of accounts receivable.

    (A)   Factoring usually indicates that a single party has bought most if not all of a company's accounts receivable. The buyer will typically be responsible for collecting the receivables. Securitization means that many parties have bought the right to a portion of a company's receivables. The seller will continue to collect the receivables and convey all cash received to the buyer.

    (B)   In some situations, it may be difficult to determine if a sale has been made or if the receivables are simply being used as security for a debt. Both buyer and seller must recognize the assets and liabilities that they control. The financial component approach is used for this determination; it specifies that any element of the receivable is considered to be sold if three criteria have been met indicating a change in control.

        (1)   The asset is isolated from the seller.

        (2)   The buyer now has the right to sell or pledge the asset.

        (3)   The seller has not retained control through agreements to repurchase or redeem the asset.

    (C)   Receivables can be sold "**with recourse.**" If a receivable is not paid by customer when due, buyer can then demand payment from seller.

        (1)   To record the sale, the seller removes receivable and records cash received. However, because of potential liability, seller must also record the fair market value of any "recourse obligation" that is expected to arise because of the failure of some customers to pay.

        (2)   The difference between the cash received and the summation of the asset lost and the recourse obligation incurred is recognized as a loss.

        (3)   If the receivable is sold without recourse so that the seller has no further obligation, the receivable is removed and the cash recognized and the difference is a loss. There is no recourse obligation.

(5)   In **discounting** a note receivable, amount to be conveyed to the seller must be computed.

    (A)   Interest to be paid on note is computed (face value times annual rate times the period of the year from date of issuance until maturity). This interest is added to face value to get maturity value of the note.

(B)   Maturity value is then multiplied by buyer's discount (profit) rate for the period of time that is remaining until maturity. The resulting figure is the profit that the buyer wants to make.

(C)   Buyer's profit is subtracted from maturity value to get price paid for the note receivable.

PROBLEMS AND SOLUTIONS
ACCOUNTS RECEIVABLE AND BAD DEBT EXPENSE

ONE - A company starts a year with an allowance balance of $8,000 (credit). During the year, $15,000 in receivables are written off as uncollectible, bad debt expense of $26,000 is recognized, and a $2,000 account previously written off as uncollectible is actually collected. The ending Allowance for Doubtful Accounts account balance is a $21,000 credit. (True or False?)

Answer - The beginning balance of $8,000 is decreased by the $15,000 write off of actual accounts. However, the $26,000 bad debt expense and the $2,000 collection of the previously written off balance will increase the allowance. These transactions leave a $21,000 credit balance ($8,000 - $15,000 + $26,000 + $2,000). (Number One is True.)

TWO - At year's end, a company has sales of $300,000, accounts receivable of $130,000, and an Allowance for Doubtful Accounts account (unadjusted) with a $2,000 credit balance. The company estimates that 4 percent of sales will be bad. The company should recognize bad debt expense of $10,000. (True or False?)

Answer - The percentage of sales method multiplies the percentage (4 percent) times the sales ($300,000). The resulting total ($12,000) is the expense to be recognized. (Number Two is False.)

THREE - At the end of the current year, a company reports sales of $400,000, accounts receivable of $130,000, and an Allowance for Doubtful Accounts account (unadjusted) with a $2,000 credit balance. The company estimates that 10 percent of its accounts receivable will be uncollectible. The company should recognize bad debt expense of $11,000. (True or False?)

Answer - The percentage of receivables method multiplies the appropriate percentage (10 percent) times the receivables ($130,000). The resulting total ($13,000) is the final balance to be reported as a credit in the Allowance for Doubtful Accounts account. Because a $2,000 credit already existed in the allowance, an increase of $11,000 must be recognized to produce the needed $13,000 balance. The increase represents the bad debt expense for the period. (Number Three is True.)

FOUR - A company starts the current year with a $16,000 credit balance in its Allowance for Doubtful Accounts account. During the year, receivables of $20,000 are written off as uncollectible. For monthly reporting purposes, bad debt expense is recognized based on 3 percent of credit sales. Total credit sales for the year were $800,000. At the end of the year, for financial statement purposes, the Allowance for Doubtful Accounts account is adjusted based on an estimated rate of 4 percent of ending receivables. The Accounts Receivable account at the end of the year was $550,000. Bad debt expense for the year is $26,000. (True or False?)

Answer - The Allowance for Doubtful Accounts account is reduced from a $16,000 credit balance to a $4,000 debit balance by the $20,000 write off of uncollectible accounts. Also during the year, bad debt expense of $24,000 is recognized based on 3 percent of credit sales of $800,000. This expense raises the allowance from a $4,000 debit balance to a $20,000 credit balance. At year's end, for external reporting, the Allowance for Doubtful Accounts account is adjusted based on the percentage of receivables method. The ending receivables balance of $550,000 is multiplied by 4 percent to arrive at a $22,000 figure. To increase the $20,000 allowance balance to $22,000, an additional bad debt expense of $2,000 must be recognized. Thus, bad debt expense will be $26,000; $24,000 is recognized during the year and an additional $2,000 is recognized at the end of the year. (Number Four is True.)

PRESENT VALUE COMPUTATIONS

(1)   The Concept of **Present Value**

    (A)   Generally accepted accounting principles state that all future cash flows must have an interest factor attached to them. Interest must be recognized virtually any time that money is paid or received over time. If cash is to be paid over time (a liability exists), interest expense is recognized; if cash is to be received (a receivable exists), interest revenue is recognized.

    (B)   The interest factor can be explicitly stated and paid, thus causing no valuation problems. For example, if a $1,000 note payable pays 9% annual cash interest, $1,000 is the principal and $90 per year is the interest. Present value is not needed; a reasonable interest rate is stated and paid.

    (C)   If a reasonable rate of interest is not stated and paid, the future cash is assumed to be part interest and part principal. For example, if land is acquired for a single payment of $2,000 to be made in two years, part of the $2,000 is viewed as principal (cost of the land) and the remainder is recorded as interest to be recognized over the two-year period.

    (D)   Present value computations are designed to compute the portion of any future cash flows that represents the principal.

        (1)   If a purchase is made that requires future cash payments but a reasonable interest rate is not stated and paid, the present value is the cost assigned to the purchase.

        (2)   For a sale with future payments that do not include a reasonable interest, the present value is the amount of the sales revenue to be recorded immediately.

    (E)   One major exception exists in connection with the use of present value. If all cash flows arise from normal business operations and are to be made within one year, present value computations are not used even if no reasonable interest rate is stated and paid.

(2)   The **calculation of present value** is based on a formula: Present Value (or Principal) is equal to the Future Cash Flows multiplied by a Conversion Rate

    (A)   Future cash flows are usually specified in an agreement or contract.

    (B)   Conversion rate comes from a table; specific rate is based on three variables.

        (1)   Number of time periods

        (2)   A reasonable interest rate (sometimes called the yield rate or effective rate or market rate)

        (3)   Whether the cash flow is a single amount or an **annuity** (which is equal payments made at equal time intervals).

    (C)   If future cash flow is a single amount, conversion rate comes from "Present Value of 1" table. If future cash flow is an annuity, "Present Value of Annuity" table is used.

    (D)   If future cash flow is several unequal payments, "Present Value of 1" table is used. A separate conversion rate is used for each payment to get individual present values. These values are added to get total present value (principal).

    (E)   If future cash flow is both a single payment and an annuity (as it would be in many notes), the conversion rate for the annuity comes from the annuity table and the conversion rate for the single amount comes from the single amount table. Again, the individual present values are added to arrive at total.

(3) Annuities

    (A) An annuity where the payments are made at the end of each period is referred to as an **Ordinary Annuity**. Interest on a payable or receivable is usually paid at the end of the period.

    (B) An annuity where the payments are made at the beginning of each period is referred to as an **Annuity Due**. Most rents and leases require payments at the beginning of the period.

    (C) If necessary, an Ordinary Annuity table can be used to solve an Annuity Due problem. Remove the first cash payment and find the conversion rate for the remaining payments using the Ordinary Annuity table. Compute the present value of these remaining payments and then add the first payment. Since it is paid immediately, it is already stated at its present value.

(4) **Net Present Value** is a term used in capital budgeting. It represents the difference between the present value of an asset's future cash flows and its cost.

    (A) Conversion rate is determined based on minimum interest rate that company wants to earn on the investment.

    (B) If present value is higher than the cost of the asset, the net present value is said to be positive and the asset is considered to be a good acquisition.

(5) Future Values

    (A) Another set of conversion rates can be used to compute the amount that a set of cash flows will be worth at a specified point in the future. For example, if $1,000 is deposited in a savings account that adds 5 percent interest per year, a future value computation can be used to determine the amount in the account at any future point in time.

    (B) Formula is: Future Value = Cash Flows multiplied by Conversion Rate. Once again, the conversion rate is based on the number of time periods, a reasonable interest rate, and whether a single amount or an annuity is involved. Conversion rate comes from a Future Value table.

PROBLEMS AND SOLUTIONS
PRESENT VALUE COMPUTATIONS

ONE - A building is acquired for $800,000, an amount that will be paid in ten years. During the interim, interest will be paid at a rate of 9 percent per year. This interest rate is considered reasonable under the circumstances. In determining the amount to record as the cost of the building, the present value of the future cash flows must be computed. (True or False?)

Answer - A present value computation is required whenever cash flows are to be paid or received in the future and interest is not being accrued at a reasonable rate. In this problem, the interest rate is considered reasonable under the circumstances. Thus, the building will be recorded at $800,000. There is no reason to compute the present value of the future cash flows. (Number One is False.)

TWO - A building is bought and the present value of the future cash flows is determined. The cash flows will occur over 7 years but do not include a reasonable rate of interest. The present value is recorded as the reported cost of the building. (True or False?)

Answer - The present value of future cash flows is the current principal of the cash flows and represents the amount to be paid for the building. Any remaining amount should be viewed as interest to be recognized over the future period of the payments. (Number Two is True.)

THREE - A building is bought for $900,000, an amount that will be paid in 6 years. The annual interest rate is 2 percent so that $18,000 will also be paid at the end of each of the six years. A reasonable interest rate is 10 percent. The present value factor for an ordinary annuity for 6 years at 10 percent is 4.4. The present value factor for an annuity due for 6 years at 10 percent is 4.8. The present value factor for a single amount in 6 years at 10 percent is .56. The building will be recorded at $583,200. (True or False?)

Answer - The $18,000 cash interest payments are made at the end of each year and, thus, form an ordinary annuity. The present value of those interest payments is $79,200 ($18,000 times 4.4). The present value of the single payment of $900,000 is $504,000 based on multiplying that amount times .56. The total present value of these two cash flows is $583,200 or $79,200 plus $504,000. (Number Three is True).

LAND, BUILDINGS, AND EQUIPMENT (FIXED ASSETS)

(1) This balance sheet classification encompasses tangible, long-lived assets that are being used to generate revenues.

(2) For reporting purposes, the cost of **fixed assets** must be determined.

    (A) For new acquisitions, all normal and necessary costs to acquire the asset and get it into a condition to be used follow the rules of **capitalization** (that is, they are added to an asset account rather than to an expense account). These amounts include the following.

        (1) Invoice price (less any discounts)

        (2) Sales taxes

        (3) Cost of delivery

        (4) Cost of installation

        (5) Payments for training employees so that they can operate or use the asset.

    (B) In certain cases, **interest costs** are also capitalized.

        (1) Interest costs incurred during construction of fixed assets and inventory if it is being specifically built for a customer should be capitalized. The interest is added to the asset account rather than being recorded as interest expense.

        (2) The amount of interest to be capitalized is calculated each year by multiplying the average accumulated expenditures to date times an interest rate.

            (a) If a specific debt is incurred to finance the construction, the interest rate on that debt is used in this computation. Otherwise, the weighted average interest rate for all of the company's outstanding debt is used.

            (b) If the calculation of capitalized interest gives a figure that is more than the actual interest incurred during the period, only the actual interest is capitalized.

    (C) **Assets received as gifts** are initially recorded at fair market value with a corresponding increase in a Donated Revenue account.

    (D) For an asset already in use, any new expenditure is only capitalized if it is a betterment in some way: the life of the asset is extended beyond the original estimation, the asset becomes more efficient or productive, or operating costs are decreased. If an expenditure simply maintains the asset at its anticipated level of productivity and length of life, the cost is recorded as a maintenance expense.

(3) Assets may be acquired (or sold) for future cash payments (a payable is created by a purchase, a receivable by a sale). If a reasonable interest rate is not stated and paid, the cost of the asset (or the revenue if it is a sale) will be the present value of the cash flows based on a reasonable interest rate.

    (A) In such cases, the asset (or sales revenue) is recorded at **present value**. The payable (or receivable) is reported at the total cash flow. A Discount account is set up for the difference. This is a contra account to the payable (or receivable).

        (1) The Discount represents the portion of the total cash flows that is viewed as interest rather than principal.

        (2) As an alternative, the payable (or receivable) could be reported as a single number net of the discount.

(B)   Over the life of the payable/receivable, the discount will gradually be reclassified (amortized) as interest.

    (1)   Reducing the discount causes an increase in the net balance of the payable/receivable.

    (2)   If payable/receivable is shown as a single net figure, recognition of interest within the cash flows increases the payable/receivable balance being reported.

(C)   Interest to be recognized each period is computed by multiplying the payable/receivable net of the discount times a reasonable interest rate. This is referred to as the **effective rate method**.

(D)   As an alternative, if the results are not materially different, the straight-line method can be used to compute interest expense. The discount is divided evenly over the periods of time that payment will be made.

(4)   **Depreciation** is the process of assigning or allocating the cost of a fixed asset as an expense to the years in which it is used to generate revenues.

    (A)   The amount is computed and recorded at the end of each year in which the asset is in use. It is also recorded at the date an asset is sold, traded, or otherwise disposed of.

        (1)   Recording entry is a debit (increase) to depreciation expense and a credit (increase) to accumulated depreciation. Depreciation expense is shown on income statement and is closed out each year. **Accumulated depreciation** is a contra-account to the asset and, hence, is reported on the balance sheet so that it is not closed at the end of every period.

        (2)   Asset's book value (or carrying value) is its cost less total accumulated depreciation recognized to date.

        (3)   For convenience, a **half-year convention** (or some variation) can be used. Only one-half year of depreciation is recorded in the year of acquisition and again in the year of disposal regardless of the exact dates of purchase or disposal.

        (4)   If an asset is not being used to generate revenues, it is reported as an "other asset" and depreciation is not reported.

    (B)   **Straight-line method** - records the same expense for each full year. Annual figure is computed as follows: (<Cost - Salvage Value>/Life).

    (C)   **Accelerated depreciation** methods record high depreciation levels in the initial years of use (when the asset is most productive and subject to quick losses of value) but lower expense levels later. Several methods are available that create this pattern of cost allocation.

        (1)   **Double declining balance method** computes the current expense as follows: (<Cost - Accumulated Depreciation> X 2/Life). Because accumulated depreciation gets larger each year, the resulting book value figure (and, hence, depreciation expense) will get smaller each year. An alternative method is 150% declining balance that uses 1.5/Life rather than 2/Life.

        (2)   **Sum of the years digits method** computes the annual expense as follows: (<Cost - Salvage Value> X Fraction). The fraction is determined as follows:

        (a)   Denominator: the sum of the years of the asset's life. An asset with a five-year life would have a denominator of 15 (5 + 4 + 3 + 2 + 1).

        (b)   Numerator: the number in the asset's life that corresponds to the current year (in descending order). For an asset with a five-year life, 5 would be used for the first year, 4 for the second, and so on.

(D)   **Group depreciation** (and the similar "composite" method) applies one straight-line rate to an entire group of assets that are all acquired in the same year but with different lives. For example, 20 different small machines might be depreciated as a group.

    (1)   In the year of acquisition, annual depreciation is computed for each asset. The total annual depreciation is divided by the total cost of these assets to get depreciation rate. Each year, this same rate is multiplied by the remaining cost of the group. Depreciation stops with the disposal of the last item in the group or when any remaining cost has been fully depreciated.

    (2)   For the disposal of an item within the group, cash received is recorded, the original cost of that particular asset is removed, and the difference is a reduction in accumulated depreciation. No gain or loss is recognized. The assumption is that all gains and losses within the group will eventually offset. Any residual gain or loss is recorded at the retirement of the last asset.

(E)   **Depletion of wasting assets** such as oil wells and gold mines is computed on the straight-line method but based on units not years.

    (1)   Rate is found by dividing the cost (less any anticipated residual value) by the number of expected units.

    (2)   When units are removed, the cost (the units times the rate) is first recorded in an Inventory account. At the eventual time of sale, the cost is reclassified from inventory to cost of goods sold.

    (3)   Because the number of units is an estimation, a new depletion rate may have to be computed each year. Estimated residual value is subtracted from remaining book value. The resulting figure is divided by the estimated number of units remaining.

    (4)   Depreciation can also be computed using an approach (known as the **units of production method**) that is similar to depletion computation. Depreciation of a taxicab, for example, could be based on the miles driven this year as a percentage of the total mileage of expected use.

(5)   Disposals - when an asset is sold, destroyed, or otherwise disposed of, depreciation is recorded to the date of disposal.

    (A)   Both the cost of the asset and the accumulated depreciation are then removed from the records.

    (B)   If the amount received is different from the book value being removed, a gain is recorded (if more is collected) or a loss (if less).

(6)   **Asset with an impaired value**.

    (A)   Impairment occurs when the total of expected net future cash inflows is less than current book value.

    (B)   If impaired, book value of asset is written down to fair market value and a corresponding loss is recorded.

     (C)   If an asset's book value is written down because of an impairment but the value subsequently increases, no write up is allowed.

     (D)   An asset that is awaiting disposal is recorded at the lower of its book value or fair market value (less any cost to dispose). Depreciation of these assets should cease.

(7)   **Nonmonetary trades** - two questions must be addressed: what value is recorded for the item received and is a gain or loss to be recognized?

     (A)   Losses are always recognized immediately and can be created in two cases. In either situation, the asset must be reduced to its actual value and a loss recorded.

          (1)   If the item given up is worth less than its book value.

          (2)   If the item received is worth less than is to be recorded.

     (B)   Rules for recording the **trade of dissimilar items**.

          (1)   Old item is removed at its book value; new item is recorded at fair market value. Fair market value of item given up is used for this purpose (because it measures the sacrifice being made to get new asset). However, if value of old item is not known, use the value of item received.

          (2)   Gain is recognized if value recorded for new item is greater than the book value of the old item. If company is issuing its own stock in the trade, no gains and losses can be recorded on the stock. Instead, additional paid-in capital is adjusted.

          (3)   If cash is paid or received in a dissimilar trade, this money must be recorded at face value.

               (a)   If new asset is recorded based on value of items given up, the cash affects the capitalized amount. (1) - If cash is paid, it is added to old asset's market value to determine recording of new asset (2) - If cash is collected, it is subtracted from old asset's market value to get recording of new asset.

               (b)   If new asset is recorded based on its own value, cash paid or received does not affect that figure but will impact the amount of gain or loss to be recognized.

     (C)   Rules for the **trade of similar items**.

          (1)   The exchange does not culminate an earnings process. Old item is removed at book value and new item is recorded at same book value. Paying cash simply increases the book value being given up.

          (2)   Gain is never recognized in a similar trade of this type.

     (D)   A unique reporting situation is created if a company exchanges similar items but also receives cash or other boot.

          (1)   This trade has characteristics of both dissimilar and similar exchanges. It is easiest to record this transaction as two separate trades.

          (2)   In order to record two trades, the book value of the item being relinquished must be split into two components. The book value must be divided based on the fair market values of the two items being received (the similar asset and the cash).

               (a)   The cash collected is compared to the equivalent portion of the old book value to determine any gain to be recorded. This portion is handled like a dissimilar trade.

               (b)   The item received is recorded at the equivalent portion of the old book value with no gain recorded. This portion is handled like a similar trade.

(3) For example, assume that land with a $7,000 book value is traded to get land worth $8,000 (80%) and cash of $2,000 (20%). The old $7,000 book value must be split into a $5,600 (80%) component and a $1,400 (20%) component. The $2,000 cash that is received is compared to the $1,400 portion of the book value to get a $600 gain. The $5,600 book value component is used as the book value for the new land.

PROBLEMS AND SOLUTIONS
LAND, BUILDINGS, AND EQUIPMENT

ONE - A building and the land on which it is constructed are acquired for $490,000. The building has an appraised value of $100,000 but no basis exists for determining the value of the land. The company making the purchase tears down the building at a cost of $40,000 in order to make room for the construction of a new and bigger building. Scrap salvaged from the old building is sold for $9,000. The Land account will be recorded by the new owner at $521,000. (True or False?)

Answer - Because the building was removed, the entire amount of $490,000 must have been paid to acquire the land. The company had no use for the old building or it would not have been razed. In order to get the land into condition for use (as a site for the new building), a net cost of $31,000 is incurred to remove the old building. Thus, the cost attributed to the land is $521,000. If an old building is not to be used, the entire cost is assigned to the land. (Number One is True.)

TWO - A company has equipment with a cost of $80,000 and an expected residual value of $10,000 and useful life of 10 years. At the beginning of the current year, the accumulated depreciation for this equipment was $20,000. Using the double declining balance method, the depreciation expense to be recognized for this year is $10,000. (True or False?)

Answer - For this asset, the $80,000 cost less the $20,000 accumulated depreciation gives a net book value of $60,000. This figure is multiplied by a fraction that is two over the asset's ten-year life. The net book value of $60,000 times 2/10 gives an expense of $12,000. In applying any declining balance method, the expected residual value does not have an impact on the allocation computation. (Number Two is False.)

THREE - An asset is bought for $90,000 and is depreciated for a few years before being sold for $36,000. If straight-line depreciation is being used, the company has a greater chance of recording a gain on the sale of the asset than if the double declining balance method is applied. (True or False?)

Answer - The straight-line method records depreciation more slowly than an accelerated method. Consequently, book value will decline more slowly. Because the net book value will always be higher than under an accelerated method, the company that uses the straight-line method has a greater chance of reporting a loss. Since

---

the book value will be higher, the amount received is more likely to be less than that figure. (Number Three is False.)

FOUR - A truck with a book value of $46,000 and a fair market value of $50,000 is traded along with cash of $8,000 for a similar truck with a fair market value of $58,000. The newly acquired truck is recorded at $54,000. (True or False?)

Answer – In recording the exchange of similar assets, the book values of the assets being surrendered are removed and the new asset is recorded at the total of these book values. Including the payment of cash does not alter this rule. The book value of the old truck was $46,000 and the book value of the cash paid was $8,000; thus, the new truck will be recorded at the $54,000 total. That amount is equal to the book value of the items surrendered. (Number Four is True.)

FIVE - A truck with a book value of $47,000 and a fair market value of $56,000 is traded for land. A gain of $9,000 should be recognized. (True or False?)

Answer – As a dissimilar trade, the land that is received is recorded at the $56,000 value of the asset surrendered. The truck is removed at its $47,000 book value. The $9,000 difference is recorded as a gain. (Number Five is True.)

SIX - A truck with a book value of $37,000 and a fair market value of $42,000 is traded for land. The newly acquired land is reported with a balance of $42,000. (True or False?)

Answer - As a dissimilar trade, the land that is received is recorded at the $42,000 value of the asset surrendered. (Number Six is True.)

BONDS AND NOTES; PAYABLES AND INVESTMENTS (IF TO BE HELD TILL MATURITY)

(1) **Bonds and notes** are formal promises to pay a certain amount of money along with a specified amount of cash interest at a certain time in the future. Can be negotiated with a single party or can be a negotiable instrument to be bought and sold at whatever price can be achieved.

    (A) **Bonds** have several unique terms.

        (1) **Serial Bond** - Interest and principal payments are made periodically

        (2) **Term Bond** - Interest is paid each period but principal is paid as a lump sum on maturity date

        (3) **Debenture Bond** - Debt is not secured by collateral or any other type of security

        (4) **Bond Indenture** - This document gives the legal terms of a bond.

    (B) **Bond issuance costs** paid by debtor (such as printing and legal fees) are reported as an asset and amortized to expense by straight-line method over life of bond. If bond is paid off early, any remaining cost must be removed.

(2) Computation of the selling price of a bond on the market. Price is usually stated as a percentage of face value (a price of 98 would mean 98 percent of face value)

    (A) If investors want an interest rate that is same as the cash rate stated on the indenture, they will pay an amount equal to the face value of the bond. **Stated interest rate** is multiplied by face value to determine annual amount of interest to be paid.

    (B) If investors want an interest rate that differs from stated interest rate, a present value computation is made to determine price to be paid. If investors want a higher rate, the bond is sold below face value and a discount recorded. If they will accept a lower rate, bond is sold above face value and a premium recorded.

    (C) A present value computation is also necessary if stated interest rate is unreasonable (such as a zero rate). Interest is assumed to be hidden inside of the note or bond.

(3) If a premium or discount is recorded on a bond, that amount must be amortized to interest over the life of bond.

    (A) Amortization entries are made at the date of each interest payment as well as at end of fiscal year.

    (B) **Effective rate method** calculates true interest by multiplying current book value of the debt (face value plus premium or minus discount) times **effective interest rate**. The difference in this interest figure and the cash interest payment reduces the discount or premium. Because of change in discount or premium, book value of the bond or note changes each time amortization is recorded.

        (1) Effective interest rate is the market rate at the time of the transaction or the rate the company could otherwise get.

    (C) **Straight-line method** is sometimes used to amortize discount or premium although effective rate method is preferred. It divides premium or discount evenly over life of bond; that amount is amortized each period. Straight-line method can be used when recognized amounts are not materially different than figures that would have been reported by the effective rate method.

       (1)   Under either method, interest to be recognized is the cash interest plus the amortization of any discount or less the amortization of any premium.

    (D)   For a long-term bond, portion that should be reported as current is equal to any principal payment in the upcoming year less amortization of any discount or plus amortization of any premium.

(4)   If a bond is called (paid off early) before its maturity date, a final amortization entry must be recorded to bring book value up to date. Bond issuance costs must be amortized as well as any discount or premium. Face value along with any remaining bond issuance costs and any unamortized discount or premium gives book value of bond.

    (A)   The difference in this book value and cash payment is recognized as a gain or loss.

    (B)   For the debtor, the gain or loss is classified as an **extraordinary item** and shown on the bottom of the income statement net of its tax effect.

(5)   Origination fees may be paid to obtain a loan. Most of these costs are reported as a discount (if paid) or a premium (if received) and amortized to income over life of the note using the effective rate method.

(6)   A bond is sometimes sold along with **detachable stock warrants** for one price. For recording, price must be allocated between debt and equity.

    (A)   If market value of only one item is known, that amount is assigned to that item. Remainder of price is allocated to other item.

    (B)   If both items have a known fair market value, price is allocated between debt and equity based on the relative market values.

    (C)   If price is paid for a **convertible debt**, entire amount is allocated to debt. Until conversion, no amount is recorded as equity. If converted, equity is recorded at book value of debt so that no gain or loss is recorded.

(7)   If a company has a debt coming due within 12 months of the balance sheet date, the debt is classified as long-term if either one of two conditions is met before the financial statements are issued.

    (A)   Debt is classified as long-term if (1) it is refinanced on a long- term basis or (2) a noncancellable agreement to refinance on a long-term basis is signed with a financially sound lending institution

(8)   A **troubled debt restructuring** occurs when a debtor faces default and the creditor gives more lenient terms in hopes of improving future collection

    (A)   If payment is made immediately with a noncash asset (such as land), the asset is first adjusted to market value so that debtor has an ordinary gain or loss. Difference between market value of asset and book value of debt is an extraordinary gain or loss for debtor and an ordinary gain or loss for creditor.

    (B)   If debt is restructured so that debtor has better terms, debtor and creditor record the restructuring differently. Debtor records a gain if new agreement calls for less to be paid (over the entire life of revised note) than is currently due (principal plus unpaid interest to date). If less is to be paid, debt is reduced to that amount and an extraordinary gain is recognized.

        (1)   If gain or loss is recognized by debtor, no future interest is recorded even if a payment is called "interest."

        (2)   If more will ever be paid than is currently owed, no gain is recorded by debtor. That excess is recognized as interest over remaining life of the payments.

(C)   For a debt restructuring, creditor computes the present value of future cash flows (specified by the restructuring) based on the original rate of interest.

        (1)   If present value is less than current debt (principal plus accrued interest), creditor has a loss for difference.

        (2)   Future interest revenue to be recognized by creditor is original interest rate times book value which is the present value of future cash flows.

PROBLEMS AND SOLUTIONS
BONDS AND NOTES; PAYABLES AND INVESTMENTS

ONE - A bond pays interest every January 1. The bond has a face value of $10,000 and a stated cash interest rate of 10 percent per year. The bond is issued on April 1 for 97 plus accrued interest. The buyer pays $9,950 to make this acquisition. (True or False?)

Answer - The bond is sold for 97 percent of its face value or $9,700. Because 3 months have passed since the previous interest date, the buyer is required to pay the accrued interest that has accumulated on the bond since January 1. Cash interest is always computed as the face value of the debt multiplied by the stated cash interest rate. The cash interest that has accrued is $10,000 times 10 percent times 3/12 of a year or $250. Thus, $9,700 is paid for the bond and $250 is paid for the accrued interest. The total payment is $9,950. (Number One is True.)

TWO - On January 1, Year One, a company issues a $10,000 bond that pays 2 percent stated cash interest each year. Interest will be paid every December 31. The buyer wants to earn interest of 8 percent. A present value computation is made and the buyer pays $7,600 for this bond. Both parties record the bond initially at $7,600. At the end of Year One, cash interest of $152 will be paid. (True or False?)

Answer - The amount of cash interest that is paid every period is the face value of the bond times the stated cash interest rate. In this case, $10,000 times 2 percent is $200. Regardless of the price paid for the bond, this amount of cash interest will be paid each year. (Number Two is False.)

THREE - On January 1, Year One, a company issues a five-year $10,000 bond that pays 4 percent stated cash interest or $400 each year. Interest will be paid every December 31. The buyer wants to earn interest of 6 percent. A present value computation is made and the buyer pays $9,150 for this bond. If the effective rate method is applied, interest of $600 is recognized in the Year One income statement. (True or False?)

Answer - When the effective rate method is used, interest is computed each year by multiplying the net book value ($9,150 in this initial year) times the effective interest rate (6%). Consequently, interest recognized on the income statement in Year One is $549. (Number Three is False.)

FOUR - On January 1, Year One, a company issues a five-year $10,000 bond that pays 4 percent stated cash interest or $400 each year. Interest will be paid every December 31. The

---

buyer wants to earn interest of 6 percent. A present value computation is made and the buyer pays $9,150 for this bond. If the effective rate method is applied, interest of $549 is recognized in Year One. At the end of that year, the net book value of the bond is $9,299. (True or False?)

Answer - Under the effective rate method, amortization of any discount or premium is the difference in the amount of cash interest for the period ($400) and the interest recognized on the income statement ($549). The $149 difference is a reduction in the discount, thus, increasing the net book value from $9,150 to $9,299. (Number Four is True.)

FIVE - On January 1, Year One, a company issues a five-year $10,000 bond that pays 4 percent stated cash interest or $400 each year. Interest will be paid every December 31. The buyer wants to earn interest of 6 percent. A present value computation is made and the buyer pays $9,150 for this bond. If the effective rate method is applied, interest of $549 is recognized in Year One and $558 in Year Two. The net book value of the bond at the end of Year Two is $9,457. (True or False?)

Answer - Amortization in Year One is $149 ($549 less $400); amortization in Year Two is $158 ($558 less $400). Total amortization for the two years is $307 ($149 plus $158). Since the bond was issued at a discount, amortization moves the net book value of the bond upwards toward the face value. The discount is being reduced so the book value increases. Therefore, the net book value is increased by $307 from $9,150 to $9,457. (Number Five is True.)

SIX - On January 1, Year One, a Bond Payable account is reported by a company. The bond has a face value of $100,000 but a Discount on Bond account is reported on that date of $13,000. In addition, a Bond Issuance Cost account is reported as an asset with an unamortized balance of $1,000. The bond is paid off early on April 1, Year One. Amortization of the discount for that three month period is $675. Amortization of the bond issuance cost for the same period is $63. If the bond is paid off for $97,000, a loss of $9,388 is recognized on the extinguishment of the debt. (True or False?)

Answer – Because of the amortization, the discount is reduced by $675 from $13,000 to $12,325. The bond issuance cost has also been reduced by $63 to $937. Therefore, the net amount to be removed from the financial records is the $100,000 face value less the $12,325 discount and the $937 bond issuance costs or $86,738. Since $97,000 was paid to retire the debt, the company reports the extra payment as a loss of $10,262. (Number Six is False.)

SEVEN - A total of $100,000 in bonds is issued. These bonds have a market value on that date of $104,000. In addition, 10,000 stock warrants are issued along with the bonds. These warrants allow the holder to buy a share of stock for $19 per share at any time during the next three years. Because of the addition of the stock warrants, the entire package is sold for $119,000. Stockholders' equity should be increased by $15,000 as a result of the sale. (True or False?)

*Answer - In this transaction, two things are issued: bonds and stock warrants.
Normally, the price would be allocated between the two based on their relative*

fair market values. Here, only one fair market value is given: the bonds are worth $104,000. Because that is the only known market value, the bonds are recorded at this amount with the residual $15,000 assigned to the stock warrants. (Number Seven is True.)

EIGHT - On December 31, Year One, a company has a $600,000 bond payable outstanding that will come due on September 1, Year Two. The company plans to issue its Year One financial statements during March of Year Two. In February Year Two, the company signs a noncancellable agreement with a financial institution to refinance $500,000 of this debt on a long-term basis when it comes due. The company hopes to get additional long-term financing of $100,000 prior to September 1, Year Two. On its December 31, Year One, balance sheet, the $600,000 liability should be shown as a current liability. (True or False?)

Answer - The company signed a noncancellable agreement to refinance a portion of the debt before the Year One financial statements were issued. Thus, this $500,000 portion of the debt should be reported as long-term. Only the $100,000 that has not been refinanced or covered by a noncancellable agreement to refinance must be reported as a current liability. (Number Eight is False.)

NINE - On January 1, Year One, company A borrows $100,000 from bank Z. The loan is due in 10 years and has an annual rate of interest of 5 percent. The 5 percent rate of interest is considered reasonable under the circumstances. Company A does not make the $5,000 interest payment in Year One when due. Company A does not pay the second $5,000 in interest in Year Two when it is due. On December 31, Year Two, company A threatens to default. Bank Z agrees to restructure the debt. Company A will pay $10,000 per year for the next 9 years or a total of $90,000. If bank Z were going to loan money to company A now, it would charge a rate of 15 percent. The present value of the nine $10,000 payments at a 5 percent rate equals $71,000. The present value of the nine $10,000 payments at a 15 percent rate equals $48,000. Company A will recognize an extraordinary gain on the restructuring of $20,000. Ignore income taxes. (True or False?)

Answer - In a troubled debt restructuring, the debtor (company A) compares the amount that is owed at that point in time with the total amount of cash that will ever be paid on the debt. If less will be paid, the difference is recognized as an extraordinary gain. In this case, company A owes $110,000, the $100,000 face value and two years of interest at $5,000 per year. After the restructuring, company A has agreed to pay a total of only $90,000. The $20,000 reduction is an extraordinary gain. The debtor bases this computation on the total amount of cash to be paid without taking into consideration the present value of those cash flows. (Number Nine is True.)

MISCELLANEOUS FINANCIAL STATEMENTS

Interim Financial Statements

(1) **Interim financial statements** are produced for any period less than one year, most frequently every three months (quarterly statements).

(2) Revenue recognition is same as in regular accounting. Revenues are recognized when earned and the transaction is substantially complete
  (A) Such income items as extraordinary items are recorded when incurred and not allocated over the entire year

(3) Expenses are recorded in order to match them against the revenues they have helped to generate.
  (A) Expenses (such as property taxes or rents) that are for longer than a single quarter must be allocated to the periods benefited.

(4) Income taxes must be anticipated and recognized each quarter.
  (A) Each quarter the effective tax rate for the entire year is estimated. This rate is multiplied times the total income to date to derive total income tax expense to date. Any tax expense previously recognized is subtracted to leave expense for current quarter.

(5) If **inventory declines in value** during a quarter, loss is not recognized if drop in value is considered temporary.
  (A) If value decline is viewed as permanent, loss is recognized.
  (B) If loss is recognized and value goes back up, a market recovery (or gain) is recorded. Market recovery cannot exceed loss that was reported.

Personal Financial Statements and Development Stage Enterprises

(1) **Personal financial statements** are prepared for individuals.
  (A) **Statement of financial condition** presents assets and liabilities at current values rather than historical cost. Difference is referred to as net worth.
    (1) Because assets and liabilities are reported at fair market value, the potential tax effects of realizing gains and losses in value must also be reported.
    (2) Estimated tax effect on potential gains/losses is reported between liabilities and net worth section of balance sheet.
  (B) A **statement of changes in net worth** is also reported.

(2) A **development stage enterprise** is a company that is working to establish its business and has not yet generated significant revenues.
  (A) Reporting process is normal except that income statement and cash flow figures are reported twice: for the current period and as cumulative amounts since the inception of the business.

PROBLEMS AND SOLUTIONS
MISCELLANEOUS FINANCIAL STATEMENTS

ONE - A company buys inventory during the first quarter of the year at a cost of $150,000. During the second quarter, the value of the inventory drops to $141,000 but the company feels that the inventory value will go back up to $150,000 in the third quarter of the year. Because of conservatism, the company must recognize a $9,000 loss in the second quarter of the year. (True or False?)

False - This loss is only temporary in nature because the company expects for the inventory to regain its value in the third quarter. Temporary declines in market value are not recognized, even in interim financial statements. No loss is recognized by this company in the second quarter of the year. (Number One is False.)

TWO - On a statement of financial condition produced for an individual, all assets are reported at market value. (True or False?)

Answer - For personal financial statements, assets and liabilities are reported at market value. (Number Two is True.)

THREE - On a set of personal financial statements, a potential tax effect must be included based on the differences in the market value and the book value of all assets and liabilities. This potential tax effect is shown between the Liability section and the Net Worth section of the statement of financial condition. (True or False?)

Answer - Because this tax effect is only potential and not yet a real liability, it is shown outside of the Liability section. It is placed between the liabilities and the net worth on the statement of financial condition. (Number Three is True.)

STOCKHOLDERS' EQUITY

(1)   Corporations issue capital stock. Acquiring these shares of stock gives the buyer the right of ownership.

    (A)   Ownership of **common stock** gives four rights

        (1)   Right to vote for members of Board of Directors

        (2)   Right to share in any dividends that are declared

        (3)   Right to share in any assets remaining after liquidation

        (4)   Right to acquire percentage of new shares issued

    (B)   Terminology in connection with capital stock.

        (1)   **Shares authorized** - total number of shares that can legally be issued by a corporation.

        (2)   **Shares issued** - number of shares that have been sold

        (3)   **Shares outstanding** - number of shares that are presently being held by the public.

        (4)   **Par value** - a value attached to a share by the company. Anyone buying a share for less than par value risks having to make up the difference if the company ever goes bankrupt

            (a)   When stock is sold, its par value is recorded in the stock account with any excess received recorded as Additional Paid-in Capital (APIC)

            (b)   Stock issued in exchange for noncash assets or services is recorded at fair market value

        (5)   **Subscribed stock** - shares that have been ordered by a potential investor but not yet fully paid. Usually, shares cannot be issued until fully paid.

    (C)   Common stockholders can give up one or more of their basic rights to the owners of a second type of stock called **preferred stock**.

        (1)   The right given up is often connected with dividend payments. Preferred stock might be given a set dividend or one that is cumulative (all past dividends must be paid before common stock can receive any dividend).

            (a)   If a **cumulative dividend** is not paid, it is referred to as a **dividends in arrears** and must be disclosed. No dividend is viewed as a liability until declared by the company's Board of Directors.

    (D)   Companies can never record a gain or loss on buying or selling their own stock. Differences increase or decrease Additional Paid-in Capital. If APIC is reduced to zero, any further reduction is recorded to the Retained Earnings account

(2)   **Treasury Stock** is the stock of a company that has been repurchased. It be accounted for by using one of three methods.

    (A)   Under the cost method, the treasury stock is recorded at cost.

        (1)   If shares are later resold above cost, APIC is increased

        (2)   If shares are later resold below cost, APIC is reduced. If APIC is not sufficient to cover difference, remainder is a reduction in retained earnings.

    (B)   Under the **par value method**, treasury stock is recorded at its par value with any APIC that was originally recorded being removed. Any difference in issuance price and the reacquisition price increases or decreases APIC. Retained earnings can be reduced.

  (1) Under either cost or par value method, treasury stock is shown as a reduction figure within the Stockholders' Equity section of the balance sheet.

  (2) Resale of shares is handled just like an original issuance

 (C) Stock can be bought back and then retired so that it is removed entirely from the records. Entry is same as repurchase entry under the par value method except that Common Stock is reduced rather than Treasury Stock.

(3) Certain instruments that have characteristics of both equity and liabilities must be presented as liabilities, such as

 (A) Mandatorily redeemable stock.

 (B) Share repurchase agreements.

(4) **Retained Earnings** account is a measure of net assets held by company that were generated originally by the operations

 (A) It is increased by net income but decreased by dividends on the date of declaration.

 (B) If company has decided to limit dividends, retained earnings is shown as two figures: unappropriated (maximum amount of dividends that would be paid) and appropriated (remainder)

(5) **Incorporation of a sole proprietorship or partnership**

 (A) All assets and liabilities are adjusted to fair market value

 (B) Stock is issued to owners based on this total fair market value

(6) **Quasi-reorganization** is a technique used by company with approval of creditors in hopes of avoiding bankruptcy

 (A) Assets and liabilities are adjusted to fair market value. Liabilities are also usually reduced by creditors. All gains and losses directly impact retained earnings.

 (B) Par value of Common Stock account is reduced with an offsetting increase in additional paid-in capital.

 (C) Negative balance in retained earnings is offset against APIC. Retained earnings is now reported as a zero balance.

(7) Dividends are distributions made to stockholders as a reward of ownership

 (A) Three dates are important: **Date of Declaration** (Board of Directors declares dividend so that it becomes a legal liability and retained earnings is reduced), **Date of Record** (ownership of stock is established. Company makes no entry but owner records a receivable), and **Date of Payment.**

 (B) **Property dividend** is a noncash distribution.

  (1) Property is adjusted by company to fair value on date of declaration with a gain or loss being recognized. Dividend is then recorded

(8) **Stock dividend** is a distribution made in the stock of the company.

 (A) Stockholders do not make a journal entry and do not record income but must reallocate book value over a greater number of shares

 (B) Company records dividend as a decrease in retained earnings and an increase in the Common Stock and APIC accounts

  (1) If stock dividend is less than 20% (owner gets less than 2 shares for every 10 being held), dividend is recorded at fair market value of newly issued shares

(2) If stock dividend is over 25%, dividend is recorded at par value of newly issued shares.

(3) If stock dividend is between 20% - 25%, company may choose to record dividend at fair value or par value of shares.

(C) In a **stock split**, the old shares are canceled and all new shares (with a new par value) are issued. No entry is necessary. Stock split does not affect stock accounts or retained earnings.

  (1) Assume that 1,000 shares outstanding with a $100 par value are split 2 for 1. The company will now have 2,000 shares outstanding with a $50 par value. Total par value does not change; it was $100,000 both before and after the split.

(9) **Stock appreciation rights** are awarded by a company to give a potential bonus to its employees. Bonus is based on increase in price of stock over a specified period of time. Company recognizes a portion of expense and liability each period. Amount is computed using ending price of stock each year.

(A) At end of each year, increase in price of stock to date is measured to provide estimation of total benefit.

(B) Estimated total benefit is multiplied by percentage of the time that has passed to give estimated benefit to date.

(C) Any previous expense that has been recognized is subtracted from estimated benefit to date to get expense for current period

(D) If price of stock has gone down, recognition of an expense reduction may be required.

(10) A **stock warrant** is the right to acquire stock at a set price

(A) If these rights are given away to owners as a dividend or in a **noncompensatory employee stock option plan**, no value is assigned. When converted into stock, normal issuance entry is recorded

  (1) Stock rights given to employees are noncompensatory if all employees share on an equal basis. The option price must be equal to market value or have only a small discount. The period in which to convert must be short.

(B) If a stock warrant is sold, the price is recorded by the company in a paid-in capital account. When converted into stock, any cash received is recorded, the stock warrant is removed, and the new stock is recorded at total of these two recorded values.

(11) Stock warrants can be issued to employees as part of a **compensatory stock option plan** to reward selected individuals. Reporting of these plans must be made by one of two methods.

(A) Rights are valued at the difference in the option price and the fair market value of the stock on the measurement date. This approach is known as the **intrinsic value method**.

  (1) **Measurement date** is the first day on which both the option price and the number of shares that can be acquired are known.

  (2) The amount of expense is equal to the value of the rights. Expense is recognized evenly over the period of time that the employee must work in the future to be entitled to the warrants.

(B) On the date when the warrants are granted, the value of the warrants (and, thus, the expense) is estimated using a computer pricing model. This estimation is based on several variables: option price, current value of stock, historical dividend rate, previous volatility of stock price, length of time that person has to convert, and alternative rates of income that are available. This approach is known as the **fair value method**.

(1) Expense is allocated to periods until employee's right to these warrants becomes vested.

(C) Company may use either method but, if first method is applied, pro forma net income information must be reported using second method.

PROBLEMS AND SOLUTIONS
STOCKHOLDERS' EQUITY

ONE - A company has 500,000 shares of authorized common stock with 90,000 shares issued and 78,000 shares outstanding. The company decides to pay a $1.00 per share cash dividend. The dividend will be $78,000. (True or False?)

True - Cash dividends are only paid to stockholders and, in this question, 78,000 shares of the stock are in the hands of the stockholders. (Number One is True.)

TWO - A company has common stock with a $10 par value. A share of this stock is issued for $19. The stock is eventually repurchased by the company for $21. The company will report a loss on this repurchase of $2. (True or False?)

False - Gains and losses are never reported in connection with stock transactions. (Number Two is False.)

THREE - A company has common stock with an authorized par value of $10 per share. This company issues 1,000 shares of this stock for $12 per share. The company later buys back 10 shares of the stock for $15 per share. Eventually, one share of this treasury stock is resold to the public for $17. The cost method is in use. At the time of sale, an Additional Paid-in Capital Account will be increased by $2. (True or False?)

Answer - Gains and losses resulting from a stock transaction cannot be reported on the issuing company's income statement. Therefore, because the stock here was resold at $2 above its acquisition price, this extra amount is reported as an increase in Additional Paid-in Capital (a stockholders' equity account). (Number Three is True.)

FOUR - Company A has an investment of 1,000 shares of company Z that it acquired for $19 per share. Company A decides to distribute these shares to its own stockholders as a property dividend. On that date, the stock is worth $25 per share. Because company A is distributing this investment as a dividend, company A records no income statement effect. (True or False?)

Answer - Whenever a noncash asset is conveyed by a company to an outside party for any reason, the asset is first adjusted to fair market value with a corresponding gain or loss being recognized on the company's income statement. In this case, the value of each of the 1,000 shares has increased by $6 so that a $6,000 gain is recognized by company A just prior to the dividend distribution. (Number Four is False.)

FIVE - A company decides to issue a 10 percent stock dividend. For this reason, the company issues 8,000 shares of its $10 par value stock with a current market value of $25 per share. In recording this dividend, the company will reduce its retained earnings by $200,000. (True or False?)

Answer - A stock dividend that is below 20-25 percent of the outstanding number of shares is recorded based on the market value of the shares issued. Because this dividend is only 10 percent, the reduction in retained earnings will be computed at the $25 fair market value for each of the 8,000 shares. Thus, the reduction in retained earnings is $200,000. (Number Five is True.)

SIX - On January 1, Year One, a company awards 1,000 stock options to Mr. A. These stock options can be converted into stock if the employee works for the company for three years from that date. After that time, Mr. A will have two additional years in which to convert. The stock options can be converted into shares of the company's common stock for cash of $20 per share. On January 1, Year One, the stock has a market value of $23 per share but that figure has risen to $30 per share by December 31, Year One. According to the intrinsic value method, the company will recognize an expense of $3,000 for Year One. (True or False?)

Answer - The total expense is $3,000; that is the difference in the option price ($20) and the market value ($23) on the measurement date (January 1, Year One) times the 1,000 options. However, that expense must be recognized over the three years that Mr. A has to work for the company to be entitled to the options. Therefore, the company will recognize $1,000 of expense in each of these three years. The expense for Year One is $1,000. (Number Six is False.)

SEVEN - According to fair value method, recognition of expense in connection with a compensatory stock option should be based on an estimation of the option's value that is determined on the date of grant. The estimation is made using a computer pricing model. (True or False?)

Answer – In applying the fair value method, a computer pricing model (such as the Black-Scholes model) must be used to calculate the value of the option. That figure is then used for expense recognition purposes. (Number Seven is True.)

EIGHT - In the quasi-reorganization of a company, its assets continue to be reported at their historical cost figures. (True or False?)

Answer - In the quasi-reorganization process, a company's assets are normally adjusted to fair market value, especially if the assets are overvalued on the company's financial records. (Number Eight is False.)

ACCOUNTING FOR LEASES

(1)   One party (the lessor) owns property while a different party (the lessee) rents and uses the property.

(2)   A lease may be recorded as a **capitalized lease** if the rights and responsibilities of ownership are conveyed to the lessee. A capitalized lease is viewed as a transfer of ownership rights. A lease is viewed as a capitalized lease if it meets any one of the following four criteria

    (A)   Title of the property transfers to lessee at the end of the lease

    (B)   Lessee has the option to buy property at end of the lease for a price that is significantly below expected market value so that there is a reasonable expectation that the price will be paid. This arrangement is referred to as a **bargain purchase option**.

    (C)   Life of the lease is 75% or more of the economic life of the item

    (D)   Present value of the minimum lease payments is 90% or more of the fair market value of the leased item

        (1)   Interest rate has to be used for this and other computations

            (a)   Lessor uses imputed interest rate built into the cash flows of the contract.

            (b)   Lessee uses its incremental borrowing rate unless the lessor's imputed interest rate is known and it is less

(3)   If none of the criteria is met, it is a rent and must be recorded as an **operating lease**

    (A)   When the lease is signed, the lessee does not record an asset or liability. As incurred, rent expense is recognized.

    (B)   Lessor retains asset on its books and records rent revenue as it is earned.

    (C)   Unless periods of time differ, revenue (lessor) and expense (lessee) should be recorded as the same amount each period.

(4)   Lessee accounts for a capitalized lease as if property were being purchased over a period of time.

    (A)   Both asset and liability are recorded at present value of **minimum lease payments**. Liability can be shown as single figure or as a payable for total payments less a Discount on Lease account to reduce net balance to present value.

        (1)   Difference between total payments and present value is interest to be recognized over life of lease. Interest is recognized each period based on effective rate method.

    (B)   Although not legally owned, lessee depreciates asset. Straight- line method is normally applied over useful life.

        (1)   If title transfers or if there is a bargain purchase option, depreciation is for life of asset. Otherwise, depreciation is for life of lease.

    (C)   Maintenance, property taxes, and the like are **executory costs**. Payments are not part of the minimum lease payments. Such payments are not included as part of the lease liability or the leased asset. Executory costs are expensed as incurred.

(5)   To account for a capitalized lease, lessor removes asset and recognizes revenue from lease. Two different methods can be used to determine pattern of revenue recognition.

    (A)   It is a **direct financing lease** if lessor is not a dealer or manufacturer of the product. Lessor leases item and does not sell it.

        (1)   Receivable and any cash immediately received are recorded.

(2)   Asset is removed from books but no immediate gain is recorded. Difference is interest to be recorded over period of payments. Initially recorded unearned interest and then amortized to interest revenue using effective rate method

(B)   It is a **sales type lease** if lessor is a dealer or manufacturer who may also sell the item.

    (1)   Receivable and any cash immediately received are recorded. Asset is removed from books. Difference is total profit.

    (2)   Normal gain on sale is immediately recorded based on sales price of item. If sales price is not known, the present value of the minimum lease payments is used.

    (3)   Any amount of the total profit in excess of the gain recorded on the sale is unearned interest to be recognized as interest over life of lease using the effective rate method

(6)   Both parties to a capitalized lease base the computation on the "**minimum lease payments**." That figure includes the annual payment plus:

(A)   For the lessor, any amount to be received as a bargain purchase option is included in the minimum lease payments because collection is expected. However, if lessor anticipates getting the asset back because the title does not transfer and there is not a bargain purchase option, the expected value of the asset when returned is also viewed as a future collection.

(B)   For the lessee, any amount to be paid as a bargain purchase option is included as part of the minimum lease payments. If, instead, the asset is to be returned to the lessor, only a value that has been guaranteed is included by the lessee.

(7)   In a capitalized lease, lessor has a receivable to report whereas lessee has a liability. On the balance sheet, a part of each balance is shown as current with the rest being long-term. The current portion is the payment to be made in the next 12 months less the amount of interest to be recognized during that period.

(8)   Lessor may have to pay direct costs such as legal fees and commissions associated with creating the lease agreement

(A)   If it is an operating lease, these costs are recorded as an asset and amortized as an expense over the life of the lease

(B)   If it is a sales type lease, cost is expensed immediately.

(C)   If it is a direct financing lease, cost is a reduction in the Unearned Interest account so that less interest revenue is recognized over the life of the lease

(9)   There can be a **sale-leaseback arrangement**. Asset is sold and then leased back to original owner. If there is a loss, seller/lessee recognizes it immediately. If there is gain, seller/lessee may have to defer recognition of the gain.

(A)   If only a minor portion of the property is leased back, any gain is recognized by seller/lessee immediately. A minor portion is when present value of payments is 10% or less of market value.

(B)   If substantially all of the property is leased back, the entire gain is initially deferred. Deferred gain is written off to reduce depreciation expense over the life of the lease.

(C)   If leaseback is more than a minor portion but less than substantially all, seller/lessee recognizes part of gain and defers the rest of the gain. Deferred gain is written off to reduce depreciation expense over the life of the lease. Gain to be deferred is amount up to the present value of the payments. Any additional amount is recognized immediately as a gain.

PROBLEMS AND SOLUTIONS
ACCOUNTING FOR LEASES

ONE - Company A leases property to company Z in an operating lease for $6,000 in the first year, $5,000 in the second year, and $1,000 in the third (and last) year of the lease. Company A will recognize rental revenue of $4,000 in the first year whereas company Z will recognize rental expense of $4,000 in the first year. (True or False?)

Answer - In operating leases, cash payments are sometimes different from year to year. However, unless some aspect of the lease or the leased property is different over time, the same amount of revenue and expense must be recognized in each year. In this lease, $12,000 will be paid over a three-year period. Therefore, since there is no indication that the lease or the leased property is different during these years, a revenue should be recorded by the lessor and an expense should be recorded by the lessee of $4,000 per year ($12,000 total payment allocated over three years). (Number One is True.)

TWO - In accounting for capitalized leases, an interest rate is required. An interest rate is needed to determine the amount of interest revenue or interest expense to be recognized. For all such computations, the lessor uses its own incremental borrowing rate as its interest rate. That is the interest rate that the lessor would get if this additional amount of money was being borrowed. (True or False?)

Answer - In all lease computations, the lessor uses the imputed interest rate that is built into the terms of the contract. This is the profit rate included in the contract because the money will be paid over a period of time. Conversely, the lessee will use its incremental borrowing rate for its interest computations unless the lessor's imputed interest rate is known and it is less. (Number Two is False.)

THREE - Company A leases property to company Z. It is to be reported as a capitalized lease. Company Z will pay $10,000 per year for four years. At the end of that time, the property will be returned to company A. The property has an expected useful life of 5 years. The present value of the payments is $32,000. Thus, company Z reports a capitalized asset of $32,000. Assume that the straight-line method of depreciation is being used. At the end of the asset's first year of usage, company Z should report depreciation expense of $6,400.

Answer - Depreciation should be based on the number of years that the lessor will get use from the asset. In this case, although the asset should last for 5 years, the lease is for only four years. Thus, the $32,000 capitalized value of the property should be depreciated over four years so that annual depreciation is $8,000 for company Z. (Number Three is False.)

FOUR - Company A leases property to company Z. It is a capitalized lease. Company Z will pay $10,000 per year for four years. Payments are made at the beginning of each year. Company Z has an incremental borrowing rate of 10 percent. The present value of these payments at that rate is $32,000. Thus, company Z reports a net capitalized liability of $32,000. At the end of the first year of usage, company Z should recognize interest expense of $3,200. (True or False?)

Answer - Interest is recognized based on the net liability balance for the year. At the beginning of the year, the net liability balance is $32,000. Since the lease payments are made at the end of each year, the net liability balance of $32,000 does not change during the year. Interest expense is $3,200 based on this net liability balance and the 10 percent interest rate. (Number Four is True.)

FIVE - Company A leases property to company Z. It is a capitalized lease. Company Z will pay $10,000 per year for four years. Payments are made at the beginning of each year. Company Z has an incremental borrowing rate of 10 percent. The present value of these payments is $32,000. Thus, Z reports a net capitalized liability of $32,000. At the end of the first year of usage, company Z should report a net liability balance of $24,200. (True or False?)

Answer - At the beginning of the year, the net liability balance is $32,000 but the first payment reduces that balance to $22,000. Thus, interest for the first year is 10 percent of that net liability or $2,200. Since the interest was not paid, it is compounded and increases the net liability to $24,200. Payments reduce the net liability while the recognition of interest that is not paid will increase the net liability balance. (Number Five is True.)

SIX - Company A leases property to company Z. It is a capitalized lease and is being recorded as a sales type lease. The property had a cost of $20,000 to company A. The normal sales price of this item is $26,000. Company Z is going to pay minimum lease payments of $35,000. Company A should recognize a $6,000 increase in net income immediately and the remaining $9,000 profit should be recognized as interest over the life of the lease. (True or False?)

Answer - In a sales type lease, the normal profit is recognized immediately and all additional profit is recognized as interest over the life of the lease. Because the product costs $20,000 but would typically be sold for $26,000, $6,000 is recognized as an increase in income immediately. Because $35,000 is to be received in total, the extra $9,000 ($35,000 less $26,000) is viewed as interest to be recognized over the life of the lease. (Number Six is True.)

SEVEN - Company A leases property to company Z. It is a capitalized lease and is being recorded by company A as a direct financing lease. The property had a cost of $32,000 to company A. Company Z is going to make five annual payments of $10,000 each. Company A's profit is $18,000 and part of that amount will be recognized immediately. (True or False?)

Answer - In a direct financing lease, no profit is recognized immediately. All profit ($18,000 in this example) will be recognized as interest over the life of the lease. (Number Seven is False.)

EIGHT - Company A leases property to company Z on January 1, Year One. It is a direct financing lease. The lease is for 8 years and the payments are $10,000 per year payable at the end of each year. The property had a cost to company A of $53,000. The imputed interest rate that company A has built into the terms of the contract is 10 percent per year. Company A recognizes interest revenue of $5,300 at the end of Year One. Company A should recognize interest revenue of $4,300 at the end of the second year of the lease. (True or False?)

Answer - As a direct financing lease, the $27,000 to be received in excess of the cost of the property is recorded as an Unearned Interest Revenue (a contra account to the lease receivable). Subsequently, the $80,000 total receivable will be reduced by the $10,000 payment made at the end of Year One so that the receivable balance during Year Two is $70,000. The Unearned Interest Revenue account will be reduced by the $5,300 in interest recognized in Year One so that the balance is no longer $27,000 but is reduced to $21,600. For Year Two, the $70,000 receivable less the $21,600 Unearned Interest Revenue gives a net receivable balance of $48,400. The interest rate is 10 percent so that $4,840 should be recognized as interest in Year Two. (Number Eight is False.)

MISCELLANEOUS ACCOUNTING CONCEPTS

(1) The FASB issued several **Statements of Financial Accounting Concepts** to create a **Conceptual Framework**. It sets goals for accounting but not absolute rules. Concepts Statement Number 2 created a structure to describe useful information.

    (A) According to Concepts Statement Number 2, the one constraint for all accounting information is that the benefits derived from using the information must outweigh the cost of getting it

    (B) To be useful for decision-making, information should have several qualities.

        (1) It should be relevant; the information can affect the decision-making process. **Relevance** has three ingredients.

            (a) Timeliness - it is received quickly enough to impact a decision.

            (b) Predictive Value - it helps to estimate future cash flows

            (c) Feedback Value - it confirms or corrects previous predictions of cash flows

        (2) It should be reliable; it can be trusted. **Reliability** has three ingredients.

            (a) Verifiability - it is objective and can be proven

            (b) Neutral - it is free from bias

            (c) Representational Faithfulness - the reporting does mirror the actual event or transaction

(2) Statement of Financial Accounting Concepts 6 establishes definitions for reporting the elements of financial statements. Several of these definitions include the following.

    (A) Asset - probable future economic benefit controlled by entity

    (B) Liability - probable future sacrifice of an economic benefit that arises from a present obligation which resulted from a past transaction or event.

    (C) Comprehensive income - change in equity during a period from all nonowner sources

    (D) Revenues - increases in net assets during a period from delivering goods or services as part of the enterprise's central operations

    (E) Expenses - decreases in net assets during a period in connection with generating revenues from the enterprise's central operations

    (F) Gains - increases in equity from peripheral transactions

    (G) Losses - decreases in equity from peripheral transactions

(3) Recognition of revenues.

    (A) Revenue is normally recognized when two factors are evident.

        (1) Earning process must be substantially complete

        (2) Assets have been received that are readily convertible into cash.

        (3) There are exceptions; revenues are recognized at other times

            (a) Revenues on long-term construction projects are frequently recognized as the work is done using the percentage of completion method.

            (b) If uncertainty exists about collection, revenues are recognized as the cash is collected using either the installment sales method or cost recovery method.

            (c) If a sales price is assured, revenue is recognized when the product is received.

(B)   If customer has the right to **return a purchase**, the point of sale is in question. Revenue is recognized when several events have occurred including the following: (1) price is set, (2) the sale is not based on some future action (such as the resale of the item), and (3) amount of returns is subject to reasonable estimation. Revenue is recognized but also a contra account (Sales Returns) is estimated and recognized.

(4)   For adequate disclosure, **Summary of Significant Accounting Policies** (usually first footnote or presented just in front of the footnotes) indicates the accounting method being used when alternative methods are available (FIFO or LIFO as an example)

(5)   The amount of future cash payments must be disclosed. The amount to be paid as a result of present **long-term liabilities** in each of the next 5 years must be shown as well as the cash payments required in total.

(6)   **Related party transactions** must also be disclosed.

    (A)   A related party includes the following: one who owns 10 percent or more of the reporting entity, another company over which the entity can exert significant influence, members of the management and their immediate families

    (B)   For material related party transactions, nature of relationship is disclosed along with a description and terms of the transaction and the amounts as well as the balances still due

(7)   To resolve conflicts that can arise between accounting rules, a **Generally Accepted Accounting Principles** (GAAP) Hierarchy was created to indicate which rules and pronouncements take precedent.

    (A)   There are really two hierarchies: one has five levels for businesses and the other has five levels for governments and not-for-profit organizations. Highest levels have most authority.

    (B)   Top level for businesses has three types of pronouncements: FASB Statements, APB Opinions, and AICPA Research Studies

---

PROBLEMS AND SOLUTIONS
MISCELLANEOUS ACCOUNTING CONCEPTS

ONE - Information is verifiable if it is objective and can be proven by an independent party. Verifiability is an ingredient that makes financial information reliable. (True or False?)

Answer - FASB Concepts Statement Number 2 identifies verifiability as one of the ingredients found in information that makes it reliable. (Number One is True.)

TWO - Revenues are normally recognized when the earning process is substantially completed and assets are received that are readily convertible to cash. (True or False?)

Answer - Under normal circumstances, revenues are not recognized until the earning process is substantially completed and either cash is received or some other asset is received that can be converted to cash through the normal functioning of the business. (Number Two is True.)

THREE - If uncertainty as to collection exists, revenues are not recognized at the point that the earning process is substantially completed but rather at a later point based on cash collections. (True or False?)

Answer - If uncertainty exists as to the ability to collect cash (if the buyer is in serious financial trouble, for example, or if unusual guarantees have been about the product), revenues should be recognized by either the installment sales method or the cost recovery method. Both of those methods recognize the revenue after the date of substantial completion based on the collection of cash from the customer. (Number Three is True.)

FOUR - In a set of financial statements, the Summary of Significant Accounting Policies is usually included as the first footnote or just in front of the first footnote to indicate the accounting method that was applied by the reporting entity where alternative methods were available. (True or False?)

Answer - The Summary of Significant Accounting Policies indicates the various methods used in a set of financial statements where alternative methods were available. (Number Four is True.)

FIVE - A company reports a translation adjustment because it has a subsidiary with a different functional currency. This translation adjustment would not impact the computation of net income for this company but any change in the translation adjustment during the year will be reflected in the statement of comprehensive income. (True or False?)

Answer – A translation adjustment is reported within stockholders' equity of a company's balance sheet. Therefore, in computing net income, the translation adjustment is not taken into consideration. However, any change in the translation adjustment indicates a change in net assets that did come from an investment by an owner or a distribution to an owner. Thus, the change in the translation adjustment is included in the computation of comprehensive income. (Number Five is True.)

MARKETABLE SECURITIES

(1)   If a company has significant influence over another company (usually by ownership of 20% to 50% of its voting stock), the **equity method** is applied to account for the investment (covered in a later outline)

(2)   If a company has control over another company (by ownership of over 50% of its voting stock), **consolidated financial statements** are prepared (a topic covered in a later outline).

(3)   If a company owns bonds of another company and plans to hold these investments until maturity, the bonds are recorded at cost with any discount or premium amortized using the effective rate method as described previously in the Bonds and Notes outline. Straight-line method of amortization can be used if figures are not materially different.

(4)   All other stock and bond investments are placed in one of two categories

    (A)   **Trading Securities** - stocks and bonds held for current resale.

        (1)   Portfolio is recorded at market value with change in value recorded on income statement.

        (2)   If sold, gain or loss is recognized as the difference between fair market value at the beginning of current year and the amount received.

    (B)   **Available for Sale** - stocks and bonds are not actively traded but are not held with the intention of reaching maturity. Could be sold at any time if cash is needed.

        (1)   Portfolio is recorded at market value with change in value recorded within stockholders' equity, as a part of other comprehensive income.

        (2)   If sold, gain or loss on sale is the difference in original cost and sales price

(5)   Determination of income effect or stockholders' equity effect created each year by the change in market value.

    (A)   Two "Valuation Allowance" accounts are established at the end of each year to adjust cost of each portfolio up to or down to market value. That balance remains until end of subsequent year.

    (B)   Annual change in Valuation Allowance account creates effect on net income (if created for the Trading Securities) or stockholders' equity (if created for the Available for Sale portfolio).

(6)   Securities can be transferred from one portfolio to another if the intentions of the owner changes.

    (A)   Only an investment in a debt instrument can be changed to the "held till maturity" classification. Market value (book value) of the old classification is removed and its face value is recorded in new classification along with a related discount or premium. Thus, the old and the new book values will agree. If transferred from "trading securities," the reclassification is complete. If transferred from "available for sale," any unrealized gain or loss in stockholders' equity remains. This balance is amortized to income over remaining life of the security.

    (B)   If a security is changed to either "trading securities" or "available for sale," the previous book value (along with any unrealized gain or loss in stockholders' equity) is removed and its current market value is recorded in new classification. If a difference exists, a gain or loss is recorded in the income statement (if changed to a trading security) or in stockholders' equity (if changed to an available for sale security).

(7)   Other accounting issues relating to marketable securities.
  (A)   **Cash dividends** are recorded as revenue on date of record.
  (B)   **Stock dividends** and splits are not recorded by the owner. Book value of investment is allocated over more shares.
  (C)   Receipt of stock rights is not recorded as revenue. However, if rights have a value, the book value of the investment should be divided between the stock and the rights based on their relative fair market values.
  (D)   **Liquidating dividend** is a payment by a company that does not have income. Owner reduces investment account; no income recorded.
  (E)   Life insurance policy can have a cash surrender value which is reported as an asset. Annual payment on policy less increase in cash surrender value is expense for the period.
  (F)   A **bond sinking fund** is money set aside to pay off a bond. If debt will be paid this year, sinking fund is a current asset; otherwise, the amount is a noncurrent investment.

PROBLEMS AND SOLUTIONS
MARKETABLE SECURITIES

ONE - In accounting for marketable securities, all securities must be divided into two portfolios. (True or False?)

  Answer - Marketable securities must be classified in one of three portfolios. The three portfolios for marketable securities are (1) held until maturity, (2) trading securities, and (3) available for sale. Stocks and bonds can both be included in the later two categories but only bonds can be reported as being held until maturity. (Number One is False.)

TWO - Debt securities that are to be held until maturity are reported at the cost of the investment. (True or False?)

  Answer – Historical cost is reported initially for debt securities that are to be held until maturity but any discount or premium (any difference in cost and the maturity value of the security) must be amortized over the life of the security. This amortization is computed by use of the effective rate method. The straight-line method of amortization may be used if the resulting figures are not materially different from the effective rate method. Therefore, over its life, a debt security that is to be held until maturity is reported at its cost after removing the effects of amortization. (Number Two is False.)

THREE - Company A acquires two investments on January 1, Year One classified as trading securities. By the end of the year, one of these investments (with a cost of $1,000) is worth $1,100. The other investment (with a cost of $2,000) is worth $1,700. The company should report an unrealized loss on its income statement of $300. (True or False?)

Answer - Fair market value of marketable securities is determined and reported on a portfolio basis and not based on individual stocks. The total cost in this first year is $3,000 ($1,000 plus $2,000) and the total fair market value is $2,800 ($1,100 plus $1,700). Thus, the unrealized loss is $200 ($3,000 less $2,800). Because these investments were classified as trading securities, this $200 loss is reported on the income statement. (Number Three is False.)

FOUR - Company A acquires two investments on January 1, Year One classified as available for sale. By the end of the year, one of these investments with a cost of $1,000 is worth $1,500. The other investment with a cost of $2,000 is worth $1,600. The company should report no income statement effect but the securities will be reported on the balance sheet at $3,100. (True or False?)

Answer - The total cost in this first year is $3,000 ($1,000 plus $2,000) and the total fair market value is $3,100 ($1,500 plus $1,600). Thus, the unrealized gain is $100 ($3,100 less $3,000). Because these investments were classified as available for sale, this $100 gain is reported within the stockholders' equity section of the balance sheet. The securities themselves are reported at their $3,100 fair market value. The balance sheet reporting would be the $3,000 cost plus a $100 valuation adjustment. No income statement effect would be recognized because these marketable securities were available for sale. (Number Four is True.)

LONG-TERM CONSTRUCTION CONTRACTS

(1)   For a construction job that will take over a year to complete, **percentage of completion method** is normally the method used for financial reporting purposes. It recognizes a percentage of total profit each year as the job progresses.

    (A)   A construction-in-progress account is maintained at cost plus the gain recognized to date.

    (B)   Percentage of work done is usually determined as the cost to date divided by the total of the estimated cost of the project.

    (C)   This percentage is multiplied by the total estimated profit to get the profit earned to date.

    (D)   Any previously recognized income is subtracted from profit earned to date to get profit to be recognized in current year.

    (E)   If a loss is anticipated, 100% must be immediately recognized

(2)   An alternative method to account for long-term construction projects is the **completed contract method**. It is not considered appropriate unless reasonable estimations cannot be made about a job. Usually some significant uncertainty exists.

    (A)   Cost is recorded in construction account with no income effect recognized until completed.

    (B)   Any anticipated losses must be recognized immediately.

(3)   Under either method, bills are sent out to the buyer periodically. The bills do not affect recognition of revenue. Accounts receivable and a Billings account are both recorded.

    (A)   For balance sheet reporting, Construction-In-Progress and Billings accounts are netted. If billings is higher, net amount is a liability; if construction account is higher, amount is reported as an asset.

PROBLEMS AND SOLUTIONS
LONG-TERM CONSTRUCTION CONTRACTS

ONE - A construction company begins a project that will take several years to complete. In recording the cost of this project and the profits, the company may choose to use either the completed contract method or the percentage of completion method. (True or False?)

Answer – Under certain conditions, the percentage of completion method must be used. If those conditions are not met, the completed contract method is appropriate. The company does not have a choice. Use of a specific method is based on the situation. One of the most important of the conditions for using the percentage of completion method is that the company must be able to make reasonable estimations of the degree that the project has been completed. (Number One is False.)

TWO - A company begins construction of a project that will take two years to complete. The total sales price is $10 million and the total costs are estimated initially as $9 million. Costs for the first year amount to $4 million; costs for the second year amount to $5.2

million and the job is finished. If the completed contract method is in use, a profit of $800,000 is recognized in the second year. (True or False?)

Answer – When applying the completed contract method, recognition of all profits is delayed until the job is finished. Although the profit here was estimated originally as $1 million, it eventually proved to be only $800,000. Thus this actual figure should be recognized when the work is completed in the second year. However, because of the conservative nature of accounting, if a loss is anticipated, the entire amount of the loss must be recognized immediately. (Number Two is True.)

THREE - A company begins construction of a project that will take longer than one year to complete. Costs for the first year are $600,000. The job has a sales price of $2 million. It should cost an additional $900,000 in year two to complete this project. If the percentage of completion method is being applied, the builder should recognize a profit on this job of $200,000 at the end of the first year. (True or False?)

Answer – The anticipated total cost is $1.5 million (the $600,000 expended to date plus the additional expected cost of $900,000). Because the sales price is $2 million, the company believes that it will earn a profit of $500,000. Of the total cost of $1.5 million, 40 percent has been expended to date ($600,000/$1.5 million). Using the percentage of completion method, 40 percent of the $500,000 expected profit indicates that $200,000 is recognized in this first year. (Number Three is True.)

FOUR - A company begins construction of a project that will take longer than one year to complete. The sales price is $2 million and, during the first year, the construction company recognized a profit of $220,000 by using the percentage of completion method. By the end of year two, the company has spent a total of $900,000 and anticipates that an additional $600,000 will still have to be spent to complete the work. In year two, the construction company should recognize an additional profit of $80,000. (True or False?)

True – Total cost is anticipated to be $1.5 million: the $900,000 expended to date plus the additional expected cost of $600,000. Thus, at the end of the second year, the job is 60 percent completed ($900,000 spent to date divided by the estimated total cost of $1.5 million). The expected profit is $500,000 ($2 million sales price less expected total cost of $1.5 million). Consequently, profit to be recognized to date is $300,000 ($500,000 total profit multiplied by 60 percent). Since $220,000 has been reported previously, only an additional $80,000 should be recognized in the second year ($300,000 less $220,000). (Number Four is True.)

INSTALLMENT SALES METHODS

(1) **Installment sales method** is appropriately used to recognize profits for any sale when collection will take over a year and a significant uncertainty exists.
  (A) No profit is recognized at time of sale but rather when cash is collected. Until cash is collected, all profit is recognized in a Deferred Gain account.
  (B) Profit to be recognized is the gross profit percentage times cash collected.
  (C) Gross profit percentage is the profit divided by the sales price. This same percentage multiplied times the remaining receivable balance represents the gain still deferred.
(2) **Cost recovery method** is appropriately used for any sale where collection is highly doubtful. For example, a sale is made to a company on the verge of bankruptcy.
  (A) No profit is recorded until cash equal to cost of asset is collected. For all further collections of cash, an equal amount of profit is recognized.

PROBLEMS AND SOLUTIONS
INSTALLMENT SALES METHOD

ONE - A company sells land for $4.2 million, a cash amount that will be collected over four years. Under these circumstances, the company will probably use the installment sales method in recognizing the profit on this sale when applying generally accepted accounting principles. (True or False?)

Answer – According to generally accepted accounting principles, the installment sales method is only applicable to a sale when a portion of the payment will not be made until a future time period and collection of the sales price is not reasonably assured. This method is only used for financial reporting when no basis exists for estimating the degree of collectibility of the receivable. Although it does not directly impact this part of the exam, the installment sales method is frequently used in computing income for tax purposes. (Number One is False.)

TWO - A company sells land that cost $3 million for $4 million to be received in the future. Assume that the installment sales method is being used. The gross profit percentage is 33 1/3 percent. (True or False?)

Answer – The profit on this sale is $1 million and the sales price is $4 million so that the gross profit percentage is 25 percent ($1 million profit divided by $4 million sales price). (Number Two is False.)

THREE - On January 1, a company sells land that cost $3 million for $4 million to be received in the future. The company plans to apply the installment sales method. On August 1, the company receives the first payment of $600,000. When this collection is made, the company should recognize a profit of $150,000. (True or False?)

Answer – When using the installment sales method, the profit to be recognized is always the cash collected on the receivable multiplied by the gross profit percentage. In this situation, the cash collected is $600,000 and the gross profit percentage is 25 percent ($1 million profit divided by $4 million sales price). Therefore, the profit to be recognized is $150,000 or $600,000 multiplied by 25 percent. (Number Three is True.)

FOUR - On January 1, a company sells land that cost $4 million for $5 million to be received in the future. The installment sales method is to be used by the seller. On September 1, the company receives the first payment of $900,000. After this collection is made, the company will still report a deferred gross profit of $820,000. (True or False?)

Answer – When using the installment sales method, the deferred gross profit that has not yet been recognized as profit is the remaining receivable balance multiplied by the gross profit percentage. In this problem, the remaining receivable is $4.1 million after the initial payment of $900,000. The gross profit percentage is 20 percent ($1 million profit divided by $5 million sales price). Therefore, after the collection, the deferred gross profit balance is $820,000 or the $4.1 million receivable multiplied by the 20 percent gross profit percentage. This same figure can be determined by taking the original profit of $1 million and subtracting the profit recognized on the collection or $180,000 ($900,000 cash multiplied by 20 percent gross profit percentage). (Number Four is True.)

STRUCTURE OF AN INCOME STATEMENT

(1)   An income statement can be reported by the single step format.
    (A)   All revenues and gains are listed first followed by all expenses and losses.

(2)   Income statement can also be constructed using a multiple step format.
    (A)   Revenues from major operations are listed first followed by cost of goods sold to arrive at gross profit.
    (B)   Operating expenses are subtracted next. These expenses are usually presented as two categories: (1) selling expenses such as commissions, advertising, and bad debt expense and (2) general and administrative expenses such as insurance, repairs, and accounting.
    (C)   Other revenues and expenses are reported next. This category typically reports most gains and losses as well as interest revenues and interest expense.
    (D)   Gains or losses that are unusual in nature or infrequent in occurrence are reported next.
    (E)   For most income statements, the final reduction is for income tax expense. As will be discussed in a later outline, this figure is frequently reported as two components: current expense and deferred expense.
    (F)   If a company is publicly held, earnings per share information must also be reported along with each income statement.

(3)   Regardless of the format, three figures are always reported at the bottom of the income statement net of the applicable tax effect.
    (A)   The income effect of a discontinued operation, a topic that will be covered in a later outline
    (B)   Extraordinary gains and losses.
    (C)   Cumulative effect of a change in accounting principle, a topic that will be covered in a later outline.

(4)   **Restructuring charges** are one type of unusual loss. Such charges are commonly incurred in conjunction with the exit or disposal of a location or line of business. A liability for a cost associated with an **exit or disposal activity** should be recognized and measured at fair value in the period in which the liability is incurred.

(5)   **Extraordinary items** are reported at the bottom of the income statement net of any tax effect.
    (A)   To be classified as extraordinary, gains and losses must have three characteristics.
        (1)   Must be material in size. That means being of a size and/or nature that will affect the decision making of an outside party.
        (2)   Unusual in nature
        (3)   Infrequent in occurrence
    (B)   Certain gains and losses cannot be considered extraordinary
        (1)   Write-offs of assets not caused by a specific external event such as the write off of obsolete inventory or equipment.
        (2)   Gains and losses created by changes in the value of a foreign currency
        (3)   Gains or losses resulting from a strike.

(6)   A company must now produce a **statement of comprehensive income** in order to report all changes in the net assets of a company other than investments by owners and distributions to owners.

(A)   At present, several changes in net assets are reflected in stockholders' equity instead of within net income. There are three primary examples.

    (1)   The translation of the financial statements of a foreign subsidiary creates a translation adjustment.

    (2)   Changes in the value of marketable securities classified as available for sale creates an unrealized gain or an unrealized loss.

    (3)   Recognition of a minimum liability in connection with pension plans can (but does not always) create an equity balance.

(B)   The statement of **comprehensive income** starts with net income and adjusts that figure for changes during the period in each of these equity figures. For example, if marketable securities that are available for sale go up in value, the change is not reported in net income but would be reported in comprehensive income.

(C)   The net income figure may contain items that have been recognized previously in computing comprehensive income. For example, if available for sale securities go up in one year but are sold for a gain at the start of the following year, comprehensive income increases in the first year but net income increases in the second.

    (1)   A reclassification adjustment will be reported to remove amounts from net income that have already been reported in computing comprehensive income.

(7)   A **prior period adjustment** (PPA) is a physical change in an income statement item reported in a previous time period. It is not recorded on the income statement of the current period.

(A)   Prior period adjustments are only made in a few specific cases.

    (1)   A PPA is used if an error has occurred in applying an accounting principle or if a mathematical error has been made.

    (2)   A few specific types of accounting changes are also recorded with a PPA (topic will be covered in a later outline).

    (3)   The discovery of an incorrect estimation is not handled through a PPA (topic will be covered in a later outline).

(B)   If earlier income statement is being shown, change is made directly to it. If earlier statement is not shown, change is made as an adjustment to the earliest beginning retained earnings balance being reported.

    (1)   Regardless of reporting, actual journal entry adjusts the beginning retained earnings for the current year.

PROBLEMS AND SOLUTIONS
STRUCTURE OF AN INCOME STATEMENT

ONE - A company has the following costs: freight out = $30,000, freight in = $40,000, advertising expense = $50,000, accounting expense = $60,000, bad debt expense = $20,000, sales returns = $10,000, and sales commissions = $90,000. The total amount of selling expenses to be reported on the company's income statement is $170,000. (True or False?)

Answer – The selling expenses are (1) freight out (which is the same as a delivery expense), (2) advertising expense, (3) bad debt expense, and (4) sales *commissions. These four total to $190,000. Freight in is added to the cost of the inventory being received. Accounting expense is an administrative expense. Sales returns is a contra account used to reduce the Sales account. (Number One is False.)*

TWO - Four different figures must be reported at the very bottom of a company's income statement net of their own income tax effects: (1) discontinued operations, (2) extraordinary items, (3) the cumulative effect of an accounting change, and (4) prior period adjustments. (True or False?)

Answer – Only three figures should be reported at the very bottom of an income statement net of their own tax effect: (1) discontinued operations, (2) extraordinary items, and (3) the cumulative effect of an accounting change. In contrast, prior period adjustments are changes to be reported in figures reported on previous income statements. If the earlier income statement is being shown, the actual figure is changed. If the earlier income statement is not being reported, the prior period adjustment is shown as a change (net of income tax effect) in the earliest Retained Earnings balance being reported. (Number Two is False.)

THREE - An income effect is created by an event that is both unusual in nature and infrequent in occurrence. This income effect must be reported as an extraordinary gain or loss (net of taxes) at the bottom of the income statement. (True or False?)

Answer – If two specific criteria are met, a gain or loss must be reported as an extraordinary item. These criteria are (1) the event must be unusual in nature and (2) the event must be infrequent in occurrence. (Number Three is True.)

FOUR - A company pays off a debt and suffers a loss on the transaction. Because paying off a debt is neither unusual in nature nor infrequent in occurrence, this loss should not be reported as an extraordinary item. (True or False?)

Answer – Because the timing of a debt payment can be manipulated in order to impact net income, any gain or loss on the extinguishment of a debt must be reported net of taxes as an extraordinary item. (Number Four is False.)

FIVE - Comprehensive income is a measure of the changes that occur in a company's net assets during a period of time for all reasons other than contributions from owners and distributions to owners. (True or False?)

Answer – Comprehensive income includes all changes in net assets other than those arising from contributions from owners and distributions to owners. Consequently, several changes that have been reported traditionally within stockholders' equity are used to adjust net income to arrive at comprehensive income. (Number Five is True.)

CONTINGENCIES AND OTHER LOSSES AND LIABILITIES

(1)   **Contingent losses** are caused by a past event but will only result in an actual loss if a future event also occurs. For example, a lawsuit has been filed but no actual loss exists unless jury finds the party guilty.

    (A)   If chance of a loss is probable and amount is reasonably subject to estimation, loss must be immediately recognized with an accompanying liability being recorded or an asset reduced

        (1)   If estimation is a range, the most likely figure within range must be recognized. If no figure is most likely, the lowest figure in the range is recognized with remainder of range disclosed

    (B)   If chance of loss is reasonably possible or if a reasonable estimation cannot be made, loss is disclosed but not recognized.

    (C)   If chance of loss is only remote, no disclosure or recognition is required.

    (D)   For a gain contingency, recognition is delayed until the earning process is substantially complete. Until then, only disclosure is required.

(2)   Contingencies such as **guarantees and coupons** are usually recorded because chance of loss is probable and the amount is subject to a reasonable estimation based on past history.

    (A)   Amount to be paid is estimated and recognized immediately as an expense.

    (B)   Amount that has not yet been paid is liability to be reported.

(3)   **Gift certificates** are also contingencies; company must give merchandise if redeemed.

    (A)   Initially recorded as a liability when customer acquires.

    (B)   Reclassified as a revenue when redeemed or when time expires.

(4)   Employer may have to report liability to employees for **compensated absences** such as vacations as well as holiday and sick pay.

    (A)   Expense and liability are recognized when the following have occurred

        (1)   Employee has performed services.

        (2)   Payment is probable.

        (3)   Amounts to be paid either vest (person is entitled to money without further work) or accumulate (carry over from year to year)

PROBLEMS AND SOLUTIONS
CONTINGENCIES AND OTHER LOSSES AND LIABILITIES

ONE - A company has a contingency. The company believes that it is reasonably possible that a loss of between $100,000 and $130,000 will be incurred. Because of conservatism, the company must immediately recognize a loss of $130,000. (True or False?)

Answer – Contingent losses are not recognized unless the chance of the loss occurring is considered to be probable. Thus, no income effect is recognized here because the loss is judged to be only reasonably possible. However, since occurrence is deemed to be reasonably possible, the contingency must be disclosed. Number One is false for a second reason: If a loss can only be estimated to within a range, the most likely figure within that range is recognized. If no figure within the range is judged as most likely to occur, the lowest number within the range is reported. (Number One is False.)

TWO - Company A has filed a lawsuit against company Z. At the end of Year One, company A believes that it is probable that it will win $200,000 from this legal action. On that same date, company Z believes that it is probable that it will lose $120,000. Late in Year Two, the case is resolved and company A wins $150,000. In Year Two company A will recognize a gain of $150,000 and company Z will recognize a loss of $30,000. (True or False?)

Answer – Company A has a contingent gain that will not be recognized until it is substantially completed. Substantial completion occurs in Year Two so that the entire amount of $150,000 is recognized at that time. Company Z has a contingent loss that will be recognized when it becomes probable and can be estimated. Consequently, company Z should recognize a loss of $120,000 in Year One. When the loss turns out to be $150,000 in Year Two, company Z should recognize an additional loss of $30,000. (Number Two is True.)

THREE - Jones Company sells $20,000 in gift certificates to its customers on December 31, Year One. During January of Year Two, 10 percent of the gift certificates are redeemed for merchandise costing $1,700. In January, the company should report a net profit of $300. (True or False?)

Answer – When the gift certificates are redeemed, $2,000 (10 percent of the total) will be reclassified from an Unearned Revenue account to a Revenue account. Because the cost of the goods sold is $1,700, the net profit to be reported is $300. (Number Three is True.)

FOUR - An employee of a company is entitled to three weeks of vacation each year. By the end of the current year, the employee has only taken two weeks of vacation. The company must record a liability at the end of the current year for the additional week of vacation. (True or False?)

Answer – A vacation (as well as sick days and holidays) is referred to as a compensated absence. At the end of any period, a company must accrue a liability for compensated absences if (1) the employee has performed the required services, (2) it is probable that the compensation will be taken in the future either as time off or in cash, and (3) the amounts either accumulate or vest. If future vacation time or other compensated absence does not meet all of these criteria, no liability is recognized. (Number Four is False.)

FIVE - In December of Year One, Taylor Company contracted with a printing company to produce brochures to be distributed in order to advertise Taylor's products. The cost of the brochures was $20,000. The brochures were received by Taylor on December 27, Year One, and were distributed on January 18, Year Two. Taylor received the invoice for this job on January 8, Year Two, and the amount was paid on February 1, Year Two. Taylor should recognize a liability of $20,000 on its balance sheet as of December 31, Year One. (True or False?)

Answer – Because the work has been performed by the printing company, the $20,000 should be recognized as a liability as of December 27, Year One. Payment was not made until February 1, Year Two; thus, the liability did exist on December 31, Year One. Although an invoice may contain important information, receipt does not impact the timing of the recognition of a liability. (Number Five is True.)

DEFERRED INCOME TAXES

(1)   Some revenues and expenses are recognized for external reporting in one period but tax recognition occurs in a different period. These are referred to as **temporary differences**.

    (A)   A temporary difference leads to a **deferred tax liability** if taxable income will be higher than book (accounting) income in the future. A temporary difference leads to a **deferred tax asset** if taxable income will be lower than book income in the future.

        (1)   A deferred liability indicates that an additional tax payment will be made in the future; a deferred asset indicates a future benefit since income to be taxed will be reduced.

    (B)   Examples of temporary differences that usually create less taxable income now and more taxable income later (creating a deferred tax liability) include (1) using different depreciation methods for external reporting and taxes, (2) using accrual accounting for the external reporting of sales but the installment sales method for taxes, and (3) using the equity method for the external reporting of an investment but dividends collected for taxes.

    (C)   Examples of temporary differences that usually create more taxable income now and less taxable income later (creating a deferred tax asset) include (1) estimating warranty and contingency expenses for external reporting but using actual losses for taxes, (2) estimating bad debts for external reporting but using actual losses for taxes, and (3) recognizing revenues as earned for external reporting but revenues collected in advance for taxes.

    (D)   Because of the conservative nature of accounting, recognition of a deferred tax asset requires company to also consider recognition of a contra Allowance account to reduce reported value of asset.

        (1)   A deferred tax asset indicates that future book income will be reduced to arrive at a lower taxable income. The company only gets benefit if it has book income to reduce.

        (2)   If company believes that it is more likely than not (over 50 percent likelihood) that it will have future book income for the temporary difference to reduce, no allowance is needed.

        (3)   If it is more likely than not that company will not have book income for temporary difference to reduce, allowance must be recorded to reduce reported value of deferred asset.

        (4)   Likelihood of having future book income is anticipated by looking at many factors: history of profits, law suits in progress, backlog of orders, loss of patents or other rights, gaining or losing customers, etc.

(2)   A balance sheet approach is used for recognizing deferred taxes. The amount of all future temporary differences are scheduled each year and deferred tax assets and liabilities are computed. The changes in these accounts create the income tax expense to be recognized.

(3)   Some differences between book income and taxable income will cause no future differences between book income and taxable income. Such items are known as **permanent differences** and they do not create deferred tax assets or liabilities. Examples of items that create permanent differences include the following:

(A) Municipal bond interest and life insurance proceeds are included in book income but never in taxable income.

(B) Federal taxes are expenses on the books but are not deductible for tax purposes. The same is true of life insurance premiums if the company is the beneficiary of the policy.

(C) A portion of dividends received from another domestic company is recognized but never taxed. This dividends received deduction (DRD) is 70% if less than 20% of the company is owned; the DRD is 80% if less than 80% but 20% or more of the company is owned; the DRD is 100% if 80% of more of the company is owned.

(4) **Computation of deferred income taxes** is based on a scheduling process.

(A) Items within book income for current year are listed.

(1) For each item, it should have a tax effect currently, a tax effect in the future, or no tax effect.

(B) Temporary differences from past years are also included to show how they impact either current taxable income or future taxable income.

(C) All items currently taxable are netted and multiplied by enacted tax rate to get current income tax payable and expense. These amount are recognized.

(D) For all future years, anticipated tax effects are determined and multiplied by enacted tax rates to get various deferred tax asset and liability balances. For any deferred assets, the need for an allowance is also determined.

(E) If a temporary difference relates to a noncurrent account, the deferred tax liability or asset that results is noncurrent. If it relates to a current account, the deferred tax liability or asset is current. All current deferred tax assets and liabilities are netted to arrive at a single figure to report on the balance sheet. All noncurrent deferred assets and liabilities are also netted to arrive at a single figure to report on balance sheet.

(F) At the end of each year, any previous (1) deferred tax liability, (2) deferred tax asset, and (3) allowance on any deferred tax asset balances already on the books are adjusted to the newly determined balances. The net amount of change is the deferred income tax expense figure recognized on the income statement.

PROBLEMS AND SOLUTIONS
DEFERRED INCOME TAXES

ONE - In reporting income tax expense on an income statement, a company will frequently have to report two separate figures. (True or False?)

Answer – Income tax expense is classified as either current or deferred. The income tax expense-current is the amount that has been paid currently or is now payable. The deferred portion of the expense is the amount that creates a change in the tax payments in some other year. Frequently, the deferred part of the expense reflects tax amounts that have already been incurred but will not be paid until later years. (Number One is True.)

TWO - Corporation A owns 11 percent of the outstanding stock of corporation Z and both are domestic companies. Corporation Z distributes a $100,000 dividend to corporation A, an amount that is reported as income for financial reporting purposes. Because of this dividend, the taxable income of corporation A will increase by $30,000. The remaining $70,000 will never be subject to income taxation. (True or False?)

Answer – For dividends paid by one corporation to another, a dividends received deduction is allowed for tax purposes. The company receiving the dividend reports the entire amount as revenue but also gets to take a deduction. If the owner holds less than 20 percent of the company paying the dividend, the dividends received deduction is 70 percent. In this case, corporation A will report dividend revenue of $100,000 as well as a dividends received deduction of $70,000 so that taxable income increases by only $30,000. The remaining $70,000 is never taxed. (Number Two is True.)

THREE - A company has a revenue that is shown on its income statement for financial reporting purposes in Year One but is not taxable until Year Four. A temporary tax difference has occurred. (True or False?)

Answer – When a revenue or an expense is reported in one time period for tax purposes but in a different period for financial reporting purposes, the company has a temporary tax difference. If an item shows up in both sets of records but in different time periods, a temporary tax difference has occurred. (Number Three is True.)

FOUR - On its Year One income statement, a company reports income of $100,000. Of this amount, 60 percent is taxable currently, 30 percent will be taxable at a later date, and 10 percent will never be taxable. The tax rate is 20 percent. For this year, the company should report Income Tax Expense – Current of $12,000 and Income Tax Payable – Current of $12,000. In addition, the company reports Income Tax Expense – Deferred of $6,000 and Deferred Income Tax – Liability of $6,000. (True or False?)

Answer – Of the total income, $60,000 will be taxed currently. Based on the 20 percent tax rate, both the Income Tax Expense – Current and Income Tax Payable – Current will be reported as $12,000. Another $30,000 is a temporary tax difference that will be taxed later. Based on the tax rate, the Income Tax Expense – Deferred and the Deferred Income Tax – Liability will be recognized immediately as 6,000. The remaining income of $10,000 is a permanent tax difference and is not reflected in the tax computation. Total expense to be reported is $18,000 ($12,000 current plus $6,000 deferred). (Number Four is True.)

FIVE - If a company will have more taxable income in a future period than its income computed for financial reporting purposes, a Deferred Income Tax – Liability should be reported currently. If a company will have less taxable income in a future period than its income for financial reporting purposes, a Deferred Income Tax – Asset should be reported currently. (True or False?)

Answer – If a temporary tax difference leads to an increase in taxable income in the future, a Deferred Income Tax – Liability is appropriate for the company's balance sheet. If a temporary tax difference leads to a reduction in taxable income in the future, a Deferred Income Tax – Asset is reported. (Number Five is True.)

SIX - A company has revenues of $120,000. Depreciation is its only expense. The company buys one asset for $100,000 with a two-year life. For financial reporting purposes, the straight-line method is being used so that depreciation of $50,000 is recorded each year. For tax purposes, an accelerated method is used so that $80,000 is applicable for the initial year and $20,000 for the following year. The use of accelerated depreciation creates a temporary tax difference. (True or False?)

Answer – Total expense is $100,000 in both cases so that no permanent tax difference results. However, there is a temporary tax difference of $30,000. In the subsequent year, the depreciation for reporting purposes is $50,000 but only $20,000 for tax purposes. Thus, in the future, taxable income will be higher than the net income computed for financial reporting purposes by $30,000. (Number Six is True.)

SEVEN - A company starts operations this year and recognizes both warranty expense and bad debt expense. At the end of the current year, the company will probably recognize a Deferred Income Tax – Liability balance. (True or False?)

Answer – Both warranty expense and bad debt expense are reported differently for tax purposes than they are for financial reporting purposes. Usually, the expense will be reported at a later date for tax purposes. This future reduction in taxable income creates an anticipated benefit so that a Deferred Income Tax – Asset is recognized. A Deferred Income Tax – Liability is recognized when future taxable income will be increased; however, as in this case, when future taxable income will be decreased, a Deferred Income Tax – Asset is appropriate. (Number Seven is False.)

EIGHT - A company reports revenues of $150,000 in Year One. Its only operating expense is a warranty expense estimated to be $70,000. Of that amount, $20,000 was paid in Year One with the remainder expected to be paid in Year Two. The tax rate is 20 percent and no tax payments have yet been made. No temporary tax differences have occurred in previous years. On its December 31, Year One balance sheet, the company will report an Income Tax Payable – Current account of $26,000 and a Deferred Income Tax – Asset account of $10,000. (True or False?)

Answer – On the current tax return, the company will report $150,000 in revenues and a warranty expense of $20,000 (amount paid) for a taxable income of $130,000. Based on the tax rate, Income Tax Payable – Current is $26,000. The remaining $50,000 of the warranty expense will be deductible later when paid. Thus, taxable income in the future will be lower than reported net income by that amount so that a Deferred Income Tax – Asset of $10,000 should also be reported ($50,000 temporary tax difference multiplied by 20 percent rate). (Number Eight is True.)

NINE - At the end of Year One, a company's first year of operations, a Deferred Income Tax – Liability balance of $50,000 is recognized because the company uses the installment sales method. On that same date, a Deferred Income Tax – Asset of $23,000 is recognized because warranty expense and bad debt expense will not be recognized for tax purposes until future years. The company believes that it is more likely than not that the benefit of these two expenses will never be realized. The company is very uncertain as to whether taxable income will be generated in the future that can be reduced by these expenses. Thus, an Allowance account for $23,000 is also recorded. In its income statement, the company will recognize an Income Tax Expense – Deferred figure of $50,000. (True or False?)

Answer – Recognizing the Deferred Income Tax – Liability increases the expense by $50,000. Recognizing both the Deferred Income Tax – Asset and the Allowance account anticipates that no tax benefit will be accrued. The balances are netted. Together they create no impact on income tax expense. The net effect is an expense figure of $50,000 for the year. (Number Nine is True.)

TEN - In Year One, a company ends its first year of operations and reports an Income Tax Payable – Current balance of $70,000 and a Deferred Income Tax – Liability balance of $30,000. The company ends its second year of operations and reports an Income Tax Payable – Current balance of $80,000 and a Deferred Income Tax – Liability balance of $50,000. Based on those figures, the company will report the following on its Year Two income statement: Income Tax Expense – Current of $80,000 and an Income Tax Expense – Deferred of $50,000. (True or False?)

Answer – The Income Tax Payable – Current balance for one year will be paid (within 2½ months of the end of the year if the taxpayer is a corporation) so that the balance for the subsequent year is always created solely by the expense of that year. In this case, the Income Tax Payable – Current account in the second year is $80,000 so that the Income Tax Expense – Current is also $80,000. However, any deferred asset or liability will not have been paid. The balance from one year is simply adjusted to the balance for the second year. The change in the deferred liability and deferred asset creates the expense. Since the Deferred Income Tax – Liability balance went from $30,000 (in Year One) to $50,000 (in Year Two), the Income Tax Expense – Deferred account for second year is the $20,000 increase. (Number Ten is False.)

ELEVEN - At the end of Year One, a company has a temporary tax difference created by the use of accelerated depreciation for tax purposes. A Deferred Income Tax – Liability balance is to be reported. Because of this difference, taxable income will be higher in Year Two than the company's net income computed for financial reporting purposes. The Deferred Income Tax – Liability balance should be shown as a current liability. (True or False?)

Answer – The temporary difference is caused here by the depreciation of fixed assets such as buildings or equipment. Because the buildings and equipment are noncurrent accounts on the company's balance sheet, the related Deferred Income Tax – Liability will be a noncurrent account regardless of when taxable income will be affected. (Number Eleven is False.)

EQUITY METHOD OF ACCOUNTING FOR INVESTMENTS

(1)   The **equity method** is used to account for an investment in stocks where the owner has the ability to significantly influence operating and financing decisions of the investee.

    (A)   Although the ability to apply significant influence is the only criterion, ownership of 20% to 50% of the investee's shares is usually accounted for by the equity method.

        (1)   Owner can use equity method even if less than 20% is held if owner has ability to significantly influence, for example, by having membership on the Board of Directors

        (2)   Should not use equity method even if over 20% is held if owner does not have ability to significantly influence.

(2)   In applying equity method, the investment is initially recorded at cost

    (A)   Owner recognizes income (or loss) as soon as investee earns it based on percentage of ownership. Income is recognized and book value of investment is raised (for income) or lowered (for loss).

    (B)   Because income is recognized as earned, dividends received cannot be recognized as revenue. Dividends received from investee are recorded as a reduction in the book value of the investment.

(3)   Price of investment may be in excess of investee's underlying book value. Book value is determined by taking liabilities from assets or by stockholders' equity. Figure is multiplied by percentage bought.

    (A)   Excess amount of payment may be attributed to a specific asset such as land or a building if the value of the item is greater than its book value on records of the investee. Allocation to the change in value of asset is based on percentage of the investee company that is bought.

    (B)   If any part of price that exceeds underlying book value cannot be assigned to a specific asset or liability, that remainder is assumed to be **goodwill**.

    (C)   Any allocations of excess price (unless assigned to land) must be amortized.

        (1)   If allocation is to a specific asset or liability, useful life is used. If the excess is allocated to goodwill, it should be written down if the investment is determined to be impaired.

        (2)   **Amortization** reduces investment account (allocations are not reported separately by the owner) and reduces income being reported from investee.

(4)   If a small ownership is held and then additional shares are acquired that give the ability to apply significant influence, the equity method becomes applicable in the future.

    (A)   In addition, owner must restate all previous income figures using the equity method based on the level of ownership at the time.

PROBLEMS AND SOLUTIONS
EQUITY METHOD OF ACCOUNTING FOR INVESTMENTS

ONE - A company owns 20 percent or more of another company but not more than 50 percent. The owner must use the equity method to account for this investment. (True or False?)

Answer – When 20 percent or more of another company is owned but not more than 50 percent, the equity method is usually applied. However, the 20 – 50 percent parameters are just guidelines. The official rule for applying the equity method is that the investor must have the ability to significantly influence the decision making of the investee. If a company holds 20 or more of the stock but does not have the ability to significantly influence the investee, the equity method should not be utilized. Conversely, if an investor holds less than 20 of the investee but does have significant influence, the equity method is appropriate. (Number One is False.)

TWO - Company A owns 40 percent of company Z and applies the equity method. This purchase was made on January 1, Year One, for $200,000. During Year One, company Z distributed a total of $30,000 in dividends and reported net income of $70,000. At the end of Year One, company A should report an Investment in Company Z account of $228,000. (True or False?)

Answer – Under the equity method, an investor recognizes profit from an investment as it is earned by the investee. This figure serves to raise the reported investment figure. In this case, since company Z made a profit of $70,000, company A will increase its investment by recognizing income of $28,000 (40 percent). When the equity method is applied, dividends are viewed as a transfer of capital so that the Investment balance will go down by $12,000 (40 percent of $30,000). The ending Investment in Company Z account being reported by company A will be $216,000 ($200,000 plus the $28,000 income less the $12,000 in dividends). (Number Two is False.)

THREE - Company A pays $300,000 for 30 percent of company Z and plans to apply the equity method. On that date, company Z reports a book value of $700,000. However, land owned by company Z has a book value of $100,000 when it is really worth $150,000. Goodwill of $40,000 is said to exist in the purchase price paid by company A. (True or False?)

Answer – Company Z has a book value of $700,000 but, since company A only bought 30 percent, the underlying book value of the acquired portion is $210,000. Company A paid $300,000, an amount that is $90,000 above this equivalent book value. Part of the excess payment can be attributed to the land that was worth $50,000 more than book value. However, since company A only bought 30 percent of the investee, the price paid would have only been adjusted by $15,000 (30 percent of the $50,000 excess value) to compensate for the true value of the land. An extra $90,000 was paid but the land value only explains $15,000. Thus, the remaining $75,000 is arbitrarily classified as goodwill. (Number Three is False.)

FOUR - Company A acquires 45 percent of company Z and is going to apply the equity method to this investment. Goodwill is computed in connection with the price paid by company A. Although the goodwill remains within the Investment in Company Z account, it will be amortized over a life of up to 40 years. This amortization reduces the reported income of company A. (True or False?)

Answer – The goodwill figure computed when applying the equity method remains within the investment account, but goodwill is no longer amortized. It is written down if the investment is determined to be impaired. (Number Four is False.)

FIVE - On January 1, Year One, company A acquires 30 percent of company Z. Company A has the ability to significantly influence the decisions of company Z. Thus, the equity method will be used to account for this investment. Additional cost of a building of $500,000 is computed as a component of the acquisition price. The building has a useful life of 20 years, and will be depreciated on the straight-line method. In Year One, company Z reports net income of $200,000 and pays a cash dividend of $60,000. On its Year One income statement, company A should report an Equity Income from Company Z account of $57,500. (True or False?)

Answer – Because company A is applying the equity method, income of $60,000 (30 percent of the $200,000 reported by company Z) will be reported immediately. In addition, additional depreciation must be recognized. The $500,000 allocation will be written off over 20 years at an annual rate of $2,500. This reduces the Equity Income from Company Z from $60,000 down to $57,500. Under the equity method, dividends received do not impact net income but are reported as a reduction in the Investment account. (Number Five is True.)

CONSOLIDATED FINANCIAL INFORMATION

(1)   The **consolidation process** brings together two or more sets of financial statements because the companies have common ownership. For external reporting purposes, the companies are viewed as a single entity

    (A)   Total ownership is not necessary to form a **business combination**. Only control is required which is normally established through the ownership of over 50% of the voting stock.

        (1)   If a firm is the primary beneficiary of a variable interest entity, it must consolidate even though the firm does not hold 50% voting interest.

        (2)   Subsidiaries are consolidated in total regardless of whether 100% of stock is owned. If less than 100% is held within the business combination, the outside owners are referred to as a minority interest and their ownership is reflected as a single figure in consolidated liabilities and also as a reduction in the consolidated income statement

    (B)   Consolidations can be accounted for only by the **purchase method. The pooling method** is no longer allowed.

        (1)   The fair market value of the subsidiary's assets and liabilities are used to determine allocations, goodwill can be recognized, and the subsidiary's revenues and expenses (and retained earnings) are only included from date of the merger.

(2)   A purchase is viewed as an acquisition: one company clearly buys the other. It is often compared to a parent-child relationship.

    (A)   A purchase price is determined based on the market value of the items given up and includes any direct **consolidation costs** except for stock issuance costs that are recorded as a reduction in additional paid-in capital.

    (B)   An allocation of this purchase price is made at the date of acquisition. Any difference between price paid and the equivalent portion of the underlying book value of subsidiary must be allocated. Allocation is made to specific assets and liabilities based on difference between their fair market values and book values. Book value of subsidiary is its assets minus liabilities or its total stockholders' equity.

        (1)   For example, a parent pays $100,000 over book value to acquire a subsidiary. The subsidiary has land that originally cost $50,000 but which is now worth $70,000. Of the excess purchase price, $20,000 is allocated to this land. If the parent had only bought 80% of sub, the allocation to land is just $16,000 or 80% of the increase in value.

        (2)   Any excess purchase price that cannot be allocated to specific assets and liabilities is assigned to **Goodwill**, an intangible asset that is not written off. Instead, it is periodically tested for impairment.

        (3)   If, after all allocations are made to assets and liabilities, a negative amount remains, this reduction is assigned to noncurrent assets (except for investments) based on their relative market values. If negative amount is so large that it eliminates all of these noncurrent asset accounts, a deferred credit (a liability) is established for any remainder

(C)   At date of a purchase, each consolidated asset and liability is the sum of the two book values plus or minus any allocation made of the purchase price based on the fair market value of the sub's accounts. Any goodwill is also included.

    (1)   Parent maintains an Investment account to monitor its ownership of the sub but this account is always eliminated in the consolidation process

(D)   Subsequent to the date of acquisition, the current book values of the assets and liabilities are added together along with the original allocations. However, each of these allocations (except for land and goodwill) is reduced by amortization over its useful life.

(E)   In a purchase, consolidated stockholders' equity is always the parent's balances plus any income effects relating to the subsidiary since the merger. If parent issued stock in taking over sub, those shares must be included in parent figures.

(F)   Consolidated revenues and expenses are the parent figures plus the subsidiary figures but only for the period since the merger. Amortization on any purchase price allocations must be included as expenses and any unrealized gains must be removed.

    (1)   To determine consolidated retained earnings or consolidated income, a determination of what has been included in parent's reported figures is made. No second inclusion is needed if parent has already (1) recognized its ownership percentage of the subsidiary's income, (2) removed any unrealized gains, and (3) recorded amortization expense for the period.

(3)   Some other elements of a consolidation.

    (A)   **Intercompany debt** (Accounts Receivable/Accounts Payable or Investment in Bonds/Bonds Payable) are offset against each other. All intercompany balances are removed even if ownership is below 100%.

    (B)   All balances recorded for **inventory transfers** between the parties must be removed. Both Sales and Cost of Goods Sold are reduced by the entire amount of the transfer price

    (C)   If inventory is transferred between parties, any **unrealized gain** in connection with goods still held at year's end must also be eliminated. Profit is actually being deferred until realized.

        (1)   The amount of unrealized gain remaining at end of the year is found by multiplying remaining goods times the profit. One of these figures has to be a percentage; the other has to be a dollar amount.

        (2)   Deferral of unrealized gain creates a reduction in Inventory account and an increase in Cost of Goods Sold account.

    (D)   If any other asset is transferred, all accounts must be returned to balances that would be applicable if transfer had not occurred.

        (1)   Adjustments are made to the asset account, accumulated depreciation, depreciation expense, and any gain or loss to align them with the balances that would have resulted.

    (E)   Any Investment in Subsidiary account or Income of Subsidiary account must be removed. Any intercompany dividend payments are also eliminated.

    (F)   **Minority interest balances** attributed to outside owners are computed by taking (1) the book value of the sub and (2) the reported income of the sub and multiplying both by the outside ownership percentage.

(4)   Other consolidation issues.

(A) "Combined" financial statements are consolidated statements of two or more subsidiaries without inclusion of the parent. Without the parent, no allocations or amortization are included although all intercompany figures are removed as in any consolidation

(B) **Push-down accounting** is an approach to consolidation where purchase price allocations and amortization are recorded directly on the sub's books rather than being added in each period through the consolidation process. It is supposed to make the process easier. It also enables the income reported by the subsidiary to mirror its impact on the consolidated statements.

(C) An asset is considered impaired when its book value is above the total of anticipated cash flows. However, if a fixed asset or intangible asset is acquired in a purchase combination, goodwill will often be recorded as part of the price. For impairment computation, goodwill is allocated to each of these assets based on their relative fair market values. This "adjusted" book value is compared to cash flows to determine impairment.

PROBLEMS AND SOLUTIONS
CONSOLIDATED FINANCIAL INFORMATION

ONE - The National Company is a manufacturing organization. It owns control of a subsidiary, the Plymouth Company, that serves as a finance operation. Because a manufacturing operation and a finance operation are so different in nature, consolidation is not required. (True or False?)

Answer – Only two exceptions exist to the consolidation of majority-owned subsidiaries. First, if control is only temporary, consolidation is not allowed. Second, if actual control is held by a party other than the parent company (for example, if the subsidiary is in bankruptcy), consolidation is not appropriate. Operating in different industries has no effect on the consolidation process. Therefore, unless one of the two exceptions is present, if over 50 percent of the voting stock is held, a finance operation will be consolidated with a manufacturing operation. (Number One is False.)

TWO - A business combination of two companies occurs. If the combination includes the combination of the assets, it is accounted for as a pooling. (True or False?)

Answer – SFAS 141 eliminated the pooling method in business combinations. Only the purchase method may be used. (Number Two is False.)

THREE - Company A makes a profit of $1,000 per month. Company Z makes a profit of $100 per month. On December 1, Year One, company A buys all of the outstanding stock of company Z. Company A pays an amount exactly equal to the book value of company Z. On a consolidated income statement for Year One, net income of $13,200 will be reported. (True or False?)

Answer – In a purchase, the income of the parent is included in the consolidated figures for the entire year. However, the income of the subsidiary will only be added to the consolidated balances for the period of time after the combination is created. Therefore, company A will include its net income of $12,000 for Year One but only one month of income will be included for company Z ($100). Therefore, in *this first year, consolidated net income will be $12,100. In a purchase, the subsidiary's income accounts are only included after the takeover. (Number Three is False.)*

FOUR - Company A buys all of the outstanding stock of company Z for $430,000 in cash and common stock. Company A also pays $30,000 in consolidation costs and $10,000 in stock issuance costs. The purchase price of company Z is $440,000 and company A should report an expense of $30,000. (True or False?)

Answer – In a purchase, the purchase price is the fair market value of the consideration given up to acquire the subsidiary. This figure also includes any consolidation costs. However, stock issuance costs are recorded separately as reductions to additional paid-in capital. In this problem, the purchase price of company Z will be $460,000 ($430,000 plus $30,000) with a $10,000 reduction made in additional paid-in capital. No expenses result from creating a purchase. (Number Four is False.)

FIVE - A company acquires another in a business combination. In the consolidation, management should add the book values of the two companies' assets to get the consolidated balance sheet. (True or False?)

Answer – In a purchase transaction, all of the assets of the acquired company should be recorded at fair values. If there is any excess amount of the total purchase price after this allocation, it should be recorded as goodwill. (Number Five is False.)

SIX - Company A and company Z form a business combination on January 1. Company A obtains 100 percent of the outstanding voting stock of company Z in a purchase. Company A had a building with a book value of $200,000 that was worth $230,000. Company Z had a building with a book value of $100,000 that was worth $110,000. Assume that this was not a bargain purchase. Of a consolidated balance sheet immediately after the takeover, the Buildings account will be reported as $340,000. (True or False?)

False – If 100 percent of a subsidiary is acquired in a purchase, the book value of the assets and liabilities of the parent (company A) are combined with the fair market value of the assets and liabilities of the subsidiary (company Z). The consolidated Buildings account will be $310,000: the parent's $200,000 book value plus the subsidiary's $110,000 fair market value. For a purchase, the assumption is that the parent will pay an extra $10,000 to acquire company Z because the subsidiary's building is worth that much more than market value. As an alternative approach, the consolidated Buildings account is initially the sum of the parent's book value ($200,000) plus the subsidiary's book value ($100,000) plus the allocation within the purchase price ($10,000). This approach gives the same $310,000 figure for consolidation purposes. (Number Six is False.)

SEVEN - On January 1, Year One, company A purchased all of the outstanding stock of company Z. The transaction resulted in goodwill in the amount of $100,000. This goodwill should not be amortized. (True or False?)

Answer – Goodwill is an intangible asset that is no longer amortized. Instead, it is tested for impairment periodically. (Number Seven is True.)

EIGHT - Company A and company Z were joined to create a business combination. Company A holds all of the outstanding stock of company Z. During the current year, inventory costing $150,000 is transferred from one company to the other for $200,000. Thus, gross profit on these transfers was $50,000. At the end of the year, inventory with a transfer price of $60,000 is still being held. This retained merchandise constitutes 30 percent of the amount transferred ($60,000 out of $200,000). In preparing consolidated financial statements, both the Sales account and the Cost of Goods Sold account have already been reduced by $200,000 to eliminate the intercompany transaction. No other change is needed to arrive at consolidated figures. (True or False?)

Answer – Sales and cost of goods sold do have to be reduced by $200,000 to remove the effects of the transfer. However, any time that transferred merchandise remains on hand at year end, a second elimination entry must be made to defer any unrealized gain on this inventory. The ending unrealized gain is computed by multiplying the gain on the transfer by the amount of merchandise remaining. One of these must be stated in dollars and one as a percentage. In this case, the gain on the transfer of $50,000 times the 30 percent that remains reveals an unrealized gain of $15,000. The same $15,000 unrealized gain can be determined by multiplying the gross profit percentage of 25 percent ($50,000 profit divided by $200,000 transfer price) times the $60,000 in inventory that remains. This $15,000 unrealized gain is deferred for consolidation purposes by increasing cost of goods sold and decreasing the ending inventory account. (Number Eight is False.)

NINE - Company A and company Z were joined several years ago to create a business combination. At the end of the current year, company A reports sales of $700, cost of goods sold of $500, and ending inventory of $200. On that same date, company Z reports sales of $600, cost of goods sold of $300, and ending inventory of $100. During the current year, one company sold merchandise costing $60 to the other for $100. At the end of the year, 30 percent of this merchandise remains. On consolidated financial statements, sales will be $1,200, cost of goods sold will be $712, and ending inventory will be $288. (True or False?)

Answer – To remove the intercompany transfer, both sales and cost of goods sold must be lowered by $100 (the transfer price). In addition, the effect of the unrealized gain at year's end must be eliminated by increasing cost of goods sold and reducing inventory. The $40 gross profit on these transfers ($100 price less $60 cost) is multiplied by the 30 percent remaining to get an unrealized gain of $12. Consolidated sales will be the two book values ($700 and $600) less the $100 transfer for a reported balance of $1,200. Consolidated cost of goods sold will be the two book values ($500 and $300) less the $100 transfer plus the $12 unrealized gain for a reported balance of $712. Consolidated ending inventory will be the two book values ($200 and $100) less the $12 unrealized gain for a reported balance of $288. (Number Nine is True.)

STATEMENT OF CASH FLOWS

(1) The reporting of a **statement of cash flows** (SCF) is required for each year in which an income statement is presented to show where cash was obtained and what was done with it. Any investment bought within 3 months of maturity is included as a cash item.

    (A) All cash inflows and outflows are reported within one of three classifications.

        (1) **Investing activities** are transactions involving assets that do not change in the regular course of daily operations. Examples would include the sale of equipment or the purchase of land.

        (2) **Financing activities** are transactions involving stockholders' equity or liabilities that do not change in the regular course of daily operations. Examples would include paying a dividend and issuing a bond or common stock.

        (3) **Operating activities** are transactions involving the regular course of daily operations. Examples would include paying an account payable or buying inventory.

            (a) Interest revenue, interest expense, and dividend revenue are all viewed as operating activity cash flows and not the result of investing or financing activities.

(2) To determine the cash flow effects to be reported, the changes during the year in each noncash account on the balance sheet are investigated.

    (A) Accounts such as accounts receivable, inventory, and accounts payable change in the regular course of business and are restricted to the Operating Activities column.

    (B) The reason for the change in every other balance sheet account must be identified. The cash effect for each of these transactions is determined and classified as either an investing activity or a financing activity.

        (1) In many cases, reproducing the journal entry will help to show the impact of the transaction and the change in cash.

        (2) Examples: buying a patent is a cash outflow from an investing activity, paying a note is an outflow from a financing activity, selling treasury stock is an inflow from a financing activity

        (3) Only the cash flow is reported. For example, if a car is acquired by paying cash and signing a note, only the cash outflow is reported in the SCF.

        (4) Exchanges are not included on the SCF but are separately disclosed as significant noncash transactions. Examples include land exchanged for a note and common stock issued to replace preferred stock.

        (5) Stock dividends and splits are also events that do not appear on a statement of cash flows

(3) The goal of reporting operating activities is to show the net cash inflow or outflow. There are two methods to report operating activities. The **indirect approach** starts with net income and then removes all items that are either (1) noncash balances or (2) do not occur in the regular course of business (are nonoperational).

    (A) Removal requires the subtraction of items that are included in net income as positives and the addition of items that are in net income as negatives.

(B) Noncash items include depreciation expense, amortization expense, and equity income reported in excess of the amount of dividends received.

(C) Noncash items also include the changes in operational assets and liabilities.

    (1) Examples are accounts receivable, inventory, prepaid expenses, accounts payable, and accrued expenses.

    (2) Changes in operational assets are removed by doing the opposite: an increase is subtracted, a decrease is added.

    (3) Changes in operational liabilities are removed by doing the same: an increase is added, a decrease is subtracted.

(D) Nonoperational items include most gains and losses.

(4) The **direct approach** to reporting operating activities reports the cash flows from individual types of operating transactions: cash collected from sales, cash paid for inventory purchases, cash paid for operating expenses, cash paid for taxes, etc. The various income statement accounts are converted to cash flow figures and reported.

(A) Sales less any increase in receivables during the year or plus decrease in receivables equals cash collected from sales. Can make a journal entry to simulate the recording of sales for the period as well as the change in the receivable account with the balancing figure being the cash inflow.

(B) Journal entry can be made with cost of goods sold and changes in inventory and accounts payable to derive cash paid for purchases.

(C) For any expense account, first remove any noncash item such as depreciation. Journal entry can then be made to record remaining figure and changes in related accrued expenses and prepaid expenses to arrive at cash paid for that expense.

(D) Gains and losses on the income statement are nonoperational and omitted from the reported of cash flows from operating activities.

(5) A somewhat related topic is the **conversion of cash financial records to accrual accounting**.

(A) Although accrual accounting is the appropriate generally accepted accounting principle, smaller operations often use **cash basis accounting**.

(B) Cash basis accounting is similar to the direct approach for reporting operating activities. Revenue is reported when cash is collected; expenses are reported when cash is paid.

(C) Cash basis accounting does not record several balance sheet accounts: accounts receivables, accounts payables, accrued expenses, prepayments, and inventory that has not been paid for.

(D) To change records from a cash basis to accrual accounting, two journal entries are made.

    (1) Any balance sheet accounts that were left off the records as of the first day of the current year are recorded with a balancing entry made to beginning retained earnings.

    (2) Any balance sheet accounts left off at the end of the year are recorded by adjusting the beginning balance to the year-end balance. The offsetting entry is made to the related income statement account (accounts receivable relates to sales; rent payable relates to rent expense; etc.)

PROBLEMS AND SOLUTIONS
STATEMENT OF CASH FLOWS

ONE - A statement of cash flows is divided into three sections: nonoperating cash inflows, nonoperating cash outflows, and cash flows from operations. (True or False?)

Answer – A statement of cash flows is divided into three sections: (1) cash flows from investing activities, (2) cash flows from financing activities, and (3) cash flows from operating activities. (Number One is False.)

TWO - On a statement of cash flows, cash flows from financing activities must be listed. Financing activities are liability or equity transactions that do not occur in the regular course of daily operations. (True or False?)

Answer – Financing activities (1) do not happen as part of a company's operating activities and (2) involve equities or liabilities. As an example, the issuance of a bond payable would be a financing activity as would be the acquisition of treasury stock or the distribution of a cash dividend. Equities or liabilities are involved in these cases but the transactions do not occur in the regular course of daily operations. (Number Two is True.)

THREE - Land is acquired for $300,000 by paying $20,000 in cash and signing a note payable for $280,000. On its statement of cash flows, this company should report a $300,000 cash outflow as an investing activity and a $280,000 cash inflow as a financing activity. (True or False?)

Answer – Only cash of $20,000 is paid. That amount was expended for an asset. The acquisition of land does not occur in the normal course of daily operations. Therefore, "acquisition of land" should be shown within investing activities as a cash outflow of $20,000. (Number Three is False.)

FOUR - A company buys a tract of land by signing a note. This transaction is both an investing and a financing activity. (True or False?)

Answer – Since no cash was collected or paid, it is a noncash transaction that is not included on the statement of cash flows. (Number Four is False.)

FIVE - In presenting the cash flows from operating activities, a single cash inflow or cash outflow is computed for the normal daily operations of the company. These cash flows from operating activities can be presented using either the direct method or the indirect method. (True or False?)

Answer – On a statement of cash flows, the cash flows from operating activities can be disclosed using either the direct method or the indirect method. (Number Five is True.)

SIX - A company is using the indirect approach to present cash flows from operating activities. The company reports net income of $300,000, a figure that includes depreciation expense of $40,000 and a gain on sale of land of $30,000. The company should report a net cash inflow from operating activities of $290,000. (True or False?)

Answer – The indirect approach eliminates both noncash transactions within net income (such as the depreciation expense) and effects that were not part of daily operations (such as the gain on sale of land). Depreciation expense is a negative component of net income; thus, the amount must be added back to net income to eliminate it. The gain on sale of land is a positive component of net income; the amount must be subtracted from net income to eliminate it. Net income of $300,000 plus $40,000 to eliminate the depreciation less $30,000 to eliminate the gain indicates cash flows from operating activities of $310,000. (Number Six is False.)

SEVEN - Company A is using the indirect method to present cash flows from operating activities. For the current year, company A reported net income of $360,000. During the year, accounts receivable went down by $9,000, inventory went up by $4,000, and prepaid rent went down by $1,000. The net cash inflow from operating activities is $366,000. (True or False?)

Answer – In the indirect method, increases in operational assets are subtracted from net income when looking for operational cash flows. Decreases in these same accounts are added. To derive the net cash inflow from operating activities, $9,000 (the decrease in accounts receivable) is added to the net income of $360,000. Next, the $4,000 increase in inventory is subtracted and the $1,000 drop in prepaid rent is added to arrive at a net cash inflow from operations of $366,000. (Number Seven is True.)

EIGHT - A company reports net income of $500,000. During the year, the company reported depreciation expense of $40,000 and amortization expense of goodwill of $8,000. This company also had a $13,000 gain on the sale of some land. In addition, accounts receivable went down by $4,000 during the period while inventory went up $11,000. Accounts payable went down by $7,000 while interest payable went up $2,000. The indirect method is used. The net cash inflow for this company from its operating activities is $523,000. (True or False?)

Answer – Depreciation and amortization expenses are both noncash transactions and must be removed. As negative components of net income, elimination requires an addition. The gain is from a nonoperational transaction and must also be removed. As a positive component of net income, it is subtracted. Changes in operational assets and liabilities represent noncash effects that must be removed. For operational assets, an opposite effect to the change is necessary. Thus, $4,000 is added because of the drop in accounts receivable and $11,000 is subtracted as a result of the increase in inventory. For operational liabilities, a direct effect is included for the changes so $7,000 is subtracted because accounts payable went down and $2,000 is added because interest payable went up. The net cash inflow from operating activities is $523,000 ($500,000 + $40,000 +

$8,000 - $13,000 + $4,000 - $11,000 - $7,000 + $2,000). *(Number Eight is True.)*

NINE - In using the direct method to compute cash flows from operating activities, the individual balances appearing on the income statement are converted to the amount of cash collected or paid. A company reports sales revenues of $700,000; however, accounts receivable went up during the year by $11,000. In using the direct method, the cash collected from customers would be reported as $711,000. (True or False?)

Answer – The Accounts Receivable account is directly related to the recording of sales so that the change in this asset is used in determining cash flows from sales. During this year, accounts receivable increased. Thus, more sales were made than the amount of cash collected. Since less cash was collected, the cash inflow from customers would have been $689,000 (sales of $700,000 less $11,000 increase in receivables). (Number Nine is False.)

TEN - During the current year, a company reports cost of goods sold of $400,000. For the year, inventory went down $30,000 but accounts payable went up $4,000. The cash amount paid for inventory during that year was $366,000. (True or False?)

Answer – Inventory and accounts payable are operational accounts that are both related to the recording of cost of goods sold. (1) Inventory went down so less was bought. If less inventory is acquired, cash is conserved and $30,000 less was paid. (2) Accounts payable went up. If fewer accounts payable are paid, cash is conserved and $4,000 less was paid. Only $366,000 was expended for inventory ($400,000 less $30,000 less $4,000). (Number Ten is True.)

ELEVEN - A company reports insurance expense of $25,000. Prepaid insurance on January 1 of the current year was $6,000 but at the end of the year had risen to $11,000. Using the direct method, the company should report Cash Paid for Insurance of $20,000. (True or False?)

Answer – Because the prepaid expense has gone up, the company has paid more than the expense recognized. Prepaid insurance has gone up by $5,000 so the company must have paid that much more for insurance during the period. The expense was $25,000 and the operational asset rose by $5,000 so that the cash amount paid would have been $30,000. With an expense account, the direct method requires that changes in operational assets have a direct effect on the income statement account. An increase in prepaid insurance should be added in arriving at the cash paid for insurance. (Number Eleven is False.)

INTANGIBLE ASSETS

(1) **Intangible assets** are used to generate revenues but have no physical substance.
  - (A) Most common intangibles are patents, goodwill, leasehold improvements (the right to use improvements in leased property), and organization costs.
  - (B) **Organization costs** include lawyer's and accountant's fees to get business started as well as original incorporation costs. Stock issuance costs are not capitalized but recorded as reductions in additional paid-in capital.
  - (C) Intangible assets with definite useful lives are amortized (usually on straight-line method) over lower of useful or legal life.
    - (1) Organization costs are usually amortized over a period of five years because that is minimum length for tax purposes.
    - (2) **Leasehold improvements** are amortized over the life of the improvement or the life of the lease whichever is less.
  - (D) An intangible asset that is amortized should be tested for impairment if facts and circumstances indicate that impairment may have occurred.

(2) **Goodwill** and other intangible assets with indefinite useful lives are not amortized. Instead, they are tested periodically for impairment, at least annually.
  - (A) When goodwill is acquired, it is allocated to the related reporting units (e.g., business segments).
  - (B) The goodwill assigned to a reporting unit should be tested for impairment on an annual basis and between annual tests if facts and circumstances indicate impairment may have occurred.
  - (C) The test has two steps.
    - (1) Compare the fair value of reporting unit with its carrying amount. If the carrying amount is greater than fair value, perform step (2).
    - (2) Compare implied fair value of goodwill to carrying amount. If carrying amount is greater write goodwill down to implied value.

(3) Accounting for **research and development costs**. Research is the search and discovery of new knowledge for potential profit. Development is the translation of research into a plan for a profitable product
  - (A) Research and development expenditures are expensed immediately
    - (1) This expensing includes cost of long-lived assets such as buildings and equipment if acquired for use in a specific project.
    - (2) Cost of long-lived asset acquired for research and development is not expensed immediately if it has alternative future uses. Cost is capitalized with subsequent amortization classified as a research and development expense
  - (B) Since research and development is expensed, the capitalized cost of a patent is the legal costs of establishing and successfully defending the patent.

(4) Accounting for the **development of software** that is to be sold.
  - (A) Until product reaches the stage of technological feasibility, where company has a program design or working model, all costs are recorded as research and development expenses
  - (B) After product has achieved technological feasibility, further software development costs are capitalized.

> (1) Capitalized development cost is amortized to expense each year using the greater of (1) the straight-line figure and (2) the percentage of current sales to total expected sales
>
> (C) Actual production costs are reported as inventory.

PROBLEMS AND SOLUTIONS
INTANGIBLE ASSETS

ONE - A company spends $30,000 for incorporation fees and another $10,000 for lawyers' and accountants' costs in connection with the creation of the business. The company also spends $15,000 for stock issuance costs relating to the initial sale of common stock. The company should report an Organization Costs account of $55,000 within the Intangible Assets section of its balance sheet. (True or False?)

Answer – Organization costs would be reported as $40,000. Stock issuance costs are recorded as a reduction of additional paid-in capital (or retained earnings if there is not sufficient additional paid-in capital to reduce). (Number One is False.)

TWO - Company A leases a building for 10 years from company Z. The lease is nonrenewable. Company A pays $300,000 for improvements such as walls and shelves. Company A properly records the $300,000 as leasehold improvements, an intangible asset. The walls and shelves should last for 15 years. Company A should record amortization expense of $20,000 per year. (True or False?)

Answer – Although the walls and shelves have a life of 15 years, company A only has the property leased for 10 years. Therefore, company A will only get to use these assets for that period of time. Amortization will be $30,000 per year (the cost of $300,000 divided by a ten-year life). For amortization and depreciation purposes, expense allocation should be recorded over the period of time that the party will derive benefit from the asset. (Number Two is False.)

THREE - During Year One, company A expends $100,000 for research and develop costs. At the end of the year, this work proves successful and $20,000 in legal costs are paid to get a patent. The patent is a direct result of this research and development work. At the end of Year One, the company should report $100,000 as an expense and $20,000 as an asset. (True or False?)

Answer – All research and development costs (unless for a long-lived asset with alternative uses) must be expensed as incurred. However, the cost of acquiring a patent (either as a purchase or through legal work to establish the validity of the claim) should be recorded as an intangible asset. (Number Three is True.)

FOUR - The Wall Company designs a computer software product to be sold. The product is developed and becomes a commercial success. All costs of developing this product up to the point of its sale must be expensed as a research and development cost. (True or False?)

Answer – For the development of computer software products that will be sold, all costs up to the point of technological feasibility (usually where the company has a working model) will be research and development expenses. Further software development costs from the point of technological feasibility to the creation of a product for sale are capitalized as an intangible asset. (Number Four is False.)

FIVE – Goodwill should be allocated to reporting units at acquisition and tested for impairment when it is determined that the unit will be sold. (True or False?)

Answer – Goodwill and other intangibles with indefinite useful lives should be tested for impairment at least annually, and more often if certain events occur. (Number Five is False.)

PENSION ACCOUNTING

(1)   If a company's pension is a defined benefit plan, the amount employees are entitled to receive when they retire is unknown because it is based on future factors such as length of service, salary rates, how long they live, etc. Thus, the expense incurred each year must be estimated based on assumptions about these variables.

    (A)   In a defined contribution plan, the employer contributes a set amount of money each year; that amount is the expense.

(2)   Terminology of **pension accounting** is somewhat unique.

    (A)   **Net pension cost** is the expense to be recognized and reported for a specific year

    (B)   **Funding** is amount of cash actually set aside by the employer.

    (C)   **Service cost** is the increase in the amount of pension obligation because of work done by employees in the current year

    (D)   **Projected benefit obligation** (PBO) is the total estimated liability that a company has incurred to date based on the assumptions made of the variables such as how long a person will live. One of the assumptions is what each person's highest salary will be.

        (1)   The PBO increases because of the annual service cost and interest that accrues on the PBO. PBO decreases when payments are made to retirees. PBO can go up or down if plan is amended (called a prior service cost) or if one of the assumptions is changed (called an actuarial or an unrecognized gain or loss).

    (E)   **Accumulated benefit obligation** is the total estimated liability that a company has incurred to date. It is just like PBO except that each person's current salary level is used

    (F)   **Plan assets** is total amount of assets already set aside to pay pension benefits. Funding and any income will increase the plan assets whereas payments of benefits will reduce it.

    (G)   **Prior service cost** is an increase in the projected benefit obligation because of an amendment in the plan or because of the start of the plan. PBO goes up immediately but expense is recognized through amortization over future years.

    (H)   **Actuarial/unrecognized gains and losses** are created in two ways.

        (1)   Changes in the PBO because of a change in an actuarial assumption (for example, it is estimated that people will live longer).

        (2)   The difference in the expected return on plan assets and the actual return on plan assets (as measured by the change in market value after the payments and collections are removed)

        (3)   The assumption is that actuarial/unrecognized gains and losses will even out over time; thus, they are not allowed to effect income unless they become particularly large.

(3)   Annual computation of net pension cost starts with service cost for the period and adds interest expense on PBO (based on a settlement or discount rate) and subtracts expected income on plan assets (actual procedure is to include actual return and then adjust to expected return).

(A)   In addition, net pension cost includes amortization (almost always an increase in the expense) of any prior service cost which is usually written off over the remaining service life of the employees benefited.

(B)   Net pension cost may also include amortization (can be an increase or a decrease) of any actuarial/unrecognized gain or loss. Amortization is ignored unless balance is greater than 10 percent of larger of PBO and plan assets at the beginning of the year.

(4)   Recording of net pension cost is a debit to expense and a credit to **accrued pension cost**. Funding of pension is a credit to cash and a debit to accrued pension cost. If accrued pension costs is a credit, it is reported on balance sheet as a liability. If accrued pension cost has a debit balance, it is shown as a prepaid pension cost in the asset section of the balance sheet.

(5)   A year-end **minimum liability** must be computed and additional debt may have to be recorded if above procedure does not place enough debt onto the books

    (A)   If accumulated benefit obligation exceeds the value of the plan assets, the company must report a debt at least equal to this excess

        (1)   If company already reports an accrued pension cost, it is raised (if necessary) to the minimum liability level with an offset to "Intangible Asset - Pension Costs."

            (a)   Intangible asset is not amortized; it is simply readjusted each year based on the minimum liability.

            (b)   Intangible asset cannot be larger than any unamortized prior service costs. If minimum liability is needed for a larger amount, the remainder of the debit goes to a contra stockholders' equity account.

        (2)   If company already reports a prepaid pension cost, the debt that has to be added is the minimum liability plus the amount of the prepayment.

(6)   A company can also have an obligation for **postretirement benefits** other than pensions. For example, the company might agree to pay medical insurance premiums for retired workers until their death. As employees work, this obligation is estimated and recorded as an expense in much the same way as a pension.

    (A)   A few differences with pensions do occur: the amounts are not usually funded and the obligations are less well defined and, thus, harder to estimate.

PROBLEMS AND SOLUTIONS
PENSION ACCOUNTING

ONE - At the beginning of the current year, a company has a projected benefit obligation for $800,000. At the end of the year, the company has a projected benefit obligation of $1.1 million. Of this total increase, $210,000 was the result of company employees having worked an additional year and, thus, are entitled to larger benefits. This $210,000 is known as the pension expense. (True or False?)

Answer – Any increase in the projected benefit obligation that occurs because the company employees have worked for an extra year is known as the "service cost." It is one of five components that are used in computing the pension expense each year. (Number One is False.)

TWO - A company has a projected benefit obligation on January 1, Year One, of $800,000. Because this figure is a present value amount, interest has to be recognized each year. This interest will increase the projected benefit obligation. (True or False?)

Answer – As a present value figure, the $800,000 must be multiplied by an appropriate interest rate (sometimes referred to as a discount rate or an annuity rate). The resulting interest is then compounded to increase the projected benefit obligation at the end of the year. (Number Two is True.)

THREE - Annual pension expense (often referred to as the net pension cost) is determined from five components. During the current year, service cost was $100,000, the interest on the projected benefit obligation was $30,000, and the income earned on the plan assets was $24,000. Assume that the other two components are not present in the current year. The pension expense should be reported as $154,000. (True or False?)

Answer – There are five possible components that are used in computing pension expense each year. Frequently, one or more of these components will not be present in a particular year. Here, there are three of the five components: the service cost is $100,000, interest on the projected benefit obligation is $30,000, and income on the plan assets is $24,000. Therefore, the pension expense (the net pension cost) is $106,000. The service cost and the interest on the projected benefit obligation increase the expense. Income of plan assets decreases the expense. For this year, the pension expense is $100,000 plus $30,000 less $24,000. (Number Three is False.)

FOUR - Service cost is $180,000. Actual income on plan assets is $44,000. Expected income on plan assets is $38,000. Interest on the projected benefit obligation is $25,000. Pension expense is $167,000. (True or False?)

Answer – Service cost of $180,000 plus interest on the projected benefit obligation of $25,000 less expected income on plan assets of $38,000 leads to a pension expense of $167,000. To avoid wild swings in the reported pension expense, the expected income figure is used rather than the actual income figure. The company also has an unrecognized loss here of $6,000, the reduction from the actual income to the expected income. (Number Four is True.)

FIVE - On January 1, Year One, a company has a projected benefit obligation of $900,000 and plan assets of $800,000. Company employees are threatening to strike for higher pension benefits. To avoid a strike, the company amends its defined benefit plan to give the employees additional retirement benefits. The $900,000 projected benefit obligation was an estimation derived by an actuary based on the terms of the old contract. Using the new terms, the actuary believes that the projected benefit obligation will be $1.2 million. The projected benefit obligation changed by $300,000 because the terms of the plan were amended. The $300,000 increase is referred to as an amendment cost. (True or False?)

Answer – In a defined benefit plan, a change in the amount of the projected benefit obligation because of an amendment in the terms of the plan is known as a prior service cost. (Number Five is False.)

SIX - A company starts Year One with a projected benefit obligation of $800,000. On January 1, the plan is amended and, using the new contractual terms, the projected benefit obligation is determined to be $1.2 million. If the average remaining service life of the employees working on that date is assumed to be 8 years, the company will recognize a $50,000 increase its pension expense in Year One as well as in each of the subsequent seven years. (True or False?)

Answer – The prior service cost is $400,000. The projected benefit obligation increased from $800,000 to $1.2 million because of the amendment. That amount is amortized over the remaining service life of the employees. Therefore, a $50,000 component should be recognized in pension expense for each of the next 8 years. (Number Six is True.)

SEVEN - Service cost is $210,000. Actual income on plan assets is $47,000. Expected income on plan assets is $42,000. Interest on the projected benefit obligation is $59,000. Amortization of a prior service cost is $21,000. Amortization of an excess unrecognized gain is $3,000. Pension expense is $251,000. (True or False?)

Answer – Service cost of $210,000 plus interest on the projected benefit obligation of $59,000 less expected income on plan assets of $42,000 plus $21,000 amortization of prior service cost less $3,000 amortization of excess unrecognized gain leads to a pension expense of $245,000. The amortization of the excess unrecognized gain reduces the expense because it is a gain. If an unrecognized loss were present, it would create an increase in the pension expense. (Number Seven is False.)

EIGHT - At the end of Year One, a company has a projected benefit obligation of $3.2 million, an accumulated benefit obligation of $2.1 million, and plan assets of $1.6 million. The minimum liability that should be reported by the company is $500,000. (True or False?)

True – When preparing a balance sheet, a company with a defined benefit plan must make certain that an adequate amount of liability is reported. This figure is referred to as the minimum liability and is the excess of the accumulated benefit obligation over the plan assets ($2.1 million less $1.6 million). (Number Eight is True.)

INVENTORY

(1)   **Cost of goods sold** (CGS) is computed by adding beginning inventory to purchases (including transportation-in and any other normal and necessary costs) and then subtracting ending inventory. In contrast, transportation out in not an inventory cost but a delivery expense.

  (A)   Both **inventory** and cost of goods sold can be monitored on an ongoing basis by a perpetual system or only at the end of the year by a periodic system.

    (1)   Under a **periodic system**, the costs to be expensed are not determined until the end of the year.

    (2)   Under a **perpetual system**, the next costs to be expensed are determined every time that a new transaction occurs.

  (B)   Applying costs to units sold and units retained can be done by a **FIFO** (first-in, first-out) system, **LIFO** (last-in, first-out), or averaging.

    (1)   Periodic and perpetual systems give different results except when applying FIFO.

    (2)   For averaging in a periodic system (called weighted averaging), one average is determined at the end of the year; for averaging in a perpetual system (called moving averaging), a new average is computed each time a new purchase is made.

(2)   A **cash discount** reduces inventory cost if paid within a specified time. A 2/10, n/30 discount, for example, gives a 2 percent discount if bill is paid in ten days. Remaining (net) balance must be paid in 30 days.

  (A)   Theoretically, inventory cost should be reduced even if discount is not taken since it is not a necessary cost of acquiring the inventory. This is called the net method and any discount not taken is recorded as a loss rather than being capitalized. Can also record inventory at gross figure and record separate reduction at the time discount is actually taken.

  (B)   Trade discount is a percentage reduction in the invoice price given to retailers. It is not recorded, it is just used to establish the price to be charged. If two percentages are given, the second is applied after the first is removed.

(3)   Because of obsolescence, inventory cost may have to be written down to a lower market value since accounting is conservative.

  (A)   Cost is compared to market value and the lower figure is reported.

  (B)   Replacement cost is used as market value for comparison with cost of inventory unless replacement cost lies outside of two boundaries.

    (1)   The ceiling boundary is estimated sales price less anticipated selling expenses. If replacement cost is above the ceiling, ceiling is used as market value.

    (2)   The floor boundary is estimated sales price less anticipated selling expenses and normal profit. If replacement cost is below the floor, the floor figure is used as market value.

  (C)   If goods are damaged, cost should be reduced to net realizable value.

(4)   Errors in recording and counting inventory affect reported figures.

  (A)   Errors can be made in recording the transfer of inventory, either goods being bought or sold.

(1) Transfer should be recorded at "**FOB**" point. This is point where legal title changes hands.

(2) Since ending inventory is determined by count, an error in recording a purchase or sale does not necessarily affect the reporting of ending inventory

(B) As a second problem, ending inventory can be counted incorrectly so that both ending inventory and CGS are wrong.

 (1) If ending inventory is overstated, CGS is too low, and net income is too high. If ending inventory is too low, CGS is too high, and net income is too low.

 (2) Ending inventory error automatically carries over to the next year's beginning inventory. If beginning inventory is overstated, CGS is too high, and net income is too low. If beginning inventory is too low, CGS is too low, and net income is too high.

(5) Inventory may need to be estimated for many reasons: preparation of interim financial statements, a check figure for a physical inventory count, to estimate fire and theft losses, etc.

(A) **Retail inventory method** can be used to estimate inventory but only if records are kept at both cost and retail.

 (1) Ending inventory is first estimated at its retail value by taking the beginning inventory and adding purchases and mark ups and subtracting mark downs, losses (theft and breakage, for example) and sales.

 (2) Estimated ending inventory at retail is then converted to a cost figure by multiplying it times a cost/retail ratio. Inventory at retail will not vary but there are several ways to determine the cost/retail ratio.

  (a) Average method for calculating cost/retail ratio - all cost figures (beginning inventory and purchases) are used and all retail figures (beginning inventory, purchases, mark ups, and mark downs) are used.

  (b) Conventional (or conventional-lower of cost or market) is same as averaging except that mark downs are left out of the retail part of the ratio.

  (c) FIFO is same as averaging except that beginning inventory is left out of both cost and retail figures

  (d) FIFO lower of cost or market is same as averaging except that beginning inventory is left out of both cost and retail figures and mark downs are left out of the retail part of the ratio.

(B) **Gross profit method of estimating inventory** is used when only cost figures are recorded.

 (1) Normal gross profit percentage (gross profit/sales) computed from the past is multiplied times current sales to provide an estimate of current gross profit. This figure is subtracted from sales to arrive at an estimate of the cost of inventory that has been sold in the current period.

 (2) Cost of beginning inventory is added to current purchases to get total goods available. The estimated cost of the inventory that has been sold this period is subtracted to leave the estimated cost of the inventory still on hand.

(6) **Consignment inventory** is merchandise held for sell by one party (a consignee) although the goods are owned by another (a consignor)

    (A)   Cost of consignment inventory is recorded by the owner (at cost) and not by the consignee. The party physically holding the items does not have them recorded.

    (B)   Consignor cannot record receivable until goods are sold.

(7) LIFO has some technical problems that make it difficult to use. **Dollar value LIFO** is one practical way to apply LIFO. For one thing, inventory is grouped into similar pools rather than handling items individually.

    (A)   All LIFO systems start with a base inventory which is usually the quantity when LIFO is first applied times the price on that date. If inventory increases, a new layer is added: it is the additional quantity at the latest prices. If inventory decreases, cost is removed from the most recent layers.

    (B)   When applying dollar value LIFO, the base inventory of a pool is also recorded. However, for each additional layer of inventory, the increase in quantity is measured in dollars and not units. For each additional layer, the latest price is measured as an index and not in dollars. The base inventory plus all of the added layers gives ending inventory. A layer might be a $10,000 increase in quantity times an index of 1.12 or $11,200.

    (C)   Increase in quantity for the current period is the difference between the beginning inventory measured at base year prices and the ending inventory measured at base year prices. Since the prices are held constant, any difference is caused by quantity change.

    (D)   The index for the current period is the ending inventory at ending prices divided by the ending inventory at base year prices.

PROBLEMS AND SOLUTIONS
INVENTORY

ONE - A company starts the current year with inventory costing $40,000 and ends the year with inventory costing $50,000. During this period, inventory with an invoice price of $190,000 is bought. The freight-in on this inventory was $7,000 and $2,000 more was paid for sales taxes in connection with the purchases. Cost of goods sold for the period was $209,000. (True or False?)

    Answer – Beginning inventory ($40,000) plus purchases ($199,000 after including the freight-in and taxes) less ending inventory ($50,000) leads to a cost of goods sold for the year of $189,000. (Number One is False.)

TWO - A company is using a perpetual LIFO system. It starts the year with one item costing $100. Later, on January 10, a second item is bought for $110. Then, one item is sold for $200 on January 20. Finally, on January 31, another identical item is bought for $140. The company should report a cost of goods sold for the month of January of $110. (True or False?)

    Answer – In a perpetual system, a purchase will increase inventory immediately whereas a sale will reduce inventory immediately. Here, when a sale is made after the second purchase, the cost of the goods sold is determined and recorded at that *time. On that date, the company had only two items of inventory: one costing $100 and a second costing $110. Based on the LIFO cost flow assumption, the last item (at that point in time) is transferred to cost of goods sold for a balance of $110. The ending inventory account will have two items: one costing $100 and the other costing $140 for a total of $240. In a perpetual system, the determination of which cost to transfer to cost of goods sold is made at the time of sale. (Number Two is True.)*

THREE - A company holds an item of inventory with a cost of $210. This item now has a replacement cost of $140. The company believes that it can still sell the item for $200 after expending $20 for advertising and commissions. The normal gross margin is $30. After determining the lower of cost or market value, this inventory item will be reported on the company's balance sheet at a value of $140. (True or False?)

Answer – Replacement cost ($140) is viewed as market value unless it is above a ceiling figure. In this case, the ceiling is the sales price of $200 less $20 in costs to sell the item. Thus, replacement cost is not above the ceiling figure ($180). Furthermore, replacement cost is viewed as market value unless it is below a floor figure. Here, the floor is the sales price ($200) less the cost to sell ($20) less the normal profit ($30). The floor is $150; since replacement cost ($140) is below that number, the $150 will serve as market value. Cost is $210 and market value is $150 so that the lower of cost or market value to be reported will be $150. (Number Three is False.)

FOUR - Company A sells goods to company Z with terms "FOB destination." During delivery, the truck wrecks and the goods are destroyed. Company Z must still pay company A for this merchandise. (True or False?)

Answer - The FOB point identifies the place at which title to goods is conveyed from the seller to the buyer. Unless negotiated differently, the party who holds title during delivery bears the cost of any destroyed or lost items. In this case, title had not yet been conveyed to company Z. Based on the FOB point, title would have been conveyed when the goods were received by company Z. Title had not transferred; therefore, company Z never owned the goods and is not required to pay company A. (Number Four is False.)

FIVE - Company A holds inventory that costs $10 per unit. Company A sends 100 units of this inventory to company Z to be sold on consignment for $15 per unit. For each unit sold, company Z will keep $2 and send the remaining $13 back to company A. Upon shipping the goods to company Z, company A should record a receivable of $1,500. (True or False?)

Answer – The inventory still belongs to company A and should be retained on its books at historical cost. Therefore, company A will have a Consignment Inventory account of $1,000 rather than an Accounts Receivable account of $1,500. Company Z (the consignee) does not own the goods and will not record them although a receivable must be set up if any costs have been incurred that will be reimbursed. (Number Five is False.)

SIX - A company begins the year with inventory costing $200,000. During the current year, an additional $600,000 is bought. Sales for the period are $700,000. The company usually sells its merchandise with a markup of 30 percent of the sales price. The company should estimate its current inventory as $100,000. (True or False?)

Answer – If the markup percentage is known, a company can estimate its inventory at any time by using the gross margin (gross profit) method. This company had merchandise costing $800,000 ($200,000 plus $600,000). Sales were $700,000 but that is a retail figure and not the cost of the items. The markup is 30 percent or $210,000 (30 percent of $700,000). The company can estimate cost of goods sold during the year as $490,000 ($700,000 in sales less the $210,000 markup). With inventory costing $800,000 available and cost of sales of $490,000, the company would estimate its current inventory balance as the $310,000 difference. (Number Six is False.)

SEVEN - A company reports its cost of goods sold for 1999 as $300,000 and net income as $60,000. However, in counting its ending inventory, the company omitted merchandise costing $20,000. The actual cost of goods sold was $320,000 and net income should have been reported as $40,000. (True or False?)

Answer – Because merchandise was left out of the physical count, ending inventory was understated by $20,000. In determining cost of goods sold, a formula is used: beginning inventory plus purchases less ending inventory. Ending inventory is a negative component within the computation of cost of goods sold. Since ending inventory was too low, the reduction will be understated and the resulting Cost of Goods Sold figure is overstated by $20,000. This expense was reported as $300,000 but was overstated so the actual balance should have been $280,000. The reduction in this expense causes net income to be $20,000 higher or $80,000. (Number Seven is False.)

ACCOUNTING CHANGES

(1) Companies can decide to make **changes in accounting principles** that are applied. Any change is always assumed to have occurred on the first day of the current year so that reported figures for this year are based on the new method.

    (A) The accounting problem is how to reflect the impact of the change on the figures of prior years. Most accounting changes are reported by recognizing a figure entitled "**cumulative effect of accounting change**" at the bottom of the current income statement.

        (1) No change is made in any balance shown on a prior statement.

        (2) The impact of the change on all income figures reported in prior years is totaled and reported (net of taxes) at bottom of current year income statement. This cumulative effect is shown just after any extraordinary gain or loss.

        (3) For comparability, net income totals (referred to as pro-forma income figures) for each of the past years being shown must also be disclosed using the figures that would have been appropriate if the change had been made through restatement.

    (B) Some specific changes must be made retroactively rather than through a cumulative effect. This is sometimes referred to as a **prior period adjustment**; all reported figures for prior years are physically changed to the new method. To change figures for any prior year not being reported, the earliest retained earnings figure being shown is adjusted (net of taxes). There is no cumulative effect reported on the current income statement. The following are handled as retroactive changes.

        (1) A change in the method of accounting for long-term contracts. Can be a switch from percentage of completion method to the completed contract method or vice versa.

        (2) A change from LIFO to another method of costing inventory.

        (3) A change made to correct a prior year error. The error could be a mathematical mistake or a misapplication of an accounting method.

(2) **Changes in the reporting entity** are also accounted for by restatement

    (A) A change in reporting entity is a change in the composition of consolidated statements without any change in ownership. For example, a subsidiary that used to be omitted from consolidation is now consolidated without any increase in ownership.

    (B) A pooling of interests is reported retroactively

(3) A company can change one of its estimations such as the bad debt percentage of the expected life of assets.

    (A) For **changes in estimations**, there is no cumulative effect or prior period adjustment. The past years are not impacted.

    (B) For the current year, the beginning balances for the current year are used along with the new estimations to determine figures to be reported.

    (C) If a change is both a change in an estimate and a change in a principle, it is reported as a change in an estimate.

| PROBLEMS AND SOLUTIONS |
| ACCOUNTING CHANGES |

ONE - On September 11, Year One, a company decides to change from one generally accepted method of accounting to another. When the company reports its income statement for that year, the old method will be used for the period until September 11 and the new method will be applied thereafter. (True or False?)

Answer – Regardless of how a change in accounting principles has to be handled, operations for the current year (the year in which the change is made) are always reported as if the change were made on the first day of that year. Thus, whether this decision was made on January 1, September 11, or December 31, the operations for Year One will be reported using the new method exclusively. (Number One is False.)

TWO - During Year Two, a company decides to change from one generally accepted method of accounting to another. Using the new method, the expense for Year Two will be $64,000. This same expense was reported in Year One as $44,000 using the old method. However, if the new method had been utilized during this previous year, the expense would have been $50,000. The company is now presenting comparative statements for Year One and Year Two. The expense shown for Year Two will be $64,000. The expense reported for Year One can either be $44,000 or $50,000 depending on the type of change that is being made. (True or False?)

Answer – A few changes in accounting principles are handled as prior period adjustments. In such cases, the reported balance would be restated in the statements of the prior year to $50,000. For most changes, though, the impact on all previous years is gathered and reported as a single figure in the current year. This figure is referred to as the cumulative effect of the change in accounting methods. If a cumulative effect type of change is made, the original $44,000 continues to be shown for the earlier year. (Number Two is True.)

THREE - A company makes a change in an accounting method. This particular change is handled as a cumulative effect type of change so that the impact on all previous income statements is gathered and reported at the bottom of the current income statement (net of any tax effect). This cumulative effect is the only item isolated in this manner at the bottom of an income statement. (True or False?)

Answer – Three specific income effects are isolated at the bottom of an income statement net of any related tax effect. The first of these is the results of any discontinued operation. The second is an extraordinary gain or loss. The third is the cumulative effect of a change in accounting methods. (Number Three is False.)

FOUR - A company makes a change in an accounting principle that is accounted for as a cumulative effect type of change. The entire impact of the change is reported within the income statement of the current period. (True or False?)

Answer – Regardless of the specific date of change, the current year figure will be reported based on the new method. The impact of the change on the net income of previous years will be gathered and reported at the bottom of the current income statement (net of taxes). Therefore, all changes in net income are reported within the year that the change is made. (Number Four is True.)

FIVE - A company began operations on January 1, Year One. During Year Two, this company decides to change from one generally accepted method of accounting to another. Using the new method, the expense for Year Two will be $64,000. This same expense was reported in Year One as $44,000 using the old method. However, if the new method had been utilized during this previous year, the expense would have been $50,000. The company is now producing comparative statements for Year One and Year Two. This particular change qualifies to be handled through a prior period adjustment. For Year Two, the expense will be shown as $64,000. In addition, at the bottom of the Year Two income statement, a cumulative effect of the change in accounting methods should be presented as a $6,000 reduction in income. (True or False?)

Answer – In applying a retroactive type change through a prior period adjustment, the current year figure will be shown using the new method. All previous income figures will also be changed to be consistent with the new method in use. Since all of the earlier numbers are physically changed, no cumulative effect is created or reported in any year. (Number Five is False.)

SIX - On January 1, Year One, a company buys a machine for $120,000 with an estimated life of 12 years and no salvage value. Straight-line depreciation is used. On January 1, Year Three, the company decides that the original life should have been 8 years instead of twelve. Ignore income taxes. In its income statement for Year Three, this company should report a Cumulative Effect of a Change in Accounting Methods of $10,000 as a decrease in net income. (True or False?)

Answer – This company has made a change in an estimation rather than a change in a method of accounting. A change in estimation has no impact at all on figures previously reported. Therefore, no cumulative effect is computed or recognized. (Number Six is False.)

PARTNERSHIP ACCOUNTING

(1)   A **partnership** is an association of two or more persons to carry on a business as co-owners for profit. Many aspects of accounting for a partnership are same as for a corporation but there are unique features. For example, each partner has a separate capital account, the total of which replaces the stockholders' equity section of the balance sheet.

(2)   When a new partner is admitted into a partnership, any contributions are recorded by partnership at market value but original book value is retained for tax purposes.

    (A)   A computation can be made so that new partner invests an amount that will be equal to the capital balance set up. This eliminates the need to record either goodwill or a bonus.

        (1)   The new partner's investment (NPI) can be set equal to the percentage of the business being acquired (%A) multiplied times the total capital of the business.

        (2)   Total capital would be the previous capital (PC) balance plus the new partner's investment. Thus, equation would be set up and the new investment determined algebraically. $NPI = \%A \times (PC + NPI)$ and solve for NPI

    (B)   A new partner may have to contribute assets worth more than the percentage being acquired of the total capital, especially if it is a profitable partnership.

        (1)   This difference can be recorded by **bonus method**. Partner is given a set capital balance or a percentage of total capital. Any difference from contribution (either positive or negative) is recorded to original partners' Capital accounts based on previous method of allocating profits and losses.

        (2)   This difference can also be recorded using **goodwill method**. The new partner receives a capital balance exactly equal to the contribution. The new partner's payment is then used to compute an implied value for the business as a whole. The investment is divided by the percentage acquired to get this valuation. The difference between this implied value and total capital (including the new investment) is viewed as goodwill and recorded along with an offsetting entry to the Capital accounts of the original partners based on the previous method of **allocating profits and losses**.

(3)   When revenues and expenses are closed out at the end of the year, the net profit or loss must be assigned to the partners' Capital accounts. The actual amount paid to a partner is usually set by agreement and can differ from this allocation process.

    (A)   If there is no agreement, split is always done on an even basis.

    (B)   If there is an agreement as to profit allocation but losses are not mentioned, the same method is used.

    (C)   Any agreements must be followed specifically. Can include several factors such as a salary allowance, interest, and a ratio. If more than one factor is included, the ratio is computed last

(4)   At some point, a partnership may be liquidated, the assets sold off and the debts paid with any residual amounts going to the partners.

    (A)   In liquidating noncash assets, any gains and losses are assigned to the partners based on normal profit and loss allocation.

(B) Any residual cash goes to the partners based on the final balances in their capital accounts.

(C) If enough money is set aside to pay all debts, available cash can be distributed to the partners before all noncash assets are sold. To determine distribution, maximum losses are assumed for all remaining noncash assets. If a partner has a negative capital balance after these simulated losses, that amount is also viewed as a loss to be absorbed by the remaining partners using their relative profit and loss percentages. When all remaining capital accounts have positive balances, those amounts are the safe capital amounts that can be distributed immediately.

PROBLEMS AND SOLUTIONS
PARTNERSHIP ACCOUNTING

ONE - Mr. A contributes land to help create a business as a partnership. The land had a book value to Mr. A of $8,000 but was worth $11,000 on the date of the transfer. The business should record this land at its fair market value of $11,000 with an increase in the Mr. A, Capital account of the same amount. (True or False?)

False – For financial reporting purposes, the conveyance of property to a partnership is recorded by the business at the fair market value of the item. Consequently, this land will be recorded by the partnership at the $11,000 value on that date. In contrast, for taxation purposes, the land would retain its book value of $8,000. However, in financial accounting, tax laws have no authority. (Number One is True.)

TWO - Mr. A and Ms. Z are partners who share profits and losses on a 70:30 basis respectively. Currently, Mr. A has a capital balance of $40,000 and Ms. Z has a capital balance of $20,000. The decision has been made to admit Mr. M as a third partner upon payment to the business of cash of $30,000. Mr. M will start with a 30 percent ownership in the business. If the bonus method is to be used, the total capital after the admission of Mr. M will be $100,000. (True or False?)

Answer – Under the bonus approach, total capital after an admission or departure of a partner is simply the prior capital plus or minus any change in net assets. In this case, the capital was $60,000 and Mr. M added in cash of $30,000. Total capital has increased to $90,000. (Number Two is False.)

THREE - Mr. A and Ms. Z are partners who share profits and losses on a 70:30 basis respectively. Currently, Mr. A has a capital balance of $40,000 and Ms. Z has a capital balance of $20,000. The decision has been made to admit Mr. M as a third partner upon the payment to the business of cash of $30,000. Mr. M will start off with a 30 percent ownership in the business. If the bonus method is to be used, the beginning capital account for Mr. M will be $27,000. (True or False?)

Answer – The bonus method does not adjust the total capital figure. Total capital prior to the admission of Mr. M was $60,000 ($40,000 plus $20,000). The payment to *the business of $30,000 increases total capital to $90,000. Mr. M is entitled to 30 percent of this new business so his beginning capital balance is recorded as $27,000 ($90,000 times 30 percent). In the bonus method, total capital is determined after the addition or subtraction of assets and liabilities. The new partner is then assigned the appropriate percentage of that total. (Number Three is True.)*

FOUR - Two partners have capital balances of $60,000 and $50,000. They admit a new partner into the business. This new partner pays $60,000 to the business in order to acquire a 30 percent ownership. The goodwill method (sometimes referred to as the revaluation method) is to be applied. If all assets of the business are properly valued, goodwill of $20,000 should be recognized. (True or False?)

Answer - Under the goodwill approach, after an admission of a partner, total capital is found by applying the price paid to the business as a whole. In this case, paying $60,000 for a 30 percent ownership share indicates an implied worth for the entire business of $200,000 ($60,000 divided by 30 percent). Without adjustment, total capital would be $170,000 ($110,000 capital for the old partners plus the $60,000 contribution of the new partner). Goodwill of $30,000 must be recognized to increase the capital from $170,000 to the implied value of $200,000. (Number Four is False.)

FIVE - Sam and Julie are partners with capital balances of $80,000 and $50,000 respectively. Sam works 40 hours per week in the business and Julie works 25 hours per week. Sam and Julie have an agreement whereby they will split all profits with 80 percent going to Sam and 20 percent going to Julie. In the current year, the business has a net loss of $20,000. At the end of the year, Julie's capital balance will be $40,000. (True or False?)

Answer – If an agreement exists in order to structure the allocation of profits but no mention is made of possible losses, the same process will be used in both cases. Thus, since the business lost $20,000, 80 percent of that amount ($16,000) is attributed to Sam with the remaining 20 percent to Julie ($4,000). After that, Julie's capital account will have been reduced from $50,000 to $46,000. (Number Five is False.)

SIX - A partnership has been liquidated and cash of $30,000 remains to be distributed. This cash will be given to the partners based on the ratio that they have used to allocate profits and losses. (True or False?)

Answer – A final distribution after liquidation is based on the ending capital balances of the partners, assuming that each partner has a positive balance remaining. If one or more partners reports a deficit, that amount must be contributed by that partner or the deficit must be assumed as an additional loss to be absorbed by the remaining partners. (Number Six is False.)

FINANCIAL INSTRUMENTS

(1) **Financial instruments** are cash, investments in equities, or contracts to receive or pay cash or another financial instrument.

    (A)   The term "financial instrument" includes traditional items such as accounts receivable and notes payable but also more complex arrangements such as forward currency exchange contracts.

    (B)   A **derivative** is a particular type of financial instrument that has a value based on another asset (a bond's maturity value will rise if the price of gold rises) or tied to an index (a bond's interest rate will change as the rate of inflation changes)

        (1)   All derivatives must be reported on the balance sheet. Depending on their nature, derivatives are shown as either assets or liabilities.

        (2)   All derivatives are reported at their fair values.

        (3)   Except for a few types of hedges, the change in fair value of a derivative is reported within net income for the period of the change.

    (C)   Some financial instruments have **off-balance sheet risk**; in other words, a loss can be incurred that is larger than the amount being reported. For example, (1) a company can have a commitment that is not being reported on the balance sheet that could still create a loss or (2) the company might have a payable reported as $100,000 that might actually require payment of $160,000.

    (D)   With financial instruments, there is the chance of losing the amounts reported as well as (in some cases) the chance of having additional off-balance sheet losses. The potential for these losses results from two specific types of risk.

        (1)   **Market risk** is a chance of loss resulting from a change in value. For example, a company makes a commitment to buy wheat at a set price and the price of wheat then falls below that level.

        (2)   **Credit risk** is the chance of loss resulting because another party fails to perform. For example, a company guarantees the loan of another company and the debtor fails to pay.

    (E)   Disclosure of risks associated with financial instruments.

        (1)   For financial instruments with off-balance sheet risk, the extent, nature, and terms of both market risk and credit risk must be disclosed.

        (2)   For all financial instruments, significant concentrations of credit risk must be disclosed. A significant concentration is where a large amount of performance is required of a single party or by a group of similar parties (for example, in the same industry or same geographical location.

        (3)   For all financial instruments, market value must be disclosed or an indication of why value cannot be determined.

        (4)   For derivatives, maximum potential loss must be disclosed.

| PROBLEMS AND SOLUTIONS |
| FINANCIAL INSTRUMENTS |

ONE - A company has (1) an accounts receivable of $5,000, (2) an investment in the common stock of a major company that costs $8,000 but is currently worth $11,000, and (3) a note payable for $20,000 to a local bank. All three of these balances are considered financial instruments. (True or False?)

> *Answer – A financial instrument is cash, an investment in an equity, or a contract to receive or pay cash (or another financial instrument). The note receivable, the investment in the stock of the company, and the note payable all fall under this definition. (Number One is True.)*

TWO - A derivative is a type of financial instrument, one that has a value that is based on another asset or tied to an index. (True or False?)

> *Answer – The term "derivative" is used whenever the value of a financial instrument must be derived from some other source. The value of the instrument may be based on the value of some identified asset or a particular index. (Number Two is True.)*

THREE – All derivatives must be reported on the balance sheet of the owner as either an asset or liability. Derivatives must be reported at fair value. (True or False?)

> *Answer – In order to inform readers of the presence of derivatives, they must be reported on the balance sheet. Some (a receivable, for example) are shown as assets whereas others (a payable, for example) are liabilities. All derivatives are shown at their fair value. (Number Three is True.)*

FOUR - Company A has made a commitment to buy 10,000 barrels of oil over the next year at a set price. If the price of oil falls during that period, the company will have to pay an amount above market value for the oil and will suffer a loss. In this situation, company A is facing a credit risk on this particular financial instrument (the contract to pay for the oil). (True or False?)

> *Answer – As in this case, some financial instruments can incur a loss because of a change in the value of another item (the oil in this situation). The possibility of this type of loss is known as market risk. (Number Four is False.)*

FIVE - Company A guarantees a loan for company Z. If company Z fails to repay the loan to the bank when it matures, company A will be held liable for any unpaid balance. In this situation, company A is facing a market risk on this financial instrument (the contract to pay the loan, if that becomes necessary). (True or False?)

> *Answer – This financial instrument will require payment by company A only if another party fails to perform. The possibility of this type of loss is known as credit risk. (Number Five is False.)*

SIX - A company has off-balance sheet risk in connection with a number of financial instruments. In preparing its financial statements, the company must disclose the extent, nature, and terms of both market risk and credit risk in connection with these items. (True or False?)

Answer – Off-balance sheet risk is present whenever a company can lose more on an asset or liability than is currently reported for these items on its balance sheet. Either a loss can occur in connection with an off-balance sheet item or a loss can occur that is greater than the amount actually reported for a financial instrument. The reader of the statements may be unaware of the potential for losses. Therefore, when off-balance sheet risk is present, disclosure must be made of this risk and classified as either market risk or credit risk. (Number Six is True.)

EARNINGS PER SHARE

(1) **Earnings per share** (EPS) is a common stock computation. It must be reported for each income period reported by all publicly held companies. Basically, the net income that is applicable to common stock is divided by the weighted average number of common stock shares outstanding.

    (A) Any preferred stock dividends must be subtracted from net income to get amount of income applicable to common stock.

        (1) If preferred stock is cumulative, the annual dividend is subtracted each year whether declared or not; if noncumulative, it is only subtracted when declared.

    (B) To get the weighted average of the common shares, the number of shares outstanding for a period is multiplied by that number of months. The resulting totals are added and divided by 12 to get average for the year.

        (1) For averaging purposes, shares issued as a stock dividend or split (or from a pooling of interests) are assumed as having been issued at the earliest point in the computation.

(2) The above income divided by shares is termed **basic earnings per share** and is reported by all publicly held companies. If a company has dilutive securities (that can be converted into common stock), it must also report a second figure referred to as **diluted earnings per share**. This computation gives weight to convertible items by assuming that conversion actually occurred.

    (A) To include stock options or rights in the computation of diluted earnings per share, conversion is assumed and the number of shares that would be issued is added to the weighted average number of shares.

        (1) Converting options often requires payment of cash. If conversion is assumed, the cash coming into the company is also assumed.

        (2) It is assumed that this cash is used to buy treasury stock at its average price for the period which reduces the weighted average number of outstanding shares.

    (B) To include **convertible bonds** in the computation of diluted EPS, conversion is assumed and the number of shares that would be issued is added to the weighted average number of shares.

        (1) Interest expense is a negative within net income. Assumed conversion of the bonds would eliminate the interest causing an increase (net of taxes) in income used for this computation.

    (C) To include **convertible preferred stock** in the computation of diluted EPS, conversion is assumed and the number of shares that would be issued is added to the weighted average number of shares.

        (1) Preferred stock dividends have been subtracted in arriving at the income applicable to common stock. Assumed conversion of the preferred stock would eliminate the dividends causing an increase in the income used for this computation.

(3) In computing EPS, any assumed conversion that causes the reported figure to rise is referred to as antidilutive and is not included in the computation. For earnings per share, it is just ignored.

PROBLEMS AND SOLUTIONS
EARNINGS PER SHARE

ONE - A company has one or more items outstanding that are convertible into common stock. At least one of these items is dilutive. The company will report a single earnings per share figure but it will be known as diluted earnings per share. (True or False?)

Answer – When a company has items that are convertible into common stock that will have a dilutive effect on earnings per share, the company must report two earnings per share figures: (1) basic earnings per share and (2) diluted earnings per share. (Number One is False.)

TWO - A company reports a net income of $400,000. The company has 50,000 shares of common stock outstanding as well as 20,000 shares of preferred stock. The company paid $50,000 in dividends to the holders of the common stock and $100,000 in dividends to the holders of the preferred stock. The company's basic earnings per share is $5.00. (True or False?)

Answer – Earnings per share is a residual computation to show the net income attributed to common stock after all distributions have been made to preferred stock. Therefore, the earnings portion of the calculation for basic earnings per share is the net income less dividends to preferred stock. Here, basic earnings per share would be earnings of $300,000 ($400,000 income less the dividends to preferred stockholders) divided by 50,000 shares of common stock outstanding. The company's basic earnings per share is $6.00. (Number Two is False.)

THREE - A company is computing basic earnings per share. It starts the year with 50,000 shares outstanding but issues an additional 12,000 shares on April 1 as a stock dividend. For that year, the company would use 59,000 shares in its basic earnings per share computation. (True or False?)

Answer – Theoretically, a stock dividend (as well as a stock split) is assumed to be a redivision of old shares rather than an issuance of new stock. In computing earnings per share, both a stock dividend and a stock split are assumed to have occurred on the first day of the period. The 12,000 additional shares that came from a stock dividend are viewed as having been issued on the first day of the year (regardless of the date of the dividend). Therefore, all 62,000 shares are assumed to have been outstanding for the entire year and that number is used in computing basic earnings per share. However, if any new shares had been issued during the period prior to the stock dividend, the portion of the dividend attributed to the new shares is assumed to have occurred on the date the new shares were sold. (Number Three is False.)

FOUR - A company has computed basic earnings per share to be $5.37: $537,000 in earnings divided by 100,000 shares. The company also has $1 million in convertible bonds outstanding. The bonds were sold at a discount and now have a book value of $900,000. These bonds pay a cash interest rate of 8 percent but were sold to yield a rate of 10 percent. The tax rate is 30 percent. These bonds can be exchanged for 20,000 shares of common stock. The company should also report diluted earnings per share of $4.93 (rounded). (True or False?)

Answer – When convertible items are present, their potential impact on earnings per share must be included. They are included in this computation by assuming that conversion occurred. Conversion of the bond would cause 20,000 new shares to be issued so that the number of shares increases to 120,000. Interest expense ($90,000 or 10 percent of the $900,000 book value) would not have been incurred if the bonds had been converted. Saving this interest would increase earnings from $537,000 to $627,000. With $90,000 more income, income tax expense will increase by $27,000 (30 percent of increase) which reduces earnings from $627,000 to $600,000. Thus, diluted earnings per share is $600,000 divided by 120,000 shares or $5.00. (Number Four is False.)

FIVE - A company has computed its basic earnings per share as $5.00: $500,000 in earnings divided by 100,000 shares. The company also has 10,000 shares of convertible preferred stock outstanding. Each of these shares can be exchanged for two new shares of common stock. The preferred stock pays a $4.00 per share cumulative dividend each year. This dividend was appropriately subtracted in arriving at basic earnings per share. The tax rate is assumed to be 30 percent. The company should report diluted earnings per share of $4.40. (True or False?)

Answer – When convertible items are present, their potential impact on earnings per share must be included. To include convertible preferred stock, two steps are taken in this process. First, the preferred shares are assumed to be converted so that the appropriate number of shares of common stock is added. Second, because the preferred stock is assumed converted, the required dividend would not be distributed. Thus, it is added back to net income to eliminate its effect. Dividends are not tax deductible by the company making payment so no tax effect is subtracted. Here, the 20,000 new shares (10,000 old shares at a two for one conversion ratio) are assumed issued so that the number of shares increases to 120,000. If converted, preferred dividend payments of $40,000 (10,000 shares multiplied by $4.00 per share dividend) would not be paid. The dividend is eliminated by adding it back to the company's earnings causing a rise from $500,000 to $540,000. Diluted earnings per share is $540,000 divided by 120,000 shares or $4.50. (Number Five is True.)

SIX - A company has computed its basic earnings per share to be $5.10: $510,000 in earnings divided by 100,000 common shares. The company also has 10,000 options outstanding allowing the holder to buy shares of common stock for $40 per share. The average price of this stock for the year was $50 per share. The tax rate is assumed to be 30 percent. The company should also report diluted earnings per share of $5.00. (True or False?)

Answer – When convertible items are present, the potential impact on earnings per share is included. For stock options (as well as stock rights and warrants), three steps are taken in this process. First, the stock options are assumed to be converted so that the appropriate number of shares are added to the computation. Second, *stock options frequently require payment of some money by the buyer. That money is assumed to be collected although it has no impact on the income figure in this computation. Third, money obtained from the options is assumed to be used to reacquire treasury stock (at its average price). Thus, in this case, assumed conversion of the 10,000 options would increase the number of shares from 100,000 to 110,000. Conversion of each option requires payment of $40 so the company would collect $400,000 ($40 times 10,000 stock options). Since this money is assumed to be used to buy back stock, 8,000 shares would be reacquired ($400,000 cash divided by the price of $50 per share). Diluted earnings per share is the $510,000 earnings divided by 102,000 shares (100,000 plus 10,000 less 8,000) or $5.00. No tax effect is associated with stock options in this computation. (Number Six is True.)*

FOREIGN CURRENCY BALANCES

(1)   All companies are said to have a **functional currency**. That is the currency in which most transactions are denominated. If in doubt as to identity of functional currency, several factors should be examined: the currency of primary sales markets, the currency used for major financing, the currency used to acquire materials and pay labor, etc. The dollar will be viewed here as the functional currency because it almost always is for US companies.

(2)   Prior to being reported in financial statements, figures denominated in foreign currencies must be stated at their equivalent US dollar values. Two different techniques have been established for this purpose.

    (A)   Financial statements of foreign subsidiaries of US companies are translated into US dollars for consolidation purposes if the functional currency of the sub is other than the dollar (which it normally is).

    (B)   Individual transactions of a US company made in a foreign currency are remeasured into US dollars. Although not as frequent, remeasurement is also used for the statements of a foreign sub if its functional currency is the US dollar.

(3)   Both translation and remeasurement are based on multiplying the reported foreign currency balance times a fraction which is the value of desired currency/equivalent value of the foreign currency. In either case, there are two accounting problems to address.

    (A)   Should the restatement be based on historical exchange rates or current exchange rates (called spot rates)?

    (B)   If a balance is updated using the current rate, a change occurs in the reported figure. How is this effect measured and reported?

(4)   **Translation of the financial statements of a foreign subsidiary**

    (A)   All accounts in the asset and liability sections (no exceptions) are translated into US dollars at the current exchange rate in effect on the date of the balance sheet.

    (B)   All other accounts (revenues, expenses, paid-in capital, dividends, etc.) are translated into US dollars at the historical exchange rate in effect at the time of the original recording of the account.

        (1)   Common stock, for example, is translated at rate in effect when stock was issued; dividends use the rate at the date of declaration.

        (2)   Since many income statement items (such as sales and rent expense) occur throughout the year, an average rate for the year can often be used.

        (3)   Because the date of recording is used, cost of goods sold and depreciation expense are translated at the average rate for the current year and not when the asset was bought.

    (C)   Assets and liabilities use current exchange rates; thus, their balances will continually change. The effect of these changes is accumulated and reported in a **Translation Adjustment** account that appears within stockholders' equity.

        (1)   There is no income effect created by a translation

        (2)   The translation adjustment is computed as follows.

            (a)   The January 1 balance of net assets (or the equivalent stockholders' equity) is translated at the rate on that day.

(b)   Any change in net assets during the year is translated at the rate on the date of the change. Dividends, income, and stock transactions are about the only possible changes in the net asset total

(c)   The above two translated figures are added.

(d)   The December 31 balance of net assets is translated at the rate on that date.

(e)   The value of the assets as they entered the company during the year (c) is compared to the ending value of the net assets (d). Difference is the change in value which is the translation adjustment for the year.

(5)   **Remeasurement of individual transactions** (such as purchases and sales) denominated in a foreign currency. Remeasurement is also appropriate for a subsidiary that has the same functional currency as its parent.

(A)   At the time of the original transaction, all balances are remeasured at the exchange rate on that date

(B)   Subsequently, any foreign currency monetary balances (cash, receivables, payables, and assets and liabilities reported at market value) must be remeasured at new current exchange rates.

(1)   Monetary accounts could be remeasured every day but for convenience they are remeasured at the time of subsequent transactions (a payable is collected, for example) and at the end of the fiscal period.

(2)   Any time that a monetary account is remeasured and the value changes a gain or loss is computed that is reported on the income statement (and not within the stockholders' equity).

(C)   All other accounts (such as inventory, buildings, common stock, revenues, etc.) remain at historical rates and never change. For a remeasurement, that rate is the date of the initial transaction. Thus, depreciation uses the historical rate when the asset was bought; cost of goods sold is based on the rate when the inventory was acquired.

PROBLEMS AND SOLUTIONS
FOREIGN CURRENCY BALANCES

ONE - A company has depreciation expense on its financial records of 1,000 vilsecks (a foreign currency) because of machinery bought in a foreign country. This company is now preparing financial statements and wants to state the Depreciation Expense balance in terms of U.S. dollars. There are two different methods that can be used to determine the balance to be reported in U.S. dollars. (True or False?)

Answer – For reporting purposes, any foreign currency balance (such as depreciation expense) can be stated in U.S. dollars by either (1) the translation process or (2) the remeasurement process. However, if the exchange rate between the reporting currency and the foreign currency never changes, these methods give identical results. Differences are only created when the relative value of the currencies varies over time. (Number One is True.)

TWO - A company buys inventory from a retailer in a foreign country. Based on this transaction, the company has both an Inventory balance and an Accounts Payable balance for 10,000 vilsecks (a foreign currency). In preparing financial statements, the company must state both balances in terms of U.S. dollars. For this situation, the company has to use the translation process in order to report these balances. (True or False?)

Answer – Whenever balances have been created as a result of individual transactions (such as a purchase or a sale) that are outside of a company's functional currency, the foreign currency figures should be reported in terms of U.S. dollars by means of the remeasurement process. Balances created by individual transactions of the reporting entity require remeasurement. (Number Two is False.)

THREE - Company A (a U.S. company) owns 100 percent of the outstanding common stock of company Z, an enterprise that is located in England. Consolidated financial statements are now to be produced for these companies. The functional currency for company A is the U.S. dollar and the functional currency for company Z is the British pound. Company Z has account balances denominated in British pounds. These balances must be stated in terms of U.S. dollars in order for consolidated financial statements to be produced. In this situation, the remeasurement process will be necessary to state these foreign currency balances in terms of U.S. dollars so that consolidated statements can be produced. (True or False?)

Answer – The translation process is required in this situation. The translation process is appropriate when (1) consolidated financial statements are being produced, (2) the subsidiary has balances denominated in a foreign currency, and (3) the parent and the subsidiary have different functional currencies. Because these three criteria have all been met here, translation rather than remeasurement is appropriate. (Number Three is False.)

FOUR - A company holds a receivable balance denominated in a foreign currency. For translation purposes, the current exchange rate will be used. For remeasurement purposes, the historic exchange rate (the rate when the balance was created) will be used. (True or False?)

Answer – In a translation, all assets and liabilities are stated in terms of the functional currency by using the current exchange rate (as of the date of the reporting). The receivable falls into this category; thus, the current rate is appropriate. In a remeasurement, only monetary and market value assets and liabilities utilize the current exchange rate. However, because the receivable is a monetary asset, the current rather than the historic rate would be applied. (Number Four is False.)

FIVE - A company acquired a building several years ago using a foreign currency. For translation purposes, the current exchange rate will be used to report the cost of this Building account. For remeasurement purposes, the historic exchange rate (the rate when the balance was created) is appropriate to report this Building account. (True or False?)

Answer – In a translation, all assets and liabilities are stated in terms of the functional currency by using the current exchange rate (as of the date of the reporting). A Building account falls into this category so that the current rate is appropriate. In a remeasurement, only monetary and market value assets and liabilities utilize the current exchange rate. The building represents a nonmonetary asset; thus, the historic rate is applied. (Number Five is True.)

SIX - A company buys inventory costing 100,000 vilsecks (a foreign currency) on December 1, Year One, when 20 vilsecks were equal to $1.00. Both inventory and accounts payable were initially remeasured as $5,000. On December 31, Year One, the inventory is still held and no payment has yet been made on the account payable. The value of the currencies has changed so that 25 vilsecks are now worth $1.00. If the company is producing statements in terms of the U.S. dollar (its functional currency), the inventory will still be reported at $5,000 but the account payable will now be shown as only $4,000. The company should also report a gain on its income statement of $1,000. (True or False?)

Answer - Because this is an individual transaction outside of the company's functional currency, remeasurement is appropriate. The account payable is a monetary liability and will be reported using the current exchange rate; the inventory is a nonmonetary balance that should be remeasured using the historic rate. As a monetary balance, the account payable will be reported at different balances as the exchange rate changes. In a remeasurement, this movement creates gains and losses to be reported on the income statement. The Account Payable account changed during Year One from $5,000 to $4,000. The drop in the value of the monetary liability creates a $1,000 gain to be shown on the company's income statement. In contrast, inventory is nonmonetary and the reported value will never change. Without a change in value, no gain or loss is created. (Number Six is True.)

SEVEN - A company is translating balances from a foreign subsidiary in preparing consolidated financial statements. The exchange rate has changed so that some balances are being translated at the new current rate. This process can lead to either an increase or a decrease in net income. (True or False?)

Answer – In a translation, no net income effect is produced. The net impact of changing asset and liability balances to the current exchange rate is accumulated and reported as a Translation Adjustment account within the stockholders' equity section of the balance sheet. Thus, net income is not impacted as a result of a translation. However, the change in the translation adjustment during the year will be a factor used in converting net income for the period to comprehensive income. (Number Seven is False.)

DISPOSAL OF A COMPONENT

(1) A component of a business has operations and cash flows that are clearly distinguished from the rest of the entity.

(2) If an entire segment is sold, all income effects relating to it must be shown at the bottom of the income statement (net of taxes) before extraordinary gains and losses. This section is often referred to as **Discontinued Operations.**

    (A) The income or loss from discontinued operations includes the loss or income of the component for the period, and the gain or loss on disposal.

    (B) The component is classified as discontinued operations in the first period that it meets the criteria as being "held for sale."

    (C) All figures on past income statements related to the segment must be separated and dropped to the bottom of each income statement. This reporting does not change reported income just classification.

PROBLEMS AND SOLUTIONS
DISPOSAL OF A SEGMENT

ONE - A component of a business is one with operations and cash flows that are clearly distinguished from the rest of the entity. (True or False?)

> *Answer – A component of a business that is held for sale may be presented as discontinued operations. A component of a business is one with operations and cash flows that are clearly distinguished from the rest of the entity. (Number One is True.)*

TWO - A company has sold a component of its business and will report the results of discontinued operations at the bottom of the income statement. The amount should include the income from operations and the loss on disposal net of taxes. (True or False?)

> *Answer – When a business component meets the requirement of being held for sale, it should be presented as discontinued operations. The results of operations and gain or loss on disposal should be presented, net of taxes. (Number Two is True.)*

REPORTING SEGMENTS OF AN ENTERPRISE

(1)   Company should first identify its **operating segments** based on the method the management uses to disaggregate the enterprise for the making of internal operating decisions. The factors used to determine these segments must be disclosed.

    (A)   Each operating segment must be engaged in business activities from which it earns revenues (even if only internally) and incurs expenses.

    (B)   The operating results of each operating segment must be reviewed individually by the chief operating decision-maker within the company.

    (C)   Some components of a company (central headquarters, for example, or the research and development department) may not be within any operating segment because they do not generate revenues.

    (D)   Segments may be combined if they have the same activities in the same geographic region even if company disaggregates them for internal reporting purposes.

(2)   Company must disclose information about each operating segment of a significant size. Three tests are applied and every segment that meets at least one of these tests must be included in the disclosure.

    (A)   **Revenue test** – any segment is viewed as significant if its revenue makes up 10 percent or more of the company's total. Both sales to outsiders and intersegment revenues are included.

    (B)   **Profit and loss test** – any segment is viewed as significant if its profit or loss is 10 percent of the greater of the profits of all profitable segments or the losses of all losing segments.

    (C)   **Asset test** – any segment is viewed as significant if its assets make up 10 percent or more of the company's total.

(3)   Certain disclosures are required for the company as a whole even if the company only identifies itself as having one operating segment.

    (A)   Revenue generated from external customers for each product and service.

    (B)   For domestic operations, revenues from external customers and the amount of long-lived assets. The same disclosure is required for foreign operations.

    (C)   Revenues and assets for any specific foreign country must also be disclosed if material.

    (D)   If 10 percent or more of consolidated revenues come from a single customer, that fact must be disclosed. For this test, a group of customers under common control is viewed as a single customer.

PROBLEMS AND SOLUTIONS
REPORTING SEGMENTS OF AN ENTERPRISE

ONE - In identifying operating segments for disclosure purposes, a company is required to use both an industry approach (to identify segments by product or service) and a geographic approach. (True or False?)

Answer – A company must use a management approach to determine its operating segments. Segments should be identified in the same way that management organizes the segments internally to make operating decisions and assess performance. (Number One is False.)

TWO - Extensive disclosure about the operating segments of an enterprise is required for each segment that is viewed to be of significant size. In order to determine whether a segment is significant in size, three tests have been devised. (True or False?)

Answer – In determining whether an operating segment is of significant size to warrant separate disclosure, three tests have been created: a revenue test, an operating profit or loss test, and an identifiable assets test. (Number Two is True.)

THREE - In order to ascertain whether an operating segment is of significant size to require disclosure, three tests have been created. A segment must meet all three of these tests to be considered of significant size. (True or False?)

Answer – An operating segment need only meet one of these three tests to be viewed as significant in size so that separate disclosure is required. (Number Three is False.)

FOUR - A company has $100,000 in sales to outside parties and $20,000 in intersegment sales. In determining whether a segment is of significant size, both the sales to outsiders as well as the intersegment sales are taken into consideration. (True or False?)

Answer – In deciding if an operating segment is significant, both sales to outsiders and intersegment sales are included. Thus, any segment in this company with total sales (either to outsiders or intersegment) of $12,000 or more (10 percent of the company total) would warrant disclosure. (Number Four is True.)

GOVERNMENTAL ACCOUNTING – FUND ACCOUNTING AND FINANCIAL STATEMENTS

(1) Because of the many and diverse activities of a state or local government (police and fire departments, airports, zoos, highway construction, etc.), the accounting and reporting functions are divided into a number of different funds. Each fund accounts for a specific activity and has its own unique accounting principles.

    (A) **Fund accounting** promotes **financial accountability** which is an underlying objective of government reporting. Readers of the financial statements should be able to determine the allocation of resources made to each activity and the use that the activity makes of those resources.

    (B) All funds are classified as either (1) governmental funds for public services, (2) proprietary funds where a user charge is assessed, or (3) fiduciary funds to report assets that will eventually be conveyed to a party outside of the government.

(2) Traditionally, much of government accounting (in the governmental funds) has emphasized the measurement of the **financial resources** held by each activity and the inflow and outflow of those financial resources. The accounting process was designed to monitor the source of these resources, how those resources were used by the fund, and what resources are currently held. **Modified accrual accounting** was used to determine the proper timing for recognition by recording financial resources when they became both measurable and available.

    (A) Financial resources are basically monetary assets (cash, receivables, and investments). Under this approach, liabilities are only recognized if they represent claims that require the use of current financial resources.

    (B) Focusing on financial resources allows readers to see the utilization made by government officials of the public's money. In addition, it provided a measure of **interperiod equity**, the surplus or deficit carried over to future years. For example, if financial resources generated during a period will not cover expenditures, money has to be borrowed and then repaid by taxpayers in future years.

(3) State and local governments must now report two separate sets of financial statements.

    (A) **Government-wide financial statements** move away from the financial resource approach to reporting. Instead, these statements measure all **economic resources** (all assets and all liabilities) and utilize **accrual accounting** to establish the timing of revenue and expense recognition. Thus, these statements are produced in much the same way as the statements of a for-profit business.

        (1) At least three basic columns are shown in each of the government-wide statements: a column for government activities, a column for business-type activities, and a total column. Interactivity transactions between the activities in the first two columns are shown as internal balances and eliminated in arriving at the total column.

            (a) **Governmental activities** are made up of the governmental funds. Thus, in contrast to the traditional approach to reporting, these statements measure economic resources and apply accrual accounting to the governmental funds. Most internal service funds (one of the proprietary funds) are also included as governmental activities. Any transactions between the internal service funds and the governmental funds must be eliminated, though, to avoid any double counting.

 (b) **Business-type activities** are made up of the enterprise funds which is another category within the proprietary funds.

 (c) Fiduciary funds are not reported in the government-wide financial statements because these assets must be conveyed to a party outside of the government and, therefore, are not available to be used by the government.

(2) **Statement of net assets** reports all assets and all liabilities of the governmental activities and the business-type activities (along with a total column). The difference in these assets and liabilities is known as "total net assets" and is reported within three classifications: (1) capital assets net of related debt, (2) restricted net assets that have to be used in a particular fashion, and (3) unrestricted net assets that can be used in any way.

(3) **Statement of activities** reports all revenues and expenses of the governmental activities and the business-type activities.

 (a) Direct expenses are shown by function such as "general government" and "public safety." Depreciation expense is recognized and allocated to the specific functions.

 (b) For each function, **program revenues** are netted against these expenses to arrive at individual net revenue or net expense figures. Program revenues include charges for services and grants received. For example, "health and sanitation" should net any charge received for trash collection against the direct expenses of this function to determine a net revenue or expense figure, a measure of the burden or benefit of providing this service.

 (c) A total of the net figures for all of the functions is determined and then **general revenues** are added. General revenues include property taxes and other revenues such as investment income that are not associated with a specific function.

 (d) **Special items** are also included to arrive at a "change in net assets" for the governmental activities, the business-type activities and the total government. Special items are transactions within the control of management that are either unusual in nature or infrequent in occurrence.

(B) **Fund-based financial statements** are also created to present information about each fund type. The method of reporting varies according to the type of fund being reported.

(1) For the governmental funds, a balance sheet and a statement of revenues, expenditures, and changes in fund balance are produced. These statements reflect traditional government accounting: they measure financial resources and the flow of financial resources while the timing of recognition is based on modified accrual accounting.

 (a) The **balance sheet** shows current financial resources and claims on current financial resources. The difference in these assets and liabilities is known as the "Fund Balance" and can be classified as Reserved or Unreserved based on the government's ability to make use of the financial resources. Capital assets and long-term debts are not reported.

    (b)   The **statement of revenues, expenditures, and changes in fund balance** reports, revenues, expenditures, other financing sources, other financing uses, and special items. Because expenditures are reflected here, expenses (including depreciation expense) are not reported. Capital asset outlays and long-term debt payments are reported as expenditures because they use up current financial resources.

    (c)   For these fund-based financial statements, a separate column is shown for the General Fund and any other governmental fund that is considered major. All nonmajor governmental funds are accumulated into a single column. A **major fund** is one that makes up 10 percent or more of the governmental funds and 5 percent or more of the governmental funds plus the enterprise funds.

    (d)   Because of the wide differences between the reporting for these funds in the two sets of statements, data should be presented to show how the totals for the governmental activities found on the government-wide statements reconciles with the governmental fund figures shown on the fund-based financial statements.

    (2)   For the proprietary funds, a statement of net assets is reported along with a statement of revenues, expenses, and changes in fund net assets and a statement of cash flows.

    (a)   These statements measure economic resources according to accrual accounting in the same way as in the government-wide statements.

    (b)   A separate column is shown for each enterprise fund and for the internal service funds as a whole.

    (c)   The cash flow statement has four classifications: operating activities (only the direct method can be used), noncapital financing activities (such as operating grants), capital and related financing activities (major construction and the debt incurred to finance it), and investing activities (buying and selling of investments).

    (3)   For the fiduciary funds, statement of net assets is reported along with a statement of changes in net assets.

    (4)   **Governmental Funds** account for public services (police department, fire department, and the like). There are five separate fund types within the governmental funds. These funds traditionally measure financial resources although a conversion to economic resources is necessary for government-wide financial statements. When measuring financial resources, no capital assets or long-term debts are reported. In addition, expenditures are reported when financial resources are reduced because of expenses, capital asset acquisitions, and long-term debt payments.

    (A)   The **General Fund** is used when no other fund is appropriate. It is commonly utilized to record the receipts and expenditures of financial resources by on-going public service activities such as the fire department, police department, ambulance service, etc.

(1)　Most of the unique characteristics normally associated with governmental accounting can be found in the General Fund. Budgets and encumbrances are recorded. Expenditures are recognized for fixed asset and expense costs as well as payments on long-term liabilities.

(2)　Because capital assets are omitted from the governmental funds, no depreciation is recognized.

(B)　**Special Revenue Funds** account for the receipt and expenditure of financial resources earmarked for specific operating purposes. For example, cash collected from a special tax, toll, or grant where the money must be used for a designated operating purpose would be recorded in this fund. In addition, this fund is used for gifts made to the government where both principal and any income must be utilized for a specified purpose.

(C)　**Capital Projects Funds** account for the receipt and expenditure of financial resources relating to construction or acquisition of long-lived assets. Because constructed assets are not financial resources, the actual asset is not recorded within this or any other governmental fund. Instead, the Capital Projects Fund measures the inflow and outflow of financial resources for a particular project.

(D)　**Debt Service Funds** account for the receipt and expenditure of financial resources for the payment of long-term debts and related interest. Long-term debts are not recorded in this fund until they require the use of current financial resources.

(E)　**Permanent Funds** account for resources (frequently gifts) where the principal cannot be spend but any subsequent income can be used, often for a designated purpose.

(5)　**Proprietary Funds** account for services that are financed (at least in part) by user charges. Accounting and reporting procedures are virtually identical to those found in profit oriented businesses. As with any business, they use accrual accounting and report revenues, expenses, fixed assets, depreciation, long-term liabilities, retained earnings, etc. They are designed to measure the flow of economic resources.

(A)　**Enterprise Funds** offer services to the public for a fee such as a golf course, bus service, swimming pool, etc.

(1)　Most government officials are allowed to use an enterprise fund for accounting purposes whenever an activity has a user charge.

(2)　Government officials must use an enterprise fund for accounting purposes when any one of the following occurs: the pricing policy for fees is set to recover costs, regulations specify that fees are supposed to recover costs, or debts are secured solely by the revenues generated by the activity.

(B)　**Internal Service Funds** offer services to other areas of the government for a fee such as a print shop, data processing center, motor pool, etc. As indicated, for government-wide financial statements, the internal service funds are normally included within the governmental activities after elimination of any internal exchange transactions.

(6)　**Fiduciary Funds** account for money being held by a government for a specific purpose. Use of these assets is not at the discretion of the government.

(A)　**Agency Funds** hold money to be turned over to a person or to some other government (such as money withheld from employees for social security).

(1)　Normally, only has two accounts balances: cash and the related liability. No revenues, expenses, or expenditures are reported.

(B) **Pension Trust Funds** hold money for employee retirement plans.

(C) **Investment Trust Funds** record external investment pools. Governments will sometimes pool their investments in hopes of earning a higher rate of return. Thus, a government could be holding investments actually owned by another government. If so, those investments are reported in an investment trust fund.

(D) **Private-purpose Trust Funds** record property being held for the benefit of individuals, organizations, or other governments. For example, if a person dies without heirs and a will, any property may be held in this fund until disposition occurs. Confiscated property would also be monitored in this fund.

PROBLEMS AND SOLUTIONS
GOVERNMENTAL ACCOUNTING – FUND
ACCOUNTING AND FINANCIAL STATEMENTS

ONE – A city or state government must prepare and report two entirely different sets of financial statements within its general-purpose financial statements. (True or False?)

Answer – A city or state government must produce both a governmental-wide set of financial statements for the government as a whole and a fund-based set of statements to show information broken down by funds. (Number One is True.)

TWO – In government-wide financial statements, all of the funds of the government are included. (True or False?)

Answer – Government-wide financial statements report the economic resources that can be used by the government. Hence, fiduciary funds are not included because those resources are for the benefit of parties outside of the government. All of the governmental funds and the proprietary funds do appear in the government-wide financial statements but the fiduciary funds are omitted. (Number Two is False.)

THREE – On government-wide financial statements, two columns are shown: one for governmental funds and one for proprietary funds. (True or False?)

Answer – On the government-wide statements, the activities of the government are classified as either "governmental activities" and "business-type activities." A total for the government is also shown. (Number Three is False.)

FOUR – Government-wide financial statements report governmental activities as well as business-type activities. The business-type activities are comprised of the two proprietary funds: the Enterprise Funds and the Internal Service Funds. (True or False?)

Answer – Enterprise Funds are also included as business-type activities on the government-wide financial statements. However, the Internal Service Funds are usually part of the governmental activities. Internal Service Funds are only shown as part of the business-type activities if their services are primarily rendered to Enterprise Funds. (Number Four is False.)

FIVE – On government-wide financial statements, current assets, capital assets, current liabilities, and long-term liabilities are shown for both the governmental activities and the business-type activities. (True or False?)

Answer – Government-wide financial statements are designed to measure economic resources and the changes in those economic resources. Therefore, all assets and all liabilities are reported. (Number Five is True.)

SIX – On government-wide financial statements, a statement of activities reports revenues and expenses. Revenues should be divided between program revenues and general revenues. (True or False?)

Answer – Program revenues are derived from a particular function. For example, speeding tickets created program revenues for the police department. Each reported function should net its program revenues with its expenses to determine the net burden or benefit to the government. The total net burden or benefit is determined and then combined with the government's general revenues (such as property taxes) that are not created by a specific function. In this way, the actual cost of each function is more clearly reported. (Number Six is True.)

SEVEN – On the fund-based financial statements for the governmental funds, a separate column is reported for each fund type such as the Debt Service Funds and the Capital Projects Funds. (True or False?)

Answer – When reporting the governmental funds on the fund-based statements, a separate column must be shown for the General Fund and for any other individual fund that is considered major (normally that it makes up 10 percent of all governmental funds). (Number Seven is False.)

EIGHT - On the balance sheet for the governmental funds within the fund-based financial statements, capital assets are not reported. (True or False?)

Answer – The governmental funds (for the fund-based statements) reports the amount of current financial resources on hand and the flow of those financial resources. Current financial resources are comprised primarily of cash, receivables, and investments. Therefore, on the balance sheet for these funds, no capital assets are reported since they are not current financial resources. In the same manner, liabilities are only reported if they are a claim against current financial resources. (Number Eight is True.)

NINE – There are four fund types within the governmental funds of a government. (True or False?)

> *Answer – For years there were four governmental fund types but recently a fifth has been added. The fund types are: General Fund (most ongoing service activities such as the fire department), Special Revenue Funds (financial resources specifically designed by an outside party for operating activities), Capital Projects Funds (financial resources for construction projects), Debt Service Funds (financial resources for payment of long-term liabilities), and Permanent Funds (financial resources where an outside party has specified that the principal cannot be spent, only the income). (Number Nine is False.)*

TEN – Both Enterprise Funds and Internal Service Funds are proprietary funds. As such they are accounted for in the fund-based financial statements in a way very similar to a for-profit business. An Enterprise Fund is an activity where a service is rendered to the public for a user charge. An Internal Service Fund is an activity where a service is rendered to other areas of the government for a user charge. (True or False?)

> *Answer – A subway system and a lottery are normally reported as Enterprise Funds. There is a user charge and the activity is open to the public. A government print shop and a supply room are Internal Service Funds. Again, there is a user charge but the service is provided mainly for other areas of the government and not to the public at large. (Number Ten is True.)*

GOVERNMENTAL ACCOUNTING – FINANCIAL REPORTING PROCESS

(1)   Governmental funds will normally measure current financial resources for internal reporting purposes and for the fund-based financial statements. These figures will be converted to the measurement of economic resources in order to produce the government-wide financial statements. The proprietary funds measure economic resources internally so that no similar conversion is necessary.

(2)   To stress the stewardship function of a government, a **budgetary journal entry** is physically recorded at the start of the fiscal year by the general fund and several other governmental funds. For the particular activity, it shows where resources will come from (debits) and what will be done with these resources (credits).

   (A)   An Estimated Revenues account is debited and an Appropriations (approved expenditures) account is credited. In addition, Estimated Other Financing Sources is debited and Estimated Other Financing Uses is credited (to record expected transfers and bond proceeds).

   (B)   To balance this entry, a **Budgetary Fund Balance** account (or just a Fund Balance account) is established

      (1)   A debit to this account indicates an anticipated deficit for the year whereas a credit indicates that a surplus is expected.

      (2)   The use of the term "control" with these or any other accounts means that a separate subsidiary ledger is being kept to provide more detailed information about the entries made to that specific account.

   (C)   The budgetary entry stays within the accounting system during the year and is then reversed off the books at the end of the year.

   (D)   Within the **comprehensive annual financial report**, this budgetary information is formally reported as required supplemental information (RSI). For the general fund and any other major special revenue fund that legally adopts a budget, the original budget is presented along with a final amended budget and the actual figures for the year. Rather than present this as RSI, a separate financial statement can also be presented to provide the same data.

(3)   Some governmental funds record commitments as **encumbrances**. To prevent overspending, commitments such as contracts and purchase orders are recorded when made. This is unique to governments; in a business, no formal entry is made for a commitment.

   (A)   Entry is a debit to an Encumbrances account and a credit to a Reserved for Encumbrances account (sometimes called Budgetary Fund Balance-Reserved for Encumbrances).

   (B)   When commitment becomes a liability, the encumbrance entry is reversed off the books and liability is recognized. If liability is a different amount than was expected, the original Encumbrance balance is still removed.

   (C)   Encumbrances are not reported on the government-wide financial statements. However, for the fund-based statements, recognition may be necessary for any encumbrances remaining at the end of the year. If the government plans to honor these outstanding commitments, a portion of the Fund Balance on the balance sheet is reported as Reserved for Encumbrance. This indicates that no liability yet exists but a portion of the financial resources must be held to satisfy the commitment.

(4)   On the government-wide financial statements, expenses are recognized along with asset acquisitions and debt payments. However, on the fund-based financial statements, governmental funds measure financial resources. Thus, outflows of financial resources for expenses, capital asset acquisition, and the payment of long-term debt are all monitored in an **Expenditures** account. Expenses, capital assets, and long-term debts are not separately recorded. The recognition of an expenditure is normally made when the cost becomes a legal liability. At that point, financial resources are reduced.

    (A)   For reporting purposes, expenditures can be classified in several different ways: by function (education and safety), by unit (fire department and police department), by activity (police administration and police training), by character (capital outlay and debt service), or by object (supplies and rent).

    (B)   Although depreciation expense is recognized in the government-wide financial statements, it is not reported by the governmental funds in the fund-based statements because it does not affect current financial resources.

    (C)   On government-wide statements, when a capital asset is sold, its cost and accumulated depreciation are both moved from the records and a gain or loss is recognized for the difference between the amount received and the net book value. On fund-based financial statements. A revenue is recognized for the total amount received; the capital asset was not recorded and cannot be removed.

(5)   **Capital assets** are recorded on government-wide financial statements at cost and then depreciated over their useful lives. If received by donation, they are reported at fair market value when received. For governmental funds, on the fund-based financial statements, expenditures are reported so that capital assets do not appear and depreciation is not appropriate.

    (A)   Artworks and historical treasures can be received as donations. In such cases, a revenue must be recorded based on fair market value if all eligibility requirements have been met.

    (B)   Recording of the asset in the government-wide statements is optional if three criteria are met: (1) the property is used for public exhibition, education, or research and not for financial gain, (2) the property is protected and preserved, and (3) there is a policy that the proceeds of any sale will be used to buy other items for the collection.

    (C)   If these criteria are met and the government chooses not to record the asset, an expense must be recognized to offset the reported revenue.

(6)   **Infrastructure assets** are stationary and have a relatively long life if properly maintained. Infrastructure includes bridges, roads, sidewalks and the like.

    (A)   All new infrastructure items must be capitalized at cost on the government-wide financial statements and depreciated. For the governmental funds, on the fund-based financial statements, expenditures are recorded rather than the infrastructure assets.

    (B)   For the government-wide financial statements, a **modified approach** can be used to avoid recognizing depreciation. Under this approach, the government can set a desired condition level for each network of infrastructure. All costs to keep the infrastructure at that level are then recognized as expenses instead of reporting depreciation.

    (C)   Any infrastructure assets acquired prior to GASB Statement 34 do not have to be capitalized immediately. Most governments have an additional four years to determine a book value for these previous infrastructure assets.

(7)   All of the revenues of a state or local government can be divided into four general classifications. Recognition varies by classification. Rules below are for government-wide financial statements. If reporting is for a governmental fund on the fund-based financial statement, the financial resource must also be available.

   (A)   **Derived tax revenues** – this is an assessment on an underlying transaction or event. Examples include sales taxes and income taxes. Asset (receivable or cash) and revenue are recognized in the same time period as the underlying transaction.

   (B)   **Imposed nonexchange revenues** – this is an assessment on taxpayers that is not based on an underlying transaction or event. The best example is a property tax assessment. Asset is recognized when there is an enforceable legal claim (receivable) or cash is received if that is earlier. Revenue is recognized when the proceeds are required to be used or the first period in which use is permitted. For property taxes, revenue is recognized in the period for which the tax is levied. If the cash is received before it can be used, a deferred revenue is recognized.

   (C)   **Government-mandated nonexchange transactions** – this is usually a grant or similar receipt given to a government to help pay for the cost of a legally required action. For example, this category is appropriate if the state requires a city to clean up its river and also provides funding for that purpose. The asset and revenue are both reported when all eligibility requirements have been met. In some cases, the government must spend the money first and then apply for reimbursement. Revenues are recognized in these cases when the money is properly spent.

   (D)   **Voluntary nonexchange transactions** – this is grants and donations given to a government, often for a specified purpose. Once again, the asset and revenue are recognized when all eligibility requirements have been met. Any restriction on the funds should be disclosed by showing a restriction in the net assets (government-wide financial statements) and a fund balance reserved balance in the fund-based financial statement.

(8)   In the fund-based statements for the governmental funds, some changes in financial resources are neither revenues nor expenditures. For inflows, these transactions are recorded as **Other Financing Sources** (OFS); for outflows, the title **Other Financing Uses** (OFU) is applied. This does not apply to government-wide financial statements because they do not focus on financial resources.

   (A)   A common OFS is the inflow of cash from the issuance of a bond. The governmental fund getting. The proceeds will debit cash and credit OFS. If the debt is not long-term, the liability rather than the OFS is reported. For the government-wide financial statements, cash is debited and the liability is always credited.

   (B)   Governments often transfer money from one fund to another. Recording of these transfers depends on purpose.

       (1)   **Operating transfers** are made to move unrestricted funds in response to decisions made by government officials. Fund getting the financial resources records inflow as an Other Financing Source; fund giving up the resources records outflow as an Other Financing Use. Any such transfers are eliminated on the government-wide financial statements (as internal balances) but not on the fund based financial statements.

       (2)   **Quasi-external transactions** (or **internal exchange transactions**) are transfers (usually to an Internal Service Fund) to pay for work done or

services performed. Fund getting money records inflow as a Revenue; fund losing the money records outflow as an Expenditure. These balances remain on the fund-based statements but are removed on the government-wide financial statements if the internal service funds are reported within the governmental activities.

(9)   A government can acquire assets though lease, arrangements that must frequently be capitalized.

    (A)   The criteria for requiring **capitalization of a lease** are same as used in a for-profit business.

    (B)   For government-wide financial statements, the reporting is the same as a business: the asset is reported at the present value of the minimum lease payments and subsequently depreciated over the period of use. The liability is also recorded at present value. Each payment is partially recognized as interest expense (if time has passed) with the remainder serving to reduce the liability principal.

    (C)   On fund-based financial statements, if the lease is acquired by a governmental fund, both an expenditure and an other financing source are recorded for the present value of all minimum lease payments. When payments are subsequently made, an expenditure is recorded, part for interest and part for the principal.

(10)   Government employees can earn amounts for vacations, holidays, and the like. When financial statements are being produced, any amounts due to employees for such **compensated absences** should be recognized if based on past services.

    (A)   For government-wide financial statements, the expense is recognized as the liability is incurred.

    (B)   In reporting governmental funds on the fund-based financial statements, an expenditure is recognized along with a liability but only for the amount of the debt that will be paid from current financial resources.

(11)   Construction (such as sidewalks or other improvements) may be made and charged in whole or in part to the owners of the property being benefited. These are called **special assessment projects**.

    (A)   If the government has no obligation at all for the work, the money just flows through the government from the property owners to pay for the services. All recording is restricted to an Agency Fund so that no expenditures, revenues, expenses, or capital assets are reported by the government.

    (B)   If the government has any obligation, even if it is only secondarily liable, the cost of the project is recorded as a regular construction project.

        (1)   For the government-wide financial statements, the capital asset is recorded at cost along with any related debt. This capital asset is depreciated over its estimated life. Collections from property owners are recorded as revenues.

        (2)   For the fund-based financial statements, an expenditure is recorded within the Capital Projects Funds. The proceeds from any debt issued to finance the project are reported as an other financing source whereas money paid on any long-term debt is an expenditure. Cash received from the property owners is shown as a revenue.

(12)   In government-wide financial statements, **supplies** and **prepaid expenses** are reported as in a for-profit business: the asset is recorded at cost and reclassified to expense as it is used. However, for fund-based financial statements, supplies and prepaid expenses cause

special reporting problems because they are neither financial resources nor capital assets. On the fund-based statements, there are two ways that can be used to report such assets.

(A) **Consumption method** records cost as an asset when acquired and then reclassifies this amount to an Expenditures account as the asset is consumed either by use or over time. At the end of the year, if any asset is still being reported, an equal amount of the unreserved fund balance should be switched to a fund balance—reserved for supplies (or prepaid items) to show that a portion of the assets being reported is not a financial resource which can be spent.

(B) **Purchases method** records entire cost as an expenditure when purchased. Any asset remaining at the end of the year is put directly onto the balance sheet, with an offsetting entry to a Fund Balance - Reserved for Supplies (or Prepaid Items) account.

(13) Governments often operate **solid waste landfills** and are responsible for eventual clean up costs. When a landfill reaches its total capacity, the government will have to expend funds to close and clean the site. Thus, a liability is incurred as every landfill is being used.

(A) A landfill can be recorded in an enterprise fund if there is a user charge or in the general fund if the landfill is open to the public.

(B) In the government-wide financial statements (and in the separate proprietary funds statements if accounted for in an enterprise fund), a liability should be accrued over the years based on the percentage of space that is filled. The liability to be reported is the percentage of the landfill capacity that is full times the estimated closure and postclosure costs. The annual adjustment to the liability is reported as an expense.

(C) If the landfill is reported in the general fund, the accounting on the fund-based financial statements will be different. Nothing is reported unless current financial resources are used or will be used. No long-term liability appears in the fund-based financial statements for the governmental funds.

(14) Investments in stocks and bonds must be recorded at fair market value. **Unrealized gains and losses** are reported along with realized gains and losses as a single number. Since investments are current financial resources, the accounting in the government-wide financial statements and the fund-based financial statements is basically the same.

(15) A **comprehensive annual financial report** (CAFR) must be produced by every reporting entity.

(A) A reporting entity is made up of a **primary government** and its **component units**. To qualify as a primary government, three criteria must be met: (1) – it has a separately elected governing body, (2) it is a legally separate entity, and (3) it is fiscally independent of other governments (its officials can pass its budget, set its tax rates, and issue bonded debt without approval).

(1) A component unit is a legally separate entity from the primary government but elected officials of the primary government are still financially accountable for the component unit. A museum operating within a city might be an example if city officials must approve the museum's budget.

(2) Usually, the financial figures for a component unit are shown in the government-wide financial statements but to the far right side so as to separate them from the funds of the primary government. These are called **discretely presented component units**.

(3)   A **blended component unit** is one that is so closely intertwined with the primary government that it is shown within the primary government's funds rather than being separately shown to the far right of the statement.

(B)   A special-purpose government is one that meets the criteria for a government but has specified functions such as some school systems. The reporting of such governments resembles that of a primary government except that it may have only governmental activities or business-type activities.

(16)   The first part of the CAFR is the general purpose external financial statements that can also be issued by themselves. The general purpose statements are required to have each of the following items.

(A)   **Management's Discussion and Analysis (MD&A)** - The MD&A provides a verbal explanation from city officials of the government's operations and financial position to help readers understand the measurements and results appearing in the statements.

(B)   Both sets of financial statements: **government-wide financial statements** and the **fund-based financial statements**. The two government-wide financial statements and the seven fund-based statements are identified above.

(C)   Notes to the financial statements.

(D)   **Required supplemental information (RSI)** – for example, the budgetary information described above would usually be included in this section as well as a description of the modified approach if it is being used.

(E)   In the CAFR, other information is presented beyond just these general purpose external financial statements such as combining statements for the various funds and statistical information.

(17)   Public colleges and universities are not-for-profit organizations but must following the accounting and reporting standards described above for state and local government units.

PROBLEMS AND SOLUTIONS
GOVERNMENTAL ACCOUNTING – FINANCIAL REPORTING PROCESS

ONE - In recording a budgetary entry at the beginning of a year, a governmental fund makes a debit to an Estimated Revenues account and a credit to an Appropriations account. (True or False?)

Answer – To record the budget for a governmental fund, the Estimated Revenues account is increased through a debit whereas the Appropriations account is increased through a credit. Estimated Other Financing Sources and Estimated Other Financing Uses may also be recorded. (Number One is True.)

TWO - The fire department is reported by a government within its General Fund. On Monday, the fire department orders a computer for $7,600. The computer is received on Friday at an actual cost of $7,700. In connection with producing fund-based financial statements, an Encumbrance account should be recorded on Monday and then the $7,600 should be removed on Friday. (True or False?)

Answer - Encumbrances are entered into the accounting records under certain circumstances to indicate that a fund has made a commitment of current financial resources. When the order for the computer was placed, the fire department made a commitment and an encumbrance is recorded. On Friday, the computer is received so that the commitment has become an actual liability. The encumbrance (the commitment) should be removed at that point in time at the amount that had been put on the books. (Number Two is True.)

THREE - A fire department orders a computer on Monday at an anticipated cost of $2,200. The computer is received on Friday at an actual cost of $2,240. The activities of the fire department are being recorded within the General Fund and fund-based financial statements are being developed. On Friday, an increase should be made to an Expenditures account for $2,240 along with a decrease to Cash (or an increase in Vouchers Payable if payment is to be made later). (True or False?)

Answer – Normally, whenever the current financial resources of a fund are reduced, an Expenditures account is reported. In connection with the acquisition of the computer, the payment of cash or the creation of a voucher payable will reduce the current financial resources of the fund so that an expenditure should be recorded. (Number Three is True.)

FOUR – In preparing fund-based financial statements, an expenditure is reported by a governmental fund when a transaction occurs to (1) acquire a capital asset, (2) incur an expense, or (3) pay a long-term liability. (True or False?)

Answer - In each of these three situations, the current financial resources of the fund have been reduced so that an expenditure should be recognized. The acquisition of a capital asset is recorded in a governmental fund as an expenditure. Incurring an expense is also recorded in that manner as is paying a long-term liability. (Number Four is True.)

FIVE – All of the revenues of a government can be divided into three different classifications: earned revenues, tax revenues, and grant revenues. (True or False?)

Answer – For reporting purposes, government revenues are placed in a classification system with four specific types of revenues: derived tax revenues, imposed nonexchange revenues, government-mandated nonexchange transactions, and voluntary nonexchange transactions. (Number Five is False.)

SIX – Sales taxes are viewed by a government as a derived tax revenue and should be recognized in the same period as the cash will be collected. (True or False?)

Answer – Sales taxes are classified as derived tax revenues. However, for derived tax revenues, governments should recognize the resulting revenue in the same period as the underlying transaction. For that reason, sales taxes are recognized in the same period as the sale. (Number Six is False.)

SEVEN – In Year One, a city government receives a grant from the state of $300,000 to help clean up the local river. After money is spent appropriately, the city will receive reimbursement from the state. The city spends $300,000 in Year Two and collects the money. The city should recognize the revenue in Year Two. (True or False?)

Answer – For both government-mandated nonexchange transactions and voluntary nonexchange transactions, revenues are reported when all eligibility requirements have been met. In this case, spending the money as specified is an eligibility requirement for reimbursement. Hence, the revenues cannot be recognized until the money is spent in the intended manner. (Number Seven is True.)

EIGHT - A government issues $2.3 million in long-term bonds for face value in order to finance construction of a new fire station. On the government-wide financial statements, both cash and long-term liabilities will be increased. In contrast, on fund-based financial statements, both cash and an Other Financing Sources account are increased. (True or False?)

Answer - Government-wide financial statements are much like those produced by a for-profit business. Issuing a bond increases both cash and the amount of long-term liabilities. However, for governmental funds being reported in the fund-based financial statements, only the amount and changes in current financial resources are reported. Long-term liabilities are not claims to current financial resources and are not reported. Thus, cash is increased but an "other financing source" is reported to indicate that the inflow came from a transaction other than a revenue. (Number Eight is True.)

NINE - The fiscal year for a particular city ends on December 31. On December 1, the city pays $3,000 to rent a facility for the next three months. The rental charge is $1,000 per month. The rental payment is made in connection with an activity accounted for within the governmental funds. Fund-based financial statements are being prepared. Assume that the consumption method is to be applied. At December 31, the city should report an Expenditure balance of $1,000 and a Prepaid Rent balance of $2,000. (True or False?)

Answer - Under the consumption method, prepaid expenses (as well as supplies) are recorded as expenditures at the time they are used. In this case, one month passes prior to year-end. Therefore, for fund-based financial statements, the expenditure is reported as $1,000 for that one month. The remaining $2,000 is shown as an asset even though it does not represent a current financial resource. On government-wide financial statements, the consumption is always applied except that an expense is reported rather than an expenditure. (Number Nine is True.)

TEN - A city operates a solid waste landfill. Any citizen or local company can use this facility. The landfill is reported as one of the Enterprise Funds because a user charge is assessed. The landfill should take ten years to be filled completely. At that time, the city will have to spend $200,000 to clean up the site. During Year One, 14 percent of the cubic space is filled. On fund-based financial statements, no liability is reported at this time because payment will not be made until the end of Year Ten. (True or False?)

Answer - The Enterprise Funds category is recorded like a for-profit business. Thus, its reporting is virtually the same on both government-wide financial statements and fund-based financial statements. As such, all long-term liabilities are reported. For a solid waste landfill, this liability is based on the percentage of space that has been filled to date. The liability is 14 percent of the total cost of $200,000 or $28,000. For Enterprise Funds, this liability is reported and the change in the liability is the expense to be reported each year. (Number Ten is False.)

ELEVEN – Equity investments owned by a government should be reported initially at cost and then adjusted to fair market value if that is below cost. (True or False?)

Answer – Investments in stocks and bonds owned by a government should be reported at fair market value. This recording is appropriate for both the fund-based financial statements and the government-wide financial statements. (Number Eleven is False.)

TWELVE - A component unit is an activity that is legally separate from a primary government. However, because of the close relationship of the component unit to the primary government, information about the unit must be presented through footnote disclosure. (True or False?)

Answer - A component unit is, indeed, an activity that is legally separate from a primary government. However, because the elected officials of the primary government are financially accountable for the separate organization, the financial results of a component unit are included on the face of the government-wide financial statements. This information is usually discretely presented to the far right side of each of the financial statements prepared by the primary government. However, if the activity is closely intertwined with the primary government, the financial information can actually be "blended" with that of the government. (Number Twelve is False.)

ACCOUNTING FOR NOT-FOR-PROFIT ORGANIZATIONS

(1)   Not-for-profit (NFP) organizations have several sources of authoritative accounting principles.

    (A)   Public colleges and universities such as the University of Virginia and the University of Kentucky follow the guidelines of the Governmental Accounting Standards Board (GASB). Financial reporting for these organizations follows the rules established above for governments and will not be discussed in this section.

    (B)   Private not-for-profit organizations such as the University of Richmond and the Heart Fund follow the guidelines of the Financial Accounting Standards Board (FASB). The rules described below are for private organizations.

    (C)   Private NFP's use **accrual accounting**. They record all capital assets and long-term debts. Neither budgetary entries nor encumbrances are formally recorded.

(2)   Financial statements are produced for NFPs to provide information for the various groups providing resources.

    (A)   The financial statements of a private NFP are designed to show the organization as a whole and are not intended to reflect fund accounting.

        (1)   **Statement of financial position** (balance sheet) reports all assets, all liabilities, and the balance of net assets (which is the "equity" section of the statement).

            (a)   In the Net Assets section, three totals are shown: unrestricted, temporarily restricted, and permanently restricted.

            (b)   The **unrestricted net asset** total discloses the amount of the organization's net assets (assets minus liabilities) that can be spent or used in any way that officials choose.

            (c)   The **temporarily restricted net asset** total indicates the amount of the net assets that has been restricted by the donor for a specific purpose or for a specific period of time.

            (d)   The **permanently restricted net asset** total is the amount of the net assets that has been restricted by the donor so that it must be held indefinitely. Usually income from these assets has to be used in a specified fashion.

        (2)   **Statement of activities** reports (usually in three columns) the changes during the current period in the amount of unrestricted net assets, temporarily restricted net assets, and permanently restricted net assets

            (a)   All three columns list increases first: revenues, gifts, gains and losses from sales, gains and losses in the value of investments, etc. Income generated on permanently restricted net assets is reported either in the temporarily restricted or the unrestricted net assets column depending on spending stipulations made by the donor.

            (b)   All expenses are listed solely in the column for unrestricted net assets. Expenses are reported by function: according to the specific program benefited or as support to operate the organization (fund raising and administrative costs). Depreciation expense is recorded by not-for-profit organizations.

            (c)   Just below the listing of increases, a line appears with a title such as **"net assets released from restrictions"** that shows an increase in unrestricted net assets and an equal decrease in temporarily restricted net assets. This figure reflects the amount of net assets that are no longer restricted because the funds were properly spent during the period or the time limitation was reached.

    (3)   Statement of cash flows looks like a statement produced by a for-profit business. It has three sections: operations, investing activities (asset transactions), and financing activities (liability and equity transactions).

(3)   The recording of **gifts** depends on whether the assets are unrestricted, temporarily restricted, or permanently restricted.

    (A)   A gift that has to be spent for a particular purpose (or that cannot be spent for a period of time) is recorded in the statement of activities as an increase in temporarily restricted net assets.

    (B)   When temporarily restricted amount is properly spent (or when required time passes), reclassification occurs: unrestricted net assets increase and temporarily restricted net assets decrease.

    (C)   Long-lived assets or other property received as gifts should be reported at fair market value on the date of the gift. Receipt of the asset can be recorded as an increase in unrestricted net assets. As an option, for long-lived assets, a time implied restriction can be presumed and the gifts can be reported as temporarily restricted net assets. If that is done, an amount equal to depreciation expense should be reclassified each period to reduce the temporarily restricted column and increase the unrestricted column. This same alternative is available if a long-lived asset is acquired with the use of temporarily restricted net assets.

(4)   NFPs often receive **pledges** of future gifts. If an unconditional promise of a future gift is made (the organization has no obligation to do anything), a receivable is recorded at present value. An allowance for uncollectible accounts is also set up as a contra account for any expected defaults. The difference is the increase in net assets shown on the statement of activities. This amount is viewed as unrestricted if it is to be collected this year and use has not been designated. However, it is temporarily restricted if it is to be received later. It is temporarily or permanently restricted if use has been designated.

(5)   Contributions can also be made of art works, museum pieces, etc. such as valuable paintings. No recording at all is required if (1) the items are used for research, education, or exhibition, (2) they are protected and preserved, and (3) if sold the money will be used to acquire similar items.

(6)   A donor can make a transfer to a NFP of assets that must be used or a separate specific beneficiary. Normally, at that point, the donor removes the asset from its records and recognizes an expense. The NFP recognizes the asset along with a related liability (rather than a contribution revenue) at the asset's fair market value while the eventual recipient recognizes an asset (usually a receivable) and a contribution revenue.

    (A)   However, if the donor retains the right to redirect the use of the assets or can revoke the gift, the donor continues to record the asset because it still has control. Once again, the NFP shows the asset along with a liability. The beneficiary makes no entry (until received) since the gift may never be obtained.

    (B)   If the NFP is given variance powers so that the beneficiary could be changed, the donor records an expense and removes the asset. Because of its control, the NFP recognizes the asset along with a contribution revenue (rather than a liability). The beneficiary will not recognize the asset until received because of the uncertainty. **Variance powers** means the NFP can ignore the donor's instructions about the gift without seeking further approval.

(7)   Contributions can also be made of **donated services**; a person can do work for an NFP organization for free or for a reduced payment.

    (A)   The value of the work donated is recorded as both a revenue and an expense but only if the work enhances a nonfinancial asset or it (1) requires a specialized skill, (2) is provided by people with that skill, and (3) would be bought if not otherwise provided.

    (B)   If these rules are not met, donated services are not recorded.

(8)   Private not-for-profit organizations often charge **membership dues**.

    (A)   If members receive substantive benefits for these dues, they should be recorded as membership revenues by the NFP.

    (B)   If members receive only negligible benefits for these dues, they should be reported as contribution revenues.

(9)   Investments in stocks and bonds are adjusted to fair market value at the end of each year. Increases and decreases appear on the statement of activities. The net asset column that is affected is based on the restrictions (if any) attached to the investments and their changes in value.

(10)   If students in colleges and universities are given **scholarships**, the entire tuition charge is recorded as a revenue. The scholarship is then recorded as a direct reduction to the revenue (rather than being reported separately as an expense). The two are netted together for reporting purposes.

(11)   Voluntary health and welfare organization (VHWOs) and other types of charities report a separate **statement of functional expenses** in order to provide additional information about the use made of money. This statement is allowed for all NFPs but is required of VHWOs. Expenses are split between "program service expenses" (doing the stated work of the charity) and "supporting service expenses" (operating the charity and fund raising).

(12)   If a charity issues a fund-raising mailing along with other information, all mailing costs are considered to be fund-raising expenses unless certain criteria are met. If there is a specific call for action and the mailing is not directed solely at potential donors, some of the mailing costs may be considered a program service cost.

PROBLEMS AND SOLUTIONS
ACCOUNTING FOR NOT-FOR-PROFIT ORGANIZATIONS

ONE - For a statement of financial position prepared for a private not-for-profit organization, a Net Assets section is reported rather than an Equity section. The Net Assets section is divided into three distinct sections. (True or False?)

Answer - The Net Assets section of the statement of financial position shows the amount of (1) unrestricted net assets, (2) temporarily restricted net assets, and (3) permanently restricted net assets. (Number One is True.)

TWO - The board of trustees of a private not-for-profit organization votes to set $800,000 in cash aside for the future acquisition of a new building. Based on this decision, the unrestricted net assets of the reporting entity are decreased by $800,000 while the temporarily restricted net assets are increased by $800,000. (True or False?)

Answer – This money is not subject to any donor restriction. Therefore, the entire $800,000 should remain within the unrestricted net assets although the amount may be labeled to indicate the intended use. The restricted categories are only used when donors have placed restrictions on the use of assets. (Number Two is False.)

THREE - A donor gives a private not-for-profit organization investments worth $300,000. The investments must be held forever although any subsequent income earned must be used to buy library books for children. During the initial year, income of $10,000 was generated but no books have yet been acquired. In the statement of activities, an increase of $310,000 should be shown in the permanently restricted net assets of the organization. (True or False?)

Answer - Although the $300,000 cannot be spent because of the donor restriction, the $10,000 should be used eventually for the purpose designated. Thus, in the statement of activities, permanently restricted net assets are increased by $300,000 whereas temporarily restricted net assets go up by $10,000. (Number Three is False.)

FOUR - Investments are bought at the beginning of the current year by a private not-for-profit organization. These investments are classified within unrestricted net assets. One of the investments is sold at a realized gain of $5,000. The other investments go up in value by $7,000. On its statement of activities, realized and unrealized gains of $12,000 should be reported. (True or False?)

Answer - Investments are reported by private not-for-profit organizations at fair market value. Thus, both the realized gain of $5,000 and the unrealized gain on market appreciation of $7,000 should be reported within the statement of activities. (Number Four is True.)

FIVE - A private not-for-profit organization receives unconditional promises from donors that amount to $10,000 and should be collected within a few months. The organization believes that 20 percent of these pledges will never be collected. Within the statement of activities, the organization will recognize net contributions of $8,000 as an increase under the category of revenues and other support. (True or False?)

Answer - Unconditional promises must be recognized by private not-for-profit organizations. These amounts are reported net of any estimated uncollectible amounts. (Number Five is True.)

SIX - A private not-for-profit organization receives a gift of a painting by a well-known artist. The painting is valued at $140,000. It will be protected and preserved by the organization and placed in a permanent exhibition with other similar works. The organization must report an increase in its net assets of $140,000. (True or False?)

> *Answer - The recording of art works and historical treasures is optional for private not-for-profit organizations. They can be recorded or they can be omitted from the financial statements. Donations will qualify as art works and historical treasures if (1) they are added to a collection for public exhibition, education, or research; (2) they are protected and preserved; and (3) they are ever sold, any receipts will be used to acquire other collection items. This gift qualifies as an art work; thus, recording is optional. (Number Six is False.)*

SEVEN - A doctor volunteers to work for a private not-for-private organization. The NFP performs medical operations on individuals who have no money. The doctor's services are valued at $5,000 but the doctor accepts no pay. In its statement of activities, the organization should report both a contribution of $5,000 and an expense of $5,000. These amounts will appear as changes in unrestricted net assets. (True or False?)

> *Answer - Donated services are recognized as both a revenue and an expense if the service (1) creates or enhances a nonfinancial asset or (2) requires a specialized skill possessed by the donor and would have had to be purchased if not donated. The gift of the medical services meets the second of these two requirements so that recognition must be made. (Number Seven is True.)*

INDEX

TABLE OF CONTENTS
REGULATION

REGULATION

TOPIC	For additional information see Wiley CPA Examination Review
Professional Responsibilities	Module 21
Federal Securities Regulations	Module 22
Sarbanes-Oxley Act	Module 22
Contracts	Module 23
Agency	Module 29
Sales	Module 24
Secured Transactions	Module 26
Negotiable Instruments	Module 25
Bankruptcy	Module 27
Debtor and Creditor Rights	Module 28
Real Property	Module 31
Employment Laws and Environmental Regulations	Module 30
Insurance	Module 32
Overview of Individual Income Taxes	Module 33
Individual Income Taxes – Income	Module 33
Individual Income Taxes – Exchanges	Module 34
Individual Income Taxes – Deductions for Adjusted Gross Income	Module 33
Individual Income Taxes – Itemized Deductions	Module 33
Individual Income Taxes – Tax Credits	Module 33
Income Taxation of Partnerships and S Corporations	Module 35
Corporate Income Taxes – Income	Module 36
Corporate Income Taxes – Expenses	Module 36
Corporate Income Taxes – Other Areas	Module 36
Other Taxation Areas	Module 37

PROFESSIONAL RESPONSIBILITIES

(1)　A CPA (accountant) has a contractual obligation to his or her clients.
- (A)　Accountant owes the client whatever duties are outlined in the engagement contract.
- (B)　Accountant is not liable for the failure to detect fraud unless it would have been detected by a normal audit. By agreement, the CPA can accept greater responsibility for the detection of fraud.
- (C)　Accountant is liable to a client for **negligence**. Accountant has a duty to perform with the skill and judgment possessed by the average accountant. Courts must apply this average accountant standard. The courts can look to several sources for guidance.
  - (1)　The customs of the profession are persuasive but not conclusive.
  - (2)　Generally accepting accounting principles and generally accepted auditing standards are also persuasive evidence but not conclusive.
  - (3)　The specific circumstances of the engagement situation are the single most important factor.

(2)　The accountant has certain obligations to third parties.
- (A)　The client is in **privity of contract** with the accountant and that forms the basis of the obligations of those two parties.
- (B)　The obligation of the accountant to outside parties depends on the relationship of that party to the work done.
  - (1)　A **third party beneficiary** is an outside party who is known to the accountant and who is viewed, by both the auditor and the client, as the primary beneficiary of the work. The accountant is liable for negligence, gross negligence, or fraud.
  - (2)　A **foreseen third party limited** (or class) is one who the accountant knew would rely on the financial statements. A foreseen third party is not in privity of contract. Most courts now hold the accountant liable for negligence as well as gross negligence or fraud for damages suffered by a foreseen third party.

(3)　According to federal securities laws, the independent accountant can have **liability under the 1933 Act.**
- (A)　Any purchaser of securities may sue whether the securities were bought at the time of initial issuance or later. Third parties can sue without having privity of contract.
- (B)　Plaintiff must prove that damages were incurred and that there was a material misstatement or omission in certified financial statements within the registration statements.
- (C)　At that point, the burden of proof shifts to the accountant who has several possible defenses.
  - (1)　Proving that generally accepted accounting principles were followed can be a valid defense but not always.
  - (2)　Proving that the plaintiff knew that the financial statements were incorrect is a valid defense.
  - (3)　Proving that the misstatement did not cause the loss is a valid defense.

        (4)   The **due diligence defense** can also be used. Under this defense, the accountant shows that a reasonable investigation was performed and that the accountant had reasonable grounds to believe that the statements were true.

    (D)   The **statute of limitations** is one year from the date that the false statement or omission is discovered. The statute of limitations cannot extend beyond three years from the date that the security was offered to the public.

    (E)   The amount of damages is the difference between the price paid for the securities and the value on the date that the suit is filed.

    (F)   The accountant's responsibility extends to the date that the registration statement is issued so that there is liability for errors due to changes that arise after the end of fieldwork but prior to the registration statement becoming effective.

  (4)   The accountant may also have **liability under the 1934 Act**. Either the purchaser or seller of registered securities may sue.

    (A)   Under Section 10, the burden of proof is more on the plaintiff who must prove each of the following.

        (1)   Plaintiff must prove damages in connection with purchase or sale of securities.

        (2)   Plaintiff must prove that there was a material misstatement or omission in information released by the company.

        (3)   Plaintiff must prove justifiable reliance on the financial information.

        (4)   Plaintiff must prove intent to deceive, manipulate, or defraud. Proof of **gross negligence** by the CPA may satisfy this requirement.

  (5)   Accountant can incur **criminal liability**.

    (A)   For willful violations of either the 1933 Act or the 1934 Act.

    (B)   For willful preparation of a false tax return.

  (6)   Accountant's **working papers** belong to the accountant. Most states do not recognize the working papers as privileged communication between the accountant and the client. Even in states where such a privilege is recognized, accountant must comply with a court order to produce information.

  (7)   Members of the American Institute of Certified Public Accountants (AICPA) must comply with that organization's **code of professional conduct**. A code of conduct is a mark of a true profession; it informs the public of what can be expected from members of that profession.

    (A)   Maintenance of **independence** is the cornerstone of the profession. It is hard to regulate independence in fact which is a state of mind. Thus, rules tend to concentrate on maintaining independence in appearance.

        (1)   To understand the independence rules, you have to understand the concept of **covered member.**

            (a)   An individual on the engagement team.

            (b)   An individual in a position to influence the attest engagement.

            (c)   A partner or manager who provides nonattest services to the attest client.

            (d)   A partner in the lead attest partner's office.

            (e)   The firm.

        (2)   Covered member can have no **direct financial interest** (such as ownership of stocks or bonds) in a client.

        (a)   Independence is not necessary in a compilation but lack of independence must be disclosed in the report.

        (b)   Independence is not necessary in doing consulting services as long as the client is not also an audit client.

    (3)   Covered member can have no material **indirect financial interest** in a client.

    (4)   Covered member can have no material or unusual loans from client.

    (5)   Client cannot owe money to audit firm from a prior year audit. One year's audit fee must be paid before the next year's report is issued. The unpaid fee is considered a direct financial interest.

(B)   Independence is not necessary in providing **consulting services** for nonaudit clients. There are a number of types of consulting services that can be offered.

    (1)   Consultations.

    (2)   Advisory services.

    (3)   Implementation services.

    (4)   Transaction services.

    (5)   Staff and other support services.

    (6)   Product services.

(C)   Consulting can also be done for audit clients but there are activities that cannot be done because they would impair independence.

    (1)   Auditor cannot make unauthorized changes in client data.

    (2)   Auditor cannot prepare source documents.

    (3)   Auditor cannot consummate transactions.

    (4)   Auditor cannot have custody of assets.

    (5)   Auditor cannot assume role of employee or management.

    (6)   Auditor cannot accept a commission from an outside party because a particular recommendation is made to a client.

(D)   A **confidential relationship** exists between the auditor and the client. All information gathered from the client must be held in confidence. There are times, however, when the auditor can share information with a third party without getting prior permission from the client.

    (1)   When a peer review of the firm's practice is being performed.

    (2)   In response to a court subpoena.

    (3)   As evidence in a disciplinary hearing involving the auditor.

    (4)   In response to information provided to the SEC by a previous client describing the reason for the change in auditors.

    (5)   In certain circumstances, information can be shared with governmental funding agencies.

(E)   Except in cases such as the following, an auditor cannot accept a **contingent fee** because it impairs independence.

    (1)   When the fee is fixed by a court such as in a bankruptcy case.

    (2)   In tax matters, where the fee is determined based on a judicial proceeding.

    (3)   When representing a client in an examination by a revenue agent.

(F)   False, misleading, or deceptive **advertising** is prohibited. Auditor can usually advertise any provable fact such as location, college degrees, and an expertise in a language.

| PROBLEMS AND SOLUTIONS |
| PROFESSIONAL RESPONSIBILITIES |

ONE – Under the Securities Act of 1933, much of the burden of proof is on the plaintiff. (True or False?)

> *Answer – Accountants may be held liable under the Securities Act of 1933 by a purchaser of securities. The plaintiff must only prove that damages were incurred and that the registration statement was misleading. Then, the burden of proof is shifted to the accountant to prove that he or she was diligent in performance of the audit. (Number One is False.)*

TWO – Accountants are in privity of contract with their audit client. Accordingly, the client can hold the accountant liable for ordinary negligence. (True or False?)

> *Answer – The client is in privity of contract with the accountant and that forms the basis of the obligations of those two parties. A client may hold an accountant responsible for ordinary negligence in performing obligations under the contract. (Number Two is True.)*

THREE – Independence rules of the AICPA apply to covered members. All partners are covered members for purposes of the independence rules. (True or False?)

> *Answer – Covered members of a firm include (1) an individual on the engagement team, (2) an individual in a position to influence the engagement, (3) a partner or manager who provides nonattest services to the attest client, (4) a partner in the lead attest partner's office, and the firm, itself. (Number Three is False.)*

FOUR – Independence is the cornerstone of the profession. Accordingly, an accountant must be independent of all clients. (True or False?)

> *Answer – Independence is required only for attest engagements. CPAs perform a number of services, such as consulting and tax services, in which independence is not required. However, objectivity is required for all accountant services. (Number Four is False.)*

FEDERAL SECURITIES REGULATIONS

(1) The **Securities and Exchange Commission** (SEC) was created by the **Securities Exchange Act of 1934** to administer that act as well as the **Securities Act of 1933** and certain other laws.

    (A) There are five commissioners. Not more than three of the commissioners can come from the same political party.

    (B) The SEC has power to make rules that have the same force and effect as laws enacted by Congress.

    (C) The SEC can carry out investigations. It has broad powers in this area, including subpoena power and the authority to conduct secret investigations.

    (D) The SEC also has enforcement powers. In civil cases, for example, it can revoke registration of securities. In criminal cases, it can impose fines and jail sentences. It can also issue injunctions.

(2) The Securities Act of 1933 governs the original issuance of securities. The 1933 Act differs from the 1934 Act which deals primarily with transactions that occur after the initial issuance.

    (A) The objective of the 1933 Act is to assure the public of having information necessary to evaluate securities. The SEC does not attempt to ensure the soundness of securities or to rate securities.

        (1) The 1933 Act makes it unlawful to use interstate commerce or the mail to do the following.

            (a) Sell securities unless a **registration statement** is in effect.

            (b) Sell securities not accompanied by a **prospectus**.

            (c) Make material misstatements.

        (2) A number of parties can be liable for unlawful actions committed in connection with the issuance of securities: underwriters of the securities, the issuer of the securities, directors or partners, and experts (such as CPAs and lawyers) whose work has been used.

            (a) A **security** is any stock or similar security or any security that is convertible into such a security or that carries any warrant or right to subscribe to or purchase such warrant or right or security. Usually includes any note, stock, bond, debenture, investment contract, limited partnership interest, treasury stock, etc.

            (b) An **issuer of a security** would include every person who issues or proposes to issue any security.

            (c) The term "person" encompasses individuals, corporations, partnerships, associations, etc.

            (d) An **underwriter** is any person who has purchased securities from an issuer with a view to their public distribution.

    (B) The basic rule is that no sale of securities shall occur in interstate commerce or by use of the mail without SEC registration and without furnishing every prospective purchaser with a prospectus. Interstate commerce refers to trade or commerce in securities or any transportation or communication relating thereto among or between the states and territories of the U.S. or between those states and territories and foreign countries.

(1)   A **registration statement** must be filed with the SEC before the initial sale of securities in interstate commerce. It includes financial statements and all other relevant information about the registrant together with a prospectus.

(2)   A **prospectus** is any notice, circular, advertisement, letter or other communication that offers any security for sale or confirms the sale of any security. Prospectus rules are designed to ensure that every potential buyer has appropriate information available about the issuer.

      (a)   A communication sent after the effective date of the registration statement shall not be deemed a prospectus if a written prospectus has been previously or is being contemporaneously provided to the person to whom the communication was made.

      (b)   A notice, circular, advertisement, or letter of communication shall not be deemed a prospectus if it states from whom a written prospectus may be obtained and contains other information deemed appropriate by the commission.

(C)   There are **exempt securities**; these are exceptions to the basic rule about the need for registration. In fact, many organizations attempt to structure the issuance of securities so that the sale is exempt from the rigorous requirements of registration within the securities laws.

(1)   Securities issued by certain specific types of entities are exempt. These include securities issued by a state government, the federal government, banks, savings and loan associations, farmers, co-ops, charities, and bankruptcy trustees.

(2)   Intrastate offerings are exempt. The issuer and all purchasers and all offerees must be residents of the same state. Issuer must do 80% of its business in that state.

      (a)   Such securities are usually regulated by **"Blue Sky" laws**. This term refers to the various securities regulations applied by individual states.

(3)   Small issues of not more than $5 million in a 12 month period fall under the filing requirements of **Regulation A**.

      (a)   The SEC must be notified of the sale.

      (b)   Each offeree must be supplied with an **offering circular** that contains financial information about the corporation and a description of the securities. Financial statements need not be audited.

(4)   **Casual sales** are exempt. A casual sale is one by a party that is not the issuer, an underwriter, a dealer, or a controlling person.

      (a)   A **dealer** is any person who engages either for all or part of his or her time directly or indirectly as an agent, broker, or principal in the business of offering, buying, selling, or otherwise dealing or trading in securities issued by another.

      (b)   A **controlling person** is any person who directly or indirectly controls the issuer or any person under direct or indirect common control with the issuer. The person has the power, either directly or indirectly, to influence the management or the policies of the issuer. Factors indicating control are: stock ownership and actual practical control. Because control is broadly construed to include any person capable of exerting influence, even a 5% owner who is an officer or director could be a controlling person.

    (5)   **Rule 504 of Regulation D** exempts issuance of securities of up to $1 million in a 12 month period to an unlimited number and type of investors.

        (a)   There is no restriction on resale of the securities.

        (b)   Audited balance sheets need not be supplied to potential investors.

        (c)   The SEC must be notified within 15 days of the first sale.

        (d)   General advertising is allowed.

    (6)   **Rule 505 of Regulation D** exempts issuance of up to $5 million in a 12 month period.

        (a)   No general solicitation is permitted.

        (b)   Sales can be made to no more than 35 nonaccredited investors and to an unlimited number of accredited investors. **Accredited investors** include banks, savings and loan associations, insurance companies, individuals having a net worth of at least $1 million or annual income of $200,000, etc.

        (c)   Resale of securities must be restricted for two years.

        (d)   If securities are sold to nonaccredited investors, audited balance sheets must be supplied.

    (7)   **Rule 506 of Regulation D** exempts the issuance of an unlimited amount of securities in a **private placement**.

        (a)   Requirements are similar to those established under Rule 505. However, any nonaccredited investors must be **sophisticated investors** or represented by a sophisticated investor.

        (b)   A sophisticated investor is one with knowledge and experience in financial matters.

    (8)   Sales under Rule 505 or 506 of Regulation D are restricted as to resale. These securities (as well as securities sold by a controlling person) may not be resold unless either registered with the SEC (unless exempted by securities laws) or sold per the **safe harbor provisions of Rule 144**. There are several requirements within the safe harbor provisions.

        (a)   Adequate information must be available about the issuer.

        (b)   Notice must be given to the SEC.

        (c)   Only limited amounts of securities can be sold.

        (d)   Ownership must be for at least two years. This includes any period of beneficial ownership where the securities are held in the names of the party's spouse or minor children, in a trust in which the party or any member of the party's family has an interest, and a trust created by the party who has retained a power to revoke and where that trust contains 20% or more of the security.

  (3)   There are a number of requirements for the registration of securities.

    (A)   Certain information must be included in the **registration statement.**

        (1)   Names of issuer, directors, officers, underwriters, and large shareholders.

        (2)   Description of property, business, and capitalization of issuer.

        (3)   Description of security being offered and the use to be made of the proceeds.

- (4) Financial statements audited by an independent CPA. The balance sheet should not be more than 90 days old. There should be profit and loss statements for 3 years.
- (5) Other material information such as the risks associated with the securities and information about the management.
- (B) **Prospectus** must be filed with the registration statement. It contains the same information but in summary form.
- (C) Upon filing, there is a 20 day waiting period during which time the SEC reviews the registration statement.
  - (1) SEC can ask for amendments which starts a new 20 day waiting period.
  - (2) At the end of the 20 day period, the registration statement becomes effective. The SEC can accelerate the 20 day period.
  - (3) A **stop order** can be issued to suspend the effectiveness if the statements appear to be incomplete or misleading.
- (D) During the 20 day waiting period, oral offers can be made to buy or sell the security. Written offers can also be made in this period but they must be accompanied by a **preliminary prospectus** (one that has been filed but not made effective yet) which is often referred to as a **"red herring" prospectus**.

(4) **Section 17 of the 1933 Act** prohibits fraudulent schemes and material misstatement by persons who offer or sell securities. This law applies regardless of whether registration is required. The investor must prove both material misstatement and damages. Unlike common law fraud, Section 17 does not require a showing that the misstatements were intentional or that the party suing relied on the misstatements in deciding to buy the securities.
- (A) If convicted, criminal penalties include a fine of up to $10,000 and/or imprisonment of up to five years.
- (B) In civil cases, the investor can recover the difference between the price paid for the securities and the fair market value when the suit is filed.
- (C) The statute of limitations is one year after the misstatement was discovered or should have been discovered. In no event is the statute of limitation more than three years from the date that the securities are offered to the public.

(5) **Section 11 of the 1933 Act** imposes liability on those experts whose opinions appear in a registration statement.
- (A) The expert need not be negligent to be held liable.
- (B) The burden of proof is put on to the expert who may use the due diligence defense to avoid liability.
  - (1) In the **due diligence defense**, the expert shows that he or she had reasonable grounds after a reasonable investigation to believe that the statements made were true and did not contain any omissions of material facts when the registration statement became effective.
  - (2) Any defendants other than the issuer can also use the due diligence defense by indicating that they relied on the expert and did believe that there were no misstatements or material omissions of fact.

(6) The 1934 Act regulates the sale of securities after initial issuance. The 1934 Act also requires that certain companies and other entities file on a regular periodic basis with the SEC. In this way, information is continuously available to the public.
- (A) The following must file because of the 1934 Act.
  - (1) National securities exchanges.

(2) Brokers and dealers doing business in interstate commerce.

(3) Corporations that are traded on national exchanges.

(4) Corporations having securities traded in interstate commerce that have $5 million in assets and 500 or more shareholders.

(B) Companies that qualify under the 1934 Act must file certain reports with the SEC.

(1) The **Form 10-K** is an annual report.

(2) The **Form 10-Q** is a quarterly report.

(3) The **Form 8-K** discloses certain material events such as a change in control or a change in auditors.

(4) Officers and directors must file a report of changes in ownership.

(C) It is unfair for inside parties to trade on inside information. Thus, **insider trading** rules have been created. Insiders are the directors and officers of the issuer and every person who is directly or indirectly the beneficial owner of more than 10% of any class of an equity security which is registered pursuant to the 1934 Act.

(1) Insiders who trade on inside information commit fraud unless inside information is disclosed to the other party in the transaction. This rule also applies to people who rely on tips from insiders.

(2) Profits on trades within a 6 month time (**short swing trades**) made by insiders must be forfeited to the corporation even though inside information was not relied upon in the trade.

(a) Transactions of less than $3,000 are exempt.

(b) This rule does not apply to people who rely on tips from insiders.

(3) Insiders must disclose amount of equity securities held. Any changes in ownership must be reported within 10 days.

(7) **Sections 10(b) and rule 10(b)(5) of the 1934 Act** contain anti-fraud provisions.

(A) "**Fraud**" under the 1934 Act (unlike 1933 Act fraud) resembles common law fraud. To recover one must prove (1) misstatement or omission, (2) of a material fact, (3) made with intent to deceive or through gross negligence, (4) reliance by the injured part, and (5) damages.

(B) Fraudulent schemes are prohibited. Fraudulent misstatements or omissions of material facts in connection with the sale of securities are prohibited.

(C) The test of materiality is whether a reasonable person would attach importance to the fact in determining his or her course of action in the transaction.

(D) Under the Hochfelder case, there is no liability for mere negligence.

(E) The SEC can take a number of actions as a result of fraud in connection with the 1934 Act. An injunction can be issued to temporarily or permanently suspend trading of a security. It can also impose a fine of up to $10,000 and imprisonment for up to two years.

(F) Private parties can file civil suits similar to the civil actions for fraud.

(G) Sections 10(b) and rule 10(b)(5) cover all securities whether registered or unregistered. These provisions also cover all persons not just insiders or brokers.

(8) A **proxy** is a grant of authority to a party by a shareholder allowing that party to vote the owner's shares at a specified meeting. Because of the power that a proxy gives, proxy solicitation is monitored by the SEC.

(A) It is illegal to solicit proxies by use of the mail or interstate commerce without following precise rules.

(1) Proxy must identify who is making the solicitation and clearly identify each matter to be acted on at the meeting.

    (2)   **Proxy statement** must accompany proxy and must state whether it is revocable, identify the persons making the solicitation, and list matters to be voted on and by whom proposed.

    (3)   If solicitation is by management and involves an annual meeting for electing directors, an annual report must accompany proxy statement and include two years of certified financial statements.

    (B)   Proxy materials must be filed with the SEC 10 days before being sent to shareholders.

(9)   Any party making a tender offer to acquire beneficial ownership of 5% or more of a 1934 Act company must first file with the SEC to identify the purchaser and the intentions of the purchaser. Filing is required but SEC approval for the purchase is not required.

(10)   The **Foreign Corrupt Practices Act** (FCPA) is an amendment that was passed to the 1934 Act.

    (A)   The FCPA makes it illegal for any U.S. company to offer bribes to foreign public officials.

    (1)   For a business, the penalty is a fine of up to $1 million per violation.

    (2)   For an individual, the penalty is a fine of up to $10,000 and up to five years in prison per violation.

    (B)   The FCPA has antifraud and accounting requirements that only apply to companies that must register with the SEC under the provisions of the 1934 Act.

    (1)   The antifraud provisions include the following. The penalties are the same as those above. **Scienter** (knowledge that the representations are false) is not required.

    (a)   It is illegal to falsify accounting reports.

    (b)   It is illegal to make false representations in connection with an audit.

    (2)   The accounting requirements include the following. Again, the penalties are the same as those above.

    (a)   Company must maintain books that accurately reflect its transactions and disposition of assets.

    (b)   Company must maintain internal accounting control in conformity with standard practices.

PROBLEMS AND SOLUTIONS
FEDERAL SECURITIES REGULATIONS

ONE - The Securities Act of 1933 governs the original issue of securities. Only common stock and preferred stock are considered "securities." (True or False?)

Answer - Securities include common stock, preferred stock, stock warrants, treasury stock, bonds, indentures, certain evidences of indebtedness, and any form that an investment in a business venture might take. The 1933 Act defines the term security broadly: "Unless the context otherwise requires, the term security means any note, stock, bonds, debenture, evidence of indebtedness, certificate of interest of participation in any profit-sharing agreement, reorganization certificate or subscription, investment contract, voting trust certificate, fractional undivided interest in oil, gas or mineral rights, or in general, any interest or instrument commonly known as a security." (Number One is False.)

TWO - The main objective of the Securities Act of 1933 is to ensure the soundness of the securities that are traded in the public marketplace. (True or False?)

Answer - The objective of the Securities Act of 1933 is to assure the public of having adequate information necessary to evaluate securities. The Securities Act of 1933 does not concern itself with the financial soundness or merit of an investment security. (Number Two is False.)

THREE - A prospectus is the basic selling document to be used in offering a registered security for sale. Most of the information in the registration statement must be contained in the prospectus. (True or False?)

Answer - A prospectus must contain a summary of the information that is contained in registration statement. (Number Three is True.)

FOUR - The Securities Act of 1933 requires that every transaction in securities be registered with the SEC or be exempt from registration. (True or False?)

Answer - This rule applies to every party, including a small investor who sells securities registered by the issuer ten years earlier. Of course, most such investors who resell securities will have an exemption from registration. (Number Four is True.)

FIVE - Securities issued by a nonprofit religious organization are exempt from registration but securities issued by charitable organizations are not exempt. (True or False?)

Answer - Securities issued by religious, charitable, educational, or fraternal organizations are exempt. (Number Five is False.)

SIX - Carpenter Manufacturing, Inc., is required by the Securities Exchange Act of 1934 to make quarterly and annual reports to the SEC. Therefore, it may not make an exempt offering. (True or False?)

Answer - A securities transaction may be exempt even for reporting corporations. It is the nature of the transaction, and not the size or public nature of the corporation, that determines whether the transaction is exempt. (Number Six is False.)

SEVEN - Regulation A of the 1933 Act governs "small issues." For such an issuance of securities, the SEC must first be notified, the purchasers must be supplied with an "offering circular," and the securities must be sold within a twelve-month period. (True or False?)

Answer - Under Regulation A, there is (1) no limit on the number of purchasers, (2) no requirement that the buyers be sophisticated, and (3) no restriction on re-sales. Regulation A is sometimes referred to as a low-level registration since the SEC must be informed and a disclosure document (the offering circular) must be filed with the SEC. There is a ten-day waiting period after the filing of the offering circular during which no offers or sales may be made. (Number Seven is True.)

EIGHT - Securities that are sold pursuant to the exemption of Rule 504 of Regulation D may be sold by use of general advertising and re-sold without restriction. (True or False?)

Answer - General advertising of any sales of securities pursuant to Rule 504 is now permitted. Resale of securities that are exempt under Rule 504 of Regulation D is not restricted. (Number Eight is True.)

NINE - Rule 506 of Regulation D allows the private placement of an unlimited amount of securities without registration as long as all purchasers and prospective purchasers have a net worth of $100,000 or more. (True or False?)

Answer - Rule 506 allows the sale of an unlimited amount of securities without registration but purchasers must be either accredited (such as banks, insurance companies, wealthy investors, or high level insiders) or must have knowledge and experience in financial matters. (Number Nine is False.)

TEN - To recover damages for fraud under the 1933 Act, one who purchases securities in a public offering must prove that he or she relied upon an offering circular, a prospectus, or a registration statement. (True or False?)

Answer - Reliance is not in element of fraud under the 1933 Act. The only elements that must be proven are material misstatement or omission plus damages. (Number Ten is False.)

ELEVEN - To be liable under insider trading rules, one must be an "insider," that is, an officer, director, or 10 percent shareholder of the business whose securities are traded. (True or False?)

Answer - There are two rules that govern insider trading. One rule prohibits "insiders" from profiting -- regardless whether they actually used inside information. Under this rule, profits made from the sale or purchase of securities within a six month period must be divested. A second rule prohibits anyone (whether an insider or not) from profiting on inside information in a securities trade. Anyone who trades on information that is not available to the general public, including a person who receives a tip, may be liable for fraud unless the inside information was also disclosed to the other party in the transaction. (Number Eleven is False.)

SARBANES-OXLEY ACT

(1)   The **Sarbanes-Oxley Act** (Public Company Accounting Reform and Investor Protection Act) establishes new requirements for public companies and their auditors.

(2)   CEOs and CFOs of most companies listed on public stock exchanges are required to certify financial statements filed with the SEC.

   (A)   Includes a requirement to certify to the quality of internal control.

(3)   Requires independent and qualified audit committees.

   (A)   Auditor must report directly to the audit committee.

(4)   Established the **Public Company Accounting Oversight Board** to establish auditing, independence, and quality control standards for auditors of public companies. Board also oversees inspections of work of auditors, and investigates and sanctions auditors for substandard performance.

(5)   Requirements on auditors of public companies.

   (A)   Establishes registration requirements for auditors of public companies.

   (B)   Prohibits auditors from performing certain nonattest services for audit clients in addition to those already prohibited by the AICPA code.

      (1)   Internal audit outsourcing.

      (2)   Actuarial services.

      (3)   Investment or broker-dealer services.

      (4)   Financial information systems design and/or implementation.

      (5)   Appraisal services.

   (C)   Allowable nonattest services must be approved by the audit committee.

   (D)   Requires retention of working papers for 5 years.

   (E)   Requires auditor certification to internal control of public companies.

PROBLEMS AND SOLUTIONS
SARBANES-OXLEY ACT

ONE – The Sarbanes-Oxley Act was designed to improve the financial reporting process. Accordingly, the requirements apply to all audits. (True or False?)

   Answer – The Sarbanes-Oxley Act amends the Securities Exchange Act of 1934. Accordingly, it applies to the audits of public companies. (Number One is False.)

TWO – To increase the independence of auditors of public companies, the Sarbanes-Oxley Act prohibits certain nonattest services for audit clients, including internal audit services. (True or False?)

   Answer – The Sarbanes-Oxley Act prohibits certain nonattest services for audit clients, including internal audit outsourcing, actuarial services, investment, or broker-dealer services, financial information systems design and/or implementation, and appraisal services. (Number Two is True.)

CONTRACTS

(1)   **Contract law** is a body of law that deals with the rights and duties of persons who voluntarily agree to be bound by mutual sets of promises and with the process through which they became mutually bound. General contract law governs transactions involving sales of real estate, sales of services, insurance contracts, and employment contracts. Within this portion of the outline, references are sometimes made to the **Uniform Commercial Code Article on Sales (Article 2)** which deals with transactions involving goods. This is so that the candidate can make comparisons between general contract law and Article 2 in those areas where the rules differ. There are several definitions that are quite important in contract law.

    (A)   **Offeree** is a person to whom an offer is made.

    (B)   **Offeror** is a person who makes an offer.

    (C)   A **quasi contract** is not actually a contract but can act like one. It serves as a remedy where someone has unjustly received a benefit but where there was no contract.

    (D)   A **void contract** is something that may look like a contract but because of lack of an offer, an acceptance, consideration, or because of illegality has no effect from its very beginning (ab initio).

    (E)   A **voidable contract** is a contract but one from which at least one of the parties can escape liability because of lack of capacity, lack of mutuality, duress, misrepresentation, undue influence, or mistake.

    (F)   An **unenforceable contract** is one that exists because it has all of the elements of a valid contract. However, at least one of the parties has a defense that can be used such as the Statute of Frauds or a material breach of contract.

(2)   The study of contract law can be divided into three areas.

    (A) -   Formation of the contract is the most important aspect of contract law.

    (B) -   Performance of the terms of the contract.

    (C) -   Remedies that are available if nonperformance of the terms occurs.

(3)   For a valid contract to exist, six elements must exist: offer, acceptance, mutual/real assent, consideration, capacity, and legality.

(4)   For there to be a valid contract, there must be an **offer**. An offer is an expression that creates within the offeree a power of **acceptance**. A power of acceptance is the ability to bind the offeror to that person's own promise. Three elements must exist for there to be a valid offer: intent, communication, and definiteness.

    (A)   There are three common instances where intent is lacking. Thus, in these cases, there is no offer.

        (1)   The offer was made in jest.

        (2)   Most advertisements are not offers but are considered invitations to others to make an offer.

        (3)   The person was only contemplating making an offer. For example, if a person writes a letter to a neighbor indicating that the person is "considering" selling his/her house, this statement is not an offer since intent is not present.

    (B)   An offer (or counteroffer) is not valid unless it is actually communicated.

(C)   There has to be **definiteness**; that is, the terms of the offer must be stated or reasonably ascertainable. The first four terms below can be stated or can, in some cases, be inferred. The fifth term (quantity) has to be stated; it cannot be inferred.

    (1)   Parties to the contract.

    (2)   Subject matter of the contract.

    (3)   Time for performance of the terms. (An offer to paint a building which does not specify a time for performance would still be a valid offer; a reasonable time would be understood.)

    (4)   Price and method of payment.

    (5)   Quantity, which is the one term that can never be inferred.

(D)   There are common instances of non-offers. These are cases where there appears to be an offer but it is not valid because either intent, communication, or definiteness is lacking.

    (1)   An advertisement is an **invitation to offer** and not an offer because it lacks intent.

    (2)   A solicitation of subcontractors is also considered a request for offers; therefore, the lowest bidder cannot claim his/her bid is an acceptance. It is the bid that is the offer.

(E)   An offer can be terminated. As an example, assume that Heath offers in writing to sell his television station, including building and transmitting tower to Dodd for $2.0 million with the offer to remain open for 45 days. There are 6 ways Heath's offer can terminate.

    (1)   The specified time can lapse; 45 days can pass before Dodd accepts.

    (2)   The subject matter can be destroyed. For example, a plane could hit the tower and topple it into the building.

    (3)   There can be a revocation by the offeror. For example, Heath can fax a memo to Dodd stating that the previous offer is revoked.

    (4)   The death or insanity of either the offeror or offeree can occur.

    (5)   Offeree can reject the offer. Dodd could write Heath that the price was too high and that Heath could keep the station.

    (6)   The offeree could make a **counteroffer**. For example, Dodd could offer $1.9 million in response to Heath's offer.

(F)   An **option contract** is an offer that is irrevocable for an agreed time and is supported by **consideration**.

    (1)   Consideration means that the offeree either pays or promises to pay the offeror to hold the offer open while the offeree decides whether to accept.

    (2)   The offer cannot be withdrawn by the offeror or terminated by a counteroffer by the offeree during the agreed option period.

(G)   A **firm offer** is one that is irrevocable for a certain period of time not because it is supported by consideration (as above), but because it meets certain Uniform Commercial Code (UCC) requirements. Firm offers can only exist if the contract is for the sale of goods; general contract law does not recognize firm offers. This area is discussed in more detail in connection with Sales.

(5)   For there to be a valid contract, there must be **acceptance**. Acceptance of an offer is any expression by the offeree of willingness to be bound by an offer.

    (A)   An acceptance can take either of two forms.

        (1)   A **bilateral contract** is one where the offeror is looking for a promise to perform as a response to the offer.

        (2)   A **unilateral contract** is where offeror is looking for performance in response to the offer.

    (B)   An acceptance must have a certain content. To constitute an acceptance, the terms of the acceptance must mirror the terms of the offer. For example, suppose an offer contains no mention of form of payment, but the "acceptance" specifies payment must be by cash or certified check. There would be no contract under general contract law. The Uniform Commercial Code does create a slight exception to this **mirror image rule** so that an acceptance of an offer to sell goods is still a valid acceptance even though it contains terms slightly different from the offer.

    (C)   As with an offer, an acceptance is not valid unless it is communicated. However, to communicate an offer, the offeree must actually receive the offer. For an acceptance to be valid, though, merely the dispatch of the acceptance is required. Unless the offeror specifies that acceptance must be received to be valid, the acceptance is valid on dispatch even if it is never received by the offeror. This is known as the **mail box rule** or early acceptance rule.

(6)   For there to be a valid contract, there has to be **genuineness of assent**. It is important that both parties intend to be bound by their promises. Normally, an offer and acceptance ensure this desire. In some cases, however, even though there is an offer and acceptance, other circumstances can make it questionable that the parties truly agreed to anything. This lack of assent can occur where one of the parties engages in unfair tactics (misrepresentation, duress, undue influence, unilateral mistake) or where the promises made are, upon closer examination, so vague that there is no fair way to enforce them (mutual mistake or lack of mutuality). Each of these conditions would cause a lack of assent so that no valid contract would exist.

    (A)   For **misrepresentation**, four elements must exist.

        (1)   There has to be a misstatement or omission.

        (2)   The misstatement or omission has to be of a material fact.

        (3)   The offeree had to rely on the misstatement or omission.

        (4)   The reliance had to be detrimental to the offeree.

    (B)   **Duress** indicates a condition of coercion.

        (1)   Physical coercion makes the contract voidable by the party that was coerced because of lack of assent.

        (2)   Economic coercion usually does not affect a contract.

    (C)   **Undue influence** can be demonstrated by some common examples. In each case, the undue influence would probably indicate a lack of assent by the offeree.

        (1)   An employer takes advantage of a trusting, young employee.

        (2)   A lawyer takes advantage of a trusting client.

        (3)   A relative takes advantage of an elderly person.

    (D)   A **unilateral mistake** is where one party knows or should realize that the other party is relying on a mistaken belief or incorrect information. The party innocently relying on this information can avoid the contract because of lack of assent. For example, assume that a contractor solicits bids and accepts a bid that is significantly lower than any other bid. In fact, the low bid was based on an unintentional error by the bidder. The bidder can avoid the contract because of lack of assent since the contractor knew or should have known that the bidder had made a mistake of some kind.

(E) **A mutual mistake** indicates a contract that contains latent ambiguities and can be avoided by either the offeror or the offeree. Because of the ambiguities, there is a lack of assent. For example, an agreement to rent "the first floor of the building at 123 Main Street for $500 per month" might be ambiguous if that building has both a ground level floor and an English basement.

(F) **A lack of mutuality** exists in a situation where a statement has been made that sounds like a promise but it does not, in reality, bind the person making the statement to do anything. For example, one party could agree to purchase all the heating oil that he or she might "wish," "want," or "desire" from the other party. Such promises are not binding because of the lack of mutuality.

(7) For there to be a valid contract, there must be some **consideration** either promised or paid. Consideration is something that is bargained for and exchanged in a contract. Courts will not examine whether the consideration being exchanged by parties is equal.

(A) Consideration comes in either of two forms: benefit or detriment.

(1) **Legal benefit** is money paid from one party to the other for goods or services. It can also be goods bartered for different goods or for services or for a promise to pay.

(2) **Legal detriment** is a situation where one party pays or promises to pay something in exchange for the other party's promise to refrain from doing something that he or she would otherwise have the legal right to do.

(B) In some situations, either benefit or determent will exist; however, it will not be legally sufficient as consideration.

(1) Love and affection are not consideration. A moral obligation is not a contractual obligation.

(2) Past consideration is not consideration.

(3) Fulfilling a pre-existing duty is not consideration.

(a) This can relate to public officials. For example, an artist promises to pay the curator of the state museum $500 if none of the artist's paintings are stolen while on exhibit. This promise is not binding because the curator already has this obligation.

(b) This can also relate to pre-existing contractual duties. Generally, this situation involves modifying a contract after the contract has been formed. Contract law says that a modification of a contract by the parties is not valid unless it is supported by consideration that is in addition to the consideration paid or promised in the original agreement. This is true even if the modification is in writing and is signed by both parties; there has to be additional consideration. The UCC does provide an exception. If the contract is for the sale of goods, it will be governed by UCC Article 2 and not by general contract law. Under UCC Article 2, modifications are valid without additional consideration as long as the modifications were in good faith.

(C) There are situations that are exceptions where consideration is not required.

(1) A charitable subscription such as a promise to contribute to a charity.

(2) A debt that has been barred by the **statute of limitations**. Although the debtor had a valid obligation to pay, the statute of limitations (the time limit for filing suit against the debtor) has run out. However, if the debtor

renews the promise to pay, it will be binding without additional consideration.

        (3)   A **composition** has occurred. An agreement has been reached by a debtor and two or more of his or her creditors whereby the creditors have agreed to accept, as payment in full, less than the total amount that was owed.

    (D)   Consideration that is not paid is not valid consideration. Indicating in a contract that the consideration has been paid is not sufficient.

    (E)   As indicated above, UCC Article 2 governs the sale of goods and changes the concept of consideration.

        (1)   New consideration is not required for modification of a new contract.

        (2)   For a firm offer, consideration is not required but the offer must be in writing and must be signed by a merchant and must be for the sale of goods.

(8)   For there to be a valid contract, the parties must have the **legal capacity** to enter into a contract. Certain parties lack legal capacity.

    (A)   A minor lacks legal capacity.

        (1)   Even contracts for necessaries such as food, shelter, clothing, tools of trade, and employment agency fees are voidable by minors, but the minor must pay a reasonable value for any items acquired.

        (2)   A minor can disaffirm a contract at any time prior to reaching the age of majority or within a reasonable period of time thereafter. One exception is that a minor cannot disaffirm a contract for the sale of land until majority is achieved.

        (3)   A minor can only ratify a contract after reaching majority.

        (4)   A minor is not required to return the other party to the status quo.

    (B)   An insane person lacks legal capacity. However, unlike a minor, an insane person who disaffirms a contract must return the other party to the status quo.

    (C)   An intoxicated person may lack legal capacity. A party who seeks to avoid a contract must have been very drunk and one of three things must have occurred.

        (1)   The other party must have taken unfair advantage of the intoxicated party or

        (2)   The other party must have induced the intoxication or

        (3)   The intoxicated party was so drunk as to have no comprehension of the transaction.

(9)   For there to be a valid contract, there must be legality, the terms cannot require any laws to be broken. For example, the parties cannot bargain to commit a crime since that action is illegal.

    (A)   Wagering statutes are sometimes broken so that the contract is not valid. This situation usually involves the lack of an **insurable interest**. If the policy holder of an insurance policy has no insurable interest in the thing or person being insured, a wager is being made and the contract is void.

    (B)   Failing to obtain a license can affect the validity of a contract depending on the purpose of the license. Two different types of **licensing statutes** are involved in contract law.

        (1)   Failure of a contracting party to be licensed where the purpose of the license is to raise money for the government does not affect the validity of the contract.

        (2)   Failure of a contracting party to be licensed where the purpose of the license is to ensure the skill of the party (such as a doctor, realtor, lawyer, or CPA) makes the contract void. The unlicensed party cannot recover even out-of-pocket costs.

    (C)   An **exculpatory clause** is a statement in a contract whereby a party will not be held responsible for damages or injuries he or she causes even if he or she is negligent. Exculpatory clauses are generally considered valid in commercial settings but invalid if a consumer is involved.

(10)   Two topics in contract law, which are unrelated to each other, concern written agreements.

    (A)   The **Statute of Frauds** states in general that a contract does not have to be in writing in order to be enforceable. However, there are a number of exceptions to this general rule. The Statute of Frauds is merely a list of those types of contracts that must be in writing to be enforceable. To be satisfactory, these written agreements must contain an adequate description of the terms of the contract (especially the quantity) and be signed by the party being charged with performance (that is, only the person being sued needs to have signed for the contract to be enforceable). The writing may be contained in more than one document. The following contracts must be in writing to be enforceable.

        (1)   A promise to answer for debts of another. For example, one person promises to pay a debt and another person guarantees that promise. The guarantee must be in writing to be enforceable.

        (2)   A contract to transfer an interest in real estate must be in writing.

        (3)   A contract which cannot, by its terms, be performed within one year from the date the agreement was made must be in writing.

        (4)   The UCC sale of goods of $500.00 or more must be in writing.

    (B)   The **parol evidence rule** also impacts written contracts. When a contract is in writing (whether it needs to be or not), this rule limits the evidence that can be introduced at trial to prove what the terms of the contract are. For the parol evidence rule to apply, the contract must be integrated, a term that means that the agreement is a complete and final statement of all terms.

        (1)   The rule keeps certain evidence from being introduced: prior or contemporaneous written or oral statements which add to or modify or vary the written contract.

        (2)   Certain exceptions exist to the parol evidence rule so that statements that normally could not be introduced can be. These exceptions occur when fraud, undue influence, duress, misrepresentation, or mistake has occurred. Another exception to the parol evidence rule is also allowed to explain an ambiguity.

        (3)   A subsequent writing such as a modification to a written contract is not affected by the parol evidence rule.

(11)   A third party can have rights in connection with a contract.

    (A)   Rights can be assigned by the parties to a contract or rights can be delegated. **Assignment** is the transfer of rights under a contract. **Delegation** is the transfer of duties under a contract. The term "assignment" sometimes refers to the transfer of the entire contract (both rights and duties).

        (1)   The law favors free assignability. Thus, assignment and delegation are generally valid unless one of two factors is present. First, if the

        nonassigning party's risk is materially changed, assignment is not allowed. Second, an obligation that involves unique personal services cannot be delegated.

        (2)   Assignment is valid immediately regardless whether the other party to the contract received notice of the assignment.

        (3)   An assignee has no better rights than the assignor did.

(B)   There are occasions where a third party (a person who is not a party to a contract) will stand to benefit from the performance of the contract. The law, however, does not always permit such third party beneficiaries to enforce the contract. Two categories of third party beneficiaries (**donee beneficiaries** and **creditor beneficiaries**) usually can enforce a contract even though they are neither the offeror nor the offeree. Third parties who are not permitted to enforce contracts are called **incidental beneficiaries.**

        (1)   A donee beneficiary exists when the purpose of the contract (such as a life insurance contract) is to bestow a gift on someone who is not a party to the contract. A third party donee beneficiary can bring an action on the contract.

        (2)   A creditor beneficiary exists when the purpose of the contract is to perform an obligation which is owed to someone who is not a party to the contract. Such a third party creditor beneficiary can bring an action on the contract.

        (3)   An incidental beneficiary exists when there is a third party beneficiary to a contract who is neither a creditor beneficiary nor a donee beneficiary. Assume, for example, that Zeke agrees to repair Zirkle's car. Abraham often rides to work in Zirkle's car. Abraham cannot sue Zeke for Zeke's failure to repair the car, even though Abraham stood to benefit from the contract between Zeke and Zirkle.

(12)   Any nonperformance of a contract is a **breach of the contract**. There are legal remedies available when a breach has been committed by one of the parties.

    (A)   There can be several levels of breach of contract.

        (1)   A **material breach** is when nonperformance is so substantial that it excuses the nonbreaching party from further performance.

        (2)   **Substantial performance** is where performance is virtually complete and complies substantially to the requirements of the contract.

        (3)   **Anticipatory repudiation** is any expression of unwillingness or inability to perform under a contract prior to the time that performance is due. In this situation, the nonbreaching party need not wait until the date on which performance is due to bring suit on the contract.

    (B)   There are times when performance of the terms of a contract are excused.

        (1)   If one party has committed a material breach, the other party is excused from performance.

        (2)   Death excuses a party from the duty to perform services but not from the contractual duty to deliver goods or convey real estate.

    (C)   If a breach of contract has occurred, there are various remedies available to the nonbreaching party.

        (1)   The nonbreaching party can be awarded monetary damages.

           (a)   The general measure of monetary damages is the amount of money that will put the nonbreaching party in the position that he or she would have occupied had there been no breach. Such damages are known as **compensatory damages**.

(b) **Punitive damages** are damages aimed at punishing the breaching party rather than merely compensating the nonbreaching party. Punitive damages usually are not allowed in breach of contract cases.

(c) **Liquidated damages** are damages for breach of contract where the monetary amount was agreed to at the time the contract was made. Courts allow such damages only if the amount is reasonable. Generally, parties agree to liquidated (pre-arranged) damage clauses where actual damages might be difficult to calculate.

(2) Under certain circumstances, the nonbreaching party can be awarded equity.

(a) Courts can award **specific performance**. The courts will order conveyance of unique items to the nonbreaching party to satisfy the terms of the contract. All real estate is unique, as are items considered to be rare.

(b) Courts can issue an injunction to prohibit certain actions by the breaching party (however, the courts cannot force involuntary servitude). For example, a court could order a person who has signed a noncompete agreement to stop competing. The court, though, could not order a plumber to finish a plumbing job because that would be involuntary servitude.

PROBLEMS AND SOLUTIONS
CONTRACTS

ONE - Thompson writes a letter to Elton stating that "I am contemplating selling my business and feel that two hundred thousand dollars would be an appropriate price. Please write back if you are interested." This is an offer. (True or False?)

Answer - This is a writing in contemplation of making an offer but the offeror does not have the intent here to make an offer. (Number One is False.)

TWO - A valid contract requires an acceptance by the offeree. Giant Builders Inc. solicited bids for interior floor covering relating to a 20 story office building that Giant was constructing. Blake was the low bidder for this job. Blake's low bid is an acceptance of Giant's offer. (True or False?)

Answer - A solicitation of subcontractors is not an offer but is rather an invitation to make offers. Therefore, Blake's bid was an offer. (Number Two is False.)

THREE - Frank offers to sell his laundry business to Johnson and states in writing that the offer will remain open until July 31st. Frank can withdraw this offer on July 15th as long as Johnson has not accepted the offer. (True or False?)

Answer - An offeror can withdraw an offer at anytime prior to acceptance unless the offer is supported by consideration (as in an option contract). For example, if Frank had accepted payment from Johnson for the option to buy the business until July 31, an early withdrawal of the offer cannot be made. (Number Three is True.)

FOUR - Arnold offers to sell his farm to Carter for $250,000. Arnold received Carter's letter stating that Carter accepted the offer except that he was only willing to pay $240,000. Carter later learned that George was also interested in the farm. Carter immediately faxed a message to Arnold accepting his offer to sell the farm for $250,000. Carter's letter arrived the day before the fax message was sent. No contract has been formed. (True or False?)

Answer - Carter's counteroffer to buy the farm for $240,000 terminated the offer made by Arnold. (Number Four is True.)

FIVE - For an offer and acceptance to be effective, there must be a genuine, knowing assent by the parties. There must have been agreement. Assume Stan entered into a contract to sell Myers two hundred acres of farmland. Stan was aware that Myers wished to grow tobacco on the land. Stan was also aware that an unusual drainage condition made the land unsuitable for tobacco farming. Stan did not disclose the drainage condition to Myers. Myers never asked Stan about the drainage of the land or about its suitability for tobacco farming. Myers later wishes to avoid the contract. Myers cannot avoid the contract. (True or False?)

Answer – Lack of assent can occur where one of the parties engages in unfair tactics (misrepresentation, duress, undue influence, or unilateral mistake). Lack of assent can also occur where the promises are so vague that they cannot be enforced (a mutual mistake or lack of mutuality). Stan's silence constitutes a misrepresentation. Myers can, therefore, avoid the contract. A misrepresentation occurs upon a misstatement or omission of any material fact that the offeree relies upon to his or her detriment. (Number Five is False.)

SIX - Mary works as Steve's secretary for 13 years. Upon her retirement, Steve promises to pay Mary $500 per month for the next six years "because of the wonderful job she has done for this company." Steve is bound by this promise. (True or False?)

Answer - Past performance is not viewed as consideration and would not support a new contract. (Number Six is False.)

SEVEN - Nelson entered into a contract with Paul to clear all of the trees from Paul's land. Prior to completing the project, Nelson told Paul that many of the trees were taller than he had expected. Therefore, Nelson demanded $500 more for the job and Paul agreed to pay. Because this agreement was made while the contract was still being performed, Paul's agreement to pay more money is binding on him. (True or False?)

Answer - A modification to a contract by the parties is not valid if it is not supported by consideration. For a modification of a contract to be binding, something new must flow to both of the parties. Paul received no new consideration here. This rule is different with regard to the sale of goods under Article 2 of the Uniform Commercial Code. (Number Seven is False.)

EIGHT - A minor may disaffirm a contract at any time prior to reaching the age of majority or within a reasonable time thereafter. (True or False?)

Answer – A minor may disaffirm a contract either before reaching the age of majority or within a reasonable time thereafter. An exception does exist: a minor cannot disaffirm a contract for the sale of real estate until after reaching the age of majority. (Number Eight is True.)

NINE - Art's son, Milton, borrowed $500 from Second Bank. Art orally promised to repay the entire debt if his son failed to make a payment. This is an unenforceable promise. (True or False?)

Answer - Under the Statute of Frauds, a promise to answer for the debt of another must be in writing to be enforceable. (Number Nine is True.)

TEN - A contract satisfies the Statute of Frauds even if it is not signed as long as it is in writing. (True or False?)

Answer - For a writing to satisfy the Statute of Frauds, the writing must adequately describe the terms of the contract and be signed by the party being charged with performance. (Number Ten is False.)

ELEVEN - The Ashville Citizens Club contracted with Riley to give a motivational speech at its annual national convention. When the convention began, Riley found himself overwhelmed with business responsibilities. He, therefore, delegated his speech making responsibilities to Johnson, the younger sister of his most famous client. Riley was in breach of his contract with the Ashville Citizens Club. (True or False?)

Answer - Although the law favors free assignability of contract rights and free delegation of contract duties, a party to a contract is not permitted to delegate unique personal services as in this case. An assignment would also not be valid if the obligation of the other party is materially changed or if the other party's risk is increased. (Number Eleven is True.)

TWELVE - Ace Heating & Air Conditioning Company contracted with Fall to upgrade the existing air conditioning system in Fall's commercial building. The price for the upgrade was $22,000. Fall completed the work within the agreed time but inadvertently failed to use a specified type of duct in some of its connections. There was no discernible difference in the working of the system because of this. Ace's final payment to Fall was to be $7,000. Ace is legally justified in withholding this payment due to Fall's breach. (True or False?)

Answer - Since Ace has substantially performed its obligations under the contract, it is entitled to payment of the $7,000 less a small amount for damages, if any, due to Ace's breach. This would be viewed as a minor breach. (Number Twelve is False.)

AGENCY

(1)   The term "**agency**" refers to a two party relationship where one party (an agent) is authorized to act on behalf of the other (a **principal**).

    (A)   Certain general characteristics are found in this type of relationship.

        (1)   In acting for a principal, the agent has a **fiduciary duty** to act for the benefit of the principal and not in the agent's own self-interest.

        (2)   The agent may be subject to the control of the principal.

            (a)   If the agent is an independent contractor, the principal has no control.

            (b)   If the agent is an employee of the principal, the agent is subject to the control of the principal.

(2)   The principal will be bound by an agent's contracts made with third parties as long as the agent has one of the following kinds of authority.

    (A)   The agent can have **actual or express authority**. The principal can expressly confer the agent with authority either orally or in writing.

    (B)   The agent can have **apparent or ostensible authority**. This authority is created when the principal leads a third party to believe that the authority exists, usually by the principal's conduct or because the appearance of authority exists. For example, the principal gives the agent a title, such as Executive Director of Procurement.

    (C)   The agent can have "after the fact" **authority by ratification**. In this situation, the principal subsequently approves a contract made by the agent.

        (1)   There are five **requirements for a ratification**.
- The principal must have capacity.
- The principal must have knowledge of the agent's act.
- The principal must have been in existence when the contract was made.
- The principal's identity must be disclosed to the other party.
- The principal must ratify before the other party to the contract withdraws.

        (2)   If the agent does not have authority to bind the principal, the other party to the contract can withdraw at any time prior to ratification.

        (3)   Upon ratification by the principal, the agent is released as if authority had existed from the start.

        (4)   If the principal accepts benefits, this action constitutes ratification. If the agent enters into a contract without authority, but the principal accepts the goods of services contracted for by the agent, the principal must pay.

(3)   A principal is liable for all torts committed by its agents in the scope of employment.

    (A)   A principal is liable if an agent committed negligence while acting in furtherance of principal's business

    (B)   If agent commits crimes or intentional torts, the principal may be liable if the actions were committed within the scope of employment and were foreseeable.

(4)   An agent will have liability to a third party for the agent's own torts and contracts.

    (A)   An agent is liable along with the principal for the agent's own torts.

    (B)   For contracts, the general rule is that the principal is liable and the agent is not as long as the agent acted within the scope of the agent's authority and the identity of the principal was fully disclosed. This rule holds regardless of how authority arose.

        (1)   If ratification occurs, the agent is not released until that point in time.

        (2)   If the existence or identity of the principal was not disclosed, the third party can hold either the principal or the agent liable but not both.

        (3)   If the principal did not actually exist when the contract was made, only the agent is liable; ratification is not permitted.

(5)   A relationship exists between the principal and the agent.

    (A)   An agent owes certain duties to its principal.

        (1)   Contractual duties are set forth in the agreement between the parties.

        (2)   There are also duties that the law imposes regardless whether there is a written contract.

            (a)   Fiduciary duty.

            (b)   Keep confidential information confidential.

            (c)   Duty to obey instructions, act only as authorized.

            (d)   Keep accounting.

            (e)   Keep property separate.

            (f)   Act with reasonable care.

        (3)   A **del credere agent** is one who promises to reimburse principal for customers who do not pay.

    (B)   A principal has certain duties to agent.

        (1)   To act in good faith.

        (2)   To refrain from thwarting agent's activities.

        (3)   Principal must compensate agent. This includes

            (a)   Established amount of pay.

            (b)   Reimbursement for expenses.

            (c)   Indemnification for damages when agent was acting at principal's direction.

(6)   The relationship between a principal and an agent can be terminated.

    (A)   A principal can fire an agent and terminate all actual authority. Principal always has the **power to terminate an agent** unless it is an **agency coupled with an interest**. However, based on their agreement, the principal may not have the right to terminate an agent. In that case, termination by the principal can lead to breach of contract.

        (1)   As an example of an agency coupled with an interest, assume that A borrows money from the First National Bank. A pledges stock as collateral and appoints the bank as A's agent to sell the stock in event of default. A cannot terminate the bank's agency which is coupled with an interest.

        (2)   Jones hires Burns as her real estate agent promising to pay Burns a 5% commission for producing a ready, willing and able buyer. The contract is for a 6 month term. Because this is not an agency coupled with an interest, Jones can fire Burns without cause before six months are over, but Jones may be liable for breach of contract.

    (B)   The relationship can be terminated by operation of law. The following occurrences automatically terminate an agency (and hence an agent's power to bind the principal). Termination is not dependent upon notification to any party.

(1) Death of either the principal or the agent.
(2) Insanity of either the principal or the agent.
(3) Bankruptcy of the principal.
(4) Illegality of agency purpose.

PROBLEMS AND SOLUTIONS
AGENCY

ONE – Davis is employed by Peters. Davis has authority to purchase inventory up to $10,000. Davis also has the title of Merchandising Vice-President. Harper, a regular supplier to Peters who has dealt with Davis, contracts through Davis to supply Peters with inventory worth $15,000. Harper is unaware that the authority of Davis is limited to $10,000. Because Davis acted outside of his actual authority, Peters will not be bound to the contract; Harper should have checked to see if authority was present. (True or False?)

Answer - Davis had apparent authority (also known as ostensible authority) to enter into the contract with Harper. Davis has a great degree of actual authority as well as a significant job title which would lead a third party to believe that Davis has actual authority for the $15,000 transaction. (Number One is False.)

TWO - A principal can ratify a contract to which it would not otherwise be bound. Upon ratification by a principal of an unauthorized contract, the agent is released as if authority had existed from the start. (True or False?)

Answer – A principal is bound by an agent's contracts with third parties as long as authority exists, such as either actual or apparent authority. This authority can also occur by ratification. Upon ratification, the agent is released as if he or she had actual authority from the outset. The principal is then bound to the contract and the agent is not. (Number Two is True.)

THREE - Arnold is injured when Butch, a delivery driver for Dragon Furniture Co., negligently runs a red light and slams his delivery vehicle into Arnold's vehicle. Arnold must choose whether to seek recovery from Butch or from Dragon Furniture Co. because he cannot sue both. (True or False?)

Answer - Both Arnold and Dragon Furniture Co. are liable for Butch's injuries. However, if a court awards a judgment in favor of Butch and against both Arnold and Dragon Furniture Co., Butch can only collect the amount awarded one time. (Number Three is False.)

FOUR - Certain occurrences automatically terminate an agency. The death of either a principal or an agent automatically terminates an agency without notice to any party. (True or False?)

Answer – The death of either the principal or the agent terminates the agency automatically without notice. Likewise, the insanity of the principal or agent or the illegality of the agency purpose would terminate the agency. For example, assume that Acme is an agent for Ball in the gambling business in a state that allows gambling. If that state passes a law making gambling illegal, the agency is terminated automatically without notice. (Number Four is True.)

SALES – UNIFORM COMMERCIAL CODE (ARTICLE 2)

(1)   Contracts for the sale of goods are governed by **Article 2 of the Uniform Commercial Code** (UCC) whereas general contract law applies to contracts for the sale of real estate, the sale of services, the sale of a business, etc.

    (A)   Most of the rules of law found in **UCC Article 2** apply to all transactions for the sale of goods. However, a few of the rules will apply only to merchants. A **merchant** is anyone who regularly deals in goods of a particular kind.

    (B)   Many of the rules governing general contract law also apply to UCC Article 2. For example, in both cases, there has to be an offer and an acceptance for a contract to be formed.

    (C)   Certain aspects of UCC Article 2 differ significantly from contract law.

        (1)   UCC Article 2 establishes rules for the creation of a **firm offer**. A firm offer is one that will remain open and binding on the offeror without consideration.

            (a)   A firm offer must be in writing.

            (b)   A firm offer must be signed by a merchant.

            (c)   The merchant must promise to keep the offer open.

            (d)   A firm offer must relate to the sale of goods.

        (2)   UCC Article 2 allows for the modification of an existing contract without additional consideration.

            (a)   Contract must be for the sale of goods.

            (b)   Modification must be made in good faith.

        (3)   Contracts for the sale of goods for $500.00 or more must be made in a signed writing that sets forth the terms to be enforceable. This is known as the Statute of Frauds. This rule does not apply in several situations even though the contract is for goods of $500.00 or more.

            (a)   A **written contract** is not required for specially manufactured goods.

            (b)   A written contract is not required to the extent goods are received and accepted by the buyer.

            (c)   A written contract is not required if an oral contract is made between merchants and, after ten days, no objection is made to a written confirmation.

(2)   There is a risk of loss while goods are in transit from the seller to the buyer. In addition, transportation costs will be incurred for shipping. The party who is required to bear both this risk and these costs is governed by intent. If intent is not specified in the contract, the **shipping terms** are used.

    (A)   FOB (**free on board**) means that the seller bears the risk of loss and the expense of shipment to get the goods to the **FOB point**.

    (B)   FAS (**free alongside ship**) means that responsibility passes to the buyer when the goods are placed alongside the ship.

    (C)   If no intent is stated and the shipping terms are not specified, the rules for assigning the risk of loss and transportation costs depend on whether the seller is a merchant.

(1)   If the seller is a merchant, responsibility passes to the buyer upon receipt of the goods.

(2)   If the seller is not a merchant, responsibility passes to the buyer upon **tender of delivery**. Tender of delivery means that the seller has offered to place the goods in the buyer's hands.

(3)   A **warranty** is any affirmation, express or implied, as to the quality, character, or suitability or fitness of goods. It also includes any representation as to title of goods.

    (A)   Regardless of whether a warranty is explicitly mentioned, a warranty of good title is given every time that a seller sells goods.

        (1)   This warranty is given even if the seller is not a merchant.

        (2)   The seller can explicitly disclaim a warranty as to good title.

        (3)   The seller is also assumed to be making a warranty that no liens exist except those that have been disclosed.

    (B)   The seller can also make warranties as to quality, character, and suitability or fitness of the goods. These are **non-title warranties**.

        (1)   An **express warranty** is one that was made by a written or oral statement. It can also be made by supplying the buyer with a model or sample of the product to be delivered.

        (2)   A warranty can also be implied. There are two types of implied warranties.

            (a)   First is the **implied warranty of merchantability**. Every merchant warrants that the goods being sold are of at least average quality, are fit for the ordinary purpose of which such goods are used, and are properly labeled.

            (b)   Second is the **implied warranty of fitness for a particular purpose**. Where the seller knows the particular purpose for which goods are to be used and that the buyer is relying on the seller's skill or judgment, there is, unless excluded or modified, an implied warranty that the goods will be fit for the designated purpose.

        (3)   An express warranty cannot be given and excluded in the same contract.

        (4)   An implied warranty (except for a title warranty) can be excluded or eliminated in one of several ways.

            (a)   The seller can indicate that the goods are sold "as is" or "with all faults."

            (b)   The seller can use clear and conspicuous language that mentions the warranty which is eliminated.

            (c)   If the buyer has the opportunity to inspect the goods, there are no implied warranties as far as defects that the inspection would have revealed.

    (C)   The **statute of limitations** specifies the time within which a suit can be filed. For breach of warranty, the statute of limitations is four years.

        (1)   By agreement of the parties, the statute of limitations can be changed.

        (2)   Even by agreement, the statute of limitations for breach of warranty cannot be longer than four years or shorter than one year.

(4)   Privity of contract describes the relationship that exists between a buyer and seller in a contract. The two parties to the contract are in privity of contract.

    (A)   Historically, a person injured because of a defect in a product could successfully sue the seller only if the injured party was the purchaser because only these two parties were in "privity of contract."

(B)   Today, privity rules vary from state to state.

    (1)   In some states, only natural persons (human beings) in the family or household of the buyer can recover for injuries because of a defect in a product.

    (2)   In other states, any natural person injured on account of a breach of warranty can recover.

    (3)   In other states, any person (including corporations that are injured) can recover.

(5)   Both the buyer and the seller have certain rights under a contract to sell goods.

    (A)   The seller's rights include the following.

        (1)   The seller has the **right of cure**. As long as the time for performance has not passed, the seller has the right to correct defects in shipments made. The seller must give timely notice of intent to cure. Thus, for example, if the wrong goods are shipped, the seller can replace the goods without breaching the contract if the time for performance has not passed.

        (2)   The seller has the right to stop shipments already in transit if the seller learns of the buyer's insolvency. The shipment must involve at least a carload or more of goods. Seller also has the right to refuse to deliver and to demand cash upon learning of seller's insolvency.

        (3)   When a buyer wrongfully rejects goods, the seller is entitled to full price recovery only where the seller is unable to resell the goods or where reasonable effort to resell would be fruitless.

    (B)   The **buyer's rights and responsibilities** include the following.

        (1)   The buyer can reject the goods if they do not conform to the contract.

        (2)   If the seller breaches the contract, the buyer has the **right to cover**. This means that the buyer can go into the market and buy substitute goods. If more was paid than the original contract price, the initial seller is responsible for the extra amount that was paid. The buyer can also recover incidental damages if any were incurred.

            (a)   Purchase of the substitute goods must be in a commercially reasonable manner but it does not necessarily have to be for the lowest possible price.

            (b)   The buyer is entitled to recovery of the difference in the contract price and the current market price even if substitute goods are not bought.

        (3)   Upon buyer's **acceptance of goods**, there is a duty to pay. A buyer is considered to have accepted a shipment of goods upon inspection or after a reasonable opportunity to inspect the goods has passed.

        (4)   A buyer's **revocation of an acceptance** is very rarely allowed. It is only allowed if it is made very soon after acceptance and involves hidden and substantial defects.

        (5)   If goods are sold C.O.D. (collect on delivery), the buyer has no right to inspect. The buyer must pay immediately. If goods are missing or defective, buyer can bring a lawsuit.

    (C)   **Recovery for breach of contract** is the same as in contract law. Payment for damages is supposed to put the nonbreaching party in the position that he or she would have occupied had there been no breach.

(D)   The statute of limitations for breach of contract is the same as discussed above for breach of warranty.

(6)   A person who is injured by a defective product can seek recovery for damages. A person can seek recovery under any one of three legal theories: negligence, breach of warranty, or strict liability.

(A)   **Negligence** is a tort relating to defective products where the seller has breached the duty of due (reasonable) care and caused harm.

(1)   Four elements must be proven.

(a)   There was a duty to exercise reasonable care.

(b)   There has been a breach of the duty to exercise reasonable care.

(c)   A damage or injury has occurred.

(d)   The breach of duty was the proximate cause of the damage or injury.

(2)   Privity of contract between the injured party and the seller or manufacturer is not required under the theory of negligence.

(3)   A disclaimer by a seller for its negligence is only valid between buyer and seller in cases that do not involve a consumer. A consumer is one who buys goods for personal, family or household purposes.

(4)   **Contributory (comparative) negligence** of the user of the product may be a defense in a negligence case. There can be a complete bar to recovery if the injured party helped cause the accident.

(B)   Recovery can also be sought based on **breach of warranty**. In such cases, the injured party asserts that either an implied or an express warranty has been breached. Frequently, the case will be based on the implied warranty of merchantability. For example, the injured party may hold that the product was not of average quality.

(1)   Privity of contract may be necessary for recovery based on breach of warranty although the modern trend is that any foreseeable party can recover.

(C)   **Strict liability** means that the manufacturer or seller who normally deals in a product of this type is liable to users without proof of fault or lack or reasonable care. Several elements must be present in order to recover under strict liability. Privity of contract between the injured party and the defendant is not required.

(1)   The product must have been defectively manufactured or designed.

(2)   The product must have been unreasonably dangerous.

(3)   The defect must have been the proximate cause of the injury.

(4)   The defendant manufactured or regularly sells the product. (This means the injured party can hold a manufacturer, retailer, or even a wholesaler liable.)

PROBLEMS AND SOLUTIONS
SALES - UNIFORM COMMERCIAL CODE (ARTICLE 2)

ONE - Article 2 of the Uniform Commercial Code (UCC) refers to state law that governs transactions involving goods. Article 2 applies only to transactions involving merchants. (True or False?)

Answer - UCC Article 2 governs transactions involving goods even if a merchant is not involved in the transaction. For example, Paul sells his piano to Les, a neighbor. This transaction is governed by UCC Article 2 although neither party is a merchant. A merchant is one who regularly deals in goods of the kind at issue. A car dealer, for example, is a merchant with respect to cars but not with respect to jewelry. (Number One is False.)

TWO - MP, a lumber distributor, offers in writing to supply American Builders, Inc., with 4,000 feet of salt-treated lumber for $.21 per foot. The offer was signed by the sales representative for MP and stated that it would remain open for 45 days. American Builders paid nothing in consideration for this offer. MP received no response from American Builders and withdrew its offer on the 40th day. American Builders faxed its order for 4,000 ft. of salt-treated lumber to MP on the 45th day. MP must sell the lumber at the agreed price of $.21 per foot. (True or False?)

Answer - MP has made a firm offer, one that cannot be withdrawn during the specified time. A firm offer is any offer for the sale of goods that (1) is made by a merchant, (2) is in writing, (3) is signed, and (4) promises to keep the offer open. The offer made my MP meets all of these criteria. No consideration needs to be paid to the offeror to create a firm offer. (Number Two is True.)

THREE - Some contracts must be in writing and signed to be enforceable. Gail promises orally to sell her sailboat to Lake for $600. Gail's promise is not enforceable because it is not in writing. (True or False?)

Answer - Any contract for the sale of goods in the amount of $500 or more must be in writing and signed to be enforceable. This is one of the rules under the Statute of Frauds. This rule is not dependent upon either party being a merchant. (Number Three is True.)

FOUR - Wolf purchased a painting from the Houston First Street Gallery for $2,000. Because of the size and fragile nature of the painting, Wolf told the owner that he would return that evening with a different vehicle to bring the painting home. That afternoon, both the gallery and Wolf's painting, were destroyed by fire. Wolf cannot recover the $2,000 that he paid for the painting. (True or False?)

Answer - When the seller is a merchant, as is the Houston First Street Gallery, the risk of loss does not pass to the buyer until the goods are actually received. In this case, the painting was merely tendered (rather than delivered) to Wolf. Therefore, the risk of loss remained with the merchant and Wolf can recover his $2,000. (Number Four is False.)

FIVE - Porter sold a used generator to Dart Builders, Inc., for $300. Porter wrote on the receipt that the sale was "as is." This language eliminates all warranties including the warranty of good title. (True or False?)

Answer - The term "as is" eliminates non-title warranties but has no effect on the warranty of title. To eliminate the warranty of title, one must specifically state that title is not warranted or must state that the goods are subject to liens. (Number Five is False.)

SIX - When a seller learns of a buyer's insolvency, the seller has the right to demand cash before delivering goods even though the contract for the sale of goods does not mention this issue. (True or False?)

Answer - The seller's right to demand cash upon learning of a buyer's insolvency arises not from the contract but is implied by the Uniform Commercial Code article on sales. (Number Six is True.)

SEVEN - Goods are shipped to a buyer who has 15 days to return them if not fully satisfied. Title to the goods passes to the buyer when the buyer takes delivery from the common carrier. (True or False?)

Answer - This is a "sale on approval." No sale occurs, and title does not pass, until the goods have been accepted. This generally occurs after the agreed time has passed and the goods are not returned. (Number Seven is False.)

EIGHT - To establish a case of negligence, one must prove that the seller had a duty, breached that duty, that damages or injuries occurred, and that the breach was the proximate cause of the injury or damages. (True or False?)

Answer - These four are the elements of a negligence case and all four must be proven. (Number Eight is True.)

NINE - Troy Bat Manufacturing, Inc. produces metal baseball bats and sells them to Gray Distributors, Inc. Gray in turn sells them to area retailers. Travis was injured when a Troy bat shattered, sending a metal splinter into his arm. Travis would have an action under strict liability against Troy Bat Manufacturing, Inc., or against the retailer that sold the bat, but not against Gray Distributors, Inc. (True or False?)

Answer - Those parties liable under the theory of strict liability include the manufacturer, the retailer, and any person who, in the regular course of business, sold the product that caused the injury, including the wholesaler. (Number Nine is False.)

SECURED TRANSACTIONS - UNIFORM COMMERCIAL CODE (ARTICLE 9)

(1)   A creditor may seek security to reduce the risk of loss on a loan or some other obligation.

    (A)   A **lien** is a claim against property that gives the lien holder the right to repossess and sell the property. There are many types of liens. A **security interest** is a voluntary lien in personal property. It gives the secured party the right to repossess and sell collateral. In other words, the lien gives the secured party the right to foreclose on property that has been provided as security for an obligation.

    (B)   **Article 9 of the Uniform Commercial Code** (UCC) governs liens that are placed on personal property or on accounts receivable and also governs sale of accounts receivable. UCC Article 9 does not govern real estate liens or mortgages.

    (C)   A **security agreement** is a contract or other agreement that gives a lien and, therefore, creates a security interest in the specified property. A security agreement need not be in writing.

    (D)   Upon **attachment**, the security interest is enforceable against the debtor. For attachment, three elements must be present.

        (1)   The debtor must have rights in the collateral. For example, a person offers to put up a car as collateral for a bank loan. The person must have rights (such as ownership) in the car.

        (2)   The secured party must have given value. In the above illustration, the bank loans money to the debtor.

        (3)   A security agreement must exist. Usually, a security agreement is drawn up and signed.

    (E)   The security interest can also be perfected. This gives the secured party priority over some other parties that might also have a claim to the collateral. Perhaps, in the previous example, the debtor later borrows money from a different lender and puts up the same car as collateral. **Perfection** provides notice of the security interest and usually gives priority in the collateral to the first lender who perfects.

        (1)   Perfection is done to protect a lien so that few other parties can supersede it.

        (2)   Generally, a security interest is perfected by filing a **financing statement** (or written notice) in the public records at the appropriate public office.

            (a)   Filing a financing statement is not necessary if the creditor takes physical possession of the collateral. At a pawn shop, for example, the creditor retains the pawned item; thus, a financing statement is not needed for perfection.

            (b)   Filing a financing statement is also not necessary if the transaction is a **purchase money security interest in consumer goods** where the seller or lender retains a security interest in property that has been sold to secure payment for that item.

        (3)   Perfection occurs upon filing or possession but does not occur before attachment. If the secured party files its financing statement within the ten days after attachment, the secured creditor has priority over any other creditor who takes an interest in the collateral during that ten day period.

(4)   Perfection normally lasts for up to five years and may be continued for an additional five years.

  (a)   When debt is fully paid, a **termination statement** can be filed to indicate the release.

  (b)   A partial release can also be made. This is most common when the debtor is going to sell a portion of the collateral and use the proceeds to pay the secured creditor.

(2)   Rules for priority are needed to resolve conflicts that are created between parties having claims to or liens on the same property.

  (A)   A perfected security interest (and a trustee in bankruptcy) take priority over an unperfected one.

  (B)   Generally, the first party to perfect its security interest takes priority. However, an exception does exist for inventory. The debtor can promote a second creditor to the first position with respect to newly acquired inventory if the first lender is properly notified and a financing statement is filed in favor the second lender before the new merchandise is received.

  (C)   A judgment occurs when the courts award a party damages. A **judgment lien** can be filed against property to secure payment of the judgment. A judgment lien is perfected only if officer of the law physically seizes the goods (that is, levies on the goods). Recordation of a judgment is irrelevant (except as to real estate).

  (D)   An unperfected security interest has priority over general creditors.

  (E)   **Buyers in the ordinary course of business** (BOCs) usually prevail over everyone whether perfected or not. Buying in the ordinary course of business means buying inventory items from a party that normally deals in such goods.

    (1)   A dealer can be either at retail or wholesale. For example, a distributor who purchases goods in the ordinary course of business from a manufacturer is a BOC.

    (2)   It is unreasonable to require that every purchaser of inventory should have to check to see if goods are subject to a security interest.

(3)   If the debtor defaults on the obligation, the secured party can take action.

  (A)   **Default** is the failure to perform in accordance with the terms of the security agreement. Default can include the failure to make payments when due, the failure to keep collateral in good repair, or the failure to maintain insurance on the collateral.

  (B)   The secured party has basic **rights upon default.**

    (1)   May retain collateral if it is already held or may take possession. Secured party can only take possession if that can be done without breaching the peace. If that is not possible, secured party must seek a court order of possession.

    (2)   After repossession, secured party can sell the collateral. Secured party must notify debtor of the sale.

      (a)   Secured party must use commercially reasonable practices for the sale. It may be a private sale; auction is not required.

      (b)   **Redemption** is the right of the debtor to pay the obligation in full prior to the sale and get the collateral back.

      (c)   If collateral is sold, any amount received in excess of the debt goes to the debtor.

(3)   Special rules relate to a security interest involving consumer goods. These rules apply if the debtor has made payments of 60% or more of the cash price (with respect to a purchase money security interest in consumer goods) or 60% or more of a nonpurchase money loan that is secured by consumer goods.

   (a)   The secured party has no right of strict foreclosure; this means that the secured party has no right to keep the collateral and cancel the debt.

   (b)   The creditor must sell the goods within 90 days or be liable for any damages.

PROBLEMS AND SOLUTIONS
SECURED TRANSACTIONS - UNIFORM COMMERCIAL CODE (ARTICLE 9)

ONE - Article 9 of the Uniform Commercial Code governs real estate mortgages. (True or False?)

Answer - Article 9 of the Uniform Commercial Code governs security interests on personal property. Article 9 also governs sales of accounts receivable. (Number One is False.)

TWO - Bayside Brick Company has been in business since 1909 without the assistance of any lending institution. Bayside Brick Company now wishes to expand its business and seeks a $150,000 loan from Heartland Bank. Heartland Bank's security interest in the current inventory of Bayside Brick will attach immediately after the president of Bayside Brick has signed the security agreement and is given a check by Heartland Bank for $150,000. (True or False?)

Answer - For attachment to occur, three things must happen. First, Bayside Brick must have rights in the collateral. Here, Bayside Brick Company already owns its inventory, thereby satisfying this element. Second, Bayside Brick must receive value. This requirement is satisfied when the loan proceeds are received. Third, there must be a security agreement. In this case, the president of Bayside Brick signed the security agreement. (Number Two is True.)

THREE - On May 11, Georgia Finance Institute loaned Tracy Transport $98,000 to purchase four used trucks. Tracy Transport spent all of the proceeds from the loan to purchase the trucks from Marks Motor Co. Tracy Transport signed a security agreement but Georgia Finance Institute failed to record its lien on the titles to the trucks. This transaction constitutes a purchase money security interest. (True or False?)

Answer - A purchase money security interest arises when a borrower uses loan proceeds to purchase the items that are the collateral for the loan. It does not matter whether the lender is the seller of the items or is a third party, such as a bank. The money must be used to buy the items that serve as the collateral. (Number Three is True.)

FOUR - Perfection refers to the strengthening of a security interest so that other parties cannot assert greater claim to collateral than the party whose security interest is perfected. Generally, perfection occurs by filing a financing statement in the appropriate state or county office. (True or False?)

> *Answer - Perfection normally occurs by filing a financing statement. It can also occur by the filing of the security agreement or can occur by taking possession of the collateral. It can also occur automatically as in the case of a purchase money security interest in consumer goods. (Number Four is True.)*

FIVE - A recorded judgment is similar to a perfected security interest and one who records a judgment takes priority over subsequently perfected security interests. (True or False?)

> *Answer - Recordation of a judgment affects real estate only. For a judgment to affect personal property, the judgment creditor must cause the sheriff to perform a levy. When the levy is executed, it is tantamount to the perfection of a security interest in personal property. (Number Five is False.)*

SIX - Only a buyer of consumer goods may qualify as a "buyer in the ordinary course of business." (True or False?)

> *Answer - Anyone who purchases from inventory in the regular course of business qualifies as a buyer in the ordinary course. One who buys six riding lawn mowers for his landscaping business is as much a buyer in the ordinary course as the person who buys a single riding mower for home use. (Number Six is False.)*

SEVEN - Default under a security agreement is the failure to perform in accordance with the terms of the security agreement. Failure to keep collateral in good repair could constitute an event of default under a security agreement. (True or False?)

> *Answer - The most significant type of default by a debtor under a security agreement is the failure to pay the underlying debt. However, other events of default include the failure to keep collateral in good repair, the failure to maintain insurance on the collateral as agreed, or (if provided in the security agreement) moving the collateral from one location to another or from one state to another. (Number Seven is True.)*

EIGHT - Wise financed the purchase of an expensive outdoor gas barbecue grill through Uniform Financial Services, Inc. Wise is in default in his payment obligations to Uniform Financial Services, Inc., which desires to repossess and sell the grill. Uniform Financial Services, Inc., need not first give notice to Wise before repossessing the grill. (True or False?)

> *Answer - A secured creditor must give notice of a sale after collateral has been repossessed but need not give notice before the repossession. A secured creditor may not, however, breach the peace when repossessing. (Number Eight is True.)*

NEGOTIABLE INSTRUMENTS

(1)   A **negotiable instrument** is a written contract that can be used as a substitute for money. In general, there are two types of negotiable instruments.

    (A)   A **promissory note** is a written promise to make payment. There are two parties to a promissory note.

        (1)   The **maker** is the party who issues the promise to pay.

        (2)   The **payee** is the party to whom the promise is made.

    (B)   A **draft** is a written order to make payment but three parties are involved. Even if a single party occupies two of these positions, it is still a three party instrument.

        (1)   The **drawer** is the party who issues the instrument.

        (2)   The **drawee** is the party who is ordered to make payment.

        (3)   The payee is the party to whom the instrument is payable.

    (C)   A **check** is one example of a draft. The owner of the account signs the check and is the drawer. The bank is the drawee. The payee will be indicated on the check. If a person makes out a check to himself, that party is both the drawer and the payee.

    (D)   A **trade acceptance** is another example of a draft. It is issued pursuant to a sale of goods as a way of extending credit to a buyer. It is an order to pay for goods at a point of time in the future. The seller is the drawer. The buyer is the drawee who will pay. The seller is also usually the payee although payment may be directed to a third party. The buyer agrees to be bound by the draft by accepting (signing) it.

(2)   A **holder in due course** of a negotiable instrument is entitled to payment despite most defenses that the maker or drawer may have. In addition, a holder in due course gets good title to the instrument.

    (A)   There are several exceptions to the rule that a holder in due course takes the negotiable instrument free of personal defenses.

        (1)   Infancy is still a defense against a holder in due course. Thus, a minor who signs a promissory note cannot be held liable.

        (2)   If the instrument was created under extreme duress.

        (3)   Bankruptcy of the party designated to make payment.

        (4)   If fraud occurred that the signer of the instrument had no opportunity to detect. This occurs when the signer was tricked in some manner. This is sometimes referred to as fraud in the factum.

    (B)   A shelter provision exists that says that a party who acquires an instrument directly or indirectly from a holder in due course can assert the rights of a holder in due course unless the acquirer was a party to a fraud or illegality involving the instrument or, as a prior holder, had notice of a defect in the instrument.

(3)   Several steps are necessary for a party to become a holder in due course of a negotiable instrument.

    (A)   A document is only considered a negotiable instrument if it has a particular form.

        (1)   It must be in writing and signed by the maker or drawer.

        (2)   It must contain an unconditional promise or order to pay.

        (3)   It must be for a sum certain in money.

        (4)   It must be payable at a definite time or on demand.

        (5)   It must be payable to order of a party or be payable to the bearer of the instrument (except for checks).

(6)   It must contain no other obligation, promise, or requirements.

(B)   The person trying to assert status as a holder in due course of the instrument must be a **holder**. The person is a holder if the instrument was properly negotiated to him. There are two steps for one to become a holder.

    (1)   First, to be a holder, one must have physical possession of the instrument.

    (2)   Second, the instrument must "run to" the possessor. This term means that the instrument has to be payable to the person who possesses it, or it must be indorsed (by the proper party) to the person who possesses it.

        (a)   A **bearer instrument** is one that is made payable to (1) cash or (2) "bearer" or (3) a specified party or the bearer of the instrument. A bearer instrument runs to any party who has physical possession of it.

        (b)   An **order instrument** is one that is payable to a particular person. The person to whom the instrument is payable can, by indorsement, cause the instrument to be payable to another person or can, by blank indorsement, convert the instrument to bearer paper.

        (c)   There are a number of different types of **indorsements**.
  - A **blank indorsement** is merely a signature.
  - A **special indorsement** indicates to whom the instrument is payable.
  - A **restrictive indorsement** limits the use of the instrument. Including "for deposit only," for example, makes the indorsement restrictive.
  - A **qualified indorsement** is one where the indorsement is without recourse. By signing in this manner, the indorser is canceling his or her contractual obligations under the instrument.

(C)   If a party has possession of a document that runs to that party and meets the six form requirements above, that party is viewed as the holder of the negotiable instrument. That party can rise to a holder in due course if five more requirements are met.

    (1)   The holder must take the instrument in good faith. There has to be honesty in fact. Thus, for example, someone who steals an instrument cannot be a holder in due course of that instrument.

    (2)   The holder must give value for the instrument. This is similar to consideration in contract law except that past consideration is valid value for a negotiable instrument whereas future consideration is not sufficient as value.

    (3)   The holder must take the instrument without notice that it is overdue.

    (4)   The holder must take the instrument without notice that it has been dishonored.

    (5)   The holder must take the instrument without notice of any defenses.

(4)   The relationship that exists between a bank and its customers is also important.

    (A)   The bank (the drawee on a check) has an obligation to a customer (the drawer of a check).

(1) Generally, a bank is obligated to follow its customer's orders. Those orders are usually that the bank should pay any check drawn by the customer as long as a holder presents the check.

(2) For this reason, a bank can pay an overdraft and then recover from its customer even if the customer is not supposed to overdraw the account.

(3) If a loss occurs because of negligence, the negligent party usually bears the loss.

(B) A bank must also follow a customer's order not to pay.

(1) An oral stop order is valid for 14 days.

(2) A written stop order is valid for six months.

(5) The parties who sign a negotiable instrument have certain legal obligations.

(A) There are two types of contractual liability. A party with **primary liability** promises to be bound by the instrument. That party has made a promise to pay the original amount to any holder of the instrument. A party with **secondary liability** promises to pay any holder if the instrument is dishonored. For example, other signers might be liable if the maker or the drawee does not pay the instrument.

(1) A maker who issues a promissory note has primary liability.

(2) An acceptor who is ordinarily a buyer of goods who signs the face of a trade acceptance, thereby agreeing to be bound by it, has primary liability.

(3) A drawer who issues a check or other draft has secondary liability.

(4) An indorser who lends his name to an instrument to provide surety has secondary liability.

(5) An indorser who signs his name to an instrument to properly negotiate it has secondary liability. However, an indorsement "without recourse" eliminates liability in most cases.

(6) A person who presents an instrument for payment and a person who transfers an instrument to another party make, by operation of law, certain warranties regarding the instrument. The warranties in these two cases differ slightly but, in general, they are as follows.

(A) The person has good title to the instrument that is being presented or transferred.

(B) All signatures are genuine or authorized.

(C) There are no known defenses to the instrument.

PROBLEMS AND SOLUTIONS
NEGOTIABLE INSTRUMENTS

ONE - The three parties to a draft are the drawer, the drawee, and the payee. (True or False?)

> *Answer - The drawer is the person who issues the draft. The drawee is the person who is ordered to pay. The payee is the person to whom the instrument is payable. (Number One is True.)*

TWO - To enable commercial paper to be freely transferable, the law established the concept of negotiability. An instrument will be considered negotiable if it contains the legend "Negotiable Instrument" anywhere on the face of the instrument. (True or False?)

Answer - For an instrument to be considered negotiable, the instrument must (1) be in writing and signed by a maker or drawer, (2) contain an unconditional promise or order to pay, (3) be for a sum certain in money, (4) be payable at a definite time or on demand, (5) be payable to order or bearer (except checks), and (6) can contain no obligations or requirements other than the obligation to pay money. (Number Two is False.)

THREE - Barnes delivers a draft to Young and Company that contains an order to pay $20,000 on June 15, Year One, "if goods have been received and inspected." Since the draft qualifies in all other respects as a trade acceptance, the condition regarding inspection of the goods will not render it non-negotiable. (True or False?)

Answer - For a draft to be considered negotiable, it must contain an unconditional promise or order to pay. Inclusion of any conditions destroys negotiability. (Number Three is False.)

FOUR - To qualify as a holder of a negotiable instrument, the instrument must be payable to or properly negotiated to the person in possession of it. For this to occur, the instrument must be payable to the person who possesses it, must be indorsed (by the proper party) to the person who possesses it, or must be payable to "cash" or to "bearer." (True or False?)

Answer - An instrument "runs to" the possessor if it is issued to him, has been indorsed to the possessor, or is bearer paper. (Number Four is True.)

FIVE - Hunt is in possession of a negotiable instrument which was originally payable to Boston. Hunt acquired the instrument by defrauding Boston. Hunt can qualify as a holder in due course, but only if he gave value for the instrument. (True or False?)

Answer - To qualify as a holder in due course of a negotiable instrument, one must, among other things, take the instrument in good faith. Good faith means honesty in fact. One cannot claim to have taken an instrument in good faith when it was obtained by fraud. (Number Five is False.)

SIX - Hill is in receipt of a draft that was issued by Kemper. The draft is due and payable in full on June 2, Year One. On June 3, Year One, Hill transferred the draft to Watson who took the instrument in good faith, for value, and without notice of any defenses to the instrument. Watson may qualify as a holder in due course of the instrument. (True or False?)

Answer - Because Watson received the instrument one day after it was due, he cannot qualify as a holder in due course. To qualify as a holder in due course, one must take the instrument without notice that it is overdue. (Number Six is False.)

SEVEN - Baker issued a check in payment for several bonds owned by Willard. Willard negotiated the check to Towne who qualified as a holder in due course. Baker filed bankruptcy before the check was cashed. Baker's bankruptcy discharge is a valid defense to Towne's claim for payment. (True or False?)

Answer - Bankruptcy of a maker or drawer is a valid defense against the claim for payment by a holder in due course. (Number Seven is True.)

EIGHT - Case issued a check in the amount of $500. Archer, a holder of the check, raised the amount of the check by $1,000 and negotiated it to a holder in due course. Case can never be liable for more than the original amount of $500. (True or False?)

Answer - Case would be liable to any holder in due course for at least $500 and could be liable for the entire altered amount if Case was negligent in the manner in which he filled out the check. For example, Case could be liable for the entire amount if the check had been written in a manner that made it easy for the amount to be raised. (Number Eight is False.)

NINE - One who transfers an instrument to another warrants that the instrument has not been materially altered and that there are no defenses of any party which can be asserted against the transferor. (True or False?)

Answer - In addition, the transferor warrants that he or she has no notice of insolvency of the maker, drawer, or acceptor. (Number Nine is True.)

TEN - Hogan writes a check on his account at First National Bank in the amount of $543 payable to French. Even though there is less than $200 in Hogan's account at First National Bank, the bank can honor the check and recover the difference from Hogan personally. (True or False?)

Answer - A bank (or savings and loan association, credit union, or trust company) can pay an overdraft and recover from its customer even if the bank prohibits the customer from overdrawing. (Number Ten is True.)

BANKRUPTCY

(1)   The **bankruptcy laws** in the U.S. have two primary goals.
    (A)   The laws seek the fair distribution of assets to creditors.
    (B)   The laws seek to discharge an honest debtor from debt.

(2)   Several basic concepts are found in bankruptcy cases.
    (A)   Creditors are stopped from taking action against the debtor (such as repossessing goods) to give the debtor time (under the control of the court) to take an organized action.
    (B)   In a **liquidation**, business is stopped and all assets are gathered and sold with the proceeds being distributed to the debtors according to their level of security or priority. If the debtor is an individual, the debts are discharged.
    (C)   In a **reorganization**, business continues under limited court supervision while a plan is created so that the company can remain in business. If properly approved, the plan is put into action. The resolution of debts is based on the provisions of the plan.

(3)   Bankruptcy laws in the U. S. are based on the **Bankruptcy Reform Act of 1978** and later amendments to it. State law does play a supporting role at times.
    (A)   The Bankruptcy Reform Act is divided into chapters, each of which sets guidelines for a specific part of the bankruptcy process.
        (1)   Chapter 1 provides definitions.
        (2)   Chapter 3 examines the administration of bankruptcy cases.
        (3)   Chapter 5 discusses debtors, creditors, and the estate.
        (4)   Chapter 7 describes a liquidation which is sometimes referred to as a straight bankruptcy.
        (5)   Chapter 9 sets guidelines for the bankruptcy of municipalities.
        (6)   Chapter 11 describes a reorganization.
        (7)   Chapter 12 covers a farmer's reorganization.
        (8)   Chapter 13 is for the reorganization of individuals.
    (B)   The **bankruptcy trustee** plays a significant role in the bankruptcy process, especially in liquidations.
        (1)   The bankruptcy trustee is not an employee of the government but is supervised by the U.S. Trustee which is a government agency.
        (2)   The bankruptcy trustee has a number of duties including the following.
            (a)   Collects the debtor's property.
            (b)   Under certain conditions, invalidates transfers made before the bankruptcy petition.
            (c)   Liquidates the debtor's property.
            (d)   Accepts or rejects lease contracts and executory contracts.
            (e)   Determines the validity of the claims made against the debtor.
            (f)   If appropriate, objects to the debtor's discharge at the end of the process.

(4)   The bankruptcy process can be commenced by the debtor (a **voluntary bankruptcy**) or by the creditors (an **involuntary bankruptcy**).
    (A)   Most debtors are eligible for a voluntary bankruptcy except banks, savings and loan associations, insurance companies, and charities.

   (1) Insolvency is not a requirement for a voluntary bankruptcy.

   (2) Upon receiving a petition, the bankruptcy court will enter an **order for relief**. The order for relief has several effects.

     (a) An automatic stay comes into effect so that creditors are prevented from taking action against the debtor. This gives the debtor some temporary relief from creditors and keeps one creditor from getting an advantage over another.

     (b) There is the creation of an estate so that the assets can be gathered and protected.

     (c) The debtor comes under the control of the bankruptcy court.

  (B) If an **involuntary bankruptcy petition** is filed by the creditors, they must prove that they have grounds for the action. Must show that debtor is not paying debts as they come due. This is known as insolvency in the equity sense.

   (1) An involuntary petition is only allowed in **chapter 7** and **chapter 11** cases. Certain debtors are excluded including farmers, banks, savings and loan associations, insurance companies, and railroads.

   (2) If debtor does not contest the petition, an order for relief is entered with the same results as in a voluntary bankruptcy.

   (3) For an involuntary petition, at least three creditors must sign and they must have total unsecured claims of $10,775 or more. If the debtor has 11 or fewer creditors, only a single creditor must sign but the unsecured claims of that creditor must still be $10,775 or more.

   (4) If an involuntary petition is filed without good cause, the debtor can recover damages including attorney fees.

(5) An **automatic stay** is created by an order for relief.

  (A) The purpose of the stay is to give the debtor breathing room from the actions of its creditors. In a liquidation, it also gives the bankruptcy trustee time to gather the assets of the business. In a reorganization, it gives the parties time to create a plan of reorganization.

  (B) The scope of the stay is very broad. It stops almost all creditor actions. It stops lawsuits, levies, garnishments, harassments, recordation of liens, and even actions by the IRS.

  (C) Certain actions are not stopped by the automatic stay. These exceptions include criminal actions, spousal and child support actions, actions by regulatory agencies, tax audits, demand for tax returns, tax assessments, and notices of tax deficiency. Other demands by taxing authorities would violate the stay.

  (D) Unless a creditor gets the court to issue a relief from the stay, the stay will continue in effect for a specific duration.

   (1) In a chapter 7 case, the stay continues until the bankruptcy is dismissed, the debtor is discharged, or the liquidation is completed.

   (2) In chapter 11, 12, and 13 cases, the stay continues until a reorganization plan is confirmed.

  (E) A creditor can ask the bankruptcy court for a relief from the stay. The creditor might request permission to enforce or perfect a lien or proceed against the debtor with a claim. Permission is only granted in limited circumstances.

   (1) Relief may be granted where there is a lack of adequate protection. Permission is granted "for cause."

(2) Relief may be granted for certain encumbered property that is not needed for reorganization.

(6) Upon the entering of an order for relief, a bankruptcy estate is created for the property.

    (A) Includes real property, personal property, tangible property, intangible property, owned by the debtor on the date bankruptcy petition is filed. Also includes the proceeds from the sale, rent, or insurance coverage of such property and can include leases and contracts to which the debtor is a party (if these have value).

    (B) Property can also be included in the bankruptcy estate because of the 180 day rule. Property will come into the estate if the debtor is entitled to it within 180 days after the petition by virtue of a life insurance policy, an inheritance, or a property settlement agreement with a spouse. Note that most property the debtor receives within 180 days of bankruptcy does not come into the estate. It is only included if received from one of these three limited categories.

    (C) Property can also be brought into the bankruptcy estate via trustee powers. Property which the debtor did not own on the date that the petition is filed can be recovered by the trustee if it was transferred shortly before the bankruptcy. In addition, certain liens and post petition transfers can also be voided.

        (1) **Preferential transfers** can be voided. The party receiving the transfer must return it to the estate. Five elements have to be present for avoidance to be appropriate.

            (a) There has to be a transfer of money or property to or for the benefit of a creditor.
- In this case, a transfer does not just mean a voluntary transfer. For example, a judgment lien placed against the debtor's property during the 90 days prior to bankruptcy can usually qualify as a preferential transfer.
- A transfer is not limited to money or property. The granting of a lien or security interest or the perfection of a lien or security interest can qualify as preferential transfer.
- If a contemporaneous transfer is made for new value, that is not a preferential transfer. Likewise, a transfer in the ordinary course of business, and (in consumer cases) transfers of not more than $600, are not considered preferential transfers.

            (b) It has to be for, or on account of, an antecedent (preexisting) debt.

            (c) Debtor had to be insolvent at the time of the transfer. (But this is usually presumed.)

            (d) Transfer had to be made within 90 days prior to the bankruptcy. If the transfer was made to an insider, it can be voided if it was made within one year prior to the bankruptcy.

            (e) The position of the creditor in relation to other creditors had to be improved by the transfer. For example, a fully secured creditor does not improve its position when it receives payment within 90 days of bankruptcy.

        (2) **Fraudulent conveyances** can be voided. The trustee can void any transfer made by the debtor during one year prior to bankruptcy if either of two events occurred.

            (a) The transfer was made with the intent to hinder or delay creditors or

> (b) The transfer was for less than adequate consideration and the debtor was insolvent or the transfer rendered the debtor insolvent.
>
> (3) Certain statutory (and other) liens and post petition transfers can be voided. For example, a landlord's lien can be voided.

(D) In addition to the property discussed above, the debtor (especially if the debtor is a business) may be a lessee of real estate or personal property. Or, the debtor may be a party to an executory (unfulfilled) contract.

    (1) Such lease rights or contract rights may be valuable. For example, the debtor may be a lessee of a commercial property under a long term lease with terms so favorable that someone would be willing to pay money to take over the lease. In such cases the trustee can sell (assign) the unexpired contract as long as any defaults are cured first.

    (2) On the other hand, if the unexpired lease or executory contract is not favorable (it is burdensome), the trustee will reject such a lease or contract, releasing the debtor from all but 12 months of the lease.

(7) The discharge of an individual debtor occurs in a **chapter 7 bankruptcy**, a liquidation.

(A) A discharge is an absolute release from personal liability for obligations. It is only available to individuals. Corporations which go through chapter 7 are liquidated and, therefore, cease to exist.

(B) The courts can deny a discharge so that no debts are discharged.

    (1) Denial can occur because of dishonesty or lack of cooperation.

    (2) Denial can occur because of a prior discharge. Only one discharge is allowed an individual under chapter 7 every six years. The time period is measured from filing date to filing date, from the filing of the previous petition to the filing of the current petition.

(C) Certain types of debts are not discharged in a chapter 7 bankruptcy. **Debts not discharged** include the following.

    (1) Certain taxes incurred within (3) years of the filing date and loans to pay such taxes.

    (2) Debts incurred through fraud or through false financial statements.

    (3) Unscheduled debts where the debtor failed to list the creditor and the debt.

    (4) Defalcation by a fiduciary, larceny, or embezzlement.

    (5) Child support and alimony payments.

    (6) Debts arising from willful or malicious torts. Injuries caused by drunk driving.

    (7) Fines and penalties owed to the government which are three years old or less.

    (8) Most educational loans.

    (9) Debts not discharged in a prior bankruptcy.

(8) In a chapter 7 bankruptcy, one general rule is that a **perfected lien** will remain undisturbed as long as the lien was not a preferential transfer or a fraudulent conveyance.

(A) Examples of such undisturbed liens would include the following.

    (1) A recorded mortgage on real estate.

    (2) A perfected security interest in goods, such as inventory.

    (3) An automatically perfected security interest in consumer goods acquired by a debtor such as furniture or a television.

(B) If the trustee sells property that is encumbered by a properly perfected lien or security interest, the proceeds must be applied to satisfy the perfected liens (or security interest) on the property sold. Any balance in excess of the debt that was secured goes into the estate for distribution to the unsecured creditors.

(9) In a chapter 7 bankruptcy, the trustee sells the debtor's property (paying perfected liens against any of the property sold) and the balance that remains, if any, goes to unsecured creditors in the **order of priorities contained in the bankruptcy code**.

   (A) If money is available, distribution is made to unsecured creditors in the following order. Each level is paid completely before moving to the next lower level. The first seven of these obligations are known generally as priority claims.

      (1) **Administrative expenses** which includes trustee's and examiner's fees, accountant's and attorney's fees, post-petition wages, and money spent to preserve the estate.

      (2) In an involuntary bankruptcy, a period of time may occur between the filing of a petition and the issuance of an order for relief. Claims may arise in the ordinary course of business during this period. These are sometimes referred to as amounts owed to **gap creditors**.

      (3) Wages up to $4,300, owed to employees of the debtor, earned within the 90 days before the filing of the bankruptcy petition. Any amounts in excess of $4,300 per employee are viewed as general unsecured claims.

      (4) Employee benefit plan contributions earned within the 180 days before the filing.

      (5) Consumer deposits up to $1,950 for undelivered goods or services. Includes goods held by the debtor on lay-away. Any amount in excess of $1,950 per person is viewed as a general unsecured claim.

      (6) Spousal and child support.

      (7) Certain taxes (usually taxes 3 years old or less.)

      (8) General unsecured claims that were filed in a timely manner.

      (9) General unsecured claims that were not filed in a timely manner.

      (10) Fines, penalties, and punitive damages.

      (11) Interest on claims.

      (12) Any remaining balance goes to the debtor.

(10) In a **chapter 11 bankruptcy**, the creditors are held off to permit the debtor (either an individual or a business) to reorganize.

   (A) A **creditors' committee** is established. It is made up of the seven largest unsecured creditors who are willing to serve in this capacity. The committee is supposed to help ensure the fairness of the process. The committee consults with the participants and makes recommendations where appropriate.

   (B) Normally, after the order for relief is entered, the debtor is permitted to continue operating the business while a plan of reorganization is being formulated. In this circumstance, the debtor is referred to as the **debtor in possession**. The creditors may ask the courts to remove the debtor if they fear that the business will be damaged.

   (C) For the first 120 days after the order for relief, only the debtor is permitted to file a **plan of reorganization** or rehabilitation.

      (1) The creditors' committee can assist the debtor in formulating a plan or, after the time limit has expired, may present its own plan to the court for consideration.

      (2) After the time limit, any interested party can file a plan. However, eventually, only one plan can be confirmed.

(D) **Voting on a reorganization plan** is done by classes. Similar creditors and shareholders are placed in groups or classes.
    (1) Confirmation of a particular plan may occur in either of two ways.
        (a) Every class accepts the plan.
        (b) The bankruptcy court can approve the plan even though some classes do not approve it but only if the court finds the plan to be fair and equitable. This process is referred to as a **cram down**.

(E) In a chapter 7 bankruptcy, a corporation cannot receive a discharge because the company has been liquidated and has ceased to operate. However, in a chapter 11 bankruptcy, the debtor continues to exist. If a reorganization plan provides for it, the court may issue a discharge.

(F) The court may convert a chapter 11 bankruptcy into a chapter 7 bankruptcy at any time if that outcome appears to be fairer to the parties involved.

(11) An individual can file for rehabilitation under **chapter 13 of the bankruptcy code**. Individuals can also reorganize under chapter 11 (if they do not qualify under chapter 13) but this is infrequent.

(A) To qualify for chapter 13, debtor must 1.) be an individual, 2.) with regular income and 3.) have unsecured debt of less than $269,250 and secured debt of less than $807,750.

(B) The plan is approved by the court and not by a vote of the creditors.

(C) Creditors may object to a plan and they will be heard by the court.

(D) Among other things, the plan must pay creditors at least as much as they would have received in a chapter 7 liquidation of the debtor.

(E) Chapter 13 plan may not last more than five years. Although a chapter 13 debtor need not repay 100% of his debts, he cannot propose to make payments for more than five years.

PROBLEMS AND SOLUTIONS
BANKRUPTCY

ONE - Bankruptcy is primarily grounded in federal law. (True or False?)

Answer - The United States Constitution empowers Congress to enact bankruptcy legislation. The most recent bankruptcy law enacted by Congress is the Bankruptcy Reform Act of 1978 (as amended) which is known as the Bankruptcy Code. (Number One is True.)

TWO - The Bankruptcy Code contains only one chapter strictly for liquidation (chapter 7); however, it contains several chapters that provide methods for reorganization or rehabilitation. (True or False?)

Answer - Chapter 9 provides for the reorganization of municipalities. Chapter 11 provides for reorganization of businesses (and some individuals). Chapter 12 provides for the reorganization of family farmers. Chapter 13 provides for the rehabilitation of individual debtors, including married couples. (Number Two is True.)

THREE - To force a debtor into an involuntary bankruptcy, the petitioning creditors must have unsecured claims that total $10,000 or more. (True or False?)

Answer - Generally, three creditors who have unsecured claims that total $10,000 or more are required to file an involuntary bankruptcy petition. If the debtor has 11 or fewer creditors, only one creditor with an unsecured claim totaling $10,000 or more is needed to file. (Number Three is True.)

FOUR - To successfully file an involuntary petition, creditors must prove that the debtor's liabilities exceed his or her assets. (True or False?)

Answer - To prevail in an involuntary bankruptcy case, creditors must prove that the debtor is not paying debts as those debts come due (equity insolvency). Insolvency in the bankruptcy sense (liabilities in excess of assets) is irrelevant. (Number Four is False.)

FIVE - Twenty days after the filing of a voluntary petition in bankruptcy, an order for relief is entered by the bankruptcy court. (True or False?)

Answer - Immediately upon the filing of a voluntary petition, the court enters an order for relief. In involuntary cases, the order for relief is typically entered 20 days after the filing of the involuntary petition. This period of time is to give the debtor time to respond to the petition filed by the creditors. (Number Five is False.)

SIX - Duane filed a petition for personal bankruptcy under chapter 7 on April 15, Year One, and received a discharge on July 26, Year One. If Duane files another chapter 7 bankruptcy on April 27, Year Seven, he will be entitled to another chapter 7 discharge. (True or False?)

Answer - Individuals are entitled to a discharge under chapter 7 every six years. The six-year time period is measured from filing date to filing date. (Number Six is True.)

SEVEN - In a chapter 7 bankruptcy proceeding, Henry's $3,500 child support obligation will not be discharged, but his $4,100 debt for alimony will be discharged. (True or False?)

Answer – Neither child support obligations nor alimony are discharged in chapter 7 proceedings. (Number Seven is False.)

EIGHT - A "gap creditor" is a creditor in an involuntary case who has extended credit to the debtor between the date of the filing of an involuntary petition and the date an order for relief is entered. (True or False?)

Answer - "Gap creditors" exist only in involuntary cases. The claim of a gap creditor is granted very high priority, higher in a Chapter 7 case than all other claims except for claims for administrative expenses (trustee fees, examiner's fees, attorney and accountant fees). (Number Eight is True.)

NINE - Wiggins, Inc. has filed a voluntary petition in chapter 7 bankruptcy. At the time of the bankruptcy, Wiggins owed its three employees their final month's pay of $3,000 each and owed sales taxes totaling $13,000. The assets in the Wiggins, Inc., case are insufficient to pay all claims. The trustee must pay the tax obligations of the debtor before paying the wages owed to its three employees. (True or False?)

Answer - Wages earned within the 90 days prior to bankruptcy (up to $4,000 per employee) have priority (after administrative expenses and "gap creditors") over all other unsecured creditors. Thus, the claims of these employees would be paid in full prior to any money being distributed to taxing authorities. (Number Nine is False.)

TEN - Unlike chapter 7 bankruptcy, which is a mechanism for liquidation, Chapter 11 is a reorganization bankruptcy. A company (or an individual) may voluntarily file for relief under chapter 11 but cannot be involuntarily petitioned into Chapter 11. (True or False?)

Answer - Chapter 11, which is available to individuals, corporations and partnerships, can be filed as a voluntary or an involuntary case. (Number Ten is False.)

ELEVEN - Within the first 120 days after filing a chapter 11 bankruptcy, only the debtor may file a plan of reorganization. (True or False?)

Answer - The 120-day period of exclusivity may, however, be extended by the court upon the request of the debtor. (Number Eleven is True.)

TWELVE - An individual must have regular income to be eligible to file for relief under chapter 13 of the bankruptcy code. (True or False?)

Answer - Although the Bankruptcy Code requires that a debtor have regular income to be eligible for chapter 13 relief, the definition of "regular income" is a broad one. Courts have ruled that one who is receiving Social Security or welfare benefits, or one who receives income from real estate commissions that vary greatly from month to month, are all eligible for chapter 13 relief. (Number Twelve is True.)

DEBTOR AND CREDITOR RIGHTS

(1)   An agreement can be created where a person (a guarantor or a surety) promises to perform an obligation owed by a debtor to a creditor. For example, a corporation could purchase a piece of equipment from a vendor on credit. The vendor agrees to make the sale after the three owners of the corporation agree to guaranty the obligation personally. Subsequently, if the corporation fails to make timely payments to the vendor or fails to perform any other obligation under the security agreement (such as maintaining adequate insurance on the equipment), the guarantors will be obligated to perform.

   (A)   Such agreements can create either a suretyship or a guaranty.

      (1)   In a **suretyship**, both the debtor and the surety have primary liability. The surety is liable without the creditor having to first make a demand on the principal debtor. The liability of the surety and the principal debtor arise under a single contract.

      (2)   In a **guaranty**, the debtor has primary liability and the guarantor has secondary liability. The guarantor is only liable if the principal debtor fails to perform its obligations to the creditor. The liability of the creditor arises from a contract that is separate from the one that created the debt originally.

      (3)   For convenience, this outline will use the term "surety" or "suretyship" to encompass both types of agreements.

   (B)   According to the **Statute of Frauds**, a suretyship agreement must be in writing because it is a promise to answer for the debt of another.

   (C)   If more than one surety exists, the creditor can proceed against any one or against all.

(2)   A creditor can have a secured interest in collateral as well as an agreement with a surety.

   (A)   The creditor does not have to proceed against the collateral before suing the surety.

   (B)   If the creditor surrenders or destroys part of the collateral, the surety is released to the extent of the loss of the collateral.

(3)   The surety has certain rights if the creditor seeks payment.

   (A)   **Exoneration** means that the surety has the right, prior to paying the debt, to try and force (usually by filing suit) the principal debtor to pay the debt.

   (B)   If the surety does have to pay, he or she has the **right of subrogation**. The surety can then step into the shoes of the creditor and have the same rights as the creditor against the debtor and collateral.

   (C)   If a co-surety does have to pay, he or she has the **right of contribution**. This right allows surety to seek reimbursement from any co-surety.

(4)   If a creditor seeks payment, the surety has certain defenses that can be used to prevent having to pay.

   (A)   In general, a surety can assert against a creditor any defense that the principal debtor could assert against the creditor. However, there are a few exceptions to that general rule.

      (1)   The bankruptcy of the principal debtor cannot be used as a defense by the surety.

        (2)   The lack of capacity of the principal debtor (for example, if the principal debtor is a minor) cannot be used as a defense by the surety.

(B)   The surety may have certain defenses against the creditor based on the creditor's own actions.

        (1)   If the creditor has released collateral, the surety is released to the extent of the value of the collateral that was released.

        (2)   If the creditor releases a co-surety, all other co-sureties are released to the same extent. For example, if A and B guaranty XYZ's $100,000 obligation to C, and C releases A (without reserving rights against B) then B is automatically released, to the extent of $50,000.

        (3)   If creditor gives principal debtor an extension of time, surety is released in full.

PROBLEMS AND SOLUTIONS
DEBTOR AND CREDITOR RIGHTS

ONE - Baxter obtained judgment against Dexter in the amount of $392. Baxter records the judgment in the jurisdiction where Dexter resides. Upon recordation of the judgment, Baxter has a perfected lien on all of Dexter's personal property. (True or False?)

Answer - The recordation of a judgment places a perfected lien against real estate in the jurisdiction in which the judgment was recorded, but has no effect on the personal property of the debtor. Recordation of a judgment is different than executing on a judgment. Recordation simply means filing a copy of the judgment paper among the real estate records. Execution refers to procedures taken such as levy and garnishment. (Number One is False.)

TWO - A lien is a claim by a creditor against real or personal property that secures payment of a debt. (True or False?)

Answer - A voluntary lien on real estate is known as a mortgage. A voluntary lien on personal property is known as a security interest. An involuntary lien can be created in several ways: a judgment lien, a mechanic's lien, a materialman's lien, an artisan's lien, etc. (Number Two is True.)

THREE - Martha owes several creditors in excess of $3,000 each. If two or more of these creditors agree to accept cash equal to 50 percent of the debt as payment in full, they will be bound by this agreement even though there is no dispute as to the validity or amounts of the debts. (True or False?)

Answer – The decision of two or more creditors to reduce their claims against a debtor is called a composition agreement, and is binding on the debtor and the creditors who agree. Although lack of consideration might seem to invalidate such an agreement, the mutual promises of two or more creditors does constitute consideration for the agreement. (Number Three is True.)

FOUR - Under the Fair Credit Reporting Act, a creditor may not report credit information to a credit reporting agency without the consent of the consumer debtor. (True or False?)

> *Answer - Creditors may report to credit reporting services any information which is accurate. The Fair Credit Reporting Act does prohibit reporting agencies from including in credit reports inaccurate or outdated information. (Number Four is False.)*

FIVE - In a surety or guarantee relationship, three parties are involved: a creditor, a principal debtor, and a surety or guarantor. The surety or guarantor promises to pay the debt of the principal debtor if the principal fails or refuses to pay. (True or False?)

> *Answer - The three parties in a contract of surety or guarantee are: the creditor, the principal debtor, and the sureties or guarantors. (Number Five is True.)*

SIX - A guarantee contract which relates to the purchase of goods for less than $500 need not be in writing to be enforceable against the guarantor. (True or False?)

> *Answer - All guarantee agreements must be in writing and signed by the guarantor to be enforceable. This rule arises under the Statute of Frauds in contract law. (Number Six is False.)*

SEVEN - Sussex Bank loans Wilson $12,000 that is payable in monthly installments over a seven-year term at 10 percent interest. Wilson's parents have both guaranteed the loan at the insistence of the bank. After two years, Sussex Bank, at the request of Wilson and without notice to any guarantors, reduces the loan rate from 10 percent to 8 percent. This loan modification will not release Wilson but will release the obligations of the parents as guarantors. (True or False?)

> *Answer - While varying the terms or conditions of a contract without approval from a surety sometimes releases the surety, a surety is not released if the modification reduces the obligation of the principal debtor. (Number Seven is False.)*

REAL PROPERTY

(1)   **Real property** is defined as land, buildings, and anything permanently annexed or affixed to land or buildings. One problem area is **fixtures**. This term refers to property which starts out as personal property but becomes so affixed to real property that it becomes part of the realty.

(2)   The extent of one's ownership interest in real estate can vary greatly. It can range from the limited right to use real estate for a short time or for a very limited purpose, to full ownership.

    (A)   **Fee simple** means ownership that is unlimited in time. It is not just for one's life but also includes the ability to transfer ownership at death. It is also unlimited in use.

    (B)   **Life estate** means ownership that is limited in time by a person's life. The party has no power over the property at death. During the person's lifetime, though, there is virtually an unlimited right to use the property. However, the life tenant cannot commit "waste" to the property.

    (C)   **Leasehold** refers to ownership which is limited in time by a period such as a term of years, months or weeks. A leasehold is unlimited in use unless it has been limited by agreement of the landlord and the tenant.

    (D)   **Easement** refers to ownership which usually is not limited in time but is severely limited in use. For example, an easement could be limited to the right to drive across property and/or pass wires and pipes under the property.

    (E)   A **license** is not truly an ownership interest in property. Rather, it is the right to use or occupy property for a very limited time and purpose. A ticket to a seat at a ball game would be an example.

(3)   Property can be co-owned by two or more persons. In such cases, ownership can be set up in several different ways.

    (A)   **Tenancy in common** involves free transferability. Any tenant can transfer his or her partial interest without consent of other tenant(s). If a co-tenant dies, his or her ownership share passes to heirs, not to other co-tenants.

    (B)   **Tenancy by the entireties** can only be by a husband and a wife. There cannot be transfer without both co-tenants joining in or consenting. If a co-tenant dies, that share of the property must go to the remaining co-tenant. A creditor can only place a lien against tenancy by entirety property if both the husband and wife are jointly obligated to the creditor.

    (C)   **Joint tenancy** allows free transferability of property without the consent of the co-tenants. Unlike tenancy in common, if a co-tenant dies, his or her ownership must go to the remaining co-tenants.

(4)   Real estate can be acquired in several different ways.

    (A)   There can be a purchase. The deed is exchanged for money or property usually pursuant to a contract. This deed is called a **bargain and sale deed**.

    (B)   There can be a **deed of gift**. The deed is given in consideration for love, affection, etc.

    (C)   The property can be obtained by **adverse possession**. This type acquisition is not created by a deed and does not require recordation of the claim. The property is taken by possession and held in this manner for a statutory period of time which is

usually 15 years. It does result in full ownership rights. There are specific requirements for this type of possession.
- (1) There must be continuous possession, although "tacking" between successive owners is permitted.
- (2) The possession must be hostile; there must be a clear indication that ownership is intended.
- (3) Possession must be open and notorious. The type of possession must give reasonable notice to the owner.
- (4) There must be actual possession.
- (5) Possession must be to the exclusion of all others.

(D) In a manner similar to adverse possession, an easement can be obtained by prescription. This is done by crossing over another person's property continuously, hostile to the owner, etc. for a statutory period of time.

(E) Property can also be acquired by will or descent.
- (1) A **will** is present if the decedent left written instructions for the transfer of his or her property after death.
- (2) If there is no will, property passes according to the **laws of descent**.

(F) Property can be obtained by the government. The property can be taken by eminent domain or it can be seized and sold to satisfy delinquent taxes.

(5) There are a number of legal guidelines concerning deeds.

(A) There are several requirements for a deed to be effectively conveyed from one party to another.
- (1) It must be signed by the grantor (the seller).
- (2) It must contain a description of the property.
- (3) It must contain the name of the grantor and the grantee (the buyer).
- (4) There must be delivery. There must be intent on the part of the grantor to pass title to the grantee.

(B) **Recordation of a deed** should be made but is not necessary for the deed to be effective. Recordation means that constructive notice is given to the world of the grantee's ownership.
- (1) Recordation is not necessary to validate the deed.
- (2) Recordation does protect the grantee against bona fide purchasers who buy the same property subsequently for value. In most cases, the second purchaser has priority if the first purchaser did not properly record. To gain priority, the second purchaser has to record first and have no knowledge of the first purchaser.

(C) There are several types of deeds.
- (1) A **general warranty deed** gives fullest warranties.
  - (a) The grantor is the true owner.
  - (b) There are no liens or claims to the property other than those disclosed in the deed.
  - (c) The grantee will have quiet enjoyment.
  - (d) The grantor will defend the title.
- (2) A **special warranty deed** is similar to a general warranty deed except that the warranties are limited to defects which occurred during the time that the grantor owned the property.
- (3) A **quitclaim deed** provides no warranties as to title. It transfers title without warranties.

(6)   Even though many mortgages purport to convey title in trust ("deed of trust") to secure the creditor, modern theory is to treat mortgages as liens rather than as a transfer of "legal title."

    (A)   The recording of mortgages follows the same theory as deeds. Recording is not necessary to validate the mortgage. However, it protects against subsequent mortgages or bona fide purchasers for value.

    (B)   At any time prior to a foreclosure sale (and for a short period after), the owner/debtor may redeem property by paying the debt in full (by the use of equity of redemption).

    (C)   A **sale of mortgaged property** can occur without paying off the mortgage first.

        (1)   The property can be sold subject to the mortgage so that the buyer is not obligated to pay the mortgage debt.

        (2)   The buyer can purchase the property and assume the mortgage. The buyer agrees to pay the mortgage debt. However, the original debtor can still be held liable.

        (3)   **Novation** can occur. The buyer can purchase the property and assume the mortgage with the creditor then releasing (in writing) the original debtor.

(7)   **Lease contracts** can also be affected by assignments and other arrangements.

    (A)   The lessee can assign the contract to a new tenant. However, unless novation occurs, the original tenant is still obligated.

    (B)   The original tenant can sublease the property to a new tenant (a sublessee). Sublessee is not directly obligated to the original landlord, only to the original tenant.

PROBLEMS AND SOLUTIONS
REAL PROPERTY

ONE - Real property includes land, buildings, and anything that is permanently annexed or affixed to the land or buildings. A fixture is something that starts out as personal property but becomes so affixed to real property that it is considered to be part of the real property. (True or False?)

    Answer - This definition is accurate for real property, including fixtures. Bricks sitting in a yard are personal property; but when mortar is applied and a wall is constructed, the bricks become a part of a building which is real property (also called realty or real estate). (Number One is True.)

TWO - A person's ownership interest in real property can vary from full and absolute ownership to a mere leasehold interest or easement. Full and absolute ownership of real estate, which is unlimited with respect to manner of usage or length of ownership, is known as a life estate. (True or False?)

    Answer - Full and absolute ownership of real estate is known as fee simple or fee simple absolute. One who has fee simple ownership of real estate (such as a typical homeowner) owns the real estate for an unlimited time (in other words, the owner can dispose of it at death by a will) and has unlimited right to use the property (as opposed to a limited right to pass electrical wires across a property or to construct a road across the property). (Number Two is False.)

THREE - Perkins is the owner of three acres of land adjoining Lower Lake. Holmes owns property which is adjacent to Perkins's property and Perkins wishes to convey to Holmes the right to pass across a small portion of Perkins's property to enable Holmes to have access to the lake. If Perkins grants such access to Holmes, Perkins and Holmes will have a joint tenancy in that portion of the property. (True or False?)

Answer - If Perkins grants access across his property to Holmes, an easement will have been created. Perkins can accomplish this by simply deeding an easement to Holmes. The easement can be recorded but does not have to be recorded to be effective between the parties. (Number Three is False.)

FOUR - Where two or more persons share ownership in the same property, their ownership is always referred to as tenancy in common. (True or False?)

Answer - Two or more persons can be co-owner's of real estate as tenants in common, as tenants by the entireties, or as joint tenants with the right of survivorship. (Number Four is False.)

FIVE - Newberry deeded his home to his sister Janice by a deed of gift which Janice failed to record. Newberry later died and his heirs assert that their claim to the property takes priority over Janice's claim because she failed to record her deed. Janice is the fee simple owner of the property and her rights to the property will not be affected by the claim of the heirs. (True or False?)

Answer - The deed from Newberry to Janice was valid without recordation. Recordation is only required to protect a grantee against the claim of a bona fide purchaser or lender for value. Because the heirs are not bona fide purchasers or lenders for value, their claim is defeated by the unrecorded deed to Janice. (Number Five is True.)

SIX - Alberta borrowed $75,000 from Cyber and orally agreed to give Cyber a mortgage on Alberta's home. The mortgage is not enforceable because it is not in writing. (True or False?)

Answer - A mortgage is an interest in real estate. Therefore, a transfer of a mortgage interest must be in writing and signed in order to satisfy the Statute of Frauds. The mortgage instrument must also include an adequate description of the property and of the debt. (Number Six is True.)

SEVEN - Brown and Brown, CPAs, are tenants under a seven-year lease. Brown and Brown wished to relocate. The lease is silent with respect to the rights of assignment or subletting. Brown and Brown, CPAs, assigns the lease to J. G. Johnson, Attorney at Law. Brown and Brown, CPAs, will be relieved of any further liability under the lease. (True or False?)

Answer - Even if Johnson is a financially responsible new tenant, Brown and Brown's assignment (although rightful) will not relieve Brown and Brown of liability. After the assignment, the landlord may look either to Brown and Brown, CPAs, or to Johnson for payment. (Number Seven is False.)

EMPLOYMENT LAWS AND ENVIRONMENTAL REGULATIONS

(1) The purpose of **workers' compensation laws** is to provide prompt compensation for job related injuries.

    (A) The theory underlying workers' compensation laws is that an injured employee is given benefits regardless of whether employer was negligent and even if employee was negligent.

    (B) There are exceptions where payment will not be made under workers' compensation laws.

        (1) Benefits will not be paid because of self inflicted wounds

        (2) Benefits will not be paid if injuries were caused by the intoxication of the employee on the job

        (3) Employee is not covered when going to and from work.

    (C) An injured employee still has some right to sue and recover from a negligent party who caused the injury.

        (1) If negligence was committed by an employer or a fellow employee, the injured party has no right to sue. In that case, workers' compensation laws cover the damage. Employee loses the right to sue employer for physical injuries unless the employer intentionally injured the employee or the employer acted maliciously

        (2) If negligence was committed by a third party, the injured party does have the right to sue the third party for damages.

        (3) If employee is injured as a result of an action by a third party, collection of benefits can still be received from workers' compensation rather than through a suit of the third party. The workers' compensation insurance company is then subrogated (steps into the shoes of the injured party) and can sue the third party for payments such as lost wages and medical expenses. If more is collected than the company's expenses, the balance goes to the employee.

    (D) To provide adequate protection for employees, payment is automatic upon satisfaction of the requirements.

        (1) Employee must report injury within short time (usually 30 days)

        (2) For up to 500 weeks, the employee can collect 2/3 of all lost wages.

        (3) All medical expenses related to the injury are covered.

        (4) The employee is compensated for the loss of a limb.

        (5) If necessary, funeral expenses are covered and certain death benefits are paid to a widow and minor children.

        (6) There is no recovery for pain and suffering.

(2) The basic programs of the **Social Security Act** include unemployment insurance, hospital insurance (Medicare), survivors and disability insurance, and old age insurance.

    (A) These programs are financed from taxes paid by employers, employees, and by self-employed individuals under the Federal Insurance Contributions Act (FICA), the Self-Employment Contributions Act, and the Federal Unemployment Tax Act (FUTA).

        (1) Taxes are imposed on "wages."

    (a)   Wages include any compensation in exchange for employment such as salaries, contingent fees, non-cash compensation, bonuses, tips, commissions, vacation pay, and "golden parachute" payments received upon termination of employment.

    (b)   Wages do not include medical and hospital expenses paid by an employer, expenses such as travel expenses that are reimbursed by the employer, insurance premiums paid by the employer, or contributions by the employer to the employee's retirement plan.

(2)   All "employees" are covered by the Act.

    (a)   An **employee** is one whose performance is subject to direct physical control by the employer on a regular basis. Officers and directors of a corporation are considered to be employees.

    (b)   An employee does not include a partner, a limited partner, or an independent contractor.

(B)   **Federal Insurance Contributions Act** (FICA) imposes social security taxes on employees, self-employed individuals, and employers.

(1)   Tax rates, which change frequently, are the same for both the employer and employees and are paid on a base amount which has been changed many times over the years by Congress.

(2)   Employer has duty to withhold employee's share of FICA from wages and to remit this along with employer's share to the government. Failure to withhold may result in employer being liable for both shares of the tax.

(3)   Employers must make timely deposits of these taxes, the frequency of which depends upon amount of payroll. Employer also must supply taxpayer identification numbers.

(4)   FICA taxes paid by employers are deductible expenses for income tax purposes.

(5)   Employers must furnish employees with written statement of wages paid and FICA contributions withheld during calendar year.

(6)   FICA is mandatory and contributions cannot be made to pension plans in lieu of FICA. However, individuals who receive private pension payments may also receive social security benefits.

(C)   Under the **Self-Employment Contributions Act**, a self-employed person must report taxable earnings and pay social security tax.

(1)   Self-employment income means the net earnings from self employment.

(2)   Self-employed individuals must pay employer's and employee's share of taxes.

(3)   Self-employed individuals can deduct half of the FICA tax paid as an adjustment to arrive at adjusted gross income on individual income tax return.

(D)   Payment of the Federal Unemployment Tax Act (FUTA) is required of any employer that employs one or more persons covered by the Act.

(1)   Employer must also pay any state unemployment taxes, but credit is given against federal unemployment tax for state unemployment taxes paid.

(2)   Employers who maintain good employment record will pay low state unemployment tax and receive additional credit against federal unemployment taxes.

(E) Old age, survivors, and disability insurance benefits are available to individuals who have worked a certain time to attain "insured status."

    (1) These benefits include the following

        (a) Survivor benefits for widow or widower and dependents

        (b) Benefits for disabled worker and dependents

        (c) Old age retirement benefits to employees and dependents.

        (d) Lump sum death benefits

    (2) Employees who are classified as "currently insured" may be eligible for limited survivor benefits, disability benefits, lump sum death benefits, including benefits to divorced spouses.

(3) Employment and **employment discrimination** are covered under several different laws.

    (A) Title VII of the Civil Rights Act of 1964 prohibits discrimination in employment on the basis of race, color, religion, sex, or national origin.

        (1) Applies to employers and labor unions having 15 or more employees that have business affairs that affect interstate commerce. Also applies to federal, state and local government employees.

        (2) **Equal Employment Opportunity Commission** (EEOC) is the federal agency charged with enforcing the Civil Rights Act. The Act is also enforced through private lawsuits by individuals.

        (3) Illegal discrimination can occur through indirect means. For example, a company that adopts a rule regarding strength requirements might adversely impact members of a protected class, resulting in sexual discrimination.

        (4) Defenses include: bona fide occupational qualifications, merit, or a system of seniority.

    (B) **Americans with Disabilities Act** (ADA) applies to employers with 15 employees or more.

        (1) Prohibits discrimination against persons with a disability in hiring, firing, compensation, or promotion. Unless an employer can show undue hardship (for example, undue expense), employer must make reasonable accommodation for individuals with a disability, which may include modifying the facility, changing the job, or buying necessary equipment.

        (2) ADA also guarantees persons with disabilities equal access to public transportation, public accommodation, and to public services that are operated by private entities.

    (C) The Equal Pay Act requires equal pay for equal work for both sexes and is enforced by the Equal Employment Opportunity Commission.

    (D) The Family and Medical Leave Act covers employees employed for at least 12 months and 1250 hours and who are employed by employer having at least 50 or more employees.

        (1) Employees are granted up to 12 weeks leave during a 12 month period on account of health problem (self or parent, spouse, or child), birth of a child, or adoption of child.

        (2) Act does not require paid leave, but requires that when employee returns, he or she must return to same or equivalent position. Returning employee cannot lose benefits.

    (E) **Fair Labor Standards Act** states that all covered employees must be paid at least minimum wage.

(1)   Employees who work more than 40 hours per week must be paid time and a half. This provision does not cover professionals, executives, or outside sales persons. Certain employees must be paid minimum wage but are not covered by overtime rules (such as taxi drivers and railroad employees).

(2)   Employees may be paid hourly, weekly, monthly, etc.

(3)   Enforcement is by the Department of Labor.

(F)   Federal Consolidated Budget Reconciliation Act (Cobra) provides that when an employee leaves employment, he or she may retain group health insurance coverage for up to 18 months. However, employee pays for the coverage and not the employer.

(G)   **Employee Retirement Income Security Act** of 1974 (ERISA) places certain requirements on pension plans.

(1)   Employer is not required by the Act to establish a pension plan.

(2)   If employer does establish a plan, this plan must meet certain standards

      (a)   Employee contributions must vest immediately.

      (b)   Employer contributions must vest after five years of employment.

      (c)   Certain investment standards are set to avoid mismanagement.

      (d)   Employer cannot postpone employee participation in plan.

      (e)   Employer must give employees annual report on plan

(H)   National Labor Relations Act allows employees to join labor organizations or participate in establishing a labor union.

(1)   Employers must bargain with the union regarding all work related issues such as firing practices, working hours and conditions, retirement, safety conditions, and pay (including sick pay and vacation pay).

(2)   Taft-Hartley Act prohibits unfair labor practices by unions such as secondary boycotts and featherbedding (requiring employers to pay employees for work not performed).

(I)   The Employee Safety-Occupational Safety Health Act was passed by Congress in 1970 to promote safety standards and ensure a safe working environment for employees.

(1)   This act applies to most employers (except governmental employers) whose businesses affect interstate commerce.

(2)   The **Occupational Safety and Health Administration** (OSHA) administers this act.

      (a)   The act requires that employers keep records of accidents and report serious accidents to OSHA.

      (b)   OSHA develops standards that it enforces in the workplace.

      (c)   OSHA may inspect workplaces but employer can require that an inspector have a warrant in order to inspect a business. "Probable cause" is necessary to obtain a warrant. Probable cause is not a high standard. Employee complaints may be sufficient for probable cause and employees making complaints may have names withheld.

(3)   Employer may not discriminate against or discharge employee for enforcing OSHA standards.

(4)   Employers may obtain temporary exemptions from some OSHA standards when employer can prove inability to comply within required time.

(5)   Permanent exemptions from some OSHA standards may also be given.

(6)   The Occupational Safety and Health Administration can issue citations, impose fines, and assess civil penalties for violations to the act.

    (a)   Employers can be forced to correct violations.

    (b)   Repeat or willful violations may result in fines. Serious violations, or violations that involve "a substantial probability" that an accident resulting from the violation will lead to death or serious harm, can result in enhanced fines.

    (c)   Willful violations that lead to an employee's death can result in criminal prosecution.

    (d)   Penalties and citations may be appealed to the Occupational Safety and Health Review Commission.

(4)   A number of **environmental regulations** have been passed over the years.

    (A)   National Environmental Policy Act (NEPA) established Council on Environmental Quality (CEQ) which ensures various environmental laws are followed. NEPA requires **environmental impact statement** be filed when federal action or proposed laws significantly affect the environment.

    (B)   The **Environmental Protection Agency** (EPA) was established to enforce laws aimed at protecting the environment. EPA has both civil and criminal enforcement capabilities.

    (C)   Comprehensive Environmental Response, Compensation, and Liability Act (CERCLA) or Superfund legislation provides for establishing a national inventory of inactive hazardous waste sites.

        (1)   It also creates a multimillion dollar **Hazardous Waste Fund** (known as Superfund) to cover the cost of eliminating or containing certain waste sites.

        (2)   Liability under CERCLA is based not on negligence or carelessness, but on "**strict liability**," that is, liability without regard to fault. Those parties liable for the cost of environmental cleanup include:

            (a)   The person who created the waste. (A person who created only a fraction of the waste at a site may be held liable for entire cleanup cost of the site. A corporation's officers or shareholders who exercised control over or handling of corporation's hazardous waste may be individually liable.)

            (b)   The person who transported the waste to the site.

            (c)   The owner or operator of the site at time of waste disposal.

            (d)   The current site owner or operator of the site.

        (3)   Emergency Planning and Community Right-to-Know Act (EPCRA) was enacted as part of the Federal Superfund Amendments and Reauthorization Act.

            (a)   It grants citizens a right-to-know about hazardous and toxic chemicals in their communities.

            (b)   Entities in control of certain quantities of extremely hazardous substances are required to notify state and local authoritative agencies and to report annually regarding the release of toxic chemicals that occur in usual business operations.

    (D)   **Clean Air Act** provides that the EPA set air quality standards for mobile (cars, trucks) and stationary (factories) sources.

       (1)   Governs gas emissions, acid rain, and toxic industrial emissions. Industrial facilities that emit air pollutants are required by this Act to install "best available" emission control technology. Environmental impact and costs are weighed in the enforcement of the Clean Air Act.

       (2)   The EPA can assess civil penalties or seek criminal sanctions.

 (E)   Federal Water Pollution Control Act (the **Clean Water Act**) is aimed at improving the quality of the nation's waterways by making water safe for recreational use and protecting wildlife living near waterways.

       (1)   The Clean Water Act controls dredging and regulates the filling of wetlands.

       (2)   Regulates the discharge of heated water by nuclear power plants.

       (3)   Industries are required by the Act to utilize "best available technology" for control and treatment of pollution, but costs and other factors can be considered.

PROBLEMS AND SOLUTIONS
EMPLOYMENT LAWS AND ENVIRONMENTAL REGULATIONS

ONE - Ernest has been employed by the Lester Company for three years. The Lester Company has failed to withhold any sums from his wages for FICA taxes. Although the Lester Company may be liable for its own contribution as well as for fines, it will not be liable for the employee's share of the unpaid taxes. (True or False?)

Answer - If an employer neglects to withhold FICA taxes, the employer may be liable for both the employee's and employer's share of taxes, resulting in a double tax. (Number One is False.)

TWO - Under the Social Security Act, wages include salary, cash and non-cash benefits but do not include reimbursed travel expenses. (True or False?)

Answer - The definition of wages under the Social Security Act include wages, contingent fees, cash and non-cash compensation, bonuses, commissions, tips, and vacation allowances. The following are not included in the definition of wages: reimbursed travel expenses, medical and hospital expenses paid by an employer, insurance premiums paid by an employer, and contributions to employee retirement plans by the employer. (Number Two is True.)

THREE - Although the Occupational Safety and Health Administration (OSHA) may assess civil penalties for violations, it may not issue an order directing an employer to correct unsafe conditions without first obtaining court approval. (True or False?)

Answer - OSHA may order employers to correct unsafe conditions and may assess civil penalties for violations, all without court intervention. (Number Three is False.)

FOUR - The provisions of the Americans with Disabilities Act apply only to businesses that are located within 200 miles of an interstate highway. (True or False?)

Answer - The Americans with Disabilities Act seeks to eliminate discrimination in any privately operated enterprise that accommodates the public. (Number Four is False.)

FIVE - Walton, Inc., which regularly employs 70 full-time workers in Georgia and Florida, pays its employees "full-time plus 10 percent" for hours worked in excess of 40 hours per week. Walton, Inc., is in violation of the Federal Fair Labor Standards Act. (True or False?)

Answer - The Federal Fair Labor Standards Act requires that workers who work more than 40 hours per week be paid time and a half. The Act applies to all businesses that operate in interstate commerce. It regulates the number of hours in the standard workweek. (Number Five is True.)

SIX - ERISA stands for the Employee Retirement Insurance Income Security Act of 1974 and requires all employers who employee 40 persons or more on a regular basis to set up pension plans for its employees. (True or False?)

Answer - The Employee Retirement Income Security Act 1974 (ERISA) does not require employers to set up pension plans for its employees. The Act provides that if an employer does set up a pension plan, it must meet certain standards, including requiring that an employee's right to the employer's contributions must vest after five years of employment. (Number Six is False.)

SEVEN - The National Environmental Policy Act requires that an environmental impact statement be prepared whenever federal action could significantly affect the environment. (True or False?)

Answer - Federal agencies are required to consider the impact on the environment that activities may have, and are often required to prepare environmental impact statements. (Number Seven is True.)

EIGHT - The "Superfund" was established to promote cleanup of hazardous waste sites. Parties that may be liable under laws relating to the Superfund include both current and past owners of sites which contain hazardous waste. (True or False?)

Answer - Parties that may be held liable under hazardous waste laws include both current and past owners of a site as well as current and past operators of the site. Also, persons involved in transporting waste to the site can be liable. (Number Eight is True.)

NINE - Thompson was a repair technician for the Auto Bus Repair Corp. Thompson was severely burned when he removed a radiator from an engine without waiting for it to cool properly. Thompson's actions were in violation of written guidelines posted by his employer. As a result, Thompson cannot recover under a workers' compensation claim. (True or False?)

Answer - Under workers' compensation laws, neither Thompson's own negligence nor his assumption of risk will prevent him from recovering compensation for his injuries. The same is true of his violation of the employer's written rules. (Number Nine is False.)

TEN - Vance was employed by the Twin Life Insurance Company as a clerk. Vance was injured when a fellow employee negligently dropped a file cabinet on Vance's foot. Vance was out of work for six months because of the injury and incurred medical bills of $1,800. Under workers' compensation laws, Vance can recover two-thirds of his pay for the time missed, all of his medical expenses, and a proportionate amount of compensation for pain and suffering. (True or False?)

Answer - Under workers' compensation laws, Vance may recover for his injuries even though the injury was the fault of a fellow employee. He may recover for lost pay (two-thirds of his regular pay for up to 500 weeks) and for all medical bills. Vance, however, cannot recover for pain and suffering. (Number Ten is False.)

INSURANCE

(1)   In an insurance contract, there has to be an **insurable interest**. This means that a relationship must exist between the insured party and the risk that is being covered. The insured party has to stand to suffer some legally recognizable loss or injury. Otherwise, the contract is simply a wager.

   (A)   For a fire or property insurance contract, an insurable interest must exist at the time that the loss is incurred. In such policies, a party can have an insurable interest in any one of several ways.

       (1)   Ownership of the insured property.

       (2)   A leasehold interest in the property.

       (3)   A future interest in the property.

       (4)   Having a secured interest in the property such as a mortgage.

   (B)   For a life insurance contract, an insurable interest need only exist at the time that the policy was issued. The person paying for the policy must have an insurable interest in the life of the insured person at the time the policy is issued. In such policies, a party can have an insurable interest in any one of several ways.

       (1)   The person is insuring his or her own life.

       (2)   The person is insuring the life of a blood relative.

       (3)   The person is insuring the life of a legal dependent.

       (4)   The person is insuring the life of an economic dependent.

(2)   In obtaining an insurance contract, the **misstatement of a warranty** can affect the contract. The **misstatement of a representation** will usually not affect the contract.

   (A)   Any statements that materially increase the risk of the insurance will be considered warranties. Warranty statements must be in writing. The misstatement of a warranty voids the insurance policy.

   (B)   Statements made by the applicant for an insurance contract (either statements made orally or in writing) that do not materially affect the risk to the insurer are representations and do not void the contract. For example, misstatement of one's place of birth does not void a life insurance policy.

   (C)   Upon expiration of a certain time period (usually two years), the insurer is prohibited from contesting the policy because of misstatement, including misstatement of warranty. This prohibition is known as the "**incontestable clause**." However, there are certain defenses such as the following that are not affected by incontestable clauses.

       (1)   Lack of insurable interest.

       (2)   Failure to pay premiums.

       (3)   Failure to file adequate proof of death within the required period of time.

       (4)   A particular risk was not covered by the policy.

(3)   The proceeds from a life insurance policy are almost always assignable. However, fire and property insurance contracts usually cannot be assigned from one owner to the next because the level of risk can vary. A claim, though, made on a fire or property insurance contract can be assigned.

(4)   The term "**subrogation**" is encountered in insurance law. It means that the insurance company, after paying the insured for damages, stands in the shoes of the insured and can

proceed against the party that caused the loss. Whether the insurer has subrogation rights depends upon the type of insurance.

(A) In fire and property insurance contracts, the right of subrogation exists.

(B) In life insurance contracts, there are no subrogation rights.

(C) In malpractice insurance contracts, there are no subrogation rights.

(D) For workman's compensation, partial subrogation exists. Subrogation is allowed against third parties (parties other than the employer or fellow employees) for lost wages and the payment of medical bills. However, subrogation is not allowed for money recovered by the employee because of pain and suffering.

(E) In cases where subrogation exists, if the injured party releases the person who caused the injury or damage, the insurance company can refuse to pay the claim.

(5) If the insured party has several policies on the same property, recovery must be pro rata from each of the policies.

(6) Many fire and property insurance contracts contain **co-insurance clauses** designed to require certain minimum coverage before the insured can receive full recovery of a partial loss. A certain percentage (often 80%) of the value of the insured property must be covered by insurance at the time of the loss. If the required amount of insurance is not held, recovery will be determined by formula.

(A) The fair market value of the property is multiplied by the required percentage to get the minimum amount of coverage.

(B) The minimum amount of coverage is divided into the actual amount of coverage to get percentage of coverage.

(C) The percentage of coverage is multiplied by the amount of damages to get the amount of recovery. However, the amount of recovery cannot be larger than the face value of the policy.

(7) Insurance contracts have several federal income tax ramifications.

(A) **Life insurance dividends** are not taxable income to the extent that they do not exceed premiums.

(B) On a **group term life insurance policy** paid by an employer for an employee, the premiums are a tax free fringe benefit to the employee if the policy is not over $50,000. The cost of any portion of a group term life insurance policy in excess of $50,000 is a taxable fringe benefit to the employee.

(C) All payments made by an employer for group term life insurance for its employees is tax deductible as long as the employer is not the beneficiary of the policy.

(D) Life insurance proceeds are not taxable income to the recipient.

PROBLEMS AND SOLUTIONS
INSURANCE

ONE - For a life insurance policy, the beneficiary must be related by blood or marriage to the insured for an insurable interest to exist. (True or False?)

Answer - To have an insurable interest, the beneficiary must be related by blood or marriage, or be an economic or legal dependent of the insured. Thus, ABC, Inc., has an insurable interest in its president Ralph Betts because the company is economically dependent on Ralph. This is known as a key-man life insurance policy. (Number One is False.)

TWO - Jefferson owns a factory building worth $400,000. His fire insurance policy contains a standard 80 percent co-insurance clause. Jefferson's only policy on the building is for $240,000. If the building is totally destroyed by fire, Jefferson will recover $240,000 from his insurance policy. (True or False?)

Answer - Based on the co-insurance clause, Jefferson is required to carry $320,000 (80 percent of the value) in insurance for complete coverage. Because Jefferson only has $240,000 in insurance, coverage is only 75 percent ($240,000/$320,000) of any loss. Thus, Jefferson should be able to collect 75 percent of the $400,000 loss or $300,000. However, recovery on all such insurance policies is limited to the face value. Jefferson will only get the $240,000 face value. (Number Two is True.)

THREE - Godfrey owns a barn that has sustained fire damage of $5,000. Godfrey had insured the barn with two fire policies. One was with JerMain Insurance Company for $10,000. The other policy was with Franklin Insurance Company for $30,000. Godfrey will recover a total of $10,000 from the two policies. (True or False?)

Answer - Under standard pro rata clauses, which most hazard policies contain, an insured party will recover for a loss on a pro rata basis from each policy. The total of these two policies is $40,000: $10,000 (or 1/4) from JerMain and $30,000 (or 3/4) from Franklin. In this instance, $1,250 (1/4 of the $5,000 loss) will be recovered from JerMain and $3,750 (3/4 of the loss) will be recovered from Franklin. An insured party is never entitled to recover more than the actual amount of a loss. (Number Three is False.)

OVERVIEW OF INDIVIDUAL INCOME TAXES

(1)   An individual completes Form 1040 in filing federal income taxes.

    (A)   Various sources of income are reported first. Usually any amounts that are earned must be reported: salary, dividends, capital gains and losses, rents, interest, sole proprietorship gains and losses, partnership gains and losses, etc.

    (B)   Specifically allowed **adjustments to income** are subtracted.

        (1)   These include (under certain conditions) **individual retirement account** (IRA) payments, retirement account payments by self-employed individuals, alimony payments, moving expenses, a portion of payments made for self-employment taxes, a portion of payments made by self-employed individuals for medical insurance, etc.

    (C)   Net figure is **adjusted gross income** (AGI).

    (D)   Next, the larger of taxpayer's **itemized deductions** or **standard deduction** should be subtracted.

        (1)   The standard deduction is based on the taxpayer's filing status but will increase each year with inflation. Because of the annual change, extensive questions about specific amounts are not likely.

        (2)   Elderly and blind taxpayers receive an increased standard deduction.

        (3)   Itemized deductions include certain payments for medical services, taxes, interest, charitable contributions, and miscellaneous items as well as casualty and theft losses.

            (a)   If AGI is high, the amount of a taxpayer's itemized deductions that can be subtracted is reduced.

    (E)   A subtraction is then made for the taxpayer's **personal exemptions**. This amount will also change with inflation over the years.

        (1)   Taxpayer is entitled to one personal exemption and, on a **joint return**, a second is received for spouse.

        (2)   An extra exemption is received for each dependent.

        (3)   If AGI is high, a taxpayer's deduction for personal exemptions is reduced.

        (4)   No personal exemption is allowed if taxpayer is claimed as a dependent on another person's tax return. In that situation, the standard deduction may also be limited.

    (F)   Remaining figure is taxable income on which tax is computed. The rate depends on filing status. Joint status and **qualifying widow/widower** have lowest rates. **Head of household** requires use of next lowest rates with highest rates applied to single taxpayers

    (G)   After an income tax figure is computed, any **tax credits** should be subtracted.

        (1)   Common credits include the child care credit, earned income credit, child tax credit, Hope scholarship credit, adoption expense credit, etc.

    (H)   Any extra taxes (such as self-employment tax or alternative minimum tax) are added to give final tax figure for taxpayer.

    (I)   Any income tax withholding, estimated tax payments, and the like are subtracted to get amount due or refund claimed.

(2)   Filing status is determined by taxpayer's status at year's end (or date of death if taxpayer died during current year). A joint return is normal if taxpayer is married although

separate returns are allowed. A single, divorced, or legally separated individual will usually fine as single.

    (A)   Qualifying widow or widower with dependent child is allowed to use same rates and standard deduction as a joint return.

        (1)   Status is permitted for the two years following the year of spouse's death. Must have dependent child living in home. It can be child, stepchild, adopted child, or foster child.

        (2)   Joint return is normally filed in year of death.

    (B)   To qualify as head of household, taxpayer must be unmarried or legally separated.

        (1)   Must maintain an unmarried child or any dependent relative in home.

        (2)   If dependent relative is a parent, that person does not have to live in taxpayer's home. Parent can live, for example, in a rest home, hospital, or own home.

(3)   For person to qualify as a **dependent** of another, five rules must be met.

    (A)   The person's gross income (not counting nontaxable income) must be below the amount of a personal exemption.

        (1)   This rule does not apply if person is taxpayer's child who is either (a) under 19 or (b) under 24 and a full-time student for at least five months during the year.

    (B)   Taxpayer must provide over one-half of person's support during the year.

    (C)   If potential dependent is married, that person cannot file a joint return.

    (D)   Person must be US citizen or person must reside in US, Canada, or Mexico.

    (E)   Must be a blood relative (includes aunts, uncles, nephews, and nieces but not cousins) or a member of taxpayer's household for entire year.

(4)   **Statute of limitations** (time limit for correction of mistakes on a tax return by the government or by the taxpayer) is normally 3 years from the due date of return. If an extension is received, it is 3 years from the date of filing.

    (A)   The period is extended to six years if income was omitted from the return equal or greater than 25 percent of reported gross income.

    (B)   For **tax fraud** cases, no statute of limitations exists.

(5)   If not enough income tax is paid through withholding, the taxpayer must make **estimated tax payments**. To encourage adequate payment, a penalty is incurred unless taxpayer pays at least 90 percent of the taxes for the current year or 100 percent of the prior year's taxes. Taxpayers with high AGI who base estimated payments on prior year's taxes must pay slightly more than 100 percent.

(6)   Anyone who prepares a tax return for compensation is a **tax preparer** and has certain responsibilities.

    (A)   Can recommend or agree with positions that are realistically possible. To meet this criterion, position must have at least a 1/3 likelihood of being sustained if challenged. Preparer can be penalized for using information where there was no realistic possibility of success. Penalty is increased if preparer was making a willful attempt to understate taxes.

    (B)   Can rely on client information without verification unless it appears incorrect, incomplete, or inconsistent.

    (C)   Can use estimates if real numbers are not available.

(7)   After IRS conducts an audit (assuming no agreement is reached), taxpayer receives a 30 day letter outlining deficiencies.

    (A)   Taxpayer can accept, appeal to appellate level of IRS, or do nothing.

(B)   If nothing is done (or if appeal does not lead to agreement), another letter is sent giving the taxpayer 90 days to file a petition with the tax court.

(C)   If petition is not filed, amount must be paid in 10 days or IRS can begin legal action to force payment.

| PROBLEMS AND SOLUTIONS |
| OVERVIEW OF INCOME TAXES |

ONE - On Form 1040, taxpayers determine the amount of their income taxes. However, before computing the amount to be paid, other taxes must be included such as the self-employment tax and the alternative minimum tax. (True or False?)

Answer - *Other taxes are paid along with income taxes on a Form 1040. Two of the most common of these other taxes are the self-employment tax and the alternative minimum tax. (Number One is True.)*

TWO - Income taxes are paid during the year through payroll withholding from salary payments. Taxpayers may also have to make estimated payments on a quarterly basis. If an insufficient amount is paid in advance, the taxpayer is subject to a penalty. An individual taxpayer can avoid this penalty by paying either 90 percent of the prior year tax or 100 percent of the current year tax. (True or False?)

Answer - *The penalty for underpayment of taxes can be avoided by an individual by paying either 90 percent of the current year tax or 100 percent of the prior year tax. A taxpayer with a relatively high level of income who bases estimated payments on the prior year tax will probably have to pay a slightly higher percentage than 100 percent. (Number Two is False.)*

THREE - During the current year, a husband dies and his wife does not remarry prior to the end of the year. For tax purposes, the wife will have to file as a single taxpayer because, at the end of the year, she was unmarried. (True or False?)

Answer - *In order for a couple to file a joint return, they must be married as of the end of the year. However, if either person or both dies during the period, they will file based on their filing status at the date of death. In this case, the couple was married when the husband died so that a joint return is still appropriate for the current year. (Number Three is False.)*

FOUR - Mr. and Mrs. Black are a married couple. Mr. Black dies in Year One. Mrs. Black does not remarry during Year Two. In that year, her daughter lives with her although the daughter is not a dependent. In addition, her dependent father lives with her. For Year Two, Mrs. Black should file as a qualifying widow. (True or False?)

Answer - *The requirements for filing as a qualifying widow or widower are that the taxpayer must pay over half of the cost of maintaining a household for a dependent child, grandchild, stepchild, or adopted child. In addition, the taxpayer cannot remarry. The daughter is not a dependent whereas the father is not a child, grandchild, etc. Therefore, Mrs. Black does not meet the requirements for this particular filing status. Mrs. Black should file as a head of household. (Number Four is False.)*

FIVE - A taxpayer's father is a citizen and resident of England. The taxpayer provides all of the support for the father who lives there in a retirement home. The father is a widower who has no income. The taxpayer cannot claim the father as a dependent. (True or False?)

Answer - To qualify as a dependent, a person must be a citizen of the US or a resident of Canada, the US, or Mexico. As a citizen and resident of England, the father cannot possibly be claimed as a dependent. (Number Five is True.)

SIX - On April 1 of Year One, a taxpayer files a tax return that was due on April 15 of that year. According to the normal statute of limitations, the government would have to file an assessment of a tax deficiency by April 1 of Year Four. (True or False?)

Answer - The normal period of assessment of a tax deficiency is three years after the due date (unless the return is filed later because of an extension). The due date in this case is April 15. Thus, the government has until April 15 of Year Four. (Number Six is False.)

INDIVIDUAL INCOME TAXES - INCOME

(1)   Virtually any income that a taxpayer strives to get is taxable: wages, interest, dividends, alimony, state income tax refunds (if tax payments were taken previously as an itemized deduction), partnership and sole proprietor income, rental income, prizes, capital gains and losses, unemployment benefits, reimbursed moving expenses, reimbursed business expenses (if no accounting is required by employer), etc.

(2)   Some income is specifically nontaxable income: welfare benefits, gifts, inheritances, child support, life insurance proceeds, compensation for injuries, etc.

    (A)   Gifts and inheritances may be taxed but that is not an income tax.

    (B)   **Social security benefits** are tax free if AGI plus tax-exempt income plus 1/2 of social security benefits are less than $32,000 (on a joint return) but 85% is taxable if this total is over $44,000 and 50% is taxable in between.

(3)   Payments or other compensation from employer are usually considered taxable as a salary. If payment is not cash, taxable income is fair value at date of transfer.

    (A)   If employer pays for **group-term life insurance** on employee, the cost of the first $50,000 in coverage is a tax free fringe benefit. The cost paid by the employer for any coverage over that amount is taxable income to the employee.

(4)   **Dividends** and **interest** revenue received by taxpayer are listed on Schedule B of the tax return. Most such inflows are fully taxed.

    (A)   Dividends on life insurance policies are not taxed.

    (B)   Stock dividends are usually not taxable unless cash could have been received instead.

    (C)   State and city bond interest is nontaxable although interest on US (federal) bonds is taxable.

    (D)   Interest on **Series EE US Savings Bonds** may be tax exempt. To qualify, bonds must be bought by and belong to taxpayer (who was over 24 when acquired) and be used to pay college costs for taxpayer, spouse, or dependent.

        (1)   Tax free exclusion is limited or lost if taxpayer's AGI is high.

(5)   Revenues and expenses from **rental activities** are reported on Schedule E.

    (A)   Revenues minus expenses gives income or loss to be reported.

    (B)   All ordinary and necessary expenses such as repairs, depreciation, insurance, etc. are allowed.

(6)   A **passive activity** is a business in which the taxpayer/owner does not materially participate. Rental activities and limited partnerships are also included in this category regardless of the owner's participation.

    (A)   All gains and losses for passive activities are netted together. If a net gain results, it is taxable income. If a net loss results, it is not deductible.

    (B)   Net passive losses can be carried over indefinitely to reduce future passive gains.

    (C)   If taxpayer is actively involved, losses from rental activities of up to $25,000 can still be deducted. This deduction is phased out if taxpayer's AGI is high.

(7)   Under a **cash accounting system**, revenues and expenses are taxable when cash or any other asset is actually conveyed. However, the creation of a receivable or payable does not affect income. According to an **accrual accounting system**, a revenue is recognized when the right to receive payment has occurred and an expense is recognized when an obligation to pay has been incurred.

(8) **Life insurance proceeds** received at death are not taxable. However, if payments are spread over a period of time, any extra amount received each year is taxable interest.

(9) Prizes and awards are taxable even if taxpayer made no attempt to win

(10) **Scholarships** are nontaxable but only if used to cover tuition and course related costs such as books and supplies. Any other amounts must be reported as taxable income.

   (A) If student has to work to earn the money (such as teach a class), it is taxable.

   (B) If student is not a degree candidate, the money is taxable.

(11) **Gambling winnings** are included as taxable income. Losses can be deducted as miscellaneous itemized deductions. Deduction for losses cannot exceed winnings.

(12) **Alimony** is taxable to recipient although child support is not taxable.

   (A) If alimony and child support are both received during the year, the child support is assumed to be received first.

   (B) Alimony is only taxable after a legal separation or divorce.

   (1) Payments must be cash and must terminate at death.

   (2) Payments must be to or for benefit of spouse.

   (3) Lump sum property settlements are not taxable.

(13) If taxpayer owns a **sole proprietorship**, all revenues and expenses are reported on Schedule C which is basically an income statement for the business. The taxpayer can deduct all expenses that were ordinary and necessary.

   (A) Proprietorship income is taxable while losses are deductible.

   (B) Business related taxes and interest that do not qualify as itemized deductions can be deducted here if ordinary and necessary. However, charitable contributions are always itemized deductions.

   (C) A loss may be so large that it cannot be deducted entirely in the current year. The resulting **net operating loss** can be carried back to reduce taxable income in the two prior years and, if a loss still results, the remainder can be carried forward to reduce taxable income for the subsequent 20 years.

PROBLEMS AND SOLUTIONS
INDIVIDUAL INCOME TAXES – INCOME

ONE - A taxpayer receives the proceeds from a $60,000 life insurance policy when the taxpayer's uncle died. This amount must be included as taxable income on the taxpayer's income tax return for that year. (True or False?)

Answer - Life insurance proceeds are never viewed as taxable income. The money is not considered to be income because it is not earned. (Number One is False.)

TWO - A taxpayer has received taxable interest income of $80,000 and social security benefits of $10,000. The taxpayer has income subject to taxation of $85,000. (True or False?)

Answer - At relatively high income levels, 85 percent of social security benefits are subject to taxation. In this situation, the taxpayer has $80,000 of interest income and $8,500 in taxable social security benefits (85 percent). The total income subject to taxation is $88,500. (Number Two is False.)

THREE - A taxpayer receives cash interest of $1,000 from a corporate bond. The same taxpayer collects $2,000 in cash interest from a bond issued by a city. Finally, the taxpayer receives $4,000 in interest from a bond issued by the federal government. The taxpayer has income subject to taxation of $1,000. (True or False?)

Answer - The interest from a corporate bond is taxable as is most interest on bonds issued by the federal government. However, interest on bonds issued by state or local governments is tax free on a federal income tax return. This taxpayer has $5,000 in income subject to taxation. (Number Three is False.)

FOUR - Smith's mother buys US Series EE Savings Bonds and immediately gives them to Smith who is 40 years of age. Several years later, Smith earns a salary of $30,000. The bonds mature and Smith receives the proceeds of $40,000 including $6,000 in interest. This money is used to pay the college costs of Smith's daughter who is his dependent. In this year, Smith has income subject to taxation of $30,000. (True or False?)

Answer - In order for interest on US Series EE Savings Bonds to qualify as tax free, the taxpayer must have bought the bonds and still own them. Smith did not buy these bonds. Therefore, the interest is taxable and Smith has income subject to taxation for this year of $36,000. If Smith had bought the bonds, the usage of the money for the college costs of Smith, his spouse, or his dependent would have caused the interest to be tax free. (Number Four is False.)

FIVE - In the current year, a taxpayer has a salary of $50,000. The taxpayer also has income from three passive activities totaling $33,000. This same taxpayer has losses from two other passive activities totaling $40,000. This taxpayer will report an adjusted gross income in the current year of $43,000 after netting the passive activities. (True or False?)

Answer - Income and losses from all passive activities are netted together. If a net passive loss exists, as it does in this case, no loss can be deducted in the current year. Thus, this taxpayer would report neither an increase nor a decrease in the taxable income of the current year due to these passive activities. Adjusted gross income will be $50,000. (Number Five is False.)

SIX - A taxpayer is a degree candidate at a college. The taxpayer receives $10,000 in financial assistance. Of this amount, $8,000 covers tuition and other educational costs whereas the remaining $2,000 is given for room and board. This taxpayer has no taxable income because of this scholarship. (True or False?)

Answer - Scholarship amounts received for tuition and other educational costs are tax free to the recipient. However, any scholarship money that is applied to other costs such as room and board is viewed as taxable. This taxpayer will have taxable income from scholarships of $2,000. (Number Six is False.)

SEVEN - A taxpayer has a salary of $50,000. The taxpayer also has $30,000 in winnings from gambling. In addition, this taxpayer has $25,000 in losses from gambling. The taxpayer will have an adjusted gross income of $80,000. (True or False?)

Answer - Gambling winnings are reported as income by a taxpayer. Losses (up to the amount of the winnings) are included separately as a miscellaneous itemized deduction. (Number Seven is True.)

EIGHT - Ted and Alice file for divorce. As part of the property settlement, Alice receives $100,000 in cash and a car valued at $12,000. In addition, she receives monthly cash alimony payments that total $20,000 in the current year and child support payments of $10,000. Alice must report taxable alimony payments of $32,000 for the year. (True or False?)

Answer - Property settlements are not viewed as taxable alimony payments. In addition, to be taxable, periodic payments must be made in cash. Finally, child support payments are not taxable. Thus, the only taxable alimony paid this year is the $20,000 amount. (Number Eight is False.)

NINE - A taxpayer does work for a customer on December 2 of Year One for $5,000. The customer has paid $1,000 and will pay the rest within 90 days. If the cash method is applied, the taxpayer reports a revenue of $1,000 in Year One; if the accrual method is applied, the taxpayer has a revenue of $5,000 in Year One. (True or False?)

Answer - Since only $1,000 has been received, a cash method taxpayer will report that amount as revenue. However, $5,000 has been earned so that an accrual method taxpayer will report that amount as revenue because the customer has an obligation to pay the entire $5,000. (Number Nine is True.)

INDIVIDUAL INCOME TAXES - EXCHANGES

(1) Gains and losses resulting from **capital asset** transactions are reported on Schedule D of the Form 1040.

    (A) Capital assets include investment property such as land, shares of stock, and bonds.

    (B) Personal properties such as furniture are also capital assets but only gains are reported for these assets, losses are not deductible.

    (C) Gains and losses are classified as short-term (held 12 months or less) or long-term.

        (1) All gains and losses are netted to arrive at a single short-term taxable figure and a single long-term taxable figure. If one of these is a net gain and the other is a net loss, a further netting is made to arrive at one taxable figure.

        (2) A net **short-term gain** is taxed at ordinary income rates whereas a net **long-term gain** is usually taxed at a maximum rate of 20 percent.

        (3) For low income taxpayers, a net long-term gain is taxed at a maximum rate of 10 percent.

    (D) If capital gains and losses are netted and a net loss results, it is deductible up to $3,000 per year. Any remaining loss is carried over indefinitely and included on future tax returns.

    (E) Some distributions from mutual funds represent capital gains.

    (F) Nonbusiness bad debts are treated as short-term capital losses.

(2) If a taxpayer trades business or investment property, a taxable gain may result.

    (A) The trade of certain types of **like-kind property** (land for land, for example) is normally not taxable. New item is recorded at basis of old property. Like-kind means same class of property.

    (B) If like-kind property is exchanged and boot (property that is not like-kind, usually cash) is received, a taxable gain may be recognized.

        (1) Taxpayer must recognize gain as the lesser of the boot received or the gain realized on the exchange.

        (2) Realized gain is the difference in basis of property given up and the fair market value of the amounts received.

        (3) If buyer assumes debt of seller, that is boot to the seller.

    (C) If property is exchanged that is not like-kind, realized gain must be recognized for tax purposes.

(3) Receipt of **inherited property** is tax-free for income tax purposes but basis must be determined if property is ever sold by the recipient.

    (A) Normally, basis is the fair market value of the property at date of decedent's death.

    (B) An alternative date must be used if it is selected by the executor of the estate. In that case, basis is value 6 months after death (or at date of conveyance if earlier than 6 months).

(4) Taxpayer can lose property by **involuntary conversion**. Property can be condemned, destroyed, or stolen.

(A)   If amount received from insurance or government is below tax basis, loss is immediately recognized. It is a capital loss if investment property was involved; it is an itemized deduction if personal property.

(B)   If payment is above basis, a gain has been earned but part (or all) of the gain may be excluded from taxable income.

    (1)   If taxpayer acquires similar **replacement property**, the amount to be taxed is the lesser of (1) the realized gain and (2) any proceeds left over after replacement. If no part of the proceeds is left, gain is not taxable.

(5)   In sales made to **related parties**, gains are taxable but losses are not deductible.

(A)   Related parties are members of taxpayer's family. Also, corporations and partnerships are related parties to a taxpayer who owns over 50 percent.

(B)   If a loss is not deductible, it can be used to decrease any later gain on eventual sale of the property to an unrelated party. The loss can reduce a subsequent gain but cannot create a loss even when property is sold to an outsider.

(6)   If a **personal residence** is sold, a gain of up to $500,000 (joint) or $250,000 (single) can be excluded.

(A)   Exclusion can only be taken once every two years.

(B)   To qualify, property must have been taxpayer's principal residence for at least two out of the previous five years.

(7)   When a **gift** is received, it has no effect on taxable income. However, if the gift is ever sold, a gain or loss may result.

(A)   To compute a taxable gain, sales price is compared with the basis of the property to the previous owner.

(B)   To compute a taxable loss, sales price is compared with the lower of (1) the previous owner's basis and (2) the fair market value of the property at the date of gift.

(C)   If gain computation arrives at a loss and loss computation gives a gain, no tax effect results from the sale. This situation occurs when property's value (1) drops between date of original purchase and the date of the gift, (2) then rises after gift is made, and (3) is still below previous owner's basis.

PROBLEMS AND SOLUTIONS
INDIVIDUAL INCOME TAXES – EXCHANGES

ONE - A taxpayer has a short-term capital gain of $4,000 and a long-term capital gain of $6,000. The entire $10,000 will be taxed at a maximum rate of 20 percent. (True or False?)

Answer - The short-term capital gain is taxed at the taxpayer's ordinary tax rate; the long-term capital gain will be taxed at a maximum tax rate of 20 percent. (Number One is False.)

TWO - A taxpayer has a $8,000 short-term capital gain and a $6,000 long-term capital loss. The individual taxpayer will report a net $2,000 short-term capital gain that will be taxed at a maximum rate of 20 percent. (True or False?)

Answer - The short-term capital gain and long-term capital loss should be netted together. The net figure takes the characteristics of the number that is larger (in absolute terms). The two are netted to create a $2,000 gain that is viewed as short-term in nature because the $8,000 gain is larger than the $6,000 loss. This short-term gain is taxed at the taxpayer's ordinary tax rate and not at a maximum of 20 percent. (Number Two is False.)

THREE - A taxpayer holds investment land with a basis of $22,000 and a fair market value of $34,000. This land is exchanged for other property that does not qualify as like-kind property. This property has a fair market value of $34,000. The taxpayer must recognize a capital gain of $12,000. (True or False?)

Answer - If a business or investment asset is exchanged for property that does not qualify as like-kind, the basis of the old asset ($22,000) is compared to the fair market value of the new property ($34,000) to determine the tax effect (a $12,000 gain). (Number Three is True.)

FOUR - A taxpayer holds investment land with a basis of $24,000 and a fair market value of $50,000. This land is exchanged for like-kind property with a fair market value of $40,000. The taxpayer also receives cash of $10,000. The taxpayer has a taxable gain of $10,000. (True or False?)

Answer - In an exchange of like-kind property, no gain or loss is recognized. However, if boot (any property that is not like-kind property) is also received, a taxable gain equal to the amount of boot ($10,000) can be recognized. This gain cannot be more than the realized gain, the excess of the fair market value of the property received ($50,000 or $40,000 plus $10,000) over the basis of the property given up ($24,000). Here, this excess is $26,000. Since the boot of $10,000 is less than the gain of $26,000, the $10,000 is the taxable amount of the gain. (Number Four is True.)

FIVE - Blue received land as an inheritance from a distant uncle. The land had a tax basis to the uncle of $56,000 but was worth $64,000 on the date of the uncle's death (January 1, Year One). Blue received title to the land on October 1, Year One, when the fair market value was $67,000. On July 1, Year One, the fair market value of this land was $66,000. The executor of the estate did not choose the alternative valuation date. The basis of the land to Blue is $64,000. (True or False?)

Answer - Unless the alternative valuation date is selected by the executor, the beneficiary uses the fair market value on the date of death as the tax basis of the property received. (Number Five is True.)

SIX - A taxpayer owns a garage that is destroyed by fire. The garage had a tax basis of $50,000 but was rendered completely worthless as a result of the fire. The taxpayer receives $60,000 from an insurance policy based on the fair market value of the garage prior to the fire. The taxpayer constructs a new garage at a cost of $71,000. The taxpayer has a taxable gain of $10,000 based on the insurance proceeds. (True or False?)

Answer - An involuntary conversion occurs when property is destroyed, damaged, stolen, or condemned. When insurance or other proceeds are received, a gain might be realized. However, if replacement property is acquired within a specified time, a part or all of the gain may be deferred for tax purposes. The taxable amount is the lesser of the gain ($10,000 in this case) and the amount of the proceeds left after the replacement. Since the replacement property here had a cost that was more than the amount received, no part of the proceeds remains. Thus, no taxable gain is reported. (Number Six is False.)

SEVEN - A taxpayer buys land for $50,000. The land drops in value to $42,000. The taxpayer sells the land to his son for $43,000. The taxpayer has no tax effect as a result of this sale. (True or False?)

Answer - Losses on related party transactions cannot be included in computing taxable income. A related party includes a spouse, brother, sister, ancestors, and lineal descendent. In addition, any corporation in which a taxpayer holds over 50 percent ownership is considered to be a related party. Thus, this loss is from a related party transaction and cannot be deducted by the taxpayer. (Number Seven is True.)

EIGHT - Mr. and Mrs. Sanborn bought their principal residence several years ago and have lived in it since that time. The residence has a tax basis of $200,000 and was sold this year for $410,000. These taxpayers are both 63 years old. They buy a replacement residence for $175,000. The Sanborns have a taxable gain on the sale of $85,000. (True or False?)

Answer - These taxpayers have no taxable gain. Married taxpayers can exclude up to $500,000 of gain on the sale of their principal residence. Thus, the $210,000 gain on the sale is excluded. They must have owned and used the residence as their principal residence for an aggregate of at least two out of the previous five years. Replacement of the residence does not affect this exclusion; the age of the taxpayers does not affect this exclusion. (Number Eight is False.)

NINE - Susan gave her friend Will an acre of land with a tax basis of $40,000 but a fair market value of $33,000. Will later sold the land for $46,000. Will must report a taxable gain of $6,000. (True or False?)

Answer - Whenever a gift is sold for an amount in excess of its previous tax basis, a taxable gain is reported for the balance received in excess of that basis. (Number Nine is True.)

INDIVIDUAL INCOME TAXES - DEDUCTIONS FOR ADJUSTED GROSS INCOME (AGI)

(1)   A number of specific items can be deducted in arriving at **adjusted gross income** (AGI). These items are allowed whether the taxpayer reports itemized deductions or takes the standard deduction.

(2)   **Alimony** is deductible by the payer if it is taxable to the recipient as discussed previously in the rules about income.

(3)   In some cases, the early withdrawal of money from a savings or investment account leads to a penalty. All income earned is taxable but the penalty is deductible in arriving at AGI.

(4)   If a self-employed individual pays **self-employment tax**, half of the payment is reported as a deduction to arrive at AGI. Deduction is allowed in same year as the income which is taxed.

(5)   If a self-employed individual pays **medical insurance** for self, spouse, and/or dependents, 100% is a deduction for AGI.

(6)   A deduction for AGI is allowed for **interest on qualified education loan**, a loan that is used to pay for the cost of tuition, fees, room, and board to attend post-secondary institution or certain vocational and other programs (at least on a half-time basis). Education expenses must have been for taxpayer, spouse, or taxpayer's dependent.

        (A)   Deduction is only for interest paid during the first 60 months that interest payments are required.

        (B)   Maximum deduction is $2,500 for 2003.

        (C)   Deduction is phased out as taxpayer's income gets high.

(7)   Deductible (Traditional) Individual Retirement Account (IRA)

        (A)   Up to $3,000 (or the amount of compensation, if less) that is put into a deductible IRA is a deduction for AGI in that year. The same amount is available to spouse as long as total compensation is at least $6,000. Alimony is viewed as compensation for this computation.

        (B)   If taxpayer is not an active participant in an employer sponsored retirement plan, the deduction can be taken each year.

        (C)   If taxpayer is an active participant in an employer sponsored retirement plan, the ability to take the deduction is phased out at relatively low AGI levels. On a joint return, if only one party is an active participant in an employer sponsored retirement plan, the other party can still take deduction unless AGI is very high.

        (D)   Any money taken out of a deductible IRA is taxable income.

                (1)   Tax is also increased by 10 percent if any money is taken out before taxpayer is 59½ years old.

                (2)   There is no 10 percent penalty on any early withdrawal if money is used to pay qualified costs of higher education or to cover the cost of a first-time home purchase. For a home purchase, only $10,000 can be removed without the penalty.

(8)   No deduction is allowed for payments to **Education IRAs**

        (A)   Nondeductible payments of up to $500 per beneficiary can be made in each tax year until beneficiary becomes 18. There can be any number of beneficiaries and no relationship is required.

        (B)   Each beneficiary is only entitled to $500 per year no matter how many people want to create these IRAs.

(C)   Distributions from the plan are tax free up to the amount of costs paid for post secondary education including tuition, fees, and some room and board costs.

(D)   In any year that the taxpayer takes either the Hope tax credit or the lifetime learning credit for a particular student, a withdrawal from an education IRA is not tax free.

(E)   There is a phase out for education IRAs but it is relatively high.

(9)   No deduction is allowed for payments to **Roth IRAs**

    (A)   A nondeductible amount of up to $3,000 per year (less any amount put into a deductible IRA) can be put into a Roth IRA.

    (B)   After the Roth IRA is five years old, all distributions are tax free as long as the person is 59½ or uses the money for a first-time home purchase (up to $10,000).

    (C)   There is a phaseout for Roth IRAs but the AGI has to be relatively high before the benefit is disallowed.

(10)   A self-employed taxpayer can deduct amounts placed in retirement plans; these plans are sometimes called **Keogh Plans** or **H.R.-10 Plans**.

    (A)   Taxpayer must generate income from either a partnership or proprietorship.

    (B)   Amount contributed to plan can be deducted up to a maximum that is the equivalent of 20 percent of self-employment income (less the deduction that is allowed for self-employment tax payments).

(11)   **Moving expenses** can be deducted if the move was employment related such as a transfer or moving to a new job. New job must be 50 miles farther from old residence than previous job was. Taxpayer can deduct the cost of physically moving goods and transporting people.

PROBLEMS AND SOLUTIONS
INDIVIDUAL INCOME TAXES – DEDUCTIONS
FOR ADJUSTED GROSS INCOME (AGI)

ONE - A taxpayer has $100,000 invested in a time deposit account. During the current year, the account earned $11,000 in interest. However, the taxpayer withdrew the funds before the maturity date and was assessed a penalty of $2,000 so that only $109,000 was received. The taxpayer still reports $11,000 as interest income for the year but also gets a $2,000 deduction in arriving at adjusted gross income. (True or False?)

Answer - A penalty for a premature withdrawal from a time deposit account is not netted against the income. Instead, this taxpayer reports the entire amount of interest as income while a separate deduction is allowed for the penalty in determining adjusted gross income. (Number One is True.)

TWO - Mr. and Mrs. Jones have total income from their jobs of over $300,000. However, neither party is an active participant in an employer-sponsored retirement plan. They have both contributed $3,000 this year to an individual retirement account (IRA). Because of the high level of income, they are not eligible to take deductions for these contributions. (True or False?)

Answer – If a taxpayer is not an active participant in an employer-sponsored retirement plan, a deduction for an IRA contribution of up to $3,000 per person can be taken. Thus, Mr. and Mrs. Jones are entitled to a total deduction (in arriving at adjusted gross income) of $6,000 for their contributions. (Number Two is False.)

THREE - Mr. Haynes is unemployed and has only $1,100 in interest income. Mrs. Haynes is employed and has compensation this year of $63,000. She is not an active participant in an employer-sponsored retirement plan. Both taxpayers contributed $3,000 to an IRA. On a joint return, they are entitled to a deduction of $6,000 in arriving at adjusted gross income. (True or False?)

Answer - On a joint return, each taxpayer can take a deduction of $3,000 for an IRA payment as long as total compensation is $6,000 or more. Thus, even though Mr. Haynes has no compensation, both of the $3,000 payments are deductible because compensation on the joint return is over $6,000. (Number Three is True.)

FOUR - A taxpayer has income of $14,000. This taxpayer contributes $1,400 to a traditional IRA. Because of this contribution, the taxpayer is not entitled to make any contribution to a Roth IRA. (True or False?)

Answer - Taxpayers are allowed to contribute up to $3,000 (or the amount of compensation, if less) to traditional and Roth IRA plans. Since only $1,400 was contributed to the traditional IRA plan, the taxpayer could put as much as $1,600 into a Roth IRA. (Number Four is False.)

FIVE - A taxpayer wants to create education IRAs for each of his six nephews and nieces. The total amount that can be contributed in any one year is $2,000. (True or False?)

Answer - A taxpayer can make contributions to education IRAs for any number of beneficiaries. The only limitation is that the amount contributed cannot exceed $500 per beneficiary per year. Since the taxpayer has six potential beneficiaries, the total contribution could be as much as $3,000 per year. (Number Five is False.)

INDIVIDUAL INCOME TAXES - ITEMIZED DEDUCTIONS

(1)   **Itemized deductions** are reported on Schedule A of the 1040 form. Taxpayers use the itemized deduction total to reduce taxable income if it is larger than the **standard deduction**. The total amount of itemized deductions must be reduced, though, if the taxpayer's AGI is high.

(2)   **Medical expenses** are included if paid for taxpayers, their dependents, and anyone who would have been a dependent except for the income test.

    (A)   All expenses made to maintain or improve health can be taken: doctors' fees, dental costs, x-rays, medical insurance, crutches, eyeglasses, etc. Prescription drugs and insulin are also included. Capital expenditures made to home for medical reasons can be included for any amount in excess of the increase in the property's fair market value.

    (B)   Some items are not allowed: cosmetic surgery, over-the-counter medicines, and any costs covered by insurance.

    (C)   The actual deduction is the cost that is in excess of 7.5 percent of AGI.

(3)   The payment of certain taxes can be deducted.

    (A)   **State and local income taxes** paid during the year are deductible but not the amount paid for federal income taxes.

        (1)   If deduction is taken in year of payment but a refund is later received, refund is taxable income in later year.

    (B)   **Real estate taxes** are deductible even if paid to foreign country.

        (1)   Taxpayer must own property to get deduction. If property is owned for just part of a year, only that portion is included.

    (C)   **Personal property taxes** are deductible if based on value of property.

(4)   **Interest expense** is an itemized deduction in certain cases.

    (A)   Interest paid on debts for both principal and second residence is deductible.

        (1)   **Interest on acquisition indebtedness** of up to $1 million is deductible. Money has to be used to buy, build, or improve house.

        (2)   **Interest on home equity indebtedness** of up to $100,000 is deductible. Money can be used for any purpose.

        (3)   No interest deduction is allowed on debt in excess of the value of the residence.

    (B)   For interest to be deductible, debt must be that of the taxpayer.

    (C)   Payment of points is deductible if amount was actually paid, was used to get money to buy, build, or improve home, was normal for that area, and was a normal amount.

    (D)   No deduction is allowed for personal interest such as that paid on credit cards, car loans, etc.

    (E)   **Interest expense to buy investments** can be deducted but expense in excess of net investment income is not deductible and must be carried forward. Net investment income includes interest, dividends, rents, and net gains on the sale of investments.

(5)   **Contributions** to qualifying domestic **charitable organizations** is deductible. Payment must be made and not just a pledge. Credit card charges are deductible.

    (A)   Dues and purchases are deductible if they exceed value of benefits received.

    (B)   Services provided to a charity are not deductible although out-of-pocket costs relating to those services are deductible.

    (C)   Property given to charity is deductible.

        (1)   For inventory or short-term capital assets, deduction is lesser of fair market value or basis (probably cost).

        (2)   For long-term capital assets, deduction is fair market value. The taxpayer does not have to report a gain if the property has appreciated in value.

    (D)   There are several limitations to the amount of charitable contributions that can be deducted in one year. Any amount that cannot be deducted is carried forward for up to five years. Computation is usually as follows.

        (1)   First, the amount to be included for the donation of long-term capital asset property is determined but only up to 30 percent of AGI in any year.

        (2)   Second, allowed deduction for long-term capital asset property is added to all other charitable contributions. This amount gives total deduction but it cannot exceed 50 percent of AGI.

(6)   **Casualty and theft losses** of property are deductible.

    (A)   A casualty is a loss created by a sudden, unexpected, or unusual event. Examples would include a fire, storm, or accident.

    (B)   Loss is measured as lesser of (1) reduction in value of property and (2) the basis of the property. Loss is reduced by any insurance payment.

    (C)   Loss from each separate incident is further reduced by $100; all losses are then combined and decreased by 10 percent of AGI to get the amount of the itemized deduction.

(7)   Several items are reported as **miscellaneous itemized deductions.**

    (A)   **Gambling losses** are deducted here but only up to the amount of the winnings that are reported as income.

    (B)   Other expenses are deductible but only for the total amount over 2 percent of AGI. These items relate to taxpayer's job or to income production or protection: unreimbursed job related expenses, union dues, safe deposit box rent, tax preparation fees, professional publications, dues in professional societies, small tools and supplies and the like. The cost of education is included but only if it is incurred to maintain or improve job skills and the education will not qualify person for new job or position. The cost of a CPA Exam Review course cannot be deducted.

PROBLEMS AND SOLUTIONS
INDIVIDUAL INCOME TAXES – ITEMIZED DEDUCTIONS

ONE - A taxpayer has adjusted gross income of $10,000 from her salary at her job. During the current year, the taxpayer has no medical expenses but did pay $900 for medical insurance. This taxpayer is entitled to a $150 itemized deduction for medical expenses. (True or False?)

Answer - Medical insurance is properly included as a medical expense. However, only the amount of medical expenses in excess of 7.5 percent of adjusted gross income can be deducted. The insurance cost here is $900, an amount $150 in excess of 7.5 percent of $10,000 (or $750). If this taxpayer had been self-employed, a

---

percentage of the medical insurance is deducted in arriving at adjusted gross income with the remainder being used to compute the taxpayer's itemized deductions. (Number One is True.)

TWO - In computing the taxes that a taxpayer can take as itemized deductions, federal taxes cannot be included. (True or False?)

Answer - Three different taxes are appropriate in computed a taxpayer's itemized deductions: (1) income taxes (but not federal taxes), (2) real estate taxes, and (3) personal property taxes. Gift taxes, social security taxes, federal income taxes, estate taxes, and sales taxes are not included as itemized deductions. (Number Two is True.)

THREE - Mr. and Mrs. Baldwin pay a $1,000 property tax on their automobile. The amount of the tax is based on the weight of the vehicle. This property tax is not deductible as an itemized deduction on their income tax return. (True or False?)

Answer - To be a deductible, a personal property tax must be based on the value of the property (it must be an ad valorem tax). This tax was based on the weight of the car and, thus, does not qualify. (Number Three is True.)

FOUR - A taxpayer incurred $3,000 of interest expense in connection with a loan to buy a car. In addition, the taxpayer paid $800 in interest on credit cards that were used to buy furniture. The taxpayer cannot include either of these payments in computing itemized deductions. (True or False?)

Answer - In determining itemized deductions, a taxpayer can only include interest on qualified residences and interest paid in connection with investment income. Neither the interest on the car loan or the furniture acquisition can be used in this computation. (Number Four is True.)

FIVE - Mr. and Mrs. Hamner own a house that had a cost of $210,000 a number of years ago. The taxpayers have no outstanding debt in connection with this residence. At the beginning of the current year, these taxpayers acquire a second residence on the river. The mortgage loan on this second home was $300,000 and the interest for the year was $23,000. The taxpayers are not entitled to an itemized deduction because the interest was incurred on a second residence. (True or False?)

Answer - Qualified residence interest includes both the taxpayer's principal residence and a second home. Since acquisition debt was not more than $1 million, the entire $23,000 qualifies as an itemized deduction. (Number Five is False.)

SIX - A taxpayer borrows money to make an investment in the stock market. Interest expense of $2,000 was incurred on the loan. Net investment income earned was $4,600. The income is included in arriving at adjusted gross income; however, the interest expense qualifies as an itemized deduction. (True or False?)

Answer - Interest expense incurred on debt to acquire investments is deductible up to the amount of net investment income (such as dividends, interest, and rents less any related expenses). Since the expense here was less than the net investment income, it can be deducted entirely. If the interest had been over $4,600, only the first $4,600 would have been deducted in the current year. The excess could then have been carried over indefinitely. (Number Six is True.)

SEVEN - Mr. Jones goes to an auction sponsored by a qualified charitable organization. He buys a cake with a fair market value of $10. Because of his support for this organization, he pays $100. Mr. Jones is entitled to a charitable contribution deduction of $90. (True or False?)

Answer - Payments for the benefit of a charitable organization that are in excess of the fair market value of the items or services received can be taken as itemized deductions. Mr. Jones paid $90 more than the value of the cake; this amount qualifies as a charitable contribution. (Number Seven is True.)

EIGHT - A taxpayer donates investment property held for several years (with a tax basis of $2,000) to a charitable organization. This property has a fair market value of $2,800. The taxpayer is eligible for a $2,800 charitable contribution deduction but must report a long-term capital gain of $800. (True or False?)

Answer – When donating investment property that has been held for longer than a year, the basic rule is that the allowed contribution is the fair market value of the property. Thus, this taxpayer is entitled to a charitable contribution of $2,800. However, since the property was not sold, no capital gain must be reported. (Number Eight is False.)

NINE - Mr. and Mrs. Anderson own a residence that has a tax basis of $99,000 but has a fair market value of $130,000. A fire destroys part of the house and reduces its fair market value to $20,000. Insurance pays them $40,000. The Andersons have a casualty loss of $59,000. (True or False?)

Answer - A casualty loss is computed as the lesser of (1) the tax basis and (2) the drop in the value of the property. In this case, the tax basis of $99,000 is below the $110,000 drop in fair market value ($130,000 less $20,000). This amount is reduced by the insurance payment of $40,000 to arrive at a casualty loss of $59,000. In computing the actual itemized deduction, the loss will be reduced by $100 and 10 percent of adjusted gross income. (Number Nine is True.)

TEN - A taxpayer has adjusted gross income of $50,000. In the current year, this taxpayer paid $300 for subscriptions to professional journals, $400 for dues to professional societies, and $500 for union dues. This taxpayer can claim a miscellaneous itemized deduction of $200. (True or False?)

Answer - Unreimbursed employee expenses are deductible as miscellaneous itemized deductions but only to the extent that they exceed 2 percent of the taxpayer's adjusted gross income. Expenses incurred in connection with professional publications, professional societies, and union dues all fall under this category as do amounts paid for small tools and supplies as well as uniforms (that cannot be adapted for general use). The taxpayer paid a total of $1,200 which is $200 in excess of 2 percent of adjusted gross income ($1,000 or 2 percent of $50,000). (Number Ten is True.)

INDIVIDUAL INCOME TAXES - TAX CREDITS

(1)   A **tax credit** is a direct decrease in an individual's income tax rather than a reduction in the amount of taxable income. There are numerous tax credits available.

(2)   A credit is allowed for payments for child or dependent care expenses.

  (A)   Credit is taken for payments made to someone to care for a dependent so that taxpayer can be gainfully employed. Payments have to be for the care of the individual.

  (B)   To qualify, dependents must be under 13 or unable to care for themselves.

  (C)   Credit is determined by taking a percentage of the amount paid.

   (1)   In determining credit, taxpayer uses payment for the year but not over $3,000 for one dependent or $6,000 for more than one dependent.

   (2)   Percentage is based on taxpayer's AGI. There are many possible percentages. If AGI is under $15,000, use 35 percent (the highest rate); if AGI is over $45,000, use 20 percent (the lowest rate).

(3)   An earned income credit is allowed for taxpayers with a relatively low amount of earned income (usually a salary) who maintain a household for a qualifying child.

  (A)   This credit is one that can create a refund from the government if the credit is larger than the amount of the taxpayer's income tax.

  (B)   A reduced earned income credit is available even if taxpayer does not have a qualifying child living in the household.

(4)   US taxpayers include foreign income on their US tax return but can take a **credit for taxes paid to foreign countries.**

(5)   A credit of up to $10,160 (for 2003) is given for qualifying adoption expenses.

  (A)   The credit is reduced and eventually eliminated for taxpayers with a high AGI.

(6)   The **child tax credit** is available for if taxpayer has qualifying children under 17.

  (A)   Taxpayers get a credit for each dependent who is their child, stepchild, foster-child, or grandchild.

  (B)   Credit phases out at high adjusted gross income levels. As the number of children increases, the higher the AGI can be before the taxpayer starts to lose the credit.

  (C)   Low income individuals may be entitled to an additional refundable credit.

(7)   Cost of post-secondary education can lead to the **Hope scholarship credit.**

  (A)   Taxpayer gets a credit for the costs of first two years of post-secondary education if paid on behalf of taxpayer, spouse, or dependent.

  (B)   Costs include tuition and related expenses but not room, board, or books.

  (C)   In each tax year, the credit is 100 percent of the first $1,000 and 50 percent of the next $1,000.

(8)   Costs of education can also entitle taxpayer to **lifetime learning credit.**

  (A)   Credit is 20 percent of qualified tuition and fees up to a maximum credit of $2,000 per return. Must be paid on behalf of taxpayer, spouse, or dependent. Can be claimed for an unlimited number of years.

  (B)   Qualified cost is the amount paid for any undergraduate or graduate program as long as person is at least half-time student. Also qualifies (whether half-time or not) if education is to acquire or improve job skills.

  (C)   A student's costs can lead to the Hope tax credit or the lifetime learning credit each year but not both. If costs are for two or more students, one credit can be taken for some and the other credit for the rest.

(D)   Ability to take either the Hope tax credit or the lifetime learning credit is lost (phased out) as income gets high.

PROBLEMS AND SOLUTIONS
INDIVIDUAL INCOME TAXES – TAX CREDITS

ONE - A taxpayer is entitled to a credit for qualifying dependent care expenses incurred to allow the taxpayer to be gainfully employed. The credit is computed by multiplying the qualifying cost incurred by a percentage. If the cost is more than $2,000 during the tax year, only $2,000 can be used in calculating this credit. (True or False?)

Answer - The actual amount of expense incurred to care for the individual will be used but only within certain limitations. If care is provided for one person, the maximum cost allowed for this computation is $3,000. If care must be given to two or more people, the maximum cost that can be included is $6,000. The actual credit will be a percentage of the appropriate cost figure. (Number One is False.)

TWO - A taxpayer is entitled to an earned income credit of $300. However, the total amount of income taxes incurred by this taxpayer is only $250. Assuming that the taxpayer has had no estimated payments or tax withholding, a refund of $50 will be received. (True or False?)

Answer - The earned income credit is refundable. In other words, if the income tax figure is reduced to zero, this credit can then create a tax refund. For this taxpayer, a refund of $50 will be received although no taxes have been paid. (Number Two is True.)

THREE -A married couple living in Virginia adopt two daughters (Anna and Lara) who were born in Nizhny-Novgorod, Russia. These taxpayers are entitled to a tax credit for qualifying adoption expenses. (True or False?)

Answer - Qualifying adoption expenses (up to a limited amount) can be taken as a tax credit. The fact that the children were not born in the United States has no impact on the basic credit. (Number Three is True.)

FOUR - A taxpayer is entitled to a tax credit (known as the Hope scholarship credit) for the costs of post-secondary school education. These costs include tuition and related expenses but not room and board. (True or False?)

Answer - The cost of tuition as well as related expenses can be used to qualify for the Hope scholarship credit. However, room and board costs are not eligible. (Number Four is True.)

FIVE - A taxpayer pays tuition costs for her son who is a college freshman. The taxpayer can take the Hope scholarship credit this year in connection with this student or the lifetime learning credit but not both. (True or False?)

Answer - For each tax year, a taxpayer may only use one of the following for each qualifying student: (1) the Hope scholarship credit, (2) the lifetime learning credit, or (3) the exclusion for distributions from an education IRA. (Number Five is True.)

INCOME TAXATION OF PARTNERSHIPS AND S CORPORATIONS

(1) **Partnerships** do not pay income taxes. The partners report their portion of income on their individual returns when earned by the partnership but, usually, not when a distribution is made. Partnerships file an informational tax return (Form 1065). Within that return, **Schedule K** is completed to indicate the income and other items assigned to each partner. Every partner receives a **Schedule K-1** that lists that effect of the partnership on that individual's tax return.

　(A) Specified partnership income items pass through directly to the income tax returns of the partners according to their percentage of ownership. Items that pass through in this manner include the following.

　　(1) Rental and royalty income

　　(2) Capital gains and losses

　　(3) Dividends and interest received

　　(4) Charitable contributions and foreign income taxes

　　(5) Section 179 expense deduction

　(B) All other revenues and expenses are netted to arrive at a single ordinary income figure which is also taxable to the partners based on the percentage of ownership.

　(C) A **guaranteed payment to a partner** is made without regard for the income earned by the business. It is income to the recipient; thus, that type of distribution is taxable to the partner. However, the partnership includes the payment as an expense in computing its ordinary income. Fringe benefits such as group-term life insurance and premiums for health plans are handled the same as guaranteed payments.

　(D) The tax year used by a partnership is normally the same as that of the partners unless a valid business reason exists for using some other date.

(2) Partnership losses are deductible by the partners but they cannot deduct more than their **at-risk basis**. This figure is the partner's investment basis in the partnership at the end of the year plus any loans made to the partnership plus the percentage of business liabilities that would have to be paid by a partner if the partnership went bankrupt.

　(A) Investment basis starts with the initial investment (and subsequent contributions) made by the partner and is then increased by ordinary partnership income and pass through income items (as well as tax-exempt income) and decreased by ordinary losses and pass through losses and expenses. Investment basis is also decreased by most distributions made to the partner.

(3) **Property contributed to a partnership** by a partner retains the same basis for tax purposes (the date as well as the amount). Partner's investment basis in partnership is increased by the basis of the property.

　(A) Usually no gain or loss is created by transfers to a partnership since the basis is retained.

　(B) If property being transferred has a liability that is also accepted by the partnership, the investment basis of the donating partner is the basis of the asset less the basis of debt. However, the at-risk balance would also include that partner's share of the liability that has just been incurred by the business.

　　(1) For example, if A gives land with a basis of $10,000 and a $6,000 liability to get a 40 percent ownership of a partnership, A's investment basis is the

$4,000 net of the two. However, the at-risk basis is $6,400: the $4,000 investment basis plus 40 percent of the partnership debt of $6,000.

    (2)   If liability is large enough, the at-risk balance could be a negative; in that case, the partner's at-risk balance is set at zero and the negative balance is a taxable gain to the donating partner.

(4)   A sale of property between a partner and a partnership is taxable. However, if partner holds over 50 percent ownership of partnership, resulting gains are taxable but losses are not deductible. The transaction is viewed as a related party transfer.

(5)   A **partnership is terminated** for tax purposes whenever only one partner remains or anytime that 50% or more of the interest changes hands within 12 months. If an interest is sold more than once during a 12 month period, it only counts once in measuring this 50% rule.

    (A)   If business is to continue, assets are assumed to be distributed and then immediately contributed to new partnership.

(6)   A distribution of cash or other assets can be made by a partnership to a partner. This is sometimes called a **nonliquidating distribution** if business will continue. Normally, this type of distribution is not taxable to either party. The partner records property received at the basis to the partnership with an equal reduction in that partner's investment basis.

    (A)   If basis of property is larger than the basis of partner's investment, partner records property at basis of the investment and investment is reduced to zero.

    (B)   If property received is cash and it is larger than investment basis, excess is a gain to the partner.

(7)   A partnership can cease operations and distribute cash and/or other assets to the partners. This transfer is referred to as a **liquidating distribution** and is normally not taxable to either party.

    (A)   If property is received without any cash, partner records this property at an amount equal to the partner's investment basis in the partnership. No tax effect is recognized.

    (B)   If cash and property are both received, cash is recorded first. Any other assets are recorded at an amount equal to the partner's investment basis (after it is reduced by the cash collected).

    (C)   If cash and/or property are received and the cash is larger than the partner's investment basis, the cash is recorded first and a gain is recognized for the amount that it exceeds the investment basis. Any other asset is recorded by the partner at a zero basis.

(8)   A business can also be established as an **S corporation**.

    (A)   Legally, this business is a corporation but it is taxed almost exactly like a partnership rather than like a corporation (a regular corporation is called **C Corporation**).

        (1)   S corporations do not pay taxes; the income passes through and is immediately taxable to the owners.

        (2)   Pass through items (very similar to those of a partnership) are reported directly on the tax return of the owners. All other income items are netted to arrive at an ordinary gain or loss that is also taxable to the owners.

        (3)   Losses are deductible up to the owner's at-risk basis. This figure is the owner's investment basis plus any loans to the business. In an S corporation, the owners are not responsible for the debts of the business.

(B)　An S corporation cannot have over 75 owners all of whom must be individuals, estates, or certain types of trusts.

PROBLEMS AND SOLUTIONS
INCOME TAXATION OF PARTNERSHIPS AND S CORPORATIONS

ONE – The JH partnership earns a net income of $30,000 during the current year. The partnership will pay income taxes on the amount earned but distributions will be tax free to the partners. (True or False?)

Answer – Distributions made by a partnership to its partners are usually tax free. However, the income earned by a partnership must be reported immediately as taxable income by the partners. The partnership does not pay income tax when the income is earned but rather the partners do. (Number One is False.)

TWO – A partnership has two partners (Smith and Jones), each of whom owns a 50 percent share. This year the partnership had $100,000 in revenues from the sale of inventory, $20,000 in interest revenue, and a $10,000 long-term capital gain. Smith will report $65,000 in income from the partnership on his individual income tax return for the year. (True or False?)

Answer – For taxation purposes, the interest revenue and capital gains and losses of a partnership pass directly through to the partners. Revenues and expenses that do not pass through are accumulated and reported as a single operating income figure for the partnership. As 50 percent owners, each partner will report $10,000 in interest revenue (50 percent), a $5,000 long-term capital gain (50 percent), and $50,000 operating income from the partnership (50 percent). (Number Two is False.)

THREE – A partnership has charitable contributions, advertising expense, and rent expense for the year. The charitable contribution will pass directly through to the tax returns of the partners. The other two items will be included in determining the ordinary operating income of the partnership. (True or False?)

Answer – For a partnership, certain items are passed through directly to the tax returns of the partners. Such items include rental income, capital gains and losses, dividend and interest revenue, and charitable contributions. Thus, any charitable contributions made by this partnership will be reported on the individual tax returns of its partners. The two remaining items do not qualify as pass through items and will be included in determining the ordinary income of the partnership. This amount will also be allocated to the partners for taxation purposes. (Number Three is True.)

FOUR – A partnership has two partners (A and Z), each of whom holds a 50 percent ownership. During the current year, the partnership earned ordinary income of $100,000. Not included in that amount is a $20,000 guaranteed payment made to Z each year. On the individual tax returns, Z will report income from the partnership of $40,000 and the guaranteed payment of $20,000. (True or False?)

Answer – A guaranteed payment is income to the recipient and a reduction for the partnership in computing ordinary income. Thus, the ordinary income of the partnership is $80,000 after removing the $20,000. Each partner is entitled to half of the income so Z must report $40,000 from the partnership as well as $20,000 from the guaranteed payment. (Number Four is True.)

FIVE – A partner holds a 30 percent ownership in a partnership and has an investment basis of $25,000. The partnership has total liabilities of $20,000. This year, the partnership reports an ordinary operating loss of $100,000. On an individual tax return, this partner can report a loss of $30,000. (True or False?)

Answer – For a partnership, a partner can deduct losses up the amount that is at-risk. This total is the investment capital plus any loans to the partnership and the partner's share of the debts of the business. Here, the investment basis is $25,000. Although the partner has not loaned money to the business, this partner is responsible for 30 percent of the liabilities ($20,000) or $6,000. Thus, this partner has an at-risk balance of $31,000. The share of the loss is 30 percent or only $30,000, an amount that can be deducted completely. (Number Five is True.)

SIX – A partnership is formed by B and Y. B contributes land with a tax basis of $18,000 and a fair market value of $24,000. For tax purposes, B records an investment basis in the partnership of $18,000. The land will also be reported by the partnership at $18,000. (True or False?)

Answer – Conveyances made between a partner and a partnership are normally recorded at the tax basis. Thus, the partnership should retain the $18,000 basis for the land and the partner (B) records the investment at the basis of the property that was contributed. (Number Six is True.)

SEVEN – Mr. Greene is a 20 percent owner of a partnership. His investment basis is $28,000. In a nonliquidating distribution, the partnership gives him cash of $10,000 and land with a basis of $12,000 and a fair market value of $16,000. The land will be reported by Greene at a basis of $12,000. (True or False?)

Answer – If a nonliquidating distribution occurs and the property has a basis below the partner's investment basis, that basis simply continues to be used. Thus, the cash will be reported by Greene at $10,000 and the land at $12,000. Because of the distribution, the Greene's investment basis will drop by $22,000 to $6,000. (Number Seven is True.)

EIGHT – Ms. Scarlet is a 30 percent owner of a partnership. Her investment basis is $33,000. In a nonliquidating distribution, the partnership gives her cash of $10,000 and land with a basis of $25,000 and a fair market value of $26,000. The land will be reported by Scarlet at a basis of $25,000. (True or False?)

Answer – If a nonliquidating distribution occurs and the property has a basis above the partner's investment basis, the property is reported at that investment basis. Thus, the cash and land must be reported by Ms. Scarlet at $33,000. Since the cash has to be shown as $10,000, the land will be reported as $23,000. The investment basis is reduced to zero. (Number Eight is False.)

NINE – Mr. Blue is a 40 percent owner of a partnership. His investment basis is $36,000. In a liquidating distribution, the partnership gives him cash of $10,000 and land with a basis of $22,000 and a fair market value of $24,000. The land will be reported by Blue at a basis of $22,000. (True or False?)

Answer – If a liquidating distribution occurs, the property conveyed normally has a basis equal to the partner's investment basis. Thus, the cash and land will be reported by Blue at a total of $36,000. The cash must be reported at $10,000 so that the land has a basis to Blue of $26,000. (Number Nine is False.)

TEN – Ms. Orange is a 20 percent owner of a partnership. Her investment basis is $24,000. In a liquidating distribution, the partnership gives her cash of $10,000 and land with a basis of $16,000 and a fair market value of $26,000. Ms. Orange has a taxable gain of $2,000. (True or False?)

Answer – If a liquidating distribution occurs, the property conveyed normally has a basis equal to the partner's investment basis. Thus, the cash and land will be reported by Ms. Orange at $24,000. The cash has to be shown as $10,000; thus, the land will be reported as $14,000. The investment basis is reduced by $24,000 and the cash and land are increased by the same amount. Therefore, no taxable gain is recognized. (Number Ten is False.)

ELEVEN – An S corporation has 10 equal owners. This year the corporation earned net income of $90,000 and made a cash distribution of $20,000. No pass through items were reported. All of the owners should report income of $9,000 on their individual tax returns. (True or False?)

Answer – The taxation of an S corporation is very similar to that of a partnership. Thus, the corporation pays no tax but the owners report the income as it is earned by the business. Pass through items are reported separately and the remaining income or loss is also reported. Because $90,000 was earned this year, each of the owners must report $9,000. Nonliquidating distributions usually have no tax effect on either a partnership or an S corporation. (Number Eleven is True.)

CORPORATE INCOME TAXES - INCOME

(1)   Corporations must file a tax return by the 15th day of the third month following the close of the taxable year. Thus, a corporation using a calendar year must file by March 15th (rather than April 15th which is the deadline for an individual). Most revenues found on a corporation's income statement are fully taxable.

   (A)   As with individuals, interest income on state and municipal bonds as well as life insurance proceeds are tax free.

   (B)   If company owns over 50 percent of another company, they are related parties. Gains on transfers are taxed but losses are not deductible. However, if a company owns 80 percent or more of another company, neither gains nor losses on transfers are reported.

(2)   When dividends are received from domestic corporations, the corporate taxpayer gets a deduction. Dividend income is recognized and then the **dividends received deduction** (DRD) is reported below the corporation's operating expenses.

   (A)   DRD is 70 percent of dividends received if less than 20 percent of outstanding stock is held. Deduction is 80 percent if company owns 20 percent to 79.99 percent of stock. Dividends are tax free if company owns 80 percent or more of the stock.

   (B)   The DRD percentage is applied to the lower of taxable net income (before the DRD deduction and any charitable contributions) or the amount of dividends received. However, the percentage is always based on dividends received if income figure is a loss or will be after the DRD is taken.

   (C)   A dividend of appreciated property (a **nonliquidating distribution**) usually generates a gain for the company making distribution; transfer is handled as if property had been sold for its market value.

   (D)   An owner receiving a property dividend (a **nonliquidating distribution**) recognizes dividend income equal to the fair market value of the item received.

(3)   Corporations also report gains and losses from **capital asset transactions** although rules are somewhat different than those used for individuals.

   (A)   Capital assets are investment property such as land (if not used in business), stocks, and bonds. However, a company can never recognize a taxable gain or loss on transactions in its own stock.

   (B)   Capital assets do not include business assets such as inventory, depreciable business property (machinery, equipment, etc.), real business property (buildings), or receivables.

   (C)   All **capital gains and losses** are combined to arrive at a single net gain or loss.

      (1)   If a net loss results, it is not deducted but can be carried back for up to 3 years and forward for up to 5 years to reduce any capital gains earned in these periods.

      (2)   Losses carried back or forward are always considered to be short-term.

      (3)   If a net capital gain results, it is immediately taxed.

(4)   **Section 1231 property** refers to assets used in a trade or business such as equipment or a warehouse. The handling of gains and losses on the sale of this property depends on whether the property is further classified as either Section 1245 or Section 1250 property.

(5)   **Section 1245 property** is depreciable personal property used in a business such as equipment, machinery, cars, trucks, etc.

(A)   If this property is sold at a gain, it is normally taxed as ordinary business income.
(B)   However, any gain in excess of the asset's accumulated depreciation is separated and classified as a Section 1231 gain which may well be reported as a capital gain (depending on what other income items are included).

(6)   **Section 1250 property** includes business land and most depreciable real business property such as an office building or warehouse. Most of any gain generated by the sale of such property is included as a Section 1231 gain.

PROBLEMS AND SOLUTIONS
CORPORATE INCOME TAXES – INCOME

ONE – Corporation AB reports sales revenue for the year of $300,000, ordinary and necessary expenses of $200,000, and dividend revenue of $20,000. These dividends were received from a domestic corporation in which AB owns 24 percent of the outstanding stock. Corporation AB has taxable income of $104,000. (True or False?)

Answer – Prior to the dividends received deduction (DRD), the corporation has income of $120,000 based on the revenues and expenses. Because AB owned between 20 percent and 79.99 percent of the other company, the DRD will be 80 percent of the $20,000 dividend or $16,000. Thus, taxable income is reduced by the DRD from $120,000 to $104,000. (Number One is True.)

TWO – The dividends received deduction (DRD) is 70 percent if a corporation owns 15 percent of another corporation but the DRD is 80 percent if 25 percent of the other company's stock is held. (True or False?)

Answer – The dividends received deduction (DRD) is 70 percent if the corporation owns less than 20 percent of the company paying the dividend. The DRD rises to 80 percent if between 20 percent and 79.99 percent of the other company's stock is held. (Number Two is True.)

THREE – The Elmhurst Co. owns investment property with a basis of $120,000 and a fair market value of $150,000. This group of assets is issued to the company's stockholders in a nonliquidating distribution. The Elmhurst Co. should recognize a capital gain of $30,000 on this distribution. (True or False?)

Answer – If property is issued to owners of a corporation in a nonliquidating distribution, the company reports the conveyance (for tax purposes) as if the property had been sold. Based on the fair market value, a sale would have generated a $30,000 capital gain for Elmhurst. (Number Three is True.)

FOUR – Corporation EFG receives property as a nonliquidating distribution from corporation WXYZ. The property had a tax basis to WXYZ of $20,000 although it was worth $23,000. For tax purposes, EFG reports a dividend revenue of $23,000 whereas WXYZ reports a capital gain of $3,000. (True or False?)

Answer – The corporation making a nonliquidating distribution reports the conveyance as if the property had been sold for its fair market value (a $3,000 gain, in this case). The corporation receiving the dividend reports income based on the fair market value of the property ($23,000). (Number Four is True.)

FIVE – A corporation issues 1,000 shares of its own common stock for $13 per share. Two years later, the company reacquires this stock for $15 per share. Two years later, the company reissues this stock for $16 per share. No taxable gain is created by the reacquisition but a taxable gain results from selling the stock back to the public. (True or False?)

Answer – No tax effect is created by transactions occurring in a company's own stock. (Number Five is False.)

SIX – A corporation has a $5,000 short-term capital gain and a $9,000 long-term capital loss. The corporation can only deduct $3,000 of the net loss in the current year. (True or False?)

Answer – Corporations are not allowed to deduct capital losses. Instead, a net loss may be carried back for three years to reduce capital gains and then carried forward for five years for the same purpose. (Number Six is False.)

SEVEN – A corporation buys a machine for $40,000 and uses it to help generate revenues. Two years later, when the machine has an adjusted tax basis of $34,000, it is sold for $41,000. The corporation reports $6,000 as ordinary business income. (True or False?)

Answer – Depreciable personal property, such as this machine, that is used in a business is referred to as Section 1245 property. Any gain on the sale of such assets is ordinary business income up to the amount of accumulated depreciation. In this case, because the cost was $40,000 and the basis was $34,000, the accumulated depreciation must have been $6,000. The property was sold at a $7,000 gain with the first $6,000 taxed as ordinary income. The remaining $1,000 will be classified as a Section 1231 gain. The handling of this gain will depend on the inclusion of other gains and losses. (Number Seven is True.)

CORPORATE INCOME TAXES - EXPENSES

(1)   Corporate expenses are deductible if ordinary and necessary.

(2)   Depreciation expense is determined by the **Modified Accelerated Cost Recovery System** (MACRS). These rules apply to property used in a trade or business (except for land) whether owned by a corporation, partnership, or proprietorship.

    (A)   Salvage value is ignored.

    (B)   New and used property are handled in the same manner.

    (C)   Personal business property is divided into six classes primarily based on expected life. Real property has two classes. The assets in each of these eight classes are depreciated over a recovery period that is usually shorter than the expected life of the assets grouped in that class.

        (1)   For personal property, four of the classes have a life of 10 years or less. These classes use the 200 percent declining balance method. The other two classes apply the 150 percent declining balance method.

        (2)   Residential rental property calculates depreciation on the straight-line method over 27 1/2 years; other real property uses the straight-line method over 39 years.

        (3)   When obtained, personal property is assumed to be acquired in the middle of the year; real property is assumed to be bought in the middle of the month of acquisition.

    (D)   Each taxpayer (corporation or individual) can elect to expense the first $100,000 (in 2003) expended for tangible personal property used in a trade or business. These assets (such as equipment) are referred to as **Section 179 property**.

        (1)   This election reduces the basis of the property for depreciation purposes.

        (2)   The availability of this immediate deduction is reduced dollar-for-dollar if total expenditures for Section 179 property during the year is in excess of $400,000.

(3)   **Organization costs** incurred during first year of a new business can be deducted over a minimum of 60 months.

    (A)   Costs include legal services, incorporation fees, fees for temporary directors, etc.

    (B)   Amortization begins with the start of business and not with payment,

    (C)   All costs in connection with issuing stock are considered adjustments to paid-in capital and cannot be expensed.

(4)   **Charitable contributions** can be deducted even though they are not ordinary and necessary costs of doing business.

    (A)   As with individuals, donations must be given to a qualifying charitable organization.

    (B)   Limit in any year is 10 percent of taxable income before deducting the dividends received deduction and before deducting the contributions.

    (C)   If corporation uses accrual accounting, deduction is allowed immediately even if not paid until first 2 1/2 months of subsequent year as long as the board of directors approved the gift during initial tax year.

    (D)   Five-year carryover applies for gifts over the limitation.

(5)   Premiums paid on a life-insurance policy for employees are deductible expenses unless company is the beneficiary.

(6)   **Casualty losses** not covered by insurance are fully deductible. That rule is different for individuals.

(7)   **Goodwill** and other intangibles (such as a going concern value acquired in the acquisition of a business) are know as **Section 197 property** and are amortized for tax purposes over a 15 year period.

(8)   **Bad debt expenses** are deductible when they actually become bad. Allowance method is not allowed for tax purposes. However, if a taxpayer is using the cash method, bad debts are not deductible because the income from the sale is never recognized.

(9)   In general, 50 percent of the cost of business meals and entertainment can be deducted.

PROBLEMS AND SOLUTIONS
CORPORATE INCOME TAXES – EXPENSES

ONE – A company buys office furniture with an estimated salvage value of $4,000 and a 12 year life. For tax purposes, the salvage value will be ignored in computing depreciation. Furthermore, depreciation will probably be computed over a life somewhat shorter than 12 years. (True or False?)

Answer – Use of the Modified Accelerated Recovery System (MACRS) is mandatory for most depreciable property. This system ignores salvage value and depreciates most assets, especially personal property, over a relatively short life. (Number One is True.)

TWO – During the current year, a company pays $167,000 for tangible personal property that will be used in that business to generate revenues. The company is entitled to an immediate deduction for part of the cost incurred in connection with this acquisition. (True or False?)

Answer – An immediate deduction is allowed in the year that tangible personal property is acquired for use in a business or trade. This property is known as Section 179 property. The allowed deduction is reduced dollar-for-dollar when the total of such acquisitions for a year exceeds $400,000. (Number Two is True.)

THREE – A company begins business operations on January 1 of the current year. The company pays $5,000 in incorporation fees and $10,000 in stock issuance costs. The maximum amount that the company can deduct in this initial year is $3,000. (True or False?)

Answer – Stock issuance costs are not viewed as organization cost; thus, no deduction is allowed in connection with the $10,000. The $5,000 paid for incorporation fees can be deducted over a minimum of 60 months (five years). At that rate, $1,000 of expense is recognized in this first year of operation. (Number Three is False.)

FOUR – A company reports revenues in Year One of $100,000 and ordinary and necessary expenses of $80,000. On December 31 of Year One, the board of directors pledges $5,000 to a qualifying charity. This gift is made on February 2 of Year Two. The company has taxable income in Year One of $18,000. (True or False?)

Answer – A company is allowed to deduct charitable contributions of up to 10 percent of its income before deducting these contributions and before the dividends received deduction. In this case, income is $20,000 so the maximum amount is $2,000.

Because the pledge was made in Year One by the board of directors and paid within the first 2 1/2 months of Year Two, the contribution is allowed in Year One. Taxable income is reduced from $20,000 to $18,000. (Number Four is True.)

FIVE – A company has revenues of $100,000 and ordinary and necessary expenses of $70,000. The company contributes $10,000 to qualifying charities. As a result, the company has $7,000 in excess contributions this year that can be carried back for three years and then forward for five years. (True or False?)

Answer – Taxable income before the charitable contribution is deducted is $30,000. Because of the 10 percent limitation, the company is entitled to a charitable contribution deduction of only $3,000. The other $7,000 can be carried forward for up to five years. (Number Five is False.)

SIX – A company pays $12,000 for insurance premiums for policies on the lives of its employees. The employees are allowed to select the beneficiary of these policies. In addition, the company pays another $8,000 for life insurance premiums on policies for these same employees where the company is the beneficiary. The company is not allowed a tax deduction for these life insurance premiums. (True or False?)

Answer – A company may take a deduction for life insurance premiums on policies unless the company is the beneficiary. Thus, in this case, the company can deduct an expense of $12,000. (Number Six is False.)

SEVEN – A company has already reported net income for financial reporting purposes of $315,000. The company has properly reported goodwill of $600,000, which is not impaired. However, the company plans to use the shortest possible amortization life for tax purposes. The company will report taxable income of $275,000. (True or False?)

Answer – For financial reporting purposes, the company would have no expense for goodwill. For tax purposes, the amortization would be $40,000 ($600,000/15 years). An extra $40,000 in expense will be taken this year for tax purposes. This extra deduction reduces income from $315,000 to $275,000. (Number Seven is True.)

EIGHT – A company is using the accrual method of reporting. A sale of $22,000 is made on account in Year One. This customer begins to undergo financial difficulties in Year Two but the $22,000 does not become uncollectible until Year Three. For tax purposes, bad debt expense of $22,000 should be recognized in Year Three. (True or False?)

Answer – For tax purposes, bad debt expenses (if the accrual method is in use) are not recognized until they actually become bad. Even if bad debts are anticipated for financial reporting, the account must be uncollectible before it can be deducted for tax purposes. If the cash method is in use, bad debt expenses are not recognized since the income from the sale was never reported. (Number Eight is True.)

CORPORATE INCOME TAXES - OTHER AREAS

(1)   An owner who transfers property to a corporation in exchange for its stock must recognize a gain if the shares received have a fair market value in excess of the tax basis of the property surrendered.

    (A)   Corporation's basis in new property is the stockholder's previous basis in this property plus any taxable gain. This computation normally gives a new basis that is equal to the fair market value of the property when conveyed.

    (B)   If stockholder controls 80 percent of the company after the transfer, no taxable gain occurs. Taxable gains and losses are normally not reported on transactions of any type with an owner of 80 percent or more of a company's stock.

(2)   A corporation with a **net operating loss** (NOL) can carry it back for up to two years to reduce previously reported taxable income and get a refund. Any remaining NOL can be carried forward for up to 20 years to reduce future taxable income. An NOL results when ordinary and necessary expenses are larger than revenues.

(3)   An **affiliated group** of corporations can elect to file a consolidated tax return. To be a member of an affiliated group, the group must own stock representing at least 80 percent of the voting power and 80 percent of the value of the subsidiary. At this level of ownership, all dividends are tax free regardless of whether a consolidated return is filed. Other advantages are only available with consolidation.

    (A)   All intercompany gains are tax free.

    (B)   One company's taxable loss may be used to reduce another's taxable profit.

(4)   Corporation must make an **alternative minimum tax** (AMT) computation and if that tax is greater than the normal tax, the extra amount must also be paid. Small corporations are exempt from the AMT.

    (A)   **Alternative minimum taxable income** (AMTI) starts with taxable income and then removes the benefits of (1) specific adjustments and (2) tax preference items. The benefits of some adjustments are removed completely while only a portion is removed for others (the ACE adjustment). AMTI is then reduced by an exemption that starts at $40,000 but fades out as income goes above $150,000. Specific rate is applied to arrive at tax.

    (B)   Adjustments removed first include amounts such as (1) part of the benefit from using accelerated depreciation methods, (2) the benefit of using installment sales method for inventory items, and (3) the benefit of applying the completed contract method.

    (C)   **Tax preference items** to be removed include (1) the amount that percentage depletion exceeds the basis of the property being depleted and (2) tax-exempt interest on private activity bonds.

    (D)   An adjusted current earnings (ACE) adjustment is then made based on 75 percent of the effect of benefits such as tax-exempt interest on municipal bond interest, the 70 percent dividends received deduction, life insurance proceeds, and the benefit of using the installment sales method for non-inventory items.

    (E)   The exemption is subtracted and the rate is applied to get the tax.

    (F)   In determining the AMT for individuals, taxable income is also affected by adjustments, preference items, and an exemption. The specific items, though, differ from those used for corporations.

(1) Adjustments include depreciation on real property in excess of straight-line method, benefit of using completed-contract method, and change needed so that medical expenses are only allowed for amounts over 10 percent of AGI. Adjustment is also needed because no deduction is allowed for (a) interest on a home equity loan, (b) personal state and local taxes, (c) income and job expenses that fall under the 2 percent guidelines, (d) the standard deduction, and (e) personal exemptions.

(2) Preference items are similar to those removed for a corporation.

(3) There is no ACE adjustment for an individual.

(4) The exemption is $58,000 on a joint return, an amount that fades out starting with income of $150,000. For a single individual, it is $40,250 and fades out beginning at income levels of $112,500.

(5) **Schedule M-1** on a corporate return requires company to reconcile its book income to its taxable income. Nontaxable income (municipal bond interest, life insurance proceeds, etc.) is subtracted; nondeductible expenses and income taxed in advance are added back.

(6) A distribution by a corporation is only considered a dividend up to the amount of company's income. For this test, income is defined as the larger of income for the current year or accumulated (retained) earnings at year's end.

(A) Any amount of distribution that is larger than this income is viewed as a return of investor's capital. This excess is not taxable to the recipient unless larger than the basis of the investment.

(7) To avoid a penalty, a corporation must make **estimated tax payments** each quarter. This amount is 25 percent of either the larger of the estimated tax for the current year or the actual tax for the prior year. If company will have a taxable income of over $1 million, estimated tax payments must be based on estimated income for the current year. Furthermore, the prior year cannot serve as the basis for estimated payments if the company had no tax liability in that year.

(8) **Uniform capitalization rules** define what costs must be capitalized (and not immediately expensed) in constructing property or purchasing inventory. Direct costs are included in the cost of the asset as are most indirect costs that benefit the asset including administrative costs and overhead.

(9) The government can assess an **accumulated earnings tax** in addition to the regular income tax.

(A) This tax is designed to discourage corporations from reducing dividend payments in order to defer paying taxes on these distributions.

(B) Accumulated earnings is a retained earnings type figure computed for tax purposes. If it gets to be excessive, the government can assess a tax on amount over a defined credit.

(C) The credit is usually "the reasonable needs" of the business although there is a set dollar alternative.

(10) If a company is a **personal holding company**, a tax is assessed in addition to the regular income tax.

(A) Basis for this tax starts with taxable income which is then reduced by the dividends paid, federal income taxes, and several other deductions.

(B) As with the accumulated earnings tax, it can be avoided by the payment of adequate dividends. Because of the similar purpose, a personal holding company is not subjected to the accumulated earnings tax.

(C)   Companies are viewed as personal holding companies if they meet two specified rules.

       (1)   Stock ownership rule is met if, during the last half of the tax year, over half of the stock is owned by 5 or fewer individuals.

       (2)   Income rule is met if 60 percent or more of company's ordinary gross income is passive (from rents, dividends, interest, etc.).

(D)   Since the rules are more objective than those for the accumulated earnings tax (which requires a determination of the reasonable needs of the taxpayer), the personal holding company tax should be self-assessed by the taxpayer whereas the accumulated earnings tax is only assessed by the government.

(11)   The following transactions can usually be carried out as tax free exchanges. If any boot is received by the taxpayer (usually cash but can be any property other than the stock being exchanged), a taxable gain must be reported for the lesser of the boot or the realized gain. Realized gain is the fair market value received in excess of the tax basis of the property being surrendered.

      (A)   **Merger** is where one company is absorbed into another and goes out of business as a separate legal entity.

      (B)   **Consolidation** is where two companies go in together to form a third (new) company.

      (C)   An acquisition can be made of 80 percent or more of a company's voting and nonvoting stock. Acquired company stays in business as a separate legal entity.

      (D)   Stock is exchanged for substantially all of the assets of a corporation.

      (E)   **Recapitalization** of a company is usually the exchange of debt for either new debt or shares of stock.

      (F)   A change such as a change in name or state of incorporation is tax free because it only affects identity, form, or place of organization.

(12)   A corporation may decide to go out of business and convey cash or other assets to its owners as a **liquidating distribution**.

      (A)   The owner records all items received at fair market value. Owner also removes the investment at its tax basis with any difference recorded as a capital gain or loss.

      (B)   Distribution of property other than cash is taxed to the corporation as if the property had been sold for its fair market value. As with a property dividend, difference between basis and fair market value is a taxable gain or loss.

      (C)   Again, if owner holds 80 percent or over of the corporation, no gain or loss is recognized by either party in connection with a liquidating distribution.

PROBLEMS AND SOLUTIONS
CORPORATE INCOME TAXES – OTHER AREAS

ONE – Mr. Kline conveys land with a tax basis of $55,000 to the Billings Company in exchange for 10,000 shares of the company's common stock. The stock is worth $67,000. This transfer gave Mr. Kline 28 percent ownership. The company will record this land at a basis of $67,000. (True or False?)

Answer – Unless a stockholder holds more than 80 percent of a company's outstanding stock after an exchange, exchanging property for stock normally creates a tax effect. Mr. Kline gave up land with a basis of $55,000 for stock valued at $67,000 and must report a $12,000 taxable gain. The company then records the land at the previous basis ($55,000) plus the taxable gain ($12,000) for a basis of $67,000. Normally, this approach means that the company will record the property at the equivalent fair market value. (Number One is True.)

TWO – A company has the following operating profits: $10,000 in Year One, $15,000 in Year Two, $20,000 in Year Three, and $25,000 in Year Four. In Year Five, the company has a net operating loss of $100,000. The company has a net operating loss carry forward to Year Six of $55,000. (True or False?)

Answer – A company can carry a net operating loss back for two years and then forward for up to 20 years. The Year Five loss will be carried back against the income in Year Three ($20,000) and Year Four ($25,000). The remaining $55,000 can then be carried forward in order to reduce future taxable income. (Number Two is True.)

THREE – A taxpayer calculates income taxes for the current year as $3,000. An alternative minimum tax computation is made that reports a tax of $3,200. The taxpayer must pay a total of $6,200 in taxes. (True or False?)

Answer – A taxpayer will pay the normal income tax as well as any part of the alternative minimum tax that exceeds this regular income tax. Because the alternative minimum tax was $200 more than the normal tax, the taxpayer must pay the $3,000 income tax plus the additional $200 for a total of $3,200. (Number Three is False.)

FOUR – In computing a corporation's alternative minimum tax, the ACE adjustment removes all of the benefits of such items as municipal bond interest and the 70 percent dividends received deduction. (True or False?)

Answer – The ACE adjustment only removes 75 percent of the tax benefits derived from such items as municipal bond interest, life insurance proceeds, and the 70 percent dividends received deduction. (Number Four is False.)

FIVE – In computing an individual's alternative minimum tax, the ACE adjustment removes a part of the benefits of such items as interest on home equity loans, the standard deduction, and personal exemptions. (True or False?)

Answer – No ACE adjustment is included in computing the alternative minimum tax of an individual taxpayer. However, an adjustment is used to remove all of the benefits of certain tax treatments such as interest on home equity loans, the standard deduction, and personal exemptions. (Number Five is False.)

SIX – A company uses MACRS for tax purposes and computes depreciation expense as $90,000. The same company uses the straight-line method for financial reporting and recognizes depreciation of $40,000. In its Schedule M-1, the company should subtract $50,000 from its income for financial purposes in order to reconcile it with taxable income. (True or False?)

Answer – For tax purposes, an additional expense of $50,000 is being recognized. Therefore, to adjust financial reporting income to taxable income, this extra expense must be subtracted. (Number Six is True.)

SEVEN – A company distributes a cash dividend of $100,000 to its stockholders during the year. The company reported income for the year of $20,000 and accumulated earnings at the end of the year of $70,000. Of the total dividend, only $90,000 should be viewed as income by the stockholders. (True or False?)

Answer – A dividend represents income to the recipient up to the larger of (1) the net income for the year or (2) accumulated earnings as of the end of the year. In this case, the $70,000 is the larger figure and is viewed as the income to be reported by the stockholders. The remaining $30,000 is a return of capital to the owners and reduces their investment basis. (Number Seven is False.)

EIGHT – A large corporation has taxable income each year in excess of $10 million. The company must make estimated tax payments each quarter. The amount of these payments can be based on the taxable income for the prior year or on the estimated amount of income for the current year. (True or False?)

Answer – A large corporation, one with taxable income of $1 million or more, must based estimated income taxes on the estimated income for the current year. (Number Eight is False.)

NINE – A company may be subjected to both the accumulated earnings tax and the personal holding company tax. (True or False?)

Answer – Both of these taxes are designed to ensure that an adequate amount of dividends are paid each year so that a company's owners cannot avoid the double taxation on dividends. Thus, assessing both taxes would be redundant. A personal holding company is not subjected to the accumulated earnings tax. (Number Nine is False.)

TEN – Mr. Koening holds an investment in JEL Company with a basis of $33,000. Because of a merger, these shares are exchanged for stock in TOH Company with a value of $36,000. Mr. Koening also collects cash of $4,000. He has a taxable gain of $7,000. (True or False?)

Answer – A merger is normally a tax free exchange as long as stock is traded for stock. However, if boot (such as the cash in this case) is received, a taxable gain must be reported as the lesser of (1) the boot or (2) the realized gain. The boot is $4,000 and the realized gain is $7,000 (the owner received property with a value of $40,000 and gave up stock with a basis of $33,000). Since the boot is the lower figure, Mr. Koening will be taxed on the $4,000. (Number Ten is False.)

OTHER TAXATION AREAS

(1) **Organizations exempt from income taxes**: they must be of a class recognized by the tax laws such as religious, educational, scientific, etc.

    (A) Must serve some common good and profits cannot benefit owners. Also, cannot exert undue political influence.

    (B) Normally, must file to get tax exempt status except for churches and organizations with receipts of $5,000 or less.

    (C) If receipts are $25,000 or more, an informational return (Form 990) must be filed (except by churches) listing total contributions, income, substantial contributors, and highest paid employees.

    (D) **Unrelated business income** (UBI) earned by a tax exempt organization is still taxed at regular rates if it exceeds $1,000.

        (1) Any business endeavor where the activity does not relate to the purpose of the organization is considered UBI.

        (2) Several types of income are not considered to be UBI.

            (a) Profits from a business that is run by volunteers

            (b) Dividends and interest unless the investments are debt financed.

            (c) Operation of legal bingo games.

            (d) Sale of items that were contributed to organization.

(2) Federal **estate tax** must be paid on transfer of property at death. Unless extension is granted, tax return must be filed within nine months of death.

    (A) If estate is not valued over an exemption amount, there is no federal estate tax. The exemption is $1 million.

    (B) Value is determined at date of death unless **alternative valuation date** is chosen by executor. This date is 6 months after death or date of conveyance whichever comes first.

    (C) In determining value, estate is reduced by funeral expenses, expenses of administering estate, debts, charitable bequests, and fair market value of amount passing to spouse.

(3) A federal **gift tax** must be paid on conveyances. An individual can give up to $11,000 per donee per year without incurring a gift tax. This exclusion is allowed for gifts of present interests and not future interests. A present interest is an unrestricted right to the immediate use of property or the income from property. If more is given but no gift tax is paid, the exemption available for federal estate tax purposes (mentioned above) is reduced so that the tax is not avoided. The exemption amount created a unified tax credit for all conveyances, both those made before death and those after death.

(4) Estates and trusts must also pay income taxes on income that they earn.

    (A) Trusts use calendar year; estates may use any fiscal year.

    (B) Taxable income is the income earned for the period less (1) an exemption, (2) conveyances of income to beneficiaries, and (3) charitable contributions.

    (C) **Distributable net income** (DNI) is the maximum amount of earned income that could be distributed to a beneficiary during the current period and be deducted by an estate or trust. It is made up of all income and expenses including tax-exempt income but does not include net capital gains allocated to the corpus.

    (D) Estates are entitled to a $600 exemption.

(E)   A **simple trust** is required to convey all income to beneficiaries when earned and gets a $300 exemption.

(F)   A **complex trust** is not required to convey all income to beneficiaries and gets a $100 exemption.

PROBLEMS AND SOLUTIONS
OTHER TAXATION AREAS

ONE – A group of local citizens begins a charity to assist homeless individuals who live in the region. These citizens solicit donations and use all monies collected for the intended purposes. This organization qualifies as tax exempt. (True or False?)

> *Answer – To be tax exempt, an organization must have a purpose that is recognized by the tax laws such as religious or educational. In addition, other stipulations are required such as that the owners cannot benefit from any profits. However, the organization must still file in order to obtain this status. Meeting the rules alone does not qualify the charity; it has to file to receive tax exempt status. (Number One is False.)*

TWO – The First National Church is a tax exempt organization that received $230,000 in donations this year and interest revenue of $12,000. The church does not have to pay income taxes but must file an informational return indicating total contributions, income, and other information. (True or False?)

> *Answer – A tax exempt organization with receipts of $25,000 or more during a year must file an information return (a 990 Form) according to the tax laws. However, because of the historical separation of church and state in this country, churches are exempted from providing such information. (Number Two is False.)*

THREE – A tax exempt organization has unrelated business income of $3,200. Despite being tax exempt, the organization must pay taxes on income of $2,200. (True or False?)

> *Answer – All unrelated business income (UBI) above a $1,000 exemption is subject to taxation. (Number Three is True.)*

FOUR – A tax exempt organization opens a grocery store to raise money for its stated goals. During the current year, the store earned profits of $23,000. The store is operated completely by volunteers. Some portion of these profits will be taxed as unrelated business income. (True or False?)

> *Answer – Normally, income earned from a business endeavor that is not related to the purpose of a tax exempt organization is unrelated business income that is subject to taxation. However, several exceptions exist. One of these exceptions is income generated from a business that is operated solely by volunteers. Thus, this income will not be taxed. (Number Four is False.)*

FIVE – An individual dies leaving an estate valued at $1,300,000. According to the person's will, $200,000 is given to charity, $200,000 is given to the spouse, and the remainder goes to that decedent's children. No federal estate taxes will have to be paid. (True or False?)

> *Answer – In determining federal estate taxes, a number of reductions are made in the value of the estate. These deductions include funeral expenses, gifts to charities, debts, and amounts conveyed to a spouse. Thus, the $1,300,000 estate is reduced to $400,000 by the conveyances to the charity and to the spouse. The remaining amount is below the federal exemption level so that no estate taxes are due. (Number Five is True.)*

SIX – A trust earns income of $10,000 during the current year. The trust computes its distributable net income (DNI) as $8,000 for the period. The trust conveys $7,000 of the income to the appropriate beneficiaries. The trust will have taxable income of $3,000. (True or False?)

> *Answer – An estate or trust can reduce its taxable income by amounts that are conveyed to a beneficiary during the current period. This deduction is limited to the figure computed as distributable net income. In this case, the $7,000 conveyed to the beneficiaries is below the $8,000 limitation. Hence, the entire conveyance can be taken as a reduction in taxable income. The beneficiaries will have taxable income of $7,000 (the amount received) and the trust will report the remaining taxable income of $3,000. (Number Six is True.)*

INDEX

TABLE OF CONTENTS
BUSINESS ENVIRONMENT AND CONCEPTS

Topic	Page

BUSINESS ENVIRONMENT AND CONCEPTS

TOPIC	For additional information see Wiley CPA Examination Review
Business Structure	Module 38
Information Technology	Module 39
Microeconomics	Module 40
Macroeconomics	Module 40
Business Strategy	Module 40
Financial Management	Module 41
Working Capital Management	Module 41
Financing Current Assets	Module 41
Capital Structure	Module 41
Risk Management	Module 42
Capital Budgeting	Module 42
Quantitative Methods	Module 45
Performance Measures	Module 43
Quality Control Principles	Module 43
Financial Planning	Module 45
Cost-Volume-Profit-Analysis	Module 45
Cost Accounting	Module 44
Variance Analysis	Module 45

BUSINESS STRUCTURE

(1) From a legal perspective, there are three basic types of business organizations, plus several hybrid types (e.g., LLCs) and special types (REITs).
  (A) A **sole proprietorship** is formed when an individual does business without incorporating or associating with a partner.
  (B) A **partnership** is formed when two or more persons carry on, as co-owners, a business for profit. May be by formal agreement, informal agreement, or no agreement at all. A partnership is not a legal entity separate from its owners.
    (1) In a **general partnership**, all partners are general partners which means that they each have unlimited liability for partnership liabilities (both contract and tort obligations).
    (2) In a **limited partnership**, some specific partners enjoy limited liability for partnership debts. A limited partnership is formed only by following statutory requirements.
  (C) A **corporation** is also formed only by following statutory requirements. Unlike a partnership, a separate legal entity is formed.
  (D) Real Estate Investment Trust (REIT) – Investors
  (E) Limited Liability Company (LLC) – Like a limited partnership except that the owners (called "members") all enjoy both the right to participate in management as well as limited liability.
(2) A partnership can be formed in any one of several ways.
  (A) There can be an explicit agreement. The agreement can be a formal document or simply an informal understanding.
  (B) The formation of a partnership can be implied by operation of law. This occurs whenever the statutory definition of a partnership (two or more persons carry on, as co-owners, a business for profit) applies to the factual situation.
    (1) For example, assume that two individuals together purchase a building and equipment and jointly market the output of the business and split the profits. Even if there is no partnership agreement of any type, the business will be considered a partnership by operation of law.
  (C) A partnership can also be formed by **estoppel**. This situation arises where one person holds another individual out to be a partner and the latter fails to deny the partnership.
(3) The authority that a partner has to bind a partnership to a contract is much like the authority found in agency law. Likewise, the responsibilities that each partner has to the other partners are also similar to those found in agency law.
  (A) As to authority, the general rule is that a partner has actual (express) and apparent (ostensible) authority to bind other partners to a contract made in the ordinary course of business. The other partners are also able to ratify a contract that has been made.
  (B) As to responsibilities, each partner has duties to every other partner that are similar to an agent's duties to a principal. These include fiduciary duties, duty to act in good faith, etc.
  (C) Because of the relationship, notice to one partner is viewed as notice to all partners.
(4) Partners can be liable for actions of other partners.
  (A) For torts, the partners are jointly and severally liable. **Joint liability** means that all partners must be sued together. **Several liability** means that a party may sue any

partner for the full amount of the claim. Thus, a partner who commits a tort in the ordinary course of partnership business has a personal liability and has created a liability for all other partners.

(B) Each partner is jointly liable with all other partners for the contracts of the partnership.

(5) Partners are co-owners of the business. There are several separate aspects to this co-ownership.

   (A) Each partner is entitled to share in the profits and surplus of the partnership.

      (1) The right to profits and surplus can be assigned to a nonpartner but the assignee does not become a partner unless admitted by unanimous vote of all partners. Profits are also subject to **attachment by creditors of the partner**.

      (2) The right to profits and surplus can be passed to heirs at the partner's death. However, partnership property such as buildings and equipment passes to the other partners.

      (3) Partners are not entitled to salaries. There is no inherent right to a salary, only to a pro rata share of profits. A partnership agreement can specify the specific method by which profits (and losses) are to be allocated.

   (B) All partners have the right to participate in the management of the business. All partners must agree before a change can be made to this right.

   (C) Each partner has the right to use specific partnership property for partnership business.

   (D) A new partner cannot be admitted without the unanimous consent of all partners.

   (E) An incoming partner is liable only for future debts of the partnership, not for existing debts. Money or property that the new partner puts into the partnership can be used to satisfy existing debts.

(6) A partnership can dissolve and wind up its affairs for any of several reasons.

   (A) **Dissolution of a partnership** can occur because of agreement of the partners or because of the withdrawal of any of the partners.

   (B) Dissolution of the partnership occurs automatically and without notice because of any of the following reasons.

      (1) Death of a partner.

      (2) Bankruptcy of a partner.

      (3) Termination as specified under the partnership agreement.

   (C) After dissolution, the partners have no authority to bind partnership except as is necessary to wind up the partnership business.

   (D) Actual business may be continued but only as a new partnership.

   (E) If the business is not continued, the assets of the business must be distributed according to set guidelines.

      (1) General creditors are paid in full first.

      (2) Debts owed to individual partners are paid next.

      (3) Any remainder is paid to the partners based on their final capital balances. If any of the final capital balances are negative, the partners must pay that much into the partnership to eliminate the deficit.

(7) A **limited partnership** must comply with the requirements of state law for a limited partnership. There must be one or more general partners and one or more limited partners. Like a general partnership, no separate entity is formed. Like shareholders in a corporation, the limited partners have limited liability.

   (A) A certificate of limited partnership must be filed to meet statutory requirements.

   (B) A limited partner is an investor only.

      (1) Cannot participate in managing the business.

      (2) Has no authority to bind the business.

      (3) Cannot use last name (surname) in the name of the partnership.

  (C) A number of events can lead to the **termination of a limited partnership**.

      (1) A judicial order.

      (2) Withdrawal, death, insolvency, or insanity of a general partner.

      (3) Termination does not result from the withdrawal, death, insolvency, or insanity of a limited partner.

      (4) Termination does not result from the transfer of a limited partner's interest to another party. The transfer by a limited partner of a partnership interest to a third party is treated as an assignment of the right to profits (if any are earned) unless the transferee is admitted as a limited partner by vote of the partners.

(8) A **corporation** is an artificial entity that comes into existence upon the proper filing of **articles of incorporation** and issuance by the state of a certificate of incorporation.

  (A) A number of different parties are involved with a corporation.

      (1) Shareholders are the owners of the corporation; shareholders elect **directors** to oversee the corporation.

      (2) Directors are elected by shareholders to direct the main course of the corporation. The directors elect officers to run day-to-day business operations. The directors are agents of the corporation; directors declare dividends.

      (3) **Officers** are chosen by the directors to run the day-to-day business of the corporation as agents for the corporation.

  (B) A corporation has several general characteristics.

      (1) It is a separate legal entity; the corporation is a separate person. It is separate from the persons who formed the corporation or who currently own it.

      (2) The owners have **limited liability**. The shareholders can lose only what they invest in the corporation (what they pay or promise to pay for the stock of the corporation).

      (3) A corporation is taxed separately from its owners because the corporation is a new, separate entity in the eyes of the taxing authorities.

      (4) A corporation is able to have **continuous life**. The corporation continues in existence even after a shareholder dies. This is true even if there is only one shareholder.

      (5) A corporation allows its owners to transfer ownership. Stock, unless restricted at issuance, is freely transferable.

  (C) A corporation is created by following the process of incorporation.

      (1) Articles of incorporation must be filed with corporation commission of the state in which incorporation is being sought. Articles of incorporation should include the following pieces of information.

         (a) Name of corporation.

         (b) Name of registered agent.

         (c) Names of incorporators.

         (d) Number of authorized shares.

      (2) **Registered agent** is appointed by the corporation to officially receive notice.

      (3) **Certificate of incorporation** is issued by the state upon proper filing of articles of incorporation and payment of all fees.

      (4) Organization meeting is the initial meeting to elect officers and directors.

      (5) By-laws are adopted by directors and officers to set structure of the corporation, to establish time and place of meetings, etc.

(6) A **de jure corporation** is one that has been correctly formed. A **de facto corporation** exists when the incorporators succeed in satisfying most requirements for incorporating but inadvertently fail to satisfy all. Corporation is still recognized.

(7) **Promoters** are individuals who undertake to form a corporation and arrange its initial capitalization. They promote the sale of stock through subscriptions. A **subscription** is a written agreement to purchase stock; it is irrevocable for 6 months.

    (a) Promoters have a fiduciary relationship with the corporation. They must act in the best interest of the new corporation and not in their own interest.

    (b) Since corporation is not yet in existence, promoters are not truly an agent of the corporation. Thus, pre-incorporation agreements are not binding on the corporation until adopted by it.

(D) To raise capital, a corporation is allowed to issue stock.

    (1) **Authorized stock** is the amount of stock that the articles of incorporation permits to be issued.

    (2) **Issued stock** is the amount of stock that has been delivered to the shareholders.

    (3) **Outstanding stock** is the amount of stock currently being held by the shareholders. It has been issued but not repurchased by the corporation as **treasury stock**.

    (4) A company will always have at least one class of stock but can also have a second class.

        (a) **Common stock** usually has the most voting rights but the least rights to dividends and to assets on liquidation of the corporation. A corporation must have common stock.

        (b) **Preferred stock** usually has less (sometimes no) voting rights but greater rights to dividends and assets on liquidation. Many companies do not issue preferred stock.

    (5) In marketing stock, valid **consideration** must be received. Buyer must pay for stock in cash, property, or services that have already been rendered. Valid consideration does not include a promise to perform services, promise to pay, or a promissory note.

    (6) If a **par value** is stated for the stock, the buyer must pay at least that amount to avoid any possible future obligation.

(E) According to the business judgment rule, officers and directors may be liable to shareholders for **negligence** committed in running the corporation, but not if they were acting in good faith in the exercise of business judgment. Corporation can indemnify officers and directors for damages suffered in such suits, including attorney's fees if approved by the court.

(F) Extraordinary transactions such as merger, consolidation, or sale of all assets must have special approval.

    (1) Directors meet and vote whether to recommend the action to the shareholders. Directors vote on and pass a resolution.

    (2) Shareholders then meet to vote whether to adopt the resolution.

    (3) If the resolution is approved by a majority of shareholders, dissenting shareholders have certain rights. A minority of shareholders cannot stop an extraordinary

transaction but they can insist on being paid fair market value for their stock. This is called "**dissenters' appraisal rights**."

(G) Shareholders have the right to inspect corporate books.
  (1) Includes minute books, stock certificate books, and general account books.
  (2) Must have purpose that is reasonably related to interest as a shareholder.
    (a) It is okay to obtain information to try and gain control of corporation.
    (b) It is not okay to obtain information to compete with corporation.
    (c) Inspection may be refused if shareholder has misused information within the previous two years.
(H) The validity of contracts between a corporation and its officers is based upon fairness and disclosure.

(9) The directors of the company declare **dividends** that are to be paid to shareholders. Once declared, dividends are considered a debt of the corporation.
  (A) Dividends are considered illegal if they do either of the following.
    (1) They render the corporation insolvent, so that is it is unable to pay debts as they come due.
    (2) They reduce the total of the assets so that there is not enough to cover the liabilities of the corporation plus any dissolution obligation to preferred shareholders.
  (B) Directors have strict liability for any illegal dividends without regard to good faith or negligence.

(10) A **dissolution will terminate a corporation's existence**. It is not complete until the winding up of affairs and distribution of assets have occurred.
  (A) A dissolution can be voluntary, that is it occurs by merger, consolidation, or the filing of articles of dissolution.
  (B) A dissolution can be involuntary if it is caused either by the failure to pay the annual assessments to the state or if fraud occurred in the original articles of incorporation.
  (C) A **judicial dissolution** can also occur. When the directors are hopelessly deadlocked, shareholders can petition the court for dissolution.

PROBLEMS AND SOLUTIONS
BUSINESS STRUCTURE

ONE - A formal agreement is required in order to form a general partnership. (True or False?)

> *Answer - Whenever two or more persons carry on, as co-owners, a business for profit and they do not incorporate the business (or file articles of limited partnership), they will be considered a general partnership. If this definition is met, a partnership has been formed even though the owners may not want or consider themselves to be in partnership and even if no formal written agreement has been made. (Number One is False.)*

TWO - Timothy, Ralph, and Zack form a general partnership to operate a pizza business. They agree that each will receive one-third of the profits of the business. During a delivery, Ralph's vehicle collides with a bus, injuring several of the passengers. Ralph was exceeding the speed limit at the time. Zack can be held personally liable and can be required to compensate fully all of the injured passengers for their injuries. (True or False?)

Answer - In a general partnership, all of the partners share unlimited liability for damages caused by any partner in the ordinary course of partnership business. For a restaurant, the delivery of pizza would be an event arising in the ordinary course of business. Thus, although not directly involved, Zack could be held liable for the damages caused by his partner Ralph. (Number Two is True.)

THREE - Every partner has the right to use specific partnership property (such as computer equipment) for personal use as long as the use does not interfere with the profitability of the partnership. (True or False?)

Answer - The rights of a partner in specific partnership property are limited to using that property (such as equipment) for partnership purposes only. (Number Three is False.)

FOUR - Hall, Gordon, Stewart, and Farmer are partners in a landscaping and tree removal service. Hall and Gordon work full-time in the business while Stewart and Farmer dedicate only 20 percent of their time to the business. No agreement has been entered into as to the division of profits. All four partners will be assigned an equal share of the profits of the business but only after allocating to each of the partners the equivalent of a minimum wage as a salary for the hours actually worked. (True or False?)

Answer - Unless agreed otherwise, partners in a partnership share all profits equally. No partner, unless otherwise agreed, is entitled to a salary or to a greater share of the profits because of greater work, money invested, or for bringing more business to the partnership. However, in many cases, the partners will agree to assign profits so as to compensate such factors. Agreement, though, is required. (Number Four is False.)

FIVE - A general partnership is being dissolved. After all loans of every type have been repaid, the partners are to receive the remainder. The remaining cash (and other assets) should be distributed based on the profit and loss ratio of the partners. (True or False?)

Answer – Any remaining assets should be distributed to the partners based on their ending capital balances. Any partner with a negative capital balance should contribute sufficient funds to eliminate the deficit. (Number Five is False.)

SIX - Sarah, Allison, and Jamie have conducted business as a limited partnership for seven years. Jamie and Allison, who financed the startup of the business, have both been limited partners and Sarah is the only general partner. Sarah now wishes to buy half of the limited partnership interest owned by Jamie. If Sarah does this, the limited partnership is destroyed because Sarah will be both a general and a limited partner. (True or False?)

Answer - The rule that a limited partnership must have at least one general partner and at least one limited partner has not been violated. A general partner can also own a limited partnership interest. Each general partner is exposed to unlimited personal liability for all of the debts of the limited partnership. (Number Six is False.)

SEVEN - A corporation is a separate person, separate from the individuals who formed the corporation or who own the corporation. Because the corporation is a separate legal entity, shareholders enjoy limited liability for the debts of the corporation. (True or False?)

Answer – Because a corporation is an entity separate from its owners, these owners (or shareholders) enjoy limited liability. They stand to lose only what they invest in the corporation: what they have paid or have promised to pay for their stock. Shareholders cannot be held personally responsible for the debts of a corporation (unless, of course, they personally guarantee an obligation). (Number Seven is True.)

EIGHT - In comparison to common stock, preferred stock has greater voting rights but less right to dividends and to assets upon liquidation of the corporation. (True or False?)

Answer – The specific rights assigned to preferred stock will depend upon the agreement specified in the stock indenture (contract). Often, common stock has greater voting rights. Preferred stock usually enjoys greater rights to assets upon liquidation and to dividends. (Number Eight is False.)

NINE - The value of the stock of Capital Corporation declined dramatically after its Board of Directors exercised poor business judgment in deciding to expand into foreign markets. Nevertheless, the corporation can indemnify the directors and pay their attorney fees in defending a lawsuit brought by the shareholders. (True or False?)

Answer - A corporation can indemnify its officers and/or directors for damages suffered in suits alleging exercise of poor business judgment and can even pay attorney fees incurred defending such suits as long as such indemnity is approved by the court. (Number Nine is True.)

TEN - Stan, a 10 percent owner of the stock of L. L. Grant Corporation, wishes to inspect the books and records of L. L. Grant Corporation in hopes of obtaining information to enable him to gain control of the corporation. Louis Grant, the company president, can rightfully deny Stan access to the books and records of the corporation. (True or False?)

Answer - It is valid to deny access to corporate books and records to someone who wishes to obtain information to compete with the corporation. However, it is not valid to deny access to a party who has purposes reasonably related to his or her interest as a shareholder, including obtaining information to gain control of the corporation. (Number Ten is False.)

INFORMATION TECHNOLOGY

Control of the Computer Function

(1) Controls used in connection with **computers** operating within an accounting system are separated into three broad classifications.
  (A) **General controls** relate to the operation of the entire computer system.
  (B) **Application controls** relate to a specific program or a specified task. Application controls are further divided into (1) programmed application controls and (2) manual follow-up of exception reports.
  (C) **User control procedures** are designed to test the completeness and accuracy of computer controls
(2) General controls are divided into four broad categories.
  (A) Controls should be in place in connection with the development of new programs.
    (1) For follow up and testing purposes, new programs should be documented usually by the creation of a detailed run manual.
    (2) New programs should be properly tested before being approved for actual use in processing data.
      (a) **Test data** can be used for this purpose. All conceivable valid and invalid situations are run through the computer to see if program reacts correctly to each.
    (3) Before a new program is put into use, all parties involved should review and authorize it. Reviewers would include management, user departments, and information system analysts.
    (4) All computer hardware should be properly programmed to ensure reliability
  (B) A detailed process should be installed to make sure that only authorized changes are made in functioning programs.
    (1) The details and reasons for all changes should be documented, reviewed, and authorized
    (2) Test data can be rerun periodically to ensure that the program still handles all known situations properly.
    (3) Programs and hardware can be designed to serve as an **integrated test facility**. Whenever a program is to be run, test data can be included to verify current processing. This approach allows for daily testing. Test data must be coded so that results will not be mixed with live data.
  (C) Access to computer, programs, and data should be adequately secured.
    (1) Computer and all files are locked and access is limited to authorized individuals
    (2) Passwords or identification numbers are used to ensure that only authorized individuals have access to the computer. Passwords and numbers are changed regularly.
  (D) The computer facility itself should be safeguarded.
    (1) Operators only have access to the portion of run manual dealing with the operating aspects of the program so that they do not have an in-depth understanding of the program.
    (2) Duplicate copies of all programs and backup information are stored at a separate location. Enough data should be kept so that the files can be reconstructed if destroyed.

(3) Programmed application controls are specifically designed so that a particular program will function properly.

    (A) **Self-checking numbers** can be used with input information. Computer uses number (employee identification, for example) in a mathematical test to verify that it is proper. One digit (called a check digit) may be placed within the number to create a mathematical verification.

    (B) **Control totals** are predetermined totals that have been computed for data. These totals can be verified at each step in process to make sure that information has not been changed.

        (1) **Item count** is total of the number of transactions to be processed

        (2) **Batch total** is a total derived from some element of the data being processed (total sales for example). Total would have some meaning or importance.

        (3) **Hash total** is a total derived from some element of the data being processed that would normally not be totaled (total of employee social security numbers, for example). Total is only computed for control purposes.

        (4) **Limit test** is an upper boundary established for processing purposes. For example, no weekly paycheck might be printed for over $2,000 without some additional testing.

        (5) **Validity test** is an internal reconciliation of data within computer to make certain that it is legitimate. For example, before printing payroll, computer can check master employee file to make sure that requested checks are only for actual employees.

(4) Some application controls are composed of manual follow up steps taken in connection with exception reports.

    (A) Whenever computer processes data that may be in error (a check request exceeds the specified limit or a self-checking digit indicates a possible problem), an **exception (or error) report** is printed and processing is halted.

    (B) A **control group** (an independent team established for review) should resolve exception report problems so that processing can continue.

(5) User control procedures are designed to ensure some human testing of computer output.

    (A) The control group and/or the department that receives output should test results before authorizing its distribution and use.

    (B) Verification is made that control totals are in agreement with actual output.

    (C) On a test basis, individual input items are verified against computer output. For example, payroll checks for a few employees could be computed manually each period to verify balances are correct.

Other Computer Areas

(1) **Electronic data interchange** (EDI) refers to transmittal of documents directly from a computer in one entity to a computer in another. The Internet is often used for this conveyance. EDI increases the speed of the transmittal and reduces the chance for clerical errors.

    (A) Authentication controls are designed to ensure proper submission and delivery of EDI communications.

    (B) Encryption makes messages unreadable to unauthorized parties to help ensure that confidential data is not misused.

(C) A value added network (VAN) refers to an organization that gathers and transmits EDI communications. Thus, some part of the communication of information exists outside of the reporting company. An example of a VAN system that enables EDI transactions is a supermarket that allows customers to use a check card to automatically transfer money from their bank accounts to that of the store.

(2) **On-line, real-time (OLRT) computer systems** pose special control problems for a company. On-line means that the computer terminal has direct access to files within main computer. Real-time means that all changes are made immediately to data without any intermediate step.

    (A) Typical examples of OLRT systems would include a savings account at a bank and a perpetual inventory system at a furniture store.

    (B) Because changes can be made from many locations, company cannot always control who makes changes. Since changes can be made without documentation, auditor has no audit trail to use in verifying that appropriate processing has taken place.

        (1) OLRT systems rely heavily on **access controls**: input or password numbers must be furnished before access is allowed, access is only allowed from approved terminals and at approved times, large changes require secondary approval.

        (2) Password numbers should be changed frequently.

        (3) Computer should be programmed to record unsuccessful attempts to enter system.

    (C) Control is improved if documentation is required which can be reconciled with computer totals periodically. Documentation may not be needed for processing but only for control purposes.

(3) **Database systems**

    (A) Database—a collection of interrelated files.

    (B) Database controls.

        (1) User departments—because users directly input data, strict controls over who is authorized to read and/or change the database are necessary.

        (2) Access controls—controls to prevent access to data.

            (a) Restricting privileges.

            (b) Logical views.

    (C) **Backup and recovery**

        (1) Backup of database and logs of transactions.

        (2) Database of replication.

        (3) Backup facility.

(4) **End-User Computing**—the end user is responsible for the development and execution of the computer application that generates the information used by the same end user.

    (A) Need to test and document applications.

    (B) Need control over access to applications and data.

    (C) Require backup of data.

(5) **Disaster recovery.**

    (A) Backup approaches.

        (1) Batch systems—grandfather-father-son approach.

        (2) On-line systems.

            (a) Checkpoint—makes a copy of database at various points.

            (b) Rollback—rollback to a point where the database is correct.

    (B) Backup facilities.

        (1) Reciprocal agreement—an agreement between two or more organizations to aid in case of disaster.

    (2) Hot site—a commercial disaster recovery service.
    (3) Cold site—similar to hot site but company provides equipment.
    (4) Internal site—large company with multiple sites for backup.
(6) Review the material on flowcharting in the Audit and Attestation section.

PROBLEMS AND SOLUTIONS
INFORMATION TECHNOLOGY

ONE – An auditor is assessing the control risk of a reporting company in connection with the operation of its computer system. General controls relate to the computer system. Application controls are created for a specific program or task. (True or False?)

Answer – Controls created in connection with the overall operation of the computer system of a company are known as general controls. In contrast, controls that are built into a particular computer program (such as a payroll program) or a specific task are called application controls. (Number One is True.)

TWO – A new computer program is being developed for a company. Before the program receives final approval, it is used to process simulated data. This same information is then processed by the program that is currently being used by the company. The results of the two runs are then compared to determine if differences exist. This type of testing of a new program is called an output test. (True or False?)

Answer – When two programs run the same data and a comparison is made, the test is known as a parallel simulation. Any differences will usually indicate a problem with one of the two programs. A similar type of testing can be performed by comparing the program's output with information that is manually derived. (Number Two is False.)

THREE – A new payroll computer program is being developed for a company. In testing this program, two payroll checks were requested for the same employee and a check was requested for an employee with an incorrect identification number. A check was also requested for an employee who had retired several months ago. The company is using the error rate approach to verify that the program is operating correctly. (True or False?)

Answer – One method of testing a computer program is to input a variety of dummy transactions to see how each one is processed. In this technique, known as the test data approach, the attempt is made to include one example of each possible valid and invalid condition. (Number Three is False.)

FOUR – Encryption is a control that attempts to prevent unauthorized use of electronic transmissions by the conversion of data into a form that is unreadable without some type of translation key. (True or False?)

Answer – One problem with reliance on the electronic transmission of information is that unauthorized parties may be able to access confidential data. To reduce the problems associated with this threat, the data may be subjected to encryption so that only appropriate use can be made of the information. (Number Four is True.)

FIVE – A value added network (VAN) is one where one computer system is linked with a second computer system within the same company to create a more efficient flow of data. (True or False?)

Answer – A value added network (VAN) is a computer service organization that provides services for electronic data interchange (EDI) messages. A VAN will transmit and store electronic messages for each of its clients so that one company can communicate directly with another. Consequently, a portion of the flow of information takes place separate from the reporting company. (Number Five is False.)

SIX – A company is running a payroll program. As part of this program, the third digit of each employee's identification number is added. Thus, any change in identification numbers would probably be spotted. This application control is referred to as a hash total. (True or False?)

Answer – A hash total is the summation of any number that would normally not be totaled. This procedure is performed purely for control purposes. Because the summation of the third digit of the employee identification number would be carried out only as a control, the result is known as a hash total. (Number Six is True.)

SEVEN – A company is running a computer payroll program for the month. A check is requested for $10,700. However, the program is not allowed to process payroll checks of over $10,000 without special approval. Because of the amount, this request should be printed out on an exception (or error) report for further investigation by the payroll department before a check can be approved. (True or False?)

Answer – Many computer programs have controls built in to prevent especially large or especially small transactions from being processed without additional authorization. This application control is known as a limit test. Information on any transaction outside of the defined limits is printed on an exception (or error) report. However, all such questionable transactions should be investigated by a control group to ensure that responsibilities have been properly segregated. (Number Seven is False.)

EIGHT – A company is running a computer payroll program for the month. Before each check is written, the employee identification number is matched with the master employee file to ascertain that the individual is a current employee of the company. This application control is known as a validity check. (True or False?)

Answer – Whenever a computer program verifies information found in one procedure against an independent source, a validity check is being performed. For example, before an invoice is paid, the computer might verify that the check is to be written to a party included on the approved vendor list. (Number Eight is True.)

NINE – As compared to traditional computing operations, end-user computing generally results in more thoroughly tested computer programs. (True or False?)

Answer – End-user computing involves the development of applications by the users of the applications. Such programs are typically not subject to the testing that is done on programs developed by Information Technology departments. (Number Nine is False.)

MICROECONOMICS

(1) The price of a good or service is determined by demand and supply.

(2) Demand is the quantity of a good or service that consumers are willing and able to purchase at a range of prices at a particular time.

   (A) A demand curve shifts when demand variables other than price change (e.g., the price of other goods and services, the price of complement products, consumer tastes, size of the market, or group boycott).

   (B) **Price elasticity of demand** measures the sensitivity of demand to a change in the product's price. It is measured with the following formula:

$$E_D = \frac{\text{Change in quantity demanded}}{\text{Average quantity}} \div \frac{\text{Change in price}}{\text{Average price}}$$

   (C) If E_D is greater than 1, demand is elastic (sensitive to price changes). If E_D is less than 1, demand is inelastic (not sensitive to price changes). If E_D is equal to 1 demand is unitary (not sensitive or insensitive to price changes).

   (D) **Income elasticity of demand** measures the change in quantity demanded of a product given a change in consumer income. The demand for normal goods goes up as income increases, while the demand for inferior goods goes down as income increases.

   (E) The **cross-elasticity of demand** measures the change in demand for a good when the price of a related or competing product is changed. If demand for the product goes up with an increase in the price of the other product, the products are substitutes. If demand goes down the products are complements.

   (F) The **law of diminishing utility** refers to the fact that as a consumer obtains more of a product the marginal utility from obtaining an additional unit of the product decreases.

   (G) The relationship between changes in personal disposable income and consumption is described by a **consumption function**. The slope of the consumption function measures the consumer's marginal propensity to consume. It illustrates the percentage of an additional dollar in income that the consumer spends. One minus the marginal propensity to consume is the marginal propensity to save.

(3) The supply curve (schedule) shows the amount of a good or service that would be supplied at various prices.

   (A) A supply curve shift occurs when supply variables other than price change (e.g., government subsidies, government price controls, prices of other goods, or price expectations).

   (B) **Elasticity of supply** measures the percentage change in quantity supplied of a product when the price changes.

   (C) Market equilibrium occurs at the intersection of the demand and supply curve. At the equilibrium price all of the supplied goods will be sold.

   (D) Government intervention can alter market equilibrium.

      (1) A price ceiling can cause too few goods to be produced causing market shortages.

      (2) A price floor can cause too many goods to be produced causing overproduction.

   (E) The products supplied by a firm depend on the firm's production costs.

      (1) In the short run, firms have both fixed and variable costs.

(2)   In the long run, all costs are variable because additional plant capacity can be added. As a firm increases its productive capacity, three outcomes are possible:
  (a)   Constant returns to scale.
  (b)   Increasing returns to scale.
  (c)   Decreasing returns to scale.
(F)   In competitive markets firms continue to produce products until marginal revenue is equal to marginal cost.

PROBLEMS AND SOLUTIONS
MICROECONOMICS

ONE – A demand curve shift occurs when the price of the product changes. (True or False?)

Answer – A demand curve shows the quantity of a good that consumers will purchase at a range of prices at a particular time. A demand curve shift occurs when a demand variable other than price changes. (Number One is False.)

TWO – If a product has a price elasticity coefficient of 1.5, the demand for the product is elastic. (True or False?)

Answer – The elasticity of demand coefficient is calculated by dividing the percentage change in quantity demanded by the percentage change in price. If the coefficient is greater than one the demand for the product is elastic. (Number Two is True.)

THREE – If the price of a product increases, demand for products that are substitutes for the product will decrease. (True or False?)

Answer – Substitute products are those that have similar utility characteristics. Therefore, if the price of a product increases, demand for substitute products will increase. (Number Three is False.)

FOUR – The law of diminishing utility indicates that as a consumer gets more of a product, total utility decreases. (True or False?)

Answer – The law of diminishing utility indicates that as a consumer gets more of a product, the marginal utility decreases. However, total utility still increases. (Number Four is False.)

FIVE – In the short run costs are fixed and variable, but in the long run all costs are variable. (True or False?)

Answer – In the long run a firm can alter its production capacity. Therefore, all costs are variable. In the short run, a firm has both fixed and variable costs. (Number Five is True.)

SIX – A firm in a competitive market should produce and sell products until marginal cost of the product is equal to its marginal revenue. (True or False?)

Answer – In a competitive market, a firm maximizes its profit by producing and selling products until marginal cost is equal to marginal revenue. (Number Six is True.)

MACROECONOMICS

(1) Macroeconomics looks at the economy as a whole.
(2) The levels of economic activity are measured with a number of benchmarks, including:
    (A) Nominal **Gross Domestic Product** (GDP)—the price of all goods and services produced by a domestic economy for a year at current market prices.
    (B) Real GDP—The price of all goods and services produced by an economy at price level adjusted prices.
    (C) **Potential GDP**—the maximum amount of production that could take place in an economy without putting pressure on the general level of prices.
    (D) Net Domestic Product (NDP)—GDP minus depreciation.
    (E) Gross National Product (GNP)—The price of all goods and services produced by labor and property supplied by the nation's residents.
    (F) Unemployment rate—the percent of the total of labor force that is unemployed at a given time. It consists of:
        (1) Frictional unemployment—the unemployment that occurs because individuals are forced or voluntarily change jobs.
        (2) Structural unemployment—the unemployment that occurs due to changes in demand for products or services, or technological advances that cause changes in needed skills.
        (3) Cyclical unemployment—the unemployment caused by economic conditions.
    (G) Inflation—the rate of increase in the price level of goods and services, usually measured on an annual basis.
    (H) Deflation—a decrease in price level.
    (I) Measures of price index (inflation) include:
        (1) **Consumer price index**—measures price changes in products bought by urban consumers.
        (2) **Producer price index**—measures price changes at the wholesale level.
        (3) **The GDP deflator**—measures price changes for net exports, investments, government expenditures and consumer spending. It is the most comprehensive measure of price level.
    (J) **Personal disposable income**—the amount of income that individuals receive and have available to purchase goods and services.
    (K) Interest rates
        (1) Real interest rates—interest rate in terms of goods.
        (2) Nominal interest rate—interest rate in terms of the nation's currency.
    (L) Government budget surplus (deficit)—the excess (deficit) of government taxes in relation to government transfer payments and purchases.
(3) An aggregate demand curve depicts the demand of consumers, businesses, government, and foreign purchasers. It looks much like the demand curve for an individual product. The aggregate supply schedule presents the relationship between goods and services supplied and the price level. **Equilibrium GDP** occurs when the output level of the economy creates just enough spending to purchase the entire output.
    (A) The **multiplier** refers to the fact that an increase in spending by consumers, businesses, or the government has a multiplied effect on equilibrium GDP. The multiplier is calculated by dividing one by the marginal propensity to save.

(B) A **business cycle** is a fluctuation in aggregate economic output that lasts for several years. Business cycles are depicted as a series of peaks and troughs. A peak marks the end of a period of economic expansion and the beginning of a contraction, and a trough marks the end of a recession and the beginning of an economic recovery. Business cycles are predicted with leading economic indicators.

(C) Investment includes expenditures for residential construction, inventories, and plant and equipment. The most important determinant of business investment is expectations about profits.

(D) **Accelerator theory** states that as economic activity increases, capital investment must be made to meet the level of increased demand. This increased capital investment in turn creates additional economic demand.

(4) Inflation has two possible causes:

(A) **Demand-pull inflation** occurs when aggregate spending exceeds the economy's full-employment output capacity.

(B) **Cost-push inflation** occurs from an increase in the cost of producing goods and services.

(5) The government regulates the economy in two ways: (1) monetary policy and (2) fiscal policy.

(A) **Monetary policy** may involve:

    (1) Change in the reserve requirements, which is the amount of cash banks must hold in reserve.

    (2) Engaging in open-market operations, which is the purchase and sale of government securities.

    (3) Change in the discount rate, which is the rate at which a bank may borrow money from the Federal Reserve.

(B) **Fiscal policy** may involve:

    (1) Changes in income taxes.

    (2) Changes in the level of government spending.

(6) International trade exists because countries have advantages with regard to the production of certain goods.

(A) **Absolute advantage** exists when it can produce the products at a lower cost than other countries.

(B) **Comparative advantage** exists when the country has no alternative uses of its resources that would involve a higher return.

(C) The balance of payments is an account summary of a nation's transactions with other nations.

(D) A foreign exchange rate is the relationship between the values of two currencies. Factors affecting exchange rates include:

    (1) Inflation.

    (2) Interest rates.

    (3) Balance of payments.

(7) Government intervention.

(A) Firms that conduct business internationally must be concerned with fluctuations in exchange rates, which can cause gains and losses. Firms can eliminate or reduce this risk by hedging.

    (1) Forward exchange market hedges—purchasing and selling currency forward exchange contracts.

    (2) Money market hedges—borrowing and lending funds of another country.

        (3)   Currency futures market hedges—purchasing and selling contracts to deliver foreign currency at a specified price.

(8) A firm that has international operations may use transfer-pricing strategy to maximize income. **Transfer pricing** is the price at which services or products are bought and sold across international borders between related parties. Firms can minimize their overall tax burden by using transfer prices to minimize net income in jurisdictions with higher tax rates.

PROBLEMS AND SOLUTIONS
MACROECONOMICS

ONE – In a period of recession, actual GDP exceeds potential GDP. (True or False?)

> *Answer – Potential GDP is the maximum amount of economic activity that can take place without putting pressure on the general price level. In a period of recession, Potential GDP exceeds actual GDP. (Number One is False.)*

TWO – Cyclical unemployment can be reduced by training employees in new skills. (True or False?)

> *Answer – Cyclical unemployment is caused by a downturn in the economy. It is reduced by economic expansion. Structural unemployment is caused by a mismatch of job requirements and employee skills in the economy. (Number Two is False.)*

THREE – The most comprehensive measure of price-level in the economy is the consumer price index. (True or False?)

> *Answer – The consumer price index measures the change in prices of goods purchased by urban consumers. The wholesale price index measures the change in prices of goods at the wholesale level. The GDP deflator measures the change in prices for net exports, investments, government expenditures and consumer spending. It is the most comprehensive measure of price level. (Number Three is False.)*

FOUR – If the marginal propensity to consume is .80 and the government increases spending by $10 million, the increase in equilibrium GDP is $50,000,000. (True or False?)

> *Answer – The multiplier measures the increase in GDP resulting from an increase in spending. The multiplier is calculated as 1/marginal propensity to save. The marginal propensity to save is equal to one minus the marginal propensity to consume. Therefore, the multiplier is equal to 5.0 (1.00/.20), and the resulting increase in GDP is $50,000,000 ($10,000,000 x 5). (Number Four is True.)*

FIVE – Demand-pull inflation occurs at high-levels of economic activity. (True or False?)

> *Answer – Demand-pull inflation occurs when aggregate spending exceeds the economy's full-employment output capacity. (Number Five is True.)*

SIX – To stimulate the economy, the Federal Reserve could decide to sell Treasury securities. (True or False?)

Answer – The Federal Reserve uses monetary policy to stimulate and control economic expansion. The sale of Treasury securities reduces the money supply and serves to contract economic activity. (Number Six is False.)

SEVEN – A country will produce a product as long as it has a comparative advantage with respect to production of the product. (True or False?)

Answer – A country has a comparative advantage with respect to the production of a product if it has no alternative use of its resources that would produce a higher return. (Number Seven is True.)

EIGHT – Assume that a firm has a receivable collectible in 90 days in Euros. To hedge the risk of a decline in the value of the Euro, the firm could sell Euros in the currency futures market. (True or False?)

Answer – To hedge a decline in the value of a receivable payable in a foreign currency, a firm could sell the currency using a currency futures contract. (Number Eight is True.)

BUSINESS STRATEGY

(1) In developing an effective business strategy, management typically assesses its economic and industry environment. Management uses the following techniques to analyze and forecast the economic environment:
   (A) Scanning—a study of all segments in the general environment.
   (B) Monitoring—a study of environmental changes identified by scanning to identify important trends.
   (C) Forecasting—developing probable projections of what might happen and its timing.
   (D) Assessing—determining changes in the firm's strategy that are necessary as a result of the information obtained.

(2) Industry analysis involves examining the nature and characteristics of the firm's industry. There are a number of different types of industries:
   (A) **Perfect (pure) competition**—a market characterized by a large number of small producers that sell a virtually identical product. Firms in these types of industries must compete on the basis of price.
   (B) **Pure monopoly**—a market in which there is a single seller of a product or service for which there are no close substitutes. A monopoly may exist for one or more of the following reasons: (1) increasing returns of scale, (2) control over the supply of raw materials, (3) patents, or (4) government franchise. A natural monopoly exists when economic or technological conditions permit only on efficient supplier. Monopolists will produce and sell products as long as average variable cost is less than marginal revenue.
   (C) **Monopolistic competition**—a market that is characterized by many firms selling a differentiated product or service. The strategies of firms in such markets tend to focus on product or service innovations, product developments, and advertising.
   (D) **Oligopoly**—a market characterized by significant barriers to entry. As a result there are few sellers of a product. Oligopolists often attempt to engage in nonprice competition. However, during economic downturns, price competition can become fierce.

(3) In analyzing the industry, management often focuses on five industry forces: (1) competitors, (2) potential entrants into the market, (3) equivalent products, (4) bargaining power of customers, and (5) bargaining power of input suppliers.

(4) Techniques for industry analysis.
   (A) Competitor analysis—involves (1) gathering information about competitors' capabilities, objectives, strategies and assumptions, and (2) using the information to understand the competitors' behavior.
   (B) Price elasticity analysis—involves using historical information to determine the price elasticity of demand for the firm's product.
   (C) Target market analysis—obtaining a thorough understanding of the market in which the firm sells its products.

(5) In developing business strategies, management will often perform a SWOT (strengths, weaknesses, opportunities, and threats) analysis.

(6) Firms generally pursue one of two basic business strategies, product differentiation or cost leadership.

(A) Product differentiation involves modification of a product to make it more attractive to the target market or to differentiate it from competitors' products. Products may be differentiated through physical characteristics, perceived differences, or support service differences.

(B) Cost leadership involves focusing on reducing the costs and time to produce, sell, and distribute a product of service. The following techniques may facilitate cost reductions:

    (1) Process reengineering—redesigning existing processes.

    (2) Lean manufacturing—identification and elimination of all types of waste in the production function.

    (3) Supply chain management—the sharing of key information from the point of sale to the final consumer back to the manufacturer, the manufacturer's suppliers, and the suppliers' suppliers. The objective is to reduce time, defects, and costs all along the supply chain.

    (4) Strategic alliances involve collaborative agreements between two or more firms.

    (5) Outsourcing involves contracting for the performance of processes by other firms.

PROBLEMS AND SOLUTIONS
BUSINESS STRATEGY

ONE – One of Porter's five forces for an industry is the bargaining power of input suppliers (True or False?)

Answer - Porter's five industry forces include (1) competitors, (2) potential entrants into the market, (3) equivalent products, (4) bargaining power of customers, and (5) bargaining power of input suppliers. (Number One is True.)

TWO – Monopolistic competition is characterized by a large number of firms producing a differentiated product. (True or False?)

Answer – Monopolistic competition is a market that is characterized by many firms selling a differentiated product or service. (Number Two is True.)

THREE – An oligopolistic market is characterized by low barriers to entry. (True or False?)

Answer – An oligopolistic market is a market characterized by significant barriers to entry. As a result there are few sellers of a product. (Number Three is False.)

FOUR – A viable business strategy for a firm in a perfectly competitive market is product differentiation. (True or False?)

Answer – In a perfectly competitive market firms sell virtually identical products. Product differentiation is not a viable business strategy. (Number Four is False.)

FIVE – Competitor analysis involves gathering information about competitors to predict their behavior. (True or False?)

> *Answer – Competitor analysis involves (1) gathering information about competitors' capabilities, objectives, strategies and assumptions, and (2) using the information to understand the competitors' behavior. (Number Five is True.)*

SIX – Product differentiation may be real or only perceived. (True or False?)

> *Answer – Products may be differentiated through physical characteristics, perceived differences, or support service differences. (Number Six is True.)*

FINANCIAL MANAGEMENT

(1) Financial management involves the following five functions: financing, capital budgeting, financial management, corporate governance, and risk-management.
  (A) The ultimate goal of management of a firm is to ethically maximize the value for its owners.
  (B) Risks and returns are inversely related.
(2) Virtually every financial decision is influenced by tax considerations. Things to remember about taxation include:
  (A) The final returns to stockholders are after tax.
  (B) Interest is tax-deductible but dividends are not.
  (C) Alternative tax accounting methods are available that affect the firm's tax liability.
  (D) Different rates apply to different types of income.
  (E) Certain tax provisions are designed to stimulate the economy.

PROBLEMS AND SOLUTIONS
FINANCIAL MANAGEMENT

ONE - Financial management involves the capital budgeting function. (True or False?)

> *Answer – Financial management includes a number of functions, including capital budgeting. Capital budgeting involves the selection of investments that meet the firm's requirements for risk and return. (Number One is True.)*

TWO – Good financial management involves investing in the highest return projects to maximize stockholder value. (True or False?)

> *Answer – High-return projects involve higher risk which may or may not be consistent with the objectives of the owners of the firm. (Number Two is False.)*

THREE – Taxation is important primarily because it affects the final return to the owners of the firm. (True or False?)

> *Answer – Taxation is important to financial managers primarily because of its effect on the firm's net income and the eventual after-tax returns to the owners of the firm. (Number Three is True.)*

WORKING CAPITAL MANAGEMENT

(1) Working capital management involves managing and financing current assets and current liabilities.

(2) The primary focus of working capital management is the cash conversion cycle of the firm, which is the length of time between when the firm makes payments and when it receives inflows. The cash conversion cycle includes:

    (A) The **inventory conversion period**—the average time required to convert materials into finished goods and sell the goods. It is equal to average inventory divided by sales per day.

    (B) The **receivables collection period**—the average time required to collect accounts receivable. It is equal to average receivables divided by credit sales per day.

    (C) The **payables deferral period**—the average time between the purchase of materials and labor and payment of cash for them. It is equal to average payables divided by purchases per day.

    (D) The formula for the cash conversion cycle is:

Inventory conversion per. + Receivables collection per. – Payables deferral per.

(3) Cash management involves holding the minimum amount of cash to meet the firm's needs.

    (A) Cash is held for two purposes: (a) for transacting business, and (b) as compensation for financial institutions.

    (B) The **float** is the time that elapses relating to mailing, processing, and clearing checks. Management's objective is to minimize the cash receipts float and maximize the cash disbursements float.

    (C) A technique for increasing the cash disbursements float is **zero-balance account**, which involves maintaining a regional bank account to which just enough funds are transferred daily to pay the checks presented.

    (D) Techniques for decreasing the cash receipts float include:

        (1) **Lock-box system**—customer payments are sent to a post office box that is maintained by a financial institution, which speeds up the deposit of the receipts.

        (2) **Concentration banking**—customers make payments to a local branch office rather than firm headquarters, and the branches make deposits to local banks. Therefore, the firm gets use of the funds more quickly. Funds are transferred to the firm's primary bank account periodically with wire transfers or official bank checks (depository transfer checks).

        (3) **Electronic funds transfer**—a system in which funds are moved electronically between accounts without the use of checks.

    (E) Cash management techniques are cost-effective if the interest savings by having use of the funds longer offset the increase in maintenance charges and fees. For example, assume that a firm can establish a lock-box system that will speed up receipt of cash collections by 2 days. The bank charges $1,000 a month for the service and the firm will save $4,000 per year in administrative costs. The firm's average daily cash receipts are equal to $150,000 and its cost of short-term funds is 6%. Should the firm establish the lock-box system? The net cost of establishing the lock-box is equal to

$12,000 ($1,000 monthly fee x 12 months) - $4,000 administrative cost savings, or $8,000. The interest savings is equal to $18,000 (6% x $300,000). Therefore, the firm will save $10,000 by establishing the lock-box system.

    (F) **International cash management** involves managing cash balances in accounts in the various countries in which the firm conducts business. Investment opportunities and prevailing interest rates vary by country.

(4) Firms hold marketable securities as a cash reserve. Therefore, the major considerations with respect to the nature of the investments are liquidity and safety. The following are typical investments that meet these criteria:

    (A) **Treasury bills and notes**—obligations of the federal government. Treasury bills are short-term and treasury notes are short-to-intermediate term.

    (B) **Federal agency securities**—obligations of federal agencies, such as the Federal Home Loan Bank.

    (C) **Certificates of deposit (CD)**—savings deposits at financial institutions. Large CDs have a secondary market.

    (D) **Commercial paper**—unsecured short-term promissory notes issued by large creditworthy corporations.

    (E) **Banker's acceptance**—a draft drawn on a bank for payment when presented to the bank. Because banker's acceptances generally have to be presented from 30 to 90 days after issuance they are often available at discounted prices as investments.

    (F) **Eurodollar certificates of deposit**—CDs offered by foreign banks to obtain dollars for the Eurodollar market.

    (G) **Money market funds**—shares in a fund that purchases higher-yielding CDs.

(5) The two goals of inventory management include: (1) to ensure adequate inventories to sustain operations, and (2) to minimize inventory costs, including holding costs, ordering and receiving costs, and costs of running out of stock.

    (A) If a firm has a seasonal demand for its product, management must decide whether to produce at a near uniform level of production all year or produce at a high level during the season of peak demand. To determine the cost-effective decision management must compare the cost of holding additional inventory under the uniform-level alternative to the additional production costs associated with the seasonal-production alternative.

    (B) A firm may also use inventory that is subject to fluctuating prices. In such cases, management should consider hedging strategies to reduce the effects of changing prices.

    (C) The **supply chain** refers to a product's production and distribution processes. It illustrates the flow of goods, services, and information from acquisition of basic raw materials through the manufacturing and distribution processes to delivery of the product to the final consumer, regardless of whether those activities occur in one or many firms. **Supply chain management** involves sharing of information among firms in the supply chain to minimize inventory levels and make the processes as efficient as possible.

    (D) The **economic order quantity** model is used to determine the inventory order quantity that minimizes inventory costs. It is calculated as follows:

$$EOQ = \sqrt{\frac{2aD}{k}}$$

where: a = cost of placing an order

D = annual demand in units

k = cost of carrying one unit of inventory for one year

(E) Determining the optimum reorder point involves balancing inventory holding costs against the stockout costs.

(F) **Materials requirements planning (MRP)** is a computerized system used to manufacture goods based on demand forecasts. A key weakness of MRP is that it is a "push through" system; products are manufactured based on the master schedule whether they are needed are not. Therefore, if the forecasts are inaccurate of there are production slowdowns, inventories will accumulate at various production stages.

(G) A **Just-in-Time (JIT)** purchasing system is a demand-pull inventory system which involves the receipt of inventories just before they are needed for production. For a JIT purchasing system to be effective, the company must select suppliers that will deliver timely, defect-free products.

(1) JIT may also be applied to production by establishing a system in which each component is completed just before it is needed by the next production stage.

(H) JIT advantages include:

(1) Lower investments in inventories and storage space.

(2) Lower inventory carrying and handling costs.

(3) Reduced risk of defective and obsolete inventory.

(4) Reduced manufacturing costs.

(5) Reduced number of high-quality suppliers.

(6) Allows the use of **backflush costing**, in which inventory costs are run directly through cost of goods sold.

(I) **Enterprise Resource Planning (ERP) systems** are enterprise-wide computerized information systems that connect all functional areas within an organization. ERP systems facilitate supply chain management by connecting the firm electronically to its suppliers and customers.

(6) Effective receivables management involves systems for deciding whether or not to grant credit and for monitoring the receivables.

(A) An overall measure of the accumulation of receivables is the days' sales outstanding which is calculated as follows:

Days' sales outstanding = Receivables/Sales per day

(B) A common management decision is whether or not to change their credit policy. In making this decision management must consider the effect of the change on sales, losses from uncollectible accounts, and accounts receivable holding costs.

PROBLEMS AND SOLUTIONS
WORKING CAPITAL MANAGEMENT

ONE – Management should hold as much cash as possible to insure liquidity of the firm. (True or False?)

Answer – A firm holds cash for two basic purposes: (1) transactions and (2) compensation to financial institutions. Cash does not produce income. Therefore, a firm should hold only enough cash to (1) take advantage of trade discounts, (2) assure that the firm maintains its credit rating, (3) take advantage of favorable business opportunities, and (4) meet emergencies. (Number One is False.)

TWO – A zero-balance account is designed to reduce the float in cash receipts. (True or False?)

Answer – A zero-balance account technique involves maintaining a regional bank account to which just enough funds are transferred daily to pay the checks presented. It is a technique to increase the float in cash disbursements. (Number Two is False.)

THREE – A firm is considering establishing a concentration banking system that will speed up receipts from customers by two days. Assuming that the firm's average daily collections are $50,000, maintenance and transfer fees are equal to $6,000 per year and the firm's short-term cost of funds is equal to 4%, the firm should not establish the concentration banking system. (True or False?)

Answer – A concentration banking system should be established if the savings in interest cost offsets the maintenance and transfer fees. In this case the interest savings would have to equal more than $6,000 per year; and it is only equal to $4,000 ([$50,000 x 2 day] x 4%). (Number Three is True.)

FOUR – Commercial paper pays a higher interest rate than Treasury bills. (True or False?)

Answer – Commercial paper is issued by large, creditworthy corporations. Therefore, it has a greater credit risk than Treasury bills issued by the U S government and, therefore, pays a higher interest rate. (Number Four is True.)

FIVE – Money market funds invest in debt and equity securities. (True or False?)

Answer – Money market funds invest in higher-yielding bank CDs, commercial paper, and other low risk securities. They do not invest in equity securities. (Number Five is False.)

SIX - The term supply chain describes the firm's processes for purchasing and manufacturing products. (True or False?)

Answer – The term supply chain describes a product's production and distribution. It illustrates the flow of goods, services, and information from acquisition of basic raw materials through the manufacturing and distribution process to delivery of the product to the consumer, regardless of whether those activities occur in one or many firms. Therefore, the supply chain is broader than the purchasing and manufacturing processes on one firm. (Number Six is False.)

SEVEN – The EOQ model balances the costs of holding goods against the cost of ordering goods. (True or False?)

> *Answer – The EOQ model minimizes the sum of ordering and carrying costs of inventory. (Number Seven is True.)*

EIGHT – An increase in the number of orders placed for inventory and a decrease in the quantity of goods on hand are characteristics of a just-in-time inventory system. (True or False?)

> *Answer – In a just-in-time system, the manufacturing process is engineered so precisely that goods should arrive at each point just as they are needed. In this way, goods do not need to be stored along the way and overall inventory quantities are reduced. In order to keep less inventory in the system, more orders are usually placed but for smaller quantities. (Number Eight is True.)*

NINE – A firm's credit criteria involves decisions about the length of time buyers are given to pay for their purchases. (True or False?)

> *Answer – A firm's credit criteria involves deciding on the required financial strength of acceptable credit customers. The length of time buyers are given to pay for their purchases is referred to as the credit period. (Number Nine is False.)*

FINANCING CURRENT ASSETS

(1) Many firms have seasonal fluctuations in demand for their products. Accordingly, current assets tend to vary in amount from month to month.

    (A) **Permanent current assets** are those that are required to operate the business in even the slowest times of the year.

    (B) **Temporary current assets** are the additional amounts of current assets that are accumulated during periods of higher production and sales.

    (C) A conservative approach is to finance permanent current assets with long-term financing sources and finance temporary current assets with short-term financing sources. However, long-term financing sources generally are more expensive, have more covenants that restrict management actions, and often have prepayment penalties.

(2) There are a number of short-term sources of funds, including:

    (A) **Accounts payable (trade credit)** is a source of funds when a firm purchases goods on credit. However, it can be expensive if the firm does not take advantage of the cash discounts available for early payment of invoices. The following formula is used to calculate the interest rate cost of not taking the discount:

$$\text{Rate} = \frac{Discount\ percent}{100\% - Discount\ percent} \ x \ \frac{365\ days}{Total\ pay\ period - Discount\ period}$$

    (B) **Short-term bank loans** are loans from financial institutions that typically mature in about 90 days and involve an interest rate tied to the prime rate or the London Interbank Offered Rate (LIBOR). These rates are referred to as nominal rates; the actual rate that a borrower receives is adjusted for the borrower's credit risk.

        (1) To calculate the interest cost when the loan is made on a discounted basis or involves a compensating balance, the interest amount should be divided by the cash available (e.g., the principal minus the discount or compensating balance).

        (2) A line of credit is an informal specification of the maximum amount that the bank will lend the borrower.

        (3) A letter of credit is an instrument that facilitates international trade. It is a promise by an importer's bank that the bank will pay for imported merchandise.

    (C) Large credit worthy borrowers can issue commercial paper to obtain short-term funds.

    (D) Accounts receivable can be used as collateral for short-term loans. These loans typically involve pledging of receivables, factoring of receivables, or asset-backed public offerings.

    (E) Inventory is also used as collateral for short-term debt, in the form of blanket inventory liens, trust receipts, or warehousing arrangements.

    (F) If a firm has a large amount of variable rate debt, management may decide to hedge the interest rate risk by selling derivatives in the financial futures market.

PROBLEMS AND SOLUTIONS
FINANCING CURRENT ASSETS

ONE – If a firm goes to a reputable financial institution, the firm will pay a nominal rate of interest. (True or False?)

> *Answer – Examples of nominal rates of interest are the prime rate and LIBOR. These rates are the ones that are charged by financial institutions to there most credit-worthy customers. Many borrowers pay the nominal rate plus several basis points to compensate the financial institution for credit risk. (Number One is False.)*

TWO – If a firm is offered credit terms of 2/10, net/30, the cost of not taking the discount is equal to 26%. (True or False?)

> *Answer – The cost of not taking the discount is calculated as follows:*

$$\frac{Discount\ percent}{100\% - Discount\ percent} \ x \ \frac{365\ days}{Total\ pay\ period - Discount\ period}$$

$$= \frac{2\%}{100\% - 2\%} \ x \ \frac{365}{30 - 10} = 37.2\%$$

> *(Number Two is False.)*

THREE – Asset-backed public offerings are debt offerings collateralized by inventory. (True or False?)

> *Answer – Asset-backed public offerings are public offerings of debt collateralized by the firm's accounts receivables. (Number Three is False.)*

FOUR – In a warehousing arrangement, inventory is maintained in the warehouse of the borrower under control of the borrower's warehouse personnel.

> *Answer – Under a warehousing arrangement, inventory is stored in a public warehouse or under the control of public warehouse personnel. The goods can only be removed with the lender's permission. (Number Four is False.)*

CAPITAL STRUCTURE

(1) Capital structure describes the firm's mix of debt and equity. In determining the appropriate mix of debt and equity, management must consider the nature of debt and equity.
  (A) Types of Debt
    (1) Private debt is in two forms: long-term loans from financial institutions and (2) private placement of unregistered bonds sold directly to accredited investors. Private debt typically is less expensive than public debt.
    (2) Public debt involves offerings of SEC registered bonds directly to investors.
    (3) Some firms also obtain funds from the Eurobond market. A Eurobond is a bond payable in the borrower's currency but sold outside the borrower's country. Since the registration and disclosure requirements for Eurobonds are less stringent than those of the SEC, the cost of issuance is less.
  (B) Debt generally has covenants that restrict the actions of management.
  (C) Debt comes with a number of security provisions, including:
    (1) **Mortgage bonds**—secured with the pledge of property.
    (2) **Collateral trust bond**—secured by financial assets.
    (3) **Debenture**—unsecured.
    (4) **Subordinated debenture**—unsecured with subordinated claims.
    (5) **Income bond**—interest payments contingent on earnings.
  (D) Methods of payment of bonds.
    (1) **Serial payments**—paid in installments.
    (2) **Sinking fund provisions**—firm makes payments to sinking fund to liquidate bonds.
    (3) **Conversion**—convertible into common stock.
    (4) **Redeemable**—may be redeemed at the holder's option.
    (5) **Call feature**—firm may force redemption.
  (E) Bond yields.
    (1) Coupon rate—the stated interest rate that the bond pays.
    (2) Current yield—the stated interest payment divided by the current price of the bond.
    (3) Yield to maturity—the interest rate that equates the future interest payments and maturity payment to the current market price.
  (F) Advantages of debt financing.
    (1) Interest is tax-deductible.
    (2) Fixed obligation.
    (3) In periods of inflation, debt is paid back in dollars with less purchasing power.
    (4) Owners do not give up control.
    (5) Debtors do not participate in excess earnings.
    (6) Debt is less costly than equity.
  (G) Disadvantages of debt financing.
    (1) Interest and principal obligations must be paid regardless of the financial position of the firm.
    (2) Debt covenants restrict management's actions.
    (3) Excessive debt increases the risk of equity.
(2) Leasing.

(A) Advantages of leasing.
    (1) A firm may be able to lease when it does not have the ability to purchase.
    (2) Less stringent provisions.
    (3) No down payment may be required.
    (4) Creditor claims of certain types of leases are restricted in bankruptcy.
    (5) The cost of a lease may be reduced if the lessor retains the tax benefits.
    (6) Operating leases do not require recognition of the liability.

(3) Equity.
  (A) Common stock.
    (1) Advantages of common stock.
      (a) The firm has no fixed obligation.
      (b) Increased equity reduces the risk of debt which reduces the firm's cost of borrowing.
    (2) Disadvantages of common stock.
      (a) Issuance costs are greater than for debt.
      (b) Ownership and control is given up.
      (c) Dividends are not tax-deductible.
      (d) Shareholders demand a higher rate of return.
      (e) Issuance of too much common stock increases the cost of capital.
  (B) Preferred stock.
    (1) Advantages of preferred stock.
      (a) No fixed obligation to pay dividends.
      (b) Increased equity reduces the cost of debt.
      (c) Common stockholders do not give up control
      (d) Preferred stockholders do not generally participate in superior earnings.
    (2) Disadvantages of preferred stock.
      (a) Issuance costs are greater than for debt.
      (b) Dividends are not tax deductible.
      (c) Dividends in arrears accumulated over time may create a burden on the firm.

(4) In deciding whether to go public a firm must balance the additional compliance costs with the advantage of creating a liquid investment for its owners.

(5) **Operating leverage** measures the degree to which a firm builds fixed costs into its operations. The degree of operating leverage (DOL) is calculated with the following formula:

$$DOL = \frac{Percent\ change\ in\ operating\ income}{Percent\ change\ in\ unit\ volume}$$

Highly leveraged firms enjoy substantial increases in income when sales volume increases, but they have greater risk.

(6) **Financial leverage** measures the extent to which the firm uses debt financing. The degree of financial leverage (DFL) is calculated with the following formula:

$$DFL = \frac{Percent\ change\ in\ EPS}{Percent\ change\ in\ EBIT}$$

Where:

EPS = Earnings per share

EBIT = Earnings before interest and taxes

(7) Management attempts to reduce the cost of capital for a firm consistent with the desired level of risk.

   (A) The **cost of debt** is equal to the interest of the loan adjusted for the fact that interest is deductible. As an example, if the firm's interest rate on a long-term debt is 8% and its marginal tax rate is 25%, the cost of debt is equal to 6% [8% x (100% - 25%)].

   (B) The **cost of preferred equity** is calculated by dividing the preferred dividend amount by the issue price of the stock. As an example, if 1,000 shares of $6.00 preferred stock is issued for $105,000, the cost of preferred stock is equal to 5.71% ($6,000/$105,000).

   (C) The **cost of common equity** is greater than that of debt or preferred equity. Common equity is raised in two ways: (1) retained earnings, and (2) issuing new common stock. The cost of equity raised by issuing new stock is somewhat higher due to floatation costs (cost of issuance). The following methods are used to estimate the cost of common equity:

      (a) **The capital asset pricing model (CAPM).**

$$CAPM = k_{RF} + (k_M - k_{RF})\, b_i$$

      where: k_{RF} = the risk free interest rate

           k_M = the market rate of interest

           b_i = the firm's beta

      (b) The **arbitrage pricing model** is similar to CAPM but the arbitrage pricing model uses a series of systematic risk factors instead of only one.

      (c) The **bond-yield-plus approach** involves adding a risk premium of 3 to 5% to the interest rate on the firm's long-term debt.

      (d) The **dividend-yield-plus-growth-rate approach** estimates the cost of equity by considering investors' expected yield on their investment.

   (D) The **weighted-average cost of capital (WACC)** is calculated by weighting each component of capital by its percentage of the total. As an example, if a firm has $100,000 in debt with a cost of 6% and $200,000 in equity with a cost of 12%, the weighted average cost of capital would be equal to 10% [($100,000/$300,000) x 6%] + [($200,000/$300,000) x 12%].

PROBLEMS AND SOLUTIONS
CAPITAL STRUCTURE

ONE – Eurobonds may be a lower cost alternative to other debt financing because they have a lower cost of issuance. (True or False?)

   Answer – Eurobonds are bonds payable in the borrower's currency that are sold in a foreign country. Because the registration and disclosure requirements for Eurobonds are less stringent than bonds issue in the US, the cost of issuance is less. (Number One is True.)

TWO – A major advantage of the issuance of debt is the tax deductibility of interest payments. (True or False?)

Answer – The advantages of the issuance of bonds include: (1) interest is tax-deductible, (2) the obligation is fixed in amount, (3) in periods of inflation, debt is paid back in dollars with less purchasing power, (4) the owners do not give up control of the firm, (5) debtors do not participate in excess earnings, and (6) debt is less costly than equity. (Number Two is True.)

THREE – A firm with a high degree of operating leverage has less earnings variability than a firm with a lower degree of operating leverage. (True or False?)

Answer – Operating leverage measures the degree to which a firm builds fixed costs into its operations. With a high percentage of fixed costs, the firm's earnings are more variable. (Number Three is False.)

FOUR – If a firm issues 1,000 shares of $7.00 preferred stock at $98,000, the cost of the preferred stock is 7%. (True or False?)

Answer – The cost of preferred stock is determined by dividing the dividend amount by the issue price. In this case the cost is equal to 7.14% ($7,000/$98,000). (Number Four is False.)

FIVE – If the risk-free interest rate is 3%, the market rate is 9% and a firm's beta is 2, the estimated cost of capital using the CAPM approach is 15%.

Answer – CAPM measures the estimated cost of capital by adding the risk-free rate to the difference between the market rate and the risk-free interest rate times the firm's beta. In this case, the firm's estimated cost of equity is equal to 15% (3% + [(9% - 3%) x beta]). (Number Five is True.)

SIX – Assume a firm has $500,000 in debt at a before-tax rate of 6%, $2,000,000 in equity at a cost of 10%, and a marginal tax rate of 40%. The firm's weighted average cost of capital is equal to 9.2%.

Answer – The weighted average cost of capital is calculated by summing the cost of the various sources of capital weighted by their proportion of the total. In this case, the weighted average cost of capital is 8.72% [($500,000/$2,500,000) x [6% x (100% - 40%)] + $2,000,000/$2,500,000 x 10%]. (Number Six is False.)

RISK MANAGEMENT

(1) There is an inverse relationship between risk and return. The greater the amount of risk the higher the expected return. Investors are considered to be **risk averse** which means that they must be compensated for increased levels of risk.

(2) When evaluating investments, management generally considers expected returns and risk.
  (A) Expected returns are often estimated based on prior history using the average return.
  (B) Measures of risk also are developed based on historical returns. The most common estimates of risk come from the variance or standard deviation of historical returns.

(3) The expected return of a portfolio of investments is calculated as the weighted average of the expected returns of the assets making up the portfolio. The variance of portfolio depends on three factors:
  (A) The percentage of the portfolio invested in each asset.
  (B) The variance of the returns of each individual asset.
  (C) The covariance among the returns of assets in the portfolio.

(4) Portfolios allow investors to diversify away unsystematic risk. Unsystematic risk is the risk that exists for one particular investment or a group of like investments. Systematic risk is the risk of the market as a whole; it cannot be diversified away. The systematic risk of a particular investment is measured by the investment's **beta.** It is measured as follows:

$$b_i = \frac{\sigma_{im}}{\sigma_m^2}$$

  where:

  σ_{im} = the covariance of the investment's returns with the returns of the overall portfolio.

  σ_m^2 = the portfolio's variance.

(5) An individual investor has a risk preference function which describes the investor's trade-off between risk and return. A portfolio that falls on the line described by this function is an **efficient portfolio.**

(6) Interest represents the cost of borrowing funds. Interest rates are determined by the amount of risk involved in making the loan.
  (A) Included in this risk are:
    (1) **Credit or default risk**—the risk that the firm will default on payment of interest or principal.
    (2) **Interest rate risk**—the risk that the value of the loan or bond will decline due to an increase in interest rates.
    (3) **Market risk**—the risk that the value of a bond or loan will decline due to a decline in the aggregate value of all assets.
  (B) The **stated interest rate** on a loan is the contractual rate charged by the lender, and the **effective annual interest rate** is the true annual return to the lender. The simple annual rate usually varies from the effective annual rate because interest is often compounded annually.
  (C) The term structure of interest rates describes the relationship between long-term, intermediate-term, and short-term interest rates. This relationship is illustrated with a yield curve.

        (1)   **Normal yield curve**—an upward sloping curve in which short-term rates are less than intermediate-term rates which are less than long-term rates.

        (2)   **Inverted yield curve**—a downward-sloping curve in which short-term rates are greater than intermediate-term rates which are greater than long-term rates.

        (3)   **Flat yield curve**—a curve in which short-term, intermediate-term and long-term rates are about the same.

        (4)   **Humped yield curve**—a curve in which intermediate-term rates are higher than both short-term and long-term rates.

  (D) **Liquidity preference theory** states that long-term rates should be higher than short-term rates because investors need a premium to entice them to hold less liquid and more price-sensitive securities.

  (E) **Market segmentation theory** states that the Treasury securities markets are segmented by the various financial institutions that purchase the securities.

  (F) **Expectations theory** explains yields on long-term securities as a function of short-term rates. Specifically, long-term rates are equal to the average of short-term rates over the long-term period.

(7) Management often uses derivatives to hedge interest rate risk.

  (A) The following types of derivatives can be used:

        (1)   **Options**—allow the holder to buy (call) or sell (put) a specific or standard commodity or financial instrument.

        (2)   **Forwards**—negotiated contracts to purchase and sell, in the future, a specific quantity of a financial instrument, foreign currency, or commodity at a specified price.

        (3)   **Futures**—forward-based standardized contracts to take delivery of a specified financial instrument, foreign currency, or commodity at a price specified at origination of the contract.

        (4)   **Currency swaps**—forward-based contracts in which two parties agree to exchange an obligation to pay cash flows in one currency for an obligation to pay in another currency.

        (5)   **Interest rate swaps**—forward-based contracts in which two parties agree to swap streams of payments over a specified period of time.

        (6)   **Swapation**—An option that provides the holder with the right to enter into a swap in the future.

  (B) For financial statement purposes, derivatives are valued at fair market value. However, if the derivative qualifies as a hedge, changes in value are used to offset changes in the value of the hedged items.

  (C) Methods of valuing derivatives

        (1)   The **Black-Scholes option-pricing model** is a mathematical model for estimating the value of stock options.

        (2)   The **zero-coupon method** is used to determine the fair value of interest rate swaps.

PROBLEMS AND SOLUTIONS
RISK MANAGEMENT

ONE – Investors are generally considered to be risk neutral. (True or False?)

Answer – A risk neutral investor is indifferent to levels of risk. Most financial theories consider investors to be risk averse, which means that investors will accept higher levels of risk but they must be compensated in terms of increased returns. (Number One is False.)

TWO – A firm has a portfolio with the following three assets and expected returns:

Asset 1	$2,000,000	6%
Asset 2	$2,000,000	9%
Asset 3	$4,000,000	12%

The expected return of the portfolio is equal to 9%. (True or False?)

Answer – The expected return of a portfolio is calculated as the weighted average of the expected returns of the individual assets making up the portfolio. In this case, the expected return is 9.75% ((6% x 2/8) + (9% x 2/8) + (12% x 4/8)). (Number Two is False.)

THREE – A balanced portfolio can be used to diversify away unsystematic risk. (True or False?)

Answer – Unsystematic risk is the risk of an individual investment or a group of related investments. Systematic risk is the risk of the market as a whole. A balanced portfolio can diversify away unsystematic risk but it cannot diversify away systematic risk. (Number Three is True.)

FOUR – The unsystematic risk of a particular investment is measured by the investment's beta. (True or False.)

Answer – Beta is calculated as the covariance of a particular investment's return with the return of the overall portfolio divided by the variance of the portfolio. Therefore, it measures the systematic risk of the investment not the unsystematic risk. (Number Four is False.)

FIVE – The risk that a bond will decline in value due to an increase in interest rates is referred to as market risk. (True or False?)

Answer – Market risk is the risk of loss on a loan or bond due to a decline in the aggregate value of all assets. Interest rate risk is the risk of loss on a loan or bond due to an increase in interest rates. (Number Five is False.)

SIX – Liquidity preference theory would predict the yield curve to be normal. (True or False?)

> *Answer – Liquidity preference theory states that investors must be paid a premium for less liquid (longer term) investments. Accordingly, the theory would predict short-term rates to be lower than intermediate-term rates which would be lower than long-term rates. This describes the normal yield curve. (Number Six is True.)*

SEVEN – To hedge an increase in short-term interest rates, a firm may use the strategy of selling Treasury bills on the futures market. (True or False?)

> *Answer – Selling Treasury bills on the futures market locks in the current short-term rate. Accordingly, this is an effective strategy for hedging increases in short-term rates. (Number Seven is True.)*

CAPITAL BUDGETING

(1) **Capital budgeting** refers to any technique used to determine the financial wisdom of a long-term investment. Two capital budgeting techniques (net present value method and the internal rate of return method) are considered theoretically superior because (1) they take into account the time value of money and (2) they rely entirely on future cash flows.

  (A) **Net present value method** computes the present value of the expected cash inflows from an investment based on the buyer's desired (or required) rate of return. Sometimes, the rate of return is the cost of the capital that will be expended.

     (1) The difference between the present value and the cost is the net present value. If present value is above cost, investment has a positive net present value which indicates that it is a good investment.

     (2) Present value is the most that would be paid for an investment. Any payment over present value would create a negative net present value.

  (B) **Internal rate of return method** (sometimes called the time-adjusted rate of return method is based on computing the exact rate of return that is being earned on an investment at a certain price.

     (1) The cost is divided by the estimated cash flows (either a single amount or one payment in an annuity) to determine the present value factor.

     (2) The present value factor is found on a chart which indicates the exact rate of return being earned. If it is equal to or above the company's desired rate of return, the investment is a good buy.

  (C) The net present value method is often considered superior to the internal rate of return method because the internal rate of return method assumes that funds generated can be reinvested at the internal rate of return of the project. Accordingly, in evaluating mutually exclusive projects, the internal rate of return method may give a suboptimal result.

(2) Some companies use capital budgeting techniques although they are considered to be inferior methods.

  (A) The **payback method** determines the length of the time that will be required for company to get its initial cash outlay back. A short payback period is considered to be better than a long payback period. Some companies require all investments to have a payback period that is within a certain time limit. However, it does not take the time value of money into account.

     (1) Cash flows can be approximated by eliminating (adding) depreciation expense from net income.

  (B) The **discounted payback method** is similar to the payback method but the future cash flows are discounted to their present values in computing the result. This is only a slight advantage over the regular payback method as neither method considers the overall profitability of the investment.

  (C) **Accounting rate of return** is computed by dividing the cost of the investment into the expected annual net income. In some cases, the current year book value is used rather than cost.

     (1) Net income can be approximated by subtracting depreciation from anticipated annual cash flows.

(D) The **residual income method** weighs the value of an investment by the size of its residual income. The cost of the investment is multiplied by a desired profit rate. Any expected income above that desired profit figure is known as residual income.

(3) In estimating cash flow, the following factors must be considered:
  (A) Remember to focus on cash flow not accounting income.
  (B) Income taxes must be included.
  (C) Depreciation is a tax deductible expense that does not reduce cash flows.
  (D) Terminal disposal price of the assets must be considered.
  (E) Use of additional working capital is an initial investment that will be recouped at the end of the investment's useful life.

(4) Risk is considered in capital budgeting using a number of techniques.
  (A) **Probability analysis** involves estimating a number of different possible cash flow outcomes and weighting each by its probability of occurrence. Then, the weighted values are summed to get the expected value.
  (B) The **risk-adjusted discount rate** technique involves adjusting the discount rate to reflect the risk of the project. High risk projects are assigned a higher hurdle discount rate.
  (C) The **time-adjusted discount rate** technique involves assigning higher hurdle discount rates to cash flows that are further in the future.
  (D) **Sensitivity analysis**, **scenario analysis**, and **simulation** techniques involve developing alternative forecasts of cash flows and evaluation of the results.
  (E) **Decision trees** are used to evaluate investments by considering the fact that most investment decisions involve a series of decisions in the future, and future cash flows are tied to the results of those decisions.
  (F) The **real options technique** views an investment as purchasing an option. It values the investment at its net present value plus or minus its option value.

PROBLEMS AND SOLUTIONS
CAPITAL BUDGETING

ONE – A company is trying to decide whether to spend $30,000 for a new piece of equipment. The payback method suggests that this investment is a wise course of action. The internal rate of return method indicates that the investment should not be made. The company will likely acquire the equipment for $30,000. (True or False?)

Answer – The internal rate of return method is considered superior to the payback method because it takes into account all cash flows as well as the time value of money. Since that method indicates that the investment is not appropriate at that price, the company should not acquire the equipment for $30,000. (Number One is False.)

TWO – A company is considering the purchase of equipment for $40,000. This investment will generate annual cash inflows of $10,000 per year for the next 6 years. The company desires a rate of return of 12 percent. At that rate, the present value of $1 in six years is .507. At that rate, the present value of an ordinary annuity of $1 over six years is 4.111. The investment has a positive net present value of $1,110. (True or False?)

Answer – Because $10,000 will be received each year, the company should utilize the present value of an ordinary annuity to compute a present value of $41,110 ($10,000 x 4.111). This present value figure exceeds the $40,000 cost by $1,110. A positive net present value such as this indicates that the acquisition is appropriate at the price quoted. (Number Two is True.)

THREE - A company is considering the purchase of equipment for $65,000. This investment will generate annual cash inflows of $10,000 per year for 10 years. The present value of an ordinary annuity of $1 over ten years at a 9 percent rate of return is 6.42. The present value of an ordinary annuity of $1 over ten years at a 10 percent rate of return is 6.14. This investment is expected to generate an internal rate of return of less than 9 percent. (True or False?)

Answer – The cost of the asset is $65,000 while the annual cash flows are $10,000 giving a present value factor of 6.50 ($65,000/$10,000) for the ten-year period. At 9 percent, the rate is 6.42 and, at 10 percent, the rate is 6.14. The internal rate of return is just below 9 percent. (Number Three is True.)

FOUR – A company is considering the purchase of equipment for $80,000. The company would like to make a return on its investment of 10 percent. In the initial year, the equipment will increase net income by $11,000. The residual income is $3,000. (True or False?)

Answer – Based on the investment of $80,000, the desired profit is $8,000 per year (10 percent). Because $11,000 is to be earned, the additional $3,000 is termed residual income. (Number Four is True.)

FIVE – A consideration of risk may be incorporated into capital budgeting techniques in a number of ways. One way is through the use of scenario analysis. (True or False?)

Answer - Scenario analysis involves developing forecasts of future cash flows based on alternative economic conditions. It is an effective way to incorporate a consideration of risk. (Number Five is True.)

QUANTITATIVE METHODS

(1) **Regression analysis** is a mathematical measure of how one dependent variable is affected by another independent variable. It is an attempt to determine whether a cause and effect relationship exists so that future outcomes can be predicted.

    (A) For example, a company might determine that each $1 increase in radio advertisement (the independent variable) will produce a $3 increase in sales revenue (the dependent variable).

(2) **High-low method** can be used to approximate future outcomes. It is not nearly as accurate as regression analysis but it is simpler and quicker to use.

    (A) Past results are gathered and only the highest and lowest outputs are selected. Both the monetary difference and the quantity difference between these two points are measured.

    (B) Dividing the monetary difference by the quantity difference gives the variable cost per unit. Any amount spent at the lowest level that is not explained by this variable cost is assumed to be the associated fixed cost.

(3) **Correlation analysis** measures how much of the change in one variable is caused by another variable (and not by other factors). A **coefficient of correlation** is computed for this purpose. If the coefficient is + 1, it means that all movement in one variable is caused by the movement in the same direction of the other variable (for example, as a person's salary goes up, the amount that person pays for a car will go up). If the coefficient is - 1, all movement in one variable is caused by the movement of the other variable in the opposite direction (for example, as the price of food rises, the amount of food purchased goes down). If the coefficient is zero, there is no relationship between the variables.

(4) **Probability analysis** is used to select one expected value based on several possibilities.

    (A) Expected value is determined based on a weighted-average calculation.

    (B) Each potential outcome is multiplied by its percentage of possibility. All of the results are added to arrive at a single expected value.

PROBLEMS AND SOLUTIONS
QUANTITATIVE METHODS

ONE – A college professor proves that a person's grade on the CPA Exam will increase as the number of hours studied for the exam increases. The professor probably used regression analysis in making this startling discovery. (True or False?)

Answer – Regression analysis mathematically measures how one dependent variable (a person's score on the CPA Exam) is affected by another variable (the number of hours of study). Thus, a change in one variable should lead to a change in the second so that future outcomes can be predicted. (Number One is True.)

TWO – During January, a company spends $14,000 to manufacture 8,000 units of a product. The following month the company produces 5,000 more units at a cost of $9,500. Using the high-low method, the fixed cost for manufacturing this item is $2,000. (True or False?)

Answer – By dividing the change in cost ($4,500) by the change in units (3,000), an accountant can predict that the variable cost is $1.50 per unit. Applying that cost to the 5,000 units produced in the most recent month, the accountant anticipates that the total variable cost was $7,500. Since the total cost for that period was actually $9,500, the remaining $2,000 is assumed to be the fixed cost associated with this product. (Number Two is True.)

THREE – A person predicts that a CPA Exam candidate has a 40 percent chance of making an 90 on a particular part of the exam, a 30 percent chance of making a 75, and a 30 percent chance of making a 60. The best estimation of this person's score is 76.5. (True or False?)

Answer – According to probability analysis, an expected value can be determined as a weighted average. The 90 is multiplied by 40 percent to get 36; the 75 is multiplied by 30 percent to get 22.5, and the 60 is multiplied by 30 percent to get 18. These three results are summed to get an expected value of 76.5. (Number Three is True.)

PERFORMANCE MEASURES

(1) Performance measures are the ways a firm measures the outcomes and activities related to achieving its strategy.

(2) There are two primary types of performance measures: financial and nonfinancial.

(3) The **balanced-scorecard** is a strategic performance measurement and management framework that measures performance in the following four perspectives:

    (A) **Financial perspective**—focuses on return on investment and other supporting financial measures.

    (B) **Customer perspective**—focuses on performance important to customers, with measures such as customer satisfaction and customer retention.

    (C) **Internal business processes perspective**—focuses on operating effectively and efficiently and includes measures such as number of defects and cycle time.

    (D) **Learning and growth perspective**—focuses on performance related to employees, infrastructure, teaming and capabilities, and includes measures such as training per employee, employee satisfaction, and information technology expenditures per employee.

(4) Components of the balanced scorecard.

    (A) Strategic objectives—a statement of what the strategy must achieve and what is critical to its success.

    (B) Performance measures—describes how success will be measured.

    (C) Baseline performance—the current level of performance.

    (D) Targets—the level of performance or rate of improvement needed.

    (E) Strategic initiatives—key action programs required to achieve strategic objectives.

(5) **Strategy maps** are diagrams of the cause-and-effect relationships between strategic objectives.

(6) **Value-based management** involves the use of value-based metrics in a strategic management system. Such metrics include:

    (A) Return on investment (ROI).

    (B) Economic profit.

    (C) Economic value added.

    (D) Cash flow ROI.

    (E) Residual income.

(7) **DuPont ROI** analysis recognizes that return on investment is the product of return on sales and asset turnover. It is calculated as follows:

ROI = (Net income/sales) x [Sales/Total assets (invested capital)]

(8) **Residual income** is equal to net income (or operating income after taxes) minus a charge for the cost of capital invested in a division.

(9) **Economic profit** is equal to accounting profit minus the cost of capital.

(10) **Economic value added (EVA)** is equal to net operating profit after taxes (NOPAT) minus the after tax weighted average cost of capital (WACC) multiplied by total assets – current liabilities.

(11) **Free cash flow** is equal to NOPAT + Depreciation and amortization – Capital expenditures – The change in working capital requirements.

(12) **Traditional financial statement measures.**

(A) Gross margin.
Gross profit/Net sales

(B) Profit margin.
Net income after interest and taxes/Net sales

(C) Return on equity.
Net income after interest and taxes/Average common stockholders' equity

(D) Receivables turnover.
Net credit sales/Average accounts receivable

(E) Inventory turnover.
Cost of goods sold/Average inventory

(F) Fixed asset turnover.
Sales/Average net fixed assets

(G) Total asset turnover.
Sales/Average total assets

(H) Current ratio.
Current assets/Current liabilities

(I) Quick ratio.
(Current assets – Inventory)/Current liabilities

(J) Debt to total assets.
Total liabilities/Total assets

(K) Debt to equity.
Total liabilities/Total equity

(L) Times interest earned.
Earnings before interest and taxes/Interest expense

(M) Price/earnings ratio.
Stock price per share/Earnings per share

(13) Benchmarking is the continuous process of comparing the levels of performance against the best levels of performance.

PROBLEMS AND SOLUTIONS
PERFORMANCE MEASURES

ONE – The balanced-scorecard is best characterized as a financial report card for a firm. (True or False?)

> *Answer - A balanced-scorecard is a strategic performance measurement and management system that uses two types of measures financial and nonfinancial. The use of both types of measures is how it gets its name. (Number One is False.)*

TWO – The strategic objectives component of the balanced-scorecard is a statement of what the strategy must achieve and what is critical to its success. (True or False?)

> *Answer – The strategic objectives component of the balanced-scorecard describes the particular strategy and how it may be achieved. (Number Two is True.)*

THREE – The DuPont ROI breaks return on investment into the two components of return on sales and asset turnover. (True or False?)

Answer – The major contribution of the DuPont ROI model is the fact that it breaks ROI into its two components: return on sales and asset turnover. (Number Three is True.)

FOUR – Residual income is a commonly used value-based measure, which is equal to net income minus preferred dividends. (True or False?)

Answer – Residual income is a commonly used value based measure. However, it is calculated as operating income after taxes minus a charge for the cost of capital invested in the division. (Number Four is False.)

FIVE – Economic value added (EVA) is a commonly used nonfinancial measure. It measures the qualitative increase in the value of the products produced by the firm. (True or False?)

Answer – Economic value added is a commonly used value based measure. It is calculated as follows:

NOPAT – [WACC x (total assets – current liabilities)]

(Number Five is False.)

QUALITY CONTROL PRINCIPLES

(1) **Total quality management (TQM)** focuses on managing the organization to excel in quality.

(2) **Six-sigma quality** is a methodology for statistical process control that focuses on reducing defects to six standard deviations from the mean or 3.4 defects per million parts.

(3) **ISO quality standards**
  (A) **ISO 9000 series**—a series of quality standards agreed upon by the International Organization for Standardization (ISO).
  (B) **ISO 14000 series**—a series of standards related to environmental control.

(4) **Quality tools and methods**
  (A) **Total quality control (management)** is the application of quality principles to all company activities and processes.
  (B) **Kaizen** is the Japanese art of continuous improvement.
  (C) **Cause-and-effect (fishbone or Ishikawa) diagrams** identify the potential causes of defects.
  (D) A **Pareto chart** is a bar graph that ranks causes of process variations by the degree of impact on quality.
  (E) **Lean manufacturing**—an operational strategy focused on achieving the shortest possible cycle time by eliminating waste.
  (F) **Theory of constraints**—refers to methods to maximize operating income when faced with some bottleneck operations.

(5) **Cost of quality** is based on the philosophy that failures have an underlying cause, prevention is cheaper than failures, and cost of quality performance can be measured. Cost of quality has four basic components:
  (A) **Prevention cost**—the cost of preventing defects, including quality training, quality engineering, audits of the quality system, etc.
  (B) **Appraisal cost**—the cost of testing and inspection.
  (C) **Internal failure cost**—the cost of products found to be defective and discovered prior to shipment to the customer.
  (D) **External failure cost**—the cost of defective products that are shipped to customers, (e.g., returns, product liability, etc).

PROBLEMS AND SOLUTIONS
QUALITY CONTROL PRINCIPLES

ONE – A major way to reduce defects is to focus on their cause. A Ishikawa diagram is useful for this process. (True or False?)

> *Answer – An Ishikawa diagram is a cause and effect tool that attempts to identify the cause of defects. (Number One is True.)*

TWO – In cost of quality methodology, the cost of product liability is classified as an internal failure cost. (True or False?)

Answer – In cost of quality methodology, internal failure cost includes the cost of products found to be defective and discovered prior to shipment to the customer. External failure cost is the cost of defective products that are shipped to customers, and includes cost of returns and product liability. (Number Two is False.)

FINANCIAL PLANNING

(1) Financial planning involves:
   (A) Analyzing the investment and financing alternatives.
   (B) Forecasting the future consequences of the alternatives.
   (C) Deciding which alternatives to undertake.
   (D) Measuring subsequent performance.
(2) Financial planning is facilitated with a financial planning model, which generates projected financial statements, operating and financial budgets, and scenario analysis.
(3) Developing sales **forecasts**.
   (A) Qualitative techniques.
      (1) Executive opinions.
      (2) Sales-force polling.
      (3) Customer surveys.
   (B) Quantitative techniques.
      (1) **Moving average**—uses average for most recent periods.
      (2) **Exponential smoothing**—moving average with more recent sales weighted more heavily.
      (3) **Decomposition of time series**—extracts seasonal and cyclical factors to arrive at trend and then reintroduces the seasonal and cyclical factors to get forecast.
      (4) **Regression analysis**—estimate sales based on observed relationships between sales and one or more predictors.
      (5) **Markov techniques**—estimate sales based on consumer behavior.
(4) Budgeting.
   (A) **Master budget** is made up of:
      (1) The **operating budget**—the budgeted income statement and supporting schedules.
      (2) The **financial budget**--the capital budget, cash budget, and the budgeted balance sheet and statement of cash flows.
   (B) **Flexible budget**—budget adjusted for sales volume.
   (C) **Responsibility accounting**—allocates revenues, assets, and costs to managers that the manager can control.

PROBLEMS AND SOLUTIONS
FINANCIAL PLANNING

ONE – The financial budget includes the budgeted income statement for a company. (True or False?)

Answer - The financial budget includes the capital budget, and the budgeted balance sheet and statement of cash flows. The operating budget includes the budgeted income statement. (Number One is False.)

TWO – The Markov technique involves forecasting sales by examining consumer behavior. (True or False?)

>   *Answer – Markov techniques attempt to forecast consumer purchasing by considering factors such as brand loyalty and brand switching behavior. (Number Two is True.)*

THREE – The "y" variable in a regression equation to forecast sales would be the variable that has found to be useful in predicting sales. (True or False?)

>   *Answer – The "y" variable in a regression equation is the dependent variable. In a model used to predict sales, the "y" variable would be sales. The "x" variables would be the predictors of sales. (Number Three is False.)*

COST-VOLUME-PROFIT ANALYSIS

(1) All of the costs incurred by a company in producing a good or service for resell purposes can be divided into two categories.

    (A) **Fixed costs** such as rent, property taxes, depreciation, insurance, etc. do not change during a period unless company's level of production goes outside of a relevant range.

        (1) This total cost is assumed to be a set figure. However, if the number of units increases or decreases significantly, changes in the company can affect the amount. For example, if a new building has to be acquired to produce additional units, both depreciation and insurance will go up even though they are viewed normally as fixed costs.

    (B) **Variable costs** such as direct materials, direct labor, electricity, etc. will change as production or sales change. The variable cost for an item might be $3.00 for every unit so that the total would depend on the number of units.

(2) **Direct (or variable) costing** can be used to compute projected net income when some type of change is being considered. It is used for internal decision making purposes.

    (A) Direct costing is not recognized as a generally accepted accounting principle (GAAP) so it cannot be used for external reporting purposes.

    (B) Direct costing anticipates future net income by subtracting both variable costs and fixed costs from revenue.

        (1) Sales minus variable costs is frequently referred to as the company's **contribution margin**.

        (2) In order to make projections at different levels, variable cost is stated as a percentage of sales whereas fixed cost is a set figure. Thus, the impact on income created by changes in factors such as sales price or fixed cost can be measured.

    (C) A company's **breakeven point** is the amount of revenues that must be generated to exactly equal expenses so that neither a profit nor loss results.

    (D) **Margin of safety** is the amount by which current (or projected) revenues exceed revenues at the breakeven point.

(3) For external reporting purposes, **absorption costing** is used.

    (A) In absorption costing, the cost of manufactured inventory includes all direct material, direct labor, and factory overhead regardless of whether the cost is fixed or variable.

    (B) Absorption costing will usually produce a different net income figure because fixed factory overhead is included as a cost of inventory (a product cost). Thus, this cost does not affect net income until the period in which the item is sold.

    (C) In contrast, direct costing views fixed factory overhead as an expense (a period cost) so that it affects income immediately.

(4) Variable and fixed cost patterns can also be used to produce a **flexible budgeting system**.

    (A) This budget is really a formula: any cost is anticipated as its fixed cost component plus its variable cost which is calculated as a percentage of revenues.

    (B) A budgeted figure can be developed for costs based on any level of output so that comparisons of budgeted to actual figures are more realistic.

PROBLEMS AND SOLUTIONS
COST-VOLUME-PROFIT ANALYSIS

ONE – A company has a contribution margin of 30 percent and fixed costs of $280,000. If the company generates revenues of $900,000, it will produce net income of $20,000. (True or False?)

> *Answer – Contribution margin (sales minus variable costs) is 30 percent of sales or $270,000. Because the fixed cost total is only $250,000, a net income of $20,000 results. (Number One is True.)*

TWO – A company has a contribution margin of 40 percent and fixed costs of $300,000. If the company generates revenues of $900,000, it has a margin of safety of $60,000. (True or False?)

> *Answer – Margin of safety is the amount by which current sales exceed sales at the breakeven point. At breakeven, no profit or loss is made because the contribution margin is equal to fixed costs. Based on the information given, 40 percent of sales must equal $300,000 at the breakeven point. Thus, the amount of sales that will generate neither a profit nor a loss will be $750,000 ($300,000/40 percent). Since current sales are $900,000, the margin of safety is $150,000. (Number Two is False.)*

THREE – A company has a contribution margin of 30 percent and fixed costs of $360,000. By increasing fixed costs by $80,000, the company's contribution margin can be raised to 40 percent. This change would decrease the breakeven point by $100,000. (True or False?)

> *Answer – At the breakeven point, contribution margin is equal to total fixed costs so that neither a profit nor a loss results. Currently, the contribution margin is 30 percent of sales revenue and fixed cost totals $360,000; thus, the breakeven point is $1.2 million ($360,000/30 percent). If the suggested change is made, contribution margin will be 40 percent and fixed costs $440,000 so that the breakeven point becomes $1.1 million ($440,000/40 percent). The breakeven point will drop by $100,000. (Number Three is True.)*

COST ACCOUNTING

(1) Cost accounting refers to any accounting method by which costs are accumulated during production so that the cost of the finished goods can be determined.

    (A) During production, all costs are accumulated in a Work-in-Process (WIP) account. When units are completed, their cost (cost of goods manufactured) is transferred to a Finished Goods account. When items are sold, cost is transferred to a Cost of Goods Sold account.

    (B) Three separate cost figures are accumulated in WIP account.

        (1) **Direct material** is the cost of any materials that are traceable to the product being manufactured.

        (2) **Direct labor** is the cost of labor that is used in the actual manufacturing process.

        (3) **Factory overhead** is any manufacturing cost other than direct material and direct labor.

    (C) Direct labor and factory overhead are sometimes combined and called **conversion costs**. Direct materials and direct labor are sometimes combined and called **prime costs**.

    (D) The costs incurred for the various types of factory overhead can take a significant amount of time to accumulate. To get usable cost figures more quickly, factory overhead is often estimated (called "applied").

        (1) A rate is determined based on some cause and effect relationship. A change in one item (the number of units, for example, or the direct labor cost) is identified that causes a change in factory overhead.

        (2) A factor (such as direct labor cost) that is believed to affect factory overhead is called a **cost driver**. As this factor increases during a period, more factory overhead cost is applied to the WIP account based on the rate in use.

        (3) Any final difference between the amount of factory overhead applied to the WIP account and the actual amount incurred is usually recorded in the Cost of Goods Sold account.

(2) **Job order cost accounting** is a system where a separate WIP account is maintained for each individual job. In this way, the resulting cost figures for a particular job should be very accurate. When the job is finished, its specific cost is transferred to finished goods. This method is used when the items being produced are individually unique such as a house, for example, or a boat.

(3) **Process cost accounting** is a system where a total cost is kept for a large number of items being mass produced. The average cost of the units is determined but the cost of any specific item is unknown.

    (A) Usually the manufacturing process is divided into departments and a separate WIP account is maintained for the items as they move through each department.

    (B) An average cost is determined for each type of cost: direct materials, direct labor, and factory overhead. In addition, if a department is any but the first, costs transferred in from previous departments must also be monitored.

    (C) For each separate type of cost, the cost is divided by the equivalent units of work done to get an average cost figure. However, the average cost per unit can be determined in either of two ways: FIFO or weighted average. These two methods compute both the costs to be included and the number of units in a different fashion.

(D) The difference in these two methods is in the handling of any beginning work-in-process, units which were started in the previous period but completed in the current period.

    (1) In a **weighted average system**, costs include all current costs plus any costs brought into the period within the beginning work-in-process. The equivalent units of work is all work that has been done on the inventory by the end of the current period: 100 percent for the finished units plus the percentage completed to date on the ending work-in-process.

    (2) In a **FIFO system**, costs include only current costs. No cost from the previous period is included. The total units of work done is just the work done in the current period: 100 percent of the finished units plus the percentage completed for the ending work-in-process less any work done on beginning work-in-process during the previous period. Removing the beginning work in process leaves just the work done in the current period

(E) Units can get spoiled or lost during production. These units can be viewed as an additional type of inventory (lost units). A cost figure can be determined in the same manner as for other inventory. The handling of that cost figure depends on the cause of the loss.

    (1) If the loss is normal, the cost of these lost units is viewed as a product cost. It is transferred to finished goods (if loss occurred at end of production) or allocated between finished goods and work-in-process if lost during production.

    (2) If the loss is abnormal, the cost of these lost units is a period cost. It is recorded as a loss in the current period.

(F) Companies that have a very short production cycle will often use a **backflush** system. All costs are initially recorded as Cost of Goods Sold. At the end of a period, the cost of ending inventory is determined and backed out of Cost of Goods Sold and into Inventory.

(4) **Activity-based costing** (ABC) is a system for determining the cost of an output. It is often used where factory overhead is a major component of the cost (such as in an organization providing a service rather than a physical product).

(A) Every separate activity from the inception of a product to its completion is identified. Overhead costs are assigned based on these activities rather than within departments. Assignment of costs is not limited to the manufacturing portion of the process but includes every activity.

(B) For each activity, a **cost driver** is identified. That is the factor that is most responsible for the creation of factory overhead. Thus, overhead should be assigned to each product in a much more accurate fashion. Rather than assigning overhead costs based on two or three departments, 20 or 30 separate cost drivers might be used. Activities utilizing the same cost driver can be grouped into cost pools to simplify the process.

(C) Activities are classified as either **value adding** (making the product better) or **nonvalue adding** (an activity such as storage that does not improve the product). Company should work to reduce or eliminate all nonvalue adding activities.

(5) In a manufacturing process, two or more products will often be produced from one process. For example, crude oil is used to produces gasoline, kerosene, heating oil, plastics, etc.

(A) The **joint costs** (the cost of the crude oil, for example) must be allocated to the various products in some logical fashion.

(B) Many methods can be used to allocate such joint production costs. For example, costs can be assigned based on the number of units or the final sales value of each product. Probably the most common approach is the **relative sales value at split off method**.

   (1) All joint costs are assigned to the individual products based on their relative sales value at the time the items are separated into their own production processes.

   (2) A variation of this method is the **net realizable value method**. Costs required by a product after it is split off are determined and subtracted from the final sales value to get the net realizable value of the product at the point when it is divided from the other products. This net realizable value is then used to allocate the joint costs.

(6) In manufacturing an item, a second product may be produced. If it is considered a joint product, the joint costs must be divided as indicated above. If the second product has only a small sales value, it will be viewed as a **by-product**. The company may choose any of a number of different methods to account for the cost of a by-product and any eventual revenues generated from it.

   (A) One technique is to assign no portion of any joint product costs to the by-product. When it is sold, the entire amount received is reported as a miscellaneous revenue or as a reduction in cost of goods sold.

   (B) A second possibility is to assign a portion of any joint costs to the by-product equal to its net realizable value (eventual sales price less any costs necessary for the sale). When sold, this inventory balance is removed so that no revenue is recognized. Less cost remains to be assigned to any joint products.

PROBLEMS AND SOLUTIONS
COST ACCOUNTING

ONE – A company starts the period with 10,000 units of inventory in work-in-process. These units are 30 percent complete at the time. During the current period, the company begins work on another 40,000 units. By the end of the period, 34,000 units have been completed and shipped to finished goods. The remaining 16,000 units are still in work-in-process although they are 80 percent completed. If a weighted-average system is in use, 46,800 equivalent units of work is assumed to have been done. If a FIFO system is in use, 43,800 equivalent units of work is assumed to have been done. (True or False?)

Answer – With a weighted-average system, all work is included. By the end of the year, 34,000 units have been completed and another 16,000 units are 80 percent complete (12,800 equivalent units of work). Thus, for the period, the equivalent number of units of work is 46,800 (34,000 plus 12,800). When a FIFO system is in use, only work done in the current period is included. Therefore, beginning work-in-process (3,000 equivalent units of work or 10,000 x 30 percent) is subtracted from the total work (46,800) to leave 43,800 units of the work that was done in the current period. (Number One is True.)

TWO – A company starts the period with $13,000 assigned to beginning work-in-process. During the period, an additional $70,000 is assigned to work-in-process. If a weighted-average system is applied, the cost used in determining cost per unit will be $83,000. If a FIFO system is used, the cost used in determining cost per unit will be $70,000. (True or False?)

Answer – When a weighted-average system is utilized, all costs are included so that $83,000 is appropriate. For a FIFO system, only the current costs are included so the appropriate figure is $70,000. (Number Two is True.)

THREE – A company starts the year with no beginning inventory. During the year, the company spends $72,000 for production costs. The company starts 40,000 units of inventory and completes 30,000. Of the remainder, 8,000 units are 50 percent complete. The other 2,000 units were lost at the end of the process. If this loss was considered abnormal, the company should immediately reduce net income by $4,000. (True or False?)

Answer – Since the company has no beginning inventory, a weighted-average system and a FIFO system will yield the same results. The company has a cost of $72,000 and equivalent units of 36,000 (30,000 units completed plus 8,000 units 50 percent complete [4,000 equivalent units] plus 2,000 units 100 percent complete because they were lost at the end of the process). The cost per unit is $2.00 ($72,000/36,000 units). Since the loss of the units was abnormal, their cost ($4,000 or 2,000 units x $2.00) is a period cost charged immediately to net income as a loss. (Number Three is True.)

FOUR – Activity-based costing is a method by which manufacturing costs are assigned in a particularly accurate fashion. (True or False?)

Answer – Activity-based costing is primarily used in assigning all overhead costs and not just production costs incurred during the manufacturing process. However, it is viewed as a more accurate method of assigning costs than other, more traditional, approaches. (Number Four is False.)

FIVE – Activity-based costing is associated with applying overhead based on the use of a mathematical direct labor output formula. (True or False?)

Answer – Activity-based costing identifies every separate activity from inception to completion of an output. Overhead is then assigned to each of these activities based on the most logical cause and effect relationship, also known as a cost driver. (Number Five is False.)

SIX – A company spends $100,000 to produce two products: A and Z. After spending another $20,000, A will sell for $140,000. After spending another $10,000, Z will sell for $90,000. Using the net realizable value method, $60,000 of the joint cost should be assigned to A. (True or False?)

Answer – At the point that these two goods are separated, A has a net realizable value of $120,000 (the final sales price of $140,000 less the $20,000 additional production cost required). At the same point, Z has a net realizable value of $80,000 (the final sales price of $90,000 less the $10,000 additional production cost required). The total of these two net realizable values is $200,000 ($120,000 plus $80,000) with A making up 60 percent of that total ($120,000/$200,000). Thus, 60 percent of the $100,000 joint cost will be assigned to A. (Number Six is True.)

SEVEN – A company spends $200,000 to produce B and Y, each of which has an equal sales value of $130,000. In this process, 1,000 pounds of a by-product (M) is also created. M can be sold for $3 per pound after spending $1 per pound for processing. None of the joint costs will be assigned to the by-product and its sales revenue will be reported as miscellaneous income. The profit on product B will be $30,000. (True or False?)

Answer – Since no part of the joint cost is assigned to M, the $200,000 is assigned evenly (based on sales value) to B and to Y. Each is assigned $100,000. If B is sold for $130,000, the profit recognized on that product is $30,000. (Number Seven is True.)

VARIANCE ANALYSIS

(1) In many manufacturing companies, a **standard cost** is determined for materials, labor, and overhead for each item being produced.

    (A) During production, standard (rather than actual) cost is recorded in work-in-process, finished goods, and cost of goods sold.

        (1) In this manner, cost figures can be determined in a timely fashion.

        (2) Differences between actual and standard figures can be determined and investigated, a process known as **variance analysis**. Remedial action can be taken quickly, if needed.

        (3) For identification purposes, differences with actual figures are recorded separately in variance accounts. At the end of the year, any balance in a variance account must be closed out. If the balance is small, it is reclassified to Cost of Goods Sold. If the balance is large, it should be allocated among work-in-process, finished goods, and cost of goods sold.

(2) In analyzing production costs, as many as eight separate variances can be calculated.

    (A) Four of these variances are **spending variances**. Too much (unfavorable) or too little (favorable) was spent for each element of cost. These are identified as a material price variance, labor rate variance, variable factory overhead spending variance, and fixed factory overhead spending variance.

    (B) Four of these variances are **quantity variances**. Too much or too little of a cost element was used in producing each unit. These are identified as a material quantity (or usage) variance, labor efficiency variance, variable factory overhead efficiency variance, and fixed factory overhead volume variance.

(3) Each of the four spending variances can be computed using three steps.

    (A) First, the actual quantity of the cost element used during the period (such as actual pounds of material put into production or actual hours worked) is multiplied by the actual unit cost (price per pound or labor cost per hour).

    (B) Second, the actual quantity of the cost element used during the period is multiplied by the standard unit cost.

    (C) The difference in these two steps is the spending variance.

        (1) For fixed factory overhead, the second computed figure is simply the single fixed overhead figure anticipated for the period.

        (2) For the material spending variance, the amount of material bought should be used if it is different than the amount of material put into production.

(4) Each of the four quantity variances can be computed using three steps.

    (A) First, the actual quantity of the cost element used during the period is multiplied by the standard unit cost.

    (B) Second, the standard quantity of the cost element is multiplied by the standard unit cost. The standard quantity is the amount that should have been used based on the actual level of production.

    (C) The difference in these two steps is the quantity variance.

        (1) For fixed factory overhead, the first computed figure is the single fixed overhead figure anticipated for the period.

(5) Four **factory overhead variances** are computed above. Two spending variances are determined and two quantity variances.

(A) There is also a three-variance method which is the same basic process except that the two fixed variances are combined into a single fixed overhead **volume variance.**

(B) There is also a two-variance method which is the same basic process except that the two variable overhead variances and the fixed overhead spending variance are all combined into a single variance which is referred to as the **controllable factory overhead variance**. The remaining fixed factory overhead variance is still used but it is now called the **noncontrollable factory overhead variance.**

PROBLEMS AND SOLUTIONS
VARIANCE ANALYSIS

ONE – A company expects to produce 1,000 units of a product. Each unit should take 2 pounds of material at $2.00 per pound. The company actually produces 1,100 units. The company uses 2,220 pounds of material that had a cost of $1.95 per pound or a total of $4,329. The company has a favorable material price variance of $111. (True or False?)

Answer – The company spent $4,329 for the materials acquired. The company expected to spend $2.00 per pound for each of these 2,220 pounds or $4,440. Since the company spent $111 less than expected ($4,440 minus $4,329), a $111 favorable material price variance exists. (Number One is True.)

TWO – A company expects to produce 1,000 units of a product. Each unit should take 2 pounds of material at $2.00 per pound. The company actually produces 1,100 units. The company uses 2,220 pounds of material that had a cost of $1.95 per pound or a total of $4,329. The company has an unfavorable material quantity (or usage) variance of $39. (True or False?)

Answer – The company used 2,220 pounds of material that should have cost $2.00 per pound or $4,440. Because the company produced 1,100 units, it should have needed only 2,200 pounds of material based on the standard or 2 pounds per unit. At $2.00 per pound, that material would have cost only $4,400. Thus, the material quantity variance is $40 ($4,440 less $4,400). Since additional material was used, the variance is unfavorable. (Number Two is False.)

THREE – A company expects to produce 2,000 units of a product. Each unit should take 4 hours of direct labor at a cost of $10 per hour. The company only produces 1,900 units and pays $11 per hour for 8,000 hours of direct labor. The labor efficiency variance is $4,400 unfavorable. (True or False?)

Answer – The company used 8,000 hours of direct labor that should have cost $10 per hour or $80,000. Because the company produced 1,900 units, it should have required only 7,600 hours based on the standard of four hours per unit. At the standard rate of $10, these hours would have had a cost of $76,000. Therefore, the labor efficiency variance is the $4,000 difference between $80,000 and $76,000. The variance is unfavorable because the company worked more hours (8,000) than was anticipated for that level of production (7,600). (Number Three is False.)

INDEX